Y0-DJN-740

MOTHERS AT WORK

PUBLIC POLICIES IN THE UNITED STATES, SWEDEN, AND CHINA

Carolyn Teich Adams

Kathryn Teich Winston

Longman

New York and London

MOTHERS AT WORK
Public Policies in the United States, Sweden, and China

Longman Inc., New York
Associated companies, branches, and representatives throughout the world.

Copyright © 1980 by Longman Inc.

All rights reserved. No part of this publication may be reproduced, stored in a retrieval system, or transmitted in any form or by any means, electronic, mechanical, photocopying, recording, or otherwise, without the prior permission of the publisher.

Developmental Editor: **Nicole Benevento**
Design: **Gloria Gentile**
Manufacturing and Production Supervisor: **Kris Becker**
Composition: **A&S Graphics, Inc.**
Printing and Binding: **Fairfield Graphics**

Library of Congress Cataloging in Publication Data

Adams, Carolyn Teich.
Mothers at work.

(Comparative studies of political life)
Includes bibliographical references and index.
1. Mothers—Employment—United States. 2. Mothers—Employment—Sweden. 3. Mothers—Employment—China. 4. Family policy—United States. 5. Family policy—Sweden. 6. Family policy—China. I. Winston, Kathryn Teich, 1946- joint author. II. Title. III. Series: Comparative studies of political life (New York)
HD6055.A3 331.4 79-18670
ISBN 0-582-28064-8

Manufactured in the United States of America
9 8 7 6 5 4 3 2 1

For our parents

CONTENTS

ACKNOWLEDGMENTS

A project of this scope owes far too many debts to be easily enumerated. Among the many teachers, colleagues, and students who have contributed to the authors' education, several individuals deserve special mention. Kathryn Winston wishes to acknowledge her intellectual and professional debts to Richard Solomon, Allen Whiting, Donald Munro, and the late Alexander Eckstein. For Carolyn Adams, Arnold Heidenheimer has been an invaluable source of intellectual guidance, professional support, and personal encouragement. Adams also wishes to thank Utica College of Syracuse University for providing a summer research grant without which the project would not have been formulated. In Sweden, the authors are particularly indebted to Ambassador Olle Dahlen of the Ministry of Foreign Affairs, Liberal Party legislator Gabriel Romanus, and Professor Alva Myrdal.

Among those who read parts or all of the manuscript, we would like to express special appreciation to Cynthia Enloe, Jo Freeman, Joyce Gelb, and Norma Diamond. Not all our readers shared all of our interpretations. We are grateful for the painstaking readings we received from our critics as well as our supporters, and we take full responsibility for whatever errors remain in the text.

1

INTRODUCTION

We are living in a time of revolutionary change in the lives of American women and their families. More women than ever before are employed outside their homes; government figures on women's labor market participation leave no doubt about that. By the end of the 1970s, fully half of American women will be in the labor force, either holding jobs or looking for them. In the three decades since the end of World War II, the proportion of American women employed outside the home has risen from less than one third to fully one half of all female adults. Even more dramatic than this general increase is the upsurge in employment among mothers, especially mothers of young children. Married mothers of children under six years old more than *doubled* their employment between 1960 and 1975, with the largest percentage increases occurring among mothers of children under three years old. Figures such as these have led one observer to conclude that "the presence or absence of young children is no longer the best predictor of whether a woman will be engaged in work for pay or not."[1] This observation implies a startling shift in the relationship between women's traditional family roles and their job roles. Or does it?

Looking beyond the mere numbers of women in the labor force, we find that, to a curious degree, the status and role definitions of women working outside the home have remained unchanged. The old French aphorism is appropriate here: "The more things change, the more they remain the same." First, working women unquestionably continue to shoulder the primary responsibility within the family for housework and child care. Research consistently shows that even mothers who work a full 40-hour week carry the main burden of household chores and child care within the family; they spend substantially more time in what Elise Boulding has called the "breeder-feeder" role than do their husbands.[2] In short, most employed women have grafted their outside jobs on to their family responsibilities instead of substituting a work role outside the home for their work roles within the home.

If women's rising employment has not seriously altered their family roles, neither has it significantly improved their economic status relative to working men's. Table 1–1 shows that between 1955 and 1975, women's earnings as a proportion of men's earnings declined significantly. The general impression that American working women have lost ground in their earning power has been confirmed by scholars and by government agencies.[3] As table 1–1 makes clear, over the two decades from 1955 to 1975, the gap between the median earnings of female and male workers widened by

TABLE 1-1. Median Earnings of Year-Round Full-Time American Workers, by Sex, 1955–75 (persons 14 years of age and over)

	Median Earnings		*Women's Median Earnings as Percent of Men's*
	Women	*Men*	
1955	$2,719	$4,252	63.9
1956	2,827	4,466	63.3
1957	3,008	4,713	63.8
1958	3,102	4,927	63.0
1959	3,193	5,209	61.3
1960	3,293	5,417	60.8
1961	3,351	5,644	59.4
1962	3,446	5,794	59.5
1963	3,561	5,978	59.6
1964	3,690	6,195	59.6
1965	3,823	6,375	60.0
1966	3,973	6,848	58.0
1967	4,150	7,182	57.8
1968	4,457	7,664	58.2
1969	4,977	8,227	60.5
1970	5,323	8,966	59.4
1971	5,593	9,399	59.5
1972	5,903	10,292	57.9
1973	6,335	11,186	57.6
1974	6,970	11,889	58.6
1975	7,504	12,758	58.8

Source: U.S. Dept. of Labor, Bureau of Labor Statistics, *U.S. Working Women: A Databook,* Bulletin 1977, p. 35.

5 percent. The average full-time woman worker in 1955 earned 64 percent of the average full-time male worker's earnings; by 1975, she was earning only 59 percent of the average male wage. How do we explain this combination of trends? On the one hand, women are entering the labor force in record numbers. On the other hand, their earning power relative to men's has declined as their participation increased, despite the 1963 Equal Pay Act.

To understand why, we must understand the structure of the American labor market. Despite magazine features on women construction workers, engineers, and astronauts, the reality is that America has a segmented labor market in which women disproportionately hold low-paid, low-prestige jobs. Segregation of the sexes into different occupational categories remains at least as strong in the 1970s as it was in 1900. Nearly two thirds of all working women are found in three sectors: clerical, service, and sales.[4] Women have a virtual monopoly (over 90 percent) on such positions as registered nurse, bank teller, typist, telephone operator, and secretary. At the other end of the occupational spectrum, women constitute only 7 percent of practicing physicians, 2 percent of engineers, 5 percent of middle managers, and 1 percent of top management. This segregation of women into low-paying jobs is inevitably reflected in the wage structure; more than 80 percent of all regularly employed women in 1974 earned under $10,000, as opposed to only 38 percent of regularly employed males.[5] Obviously, equal-pay-for-equal-work legislation can have no significant impact on wage differentials between the sexes if women are not finding "equal work" in the first place.

Up to this point in our discussion, we find virtual agreement among labor economists, sociologists, and others who have studied American working women. The female labor force occupies substantially different kinds of jobs at lower pay than working men. There is less consensus on why this situation prevails. In surveying the literature, we find not so much direct disagreement over the causes as a difference in emphasis. Some have chosen to emphasize employer discrimination against women simply on the basis of gender. This argument is especially persuasive when one looks at the relative ability of women and men to "cash in" their educational and occupational credentials for wages. The average female college graduate in the mid-1970s earned less than the average male high school dropout. Studies showing that working women, even single career women, are unable to convert their credentials into income at the same rate as working men provide strong support for the view that sex discrimination is an important cause of earning gaps.[6] Some would even argue that it is the primary cause:

> I am arguing that employer discrimination is the chief factor which produces wage gaps between men and women. . . . Men and women arrive in the labor market with essentially equal skills and competencies yet they are typically assigned different jobs even within the same firm.[7]

Others choose to emphasize women's socialization to accept self-images that are passive and nonachievement oriented. Parents, teachers, and media messages influence women from infancy to seek fulfillment in the wife-and-mother role, while motivating young men toward occupational success. According to this view, women's own preferences and attitudes (shaped, of course, by their socialization into "feminine" roles) lead them to invest less in their jobs than do their male co-workers. Some research even suggests that women associate career success with guilt and social rejection and therefore devise ways to "fail."[8] Proponents of this view argue that the "feminine" personality itself limits women's job horizons: "It is clear that men, not women, are socialized to adopt the personality characteristics that are related to success in the more prestigious and financially lucrative occupations."[9]

Still a third group of analysts points to the historical coincidence of women's mass entry into the labor market with the expansion of the service sector. A majority of the new jobs created in the 1960s and 1970s were either in the social services, with marked expansion in educational and health services, or in clerical services. It is therefore to be expected that women entering the labor force during those years are found disproportionately in such jobs.

Finally, the emphasis adopted for this study is on the career limitations women face because of their family roles. For married women, especially mothers of young children, the work experience is not the equivalent of the male work experience. Women's job expectations and job success are often constrained by their families' (and their own) perception that they are homemakers first and workers second. The limitations created by this ordering of roles take several forms. Women may leave their jobs for extended periods to bear and care for children or to care for elderly or chronically sick family members. According to Juanita Kreps, "the threat of discontinuity in a woman's worklife is perhaps the greatest single barrier to higher wages for young women." Kreps explains:

> When there is a break in woman's worklife (usually occasioned by the birth of children) the importance of this discontinuity should not be minimized. For one thing, the interruption of market work prevents the woman from building an orderly career in the same way a man does; yet when they return to work, women have to compete for jobs on the same basis as men.[10]

Besides taking women out of the labor force for extended periods, family responsibilities often motivate women to seek part-time work, which in our economy normally carries a low wage and few fringe benefits. This is another reason why women are segregated in the service industries; part-time employment is more readily available in service jobs.[11] Still another effect of women's family responsibilities was uncovered by a recent Ohio State University study of the work histories of over 18,000 American women. The study traced the career patterns of working women and found that nearly a third stayed in the same occupation in which they started, while a fifth actually experienced downward shifts in jobs. The report concluded that "marriage and childbearing increase the chances that a woman will experience downward mobility from first job to current (or last) job."[12]

SWEDISH AND CHINESE COUNTERPOINTS

American feminists, in assessing the experience of American women in the labor market, have often looked to other societies for evidence that the particular pattern of work and family roles observed in the United States is not immutable—not "human nature"—but only one of a variety of possible patterns. We may credit anthropologist Margaret Mead, in her numerous cross-cultural studies of the relationship between culture and sexuality, with raising the question whether the two sexes' family and labor roles depend on universal biological differences.[13] Sensitized by Mead and others to the variety of work-family patterns possible in human communities, feminists have shown considerable curiosity about how women live in other parts of the world. In fact, American feminism displays an "internationalist" spirit that is highly unusual in the history of American social movements. Feminist political activity in the United States has often been linked to parallel activities in other countries; American participation in the International Women's Year meetings in Mexico City in 1975 was only the most visible symbol of an international "network" on women's issues in which Americans have been active for years. Moreover, American scholars have undertaken countless research projects of women's roles and rights in foreign cultures.[14] The women's studies literature abounds with anthologies of case studies from various parts of the industrialized and developing world. Unfortunately, the investigation of foreign models has been limited mostly to case studies of individual locales, with few attempts at systematic comparison across cultures. This book is intended to help fill that gap.

Scandinavia and China provide some of the most frequently cited models of women's integration into the labor force. The pictures of both world regions painted by returning travelers, journalists, scholars, and the American media emphasize different assumptions about women's place in the national economy than are prevalent in the United States. Those assumptions are succinctly expressed by a Scandinavian sociologist:

> But even if she excels in all these respects (being a good housekeeper and hostess, a loving mother and an attractive spouse), she will reap slight social esteem, because dominant middle class opinion will insist on the superior values of choosing a career outside the home.[15]

Despite the vast geographical, social, and economic distances that separate the two regions, that statement made by a Scandinavian could be applied equally well to the People's Republic of China, with the qualification that it is not "middle class opinion" but rather party doctrine that stresses the superior value of work outside the home. As we shall see, the message of the Chinese Communist party (CCP) has varied somewhat since 1949; nonetheless, the dominant theme during most periods has been the necessity for women to engage in socially productive labor—that is, labor outside the confines of their own homes. In China, as well as in our Scandinavian example of Sweden, government social policy has encouraged women to meet society's expectation by moving out into the labor force.

The Swedish and Chinese cases are all the more intriguing because both nations have experienced such rapid change in the post–World War II era. As table 1–2 shows, the proportion of married women employed in Sweden in 1950 was significantly lower than the proportion of married women employed in the United States. During the 1950s, Sweden experienced a gradual increase in the employment of married women—an increase that accelerated rapidly in the 1960s—so that by 1965, Sweden had pulled ahead of the United States. Swedish employment had already reached the 50 percent mark (i.e., the point at which half of all married women were employed) in 1970; according to current projections, the United States will reach that mark by 1979.[16] Furthermore, the wage gap between female and male workers is narrower in Sweden than in America. In 1972 the median wage for full-time women workers in Sweden was 71 percent of the median male wage.[17] In that same year, American working women were earning slightly less than 60 percent of the median male wage. Regarding women's wages, the brightest spot in the Swedish economy is the manufacturing sector, where strong union organization has

TABLE 1-2. Percentage of Married Women (excluding divorced and widowed women) in the Work Force

	Sweden	*U.S.*
1950	16	24
1955	N.A.	28
1960	26	30
1965	37	35
1970	53	41
1975	60	44

Sources: *Statistisk Arsbok för Sverige;* and Howard Hayghe, "Families and the Rise of Working Wives: An Overview," *Monthly Labor Review* 99, no. 5 (May 1976).

narrowed wage gaps considerably over the years. From 1958 to 1974, women's average hourly wages rose from 70 to 86 percent of men's.[18]

In contrast to manufacturing jobs in Sweden, white-collar occupations continue to show much greater discrepancies between women's and men's earnings, with most estimates of the female-to-male ratio hovering around 60 percent. The postwar integration of more women, especially married women, into Sweden's labor market has been favored by government social programs to assist women in controlling their fertility, obtaining maternal and infant health services, caring for their children, and even getting occasional help with housework. We examine these programs in detail in chapter 2. The important point here is simply that Swedish social policy since 1945 has consistently encouraged women's entry into the labor force by providing them with support services and benefits to assist them in fulfilling their family roles.

The People's Republic of China, since its establishment in 1949, has also stressed getting women out of the home and into "socially productive labor." Given that women rarely even left their homes before the communists came to power, much less worked outside the home, the change has been extraordinarily swift. In rural areas, where 80 percent of the Chinese population still live, virtually all women at some point in their lives work in the fields; in cities, although the situation is far from clear, it appears that better than half of urban women at present take part in labor.[19] If men and women admittedly still do not participate equally in the work force, the improvement since 1949 has been impressive. There has been a desire to put women to work; a recognition that such a goal requires day care, communal mess halls, and other replacement services; and a definite, if sporadic, enthusiasm to establish these services. In rural areas, periodic campaigns have attacked the problem of equal pay for equal work, ameliorating if not solving it. And in the cities, women have been encouraged to move into nontraditional jobs as technicians, engineers, steel workers, and the like, which are, incidentally, also more highly paid.

All these improvements have been predicated on the notion that women's labor ought, first, to serve the collective and, second, to serve their families. Needless to say, in a society that before 1949 viewed women's labor as the exclusive property of the family, a vast amount of "reeducation" has been required—some of it effective, some of it less so. Not only have the Chinese people had to be convinced, but even party cadres have occasionally displayed "backward" behavior. Consequently, support for a change in women's status has not been uniformly strong in all areas at all times. What can be said is that, in general, the party considers women's participation in the labor force to be in the best interest of the state and the revolution, and insofar as they perceive it aiding the "greater good," they have supported it.

Compared with Sweden and China, the picture in the United States is more complicated. Unquestionably, American society attaches more esteem to work done for pay outside the home than it does to housework. The expression "just a housewife" conveys the low esteem in which the role is held, even by housewives themselves. In this respect, the United States differs little from our other two cases. The interesting difference is that American public policy has offered little assistance or encouragement to married women moving out of this low-status role and into the labor market. The basic distinction between the American approach and the approaches taken by the other two governments seems to be this: Women's programs in Sweden and China proceed from the assumption that marriage, motherhood, and employment are potentially compatible activities for women as well as men, given the appropriate social organization. American policy, on the other hand, continues to presume certain fundamental incompatibilities between women's marriage, motherhood, and work roles. Women who attempt to play multiple roles at the same time can overcome these incompatibilities only by incurring certain costs; those costs may involve paying the high price to buy adequate child care, sacrificing leisure time in order to get housework done after 5:00 P.M. or on weekends, or limiting job hours and responsibilities to those that can successfully be juggled with home responsibilities. With few exceptions, American policy makers view these necessary tradeoffs as private decisions, outside the realm of governmental concern or action. They do not see government as having any particular obligation to reduce or redistribute the costs incurred by working wives and mothers.

ON THE UTILITY OF CROSS-NATIONAL COMPARISON

Since comparative policy analysis is still a relatively new (and primitive) art, it may be useful to include a few comments on the nature of such studies.[20] The literature on comparative policy analysis has focused primarily on the central question whether government policies are better explained by features of the political system or by the economic and social environment in which government operates. While virtually all observers agree that both political and socioeconomic factors influence public policy, the debate turns on which set of factors has the stronger influence.

The political model posits that the determinant influence over policy is exerted by political variables, especially (1) the patterns of interest-group and party activity ("input" variables), (2) the structure of government itself ("institutional" variables), or (3) both. In particular, advocates of the primacy of the "input" variables have concentrated on understanding who has power and why. They have thus been concerned about the extent to which elite strata can manipulate the political system to their advantage; the relative degree of openness, pluralism, and competition in the political system; and the nature of prevailing political ideologies. If we view these "input" variables as critical, we might hypothesize, for example, that the mobilization of working women into large and highly visible interest groups would tend to be followed by government policy responsive to the needs of working women. Or we might assume, as many have, that when socialist parties are strong in a political system, government programs are more likely to promote equality for women.

The study of politics was at one time practically synonymous with the study of governmental institutions. Political science textbooks of the 1940s and 1950s were devoted primarily to the description and analysis of government structures (legislatures, executives, bureaucracies, and courts) and the distribution of powers and obligations among levels of government. With the behavioral movement that swept through the social sciences in the 1960s, the interest in government institutions waned. It has recently enjoyed a modest revival, especially among students of comparative policy, who can scarcely ignore the relevance of institutions to the policy-making process. In his introduction to *The Comparative Policy Process,* T. Alexander Smith argues vigorously:

> Institutional arrangements obviously have a profound impact on politics. . . . Political institutions are . . . crucially important, since they define the limits and levels of political battle and establish controls which first legitimize and then resolve conflict in favor of certain participants. We cannot begin to understand political man unless we understand the institutional context within which the individual operates.[21]

However, despite the continuing interest on the part of some scholars in studying parties, interest groups, and governmental institutions, the tendency among policy analysts in the last decade has been to play down the importance of political variables in favor of socioeconomic variables. One contributor to this trend has been the widely perceived decline in the importance in the West of ideological debate and conflict. Numerous Western political observers have seen politics in the postindustrial era shifting away from conflict over the nature of the "good society" toward much narrower, more technical debates over how best to implement the generally accepted consensus regarding economic and social goals.[22] In addition to the end-of-ideology theorists, another group of scholars, working in an entirely different field, has further reinforced the notion that politics plays a diminishing role in shaping public policy. Numerous comparative studies done at the level of the American states emphasize socioeconomic variables (especially economic development, usually measured by the level of wealth, industrialization, urbanization, and education) as having greater importance in determining state policies than the traditional political variables.[23]

However, both the state-level quantitative studies and the end-of-ideology writings have been done within a limited range of political systems; in the former, the universe is all American states, whereas the latter have been confined to Western postindustrial democracies. Thus we must not assume their validity for our own study, which ranges over three different political systems. On the contrary, we might expect that in comparing policy systems in which the differences are far more gross, we will find that the "input" and "institutional" variables do indeed make a difference in the substance of policy outputs.

In comparing our three case studies, we attempt to assess whether the important differences in social programs for working women are best explained by political or socioeconomic variables. As we have already observed, on both the political and environmental dimensions we are dealing with vastly differing systems. Politically, our study seeks to compare two democratic governments (the United States and Sweden) with what Alexander Groth has labeled an "innovative-mobilizational regime" (China).[24] While there are as many definitions of "democracy" as there are writers on the subject, we might all agree that democracies are distinguished from other forms of government by their procedural, rather than substantive, characteristics, and that one such procedural characteristic is the degree of open competition for control over government.[25] In both the United States and Sweden, national political leaders achieve their influence over public programs through competitive elections, though once in office, they formulate policy in different ways.

In the United States, national policy is most often the product of a collaboration among three kinds of actors: legislative committees or subcommittees, lobbyists representing particular interest groups, and bureaucrats whose offices administer the policies involved. Some of these "triangles" established to formulate policies in particular functional areas (e.g., highways, health, education) have such a permanent and visible presence in Washington that they have been labeled "policy systems."[26] These triangles hammer out the details of legislative programs, reconcile competing interests, and build the support coalition needed to carry the programs through the legislature. Compared with our other two nations, political parties in the United States play only a marginal role in the policy-making process. American parties typically approach a national campaign without any coherent, detailed program to guide Congress in setting priorities and drafting legislation. Nor do party leaders exert enough influence over their members to command a disciplined vote once bills reach the floor. Hence, federal policy reflects not so much the will of the majority party as the bargains struck within the multitude of functionally specialized "policy systems."

Moving to the implementation stage, we find in the United States that national leaders often rely on state and local governments to implement federal policy. This is particularly true in the realm of social services, where state, county, and municipal welfare agencies receive federal subsidies to deliver federally mandated services to their clients. Federal legislation, even after it has been elaborated and clarified by administrative guidelines, usually allows states and localities considerable discretion in carrying out federal policy. Predictably, federal initiatives have met particularly strong resistance from state and local agencies when they have involved dramatic social change (e.g., improved civil and economic status for minority groups).[27] Combined with the checks and balances built into the federal legislative machinery, the sharing of responsibility among several layers of semiautonomous governments completes the picture of a highly pluralistic policy process. Compared with our other two nations, America's political institutions are distinguished by their fragmentation.

It may at first seem odd to call American politics more fragmented than Swedish politics when we consider that Sweden has a total of five major national parties competing for control of the legislature. Although nominally a five-party system, Sweden has been realistically described in recent times as having three major power blocs. On the far left is the Communist party; the second bloc is the large Social Democratic party; the third is the coalition of nonsocialist parties (the Liberals, the Center, and the Moderate Unity party).[28] Having enjoyed continuous control over the national legislature since the 1930s, the Social Democratic party lost the fall election of 1976 and handed control over the legislature to a coalition that joined together the three nonsocialist parties. The coalition broke down in October 1978, and control over Sweden's government is at this writing tenuously exercised by the Liberal party, which holds a distinct minority of the seats.

The cast of characters in Swedish policy formulation is roughly the same as in the American case—that is, interest-group representatives, legislative politicians, and career bureaucrats. But the relationships among the actors, dictated by Swedish institutional arrangements, are unlike the American network of separate policy systems. Sweden's is a parliamentary form of government, in which policy-making power is concentrated in the prime minister's Cabinet, representing the party (or coalition) that controls a majority of seats in the Riksdag. The Cabinet carries the main authority and responsibility for drafting legislation. Because Sweden's national parties are more programmatic in nature than American parties, the policy of a particular Cabinet is more likely to reflect the positions taken and priorities articulated by the majority party(ies) in the previous election campaign.

Normally, Swedish policy also reflects the participation of opposition parties and interest groups via extensive consulting procedures that precede the drafting of important bills:

> Institutionalized and informal provisions for extensive consultations between the government and established economic organizations during the circulatory (or preparliamentary) stage of legislation, and membership in various administrative boards provide interest groups their most decisive avenues for interaction with political authorities.[29]

The royal commissions appointed to study important policy issues and make recommendations typically include representatives from all major parties. Moreover, Swedish law requires Cabinet ministers to consult the administrative agencies involved before they draft new legislation. The emphasis is on consensus formation and coalition building before the final legislation is drafted, thus assuring the widest possible support base in the legislature. (Such prior consultation has become even more crucial since October 1978, when government control passed from the nonsocialist coalition to the Liberal party alone.)

The persistent effort to involve bureaucratic agencies in policy formulation helps to secure their cooperation in implementation. In a departure from the structure of most parliamentary systems, Sweden assigns the responsibility for implementing national programs to a network of boards and agencies that are nominally independent from the Cabinet. In most cases, however, the cooperation of the administrative agencies is assured because they have been carefully consulted (and thereby coopted) during the drafting period. A crucial distinction between American and Swedish politics is the contrast between Sweden's unitary system and American federalism. For some programs, national boards and agencies operate their own field offices at the local level. But even in the more numerous cases where the national government relies on counties or municipalities to administer national programs, the national agencies exert much more direct control over local efforts. In sum, Sweden's political system displays much more central coordination in policy formulation and implementation than does the American system.

Not surprisingly, we find the highest degree of political coordination of all in China, whose policy goals virtually dictate a highly centralized policy process:

> Innovative-mobilizational regimes seek to change the inherited social order, popular values, traditional institutions, and the distribution of resources and gratifications in society. They organize and exhort the masses to participate in politics and seek to inculcate them with a new, more or less unified or systematic world outlook.[30]

It would be impossible to overstate the critical role of the Communist party in providing the political coordination necessary to pursue such sweeping change. While China does possess formal government structures, including a national legislative body, the National People's Congress, and government ministries to implement policy directives, the party's influence permeates every level of government. In effect, it is the party's Politburo and its select Standing Committee that initiate national policy. Their recommendations are passed to the official organs of government for ratification and implementation. Thus the circle of those with significant power to determine the direction of policy in China is very small, perhaps no more than two dozen individuals at any given moment.

Of course conflicts and competition have surfaced even within this small inner circle. On the issue of economic policy, for example, the party leadership has engaged in prolonged and intense debates—debates that, with

Mao's increasing ill health and death, erupted into a full-scale propaganda war. Nevertheless, all political factions and special interests (e.g., feminists) in China are ultimately obliged to articulate their interests within the party's framework rather than outside it. This, coupled with the small number of persons at the top of the decision-making hierarchy, produces a high degree of coordination in policy making.

From nationwide propaganda campaigns down to street-level meetings of the neighborhood residents' committees, the party invests enormous energy in activities designed to politicize the Chinese citizenry. Sinologists have hotly debated whether this high level of mobilization in China can be equated with political participation. As elections, with occasional exceptions at the lowest levels, are mostly pro forma exercises, can political participation even be said to exist in China? One of the most interesting answers to that question was given to Michael Oksenberg by a cadre of the People's Republic "in a bus bouncing along a dirt road in rural Honan." The answer concerned "investigation teams," which examine local problems at the behest of higher levels in order to facilitate the implementation of programs.

> I had inquired, "What do I have to understand in order to comprehend why you think China is a democracy? What do you have instead of elections?" He replied, "Investigation work. You must understand investigation work." [Some investigation work] concerned the eliciting of hard data, but some investigation work . . . involves opinion surveys. My Honan informant explained that these views are then aggregated—"concentrated" was his word—at each level and passed up. For this reason, he believed the highest levels represented the distilled wisdom of the masses.[31]

Local conditions are thus definitely taken into consideration in policy making.

Turning to policy implementation, we find a somewhat less clear-cut picture. China implements national programs through a system of dual bureaucracies within the party and the government that extend down through the provinces to the local level. For every level of government, a parallel body exists within the party, whose task is to guarantee that party directives are faithfully followed by government bureaucrats. Yet even with this universal system of party oversight, national leaders encounter more inertia, misunderstanding, and outright resistance than they would like from lower levels of government. Provincial and local party leaders, who often double as provincial and local governmental officials, have been known to develop power bases and sets of interests that diverge from those of national leaders. Such centrifugal tendencies, inevitable in a nation as large as China, tend to undermine the uniformly faithful adherence to national directives. Still, in comparison with our two democratic nations, China's political system must be seen as far more centralized.[32]

In addition to the political systems present in the three nations, our investigation must also consider the nature of prevailing political ideologies. Here, Sweden and China are distinguished from the United States by the influence in both nations of strong socialist parties, although admittedly Swedish Social Democrats and Chinese Communists are socialists of different stripes. Sweden's socialists are "revisionists" who have operated successfully since the turn of the century within liberal democratic structures: free elections, constitutionally defined limits on governmental power, and elaborate protections of individual civil liberties. Their goal has been the construction of a welfare state that guarantees economic productivity and personal security. The Chinese Communists are revolutionary socialists who have rejected liberal democratic forms in favor of the more collectivist forms needed to mobilize the population in support of their twin goals of modernization and social revolution. As a doctrine, Chinese Communism emphasizes social cooperation rather than electoral competition; it prizes the collective welfare above individual rights; it seeks to increase production more than personal security. The extent to which these very different varieties of socialism have influenced government programs for working women in Sweden and China is examined in chapter 4.

So far, we have been considering only the political variables that may influence social programs for working women. But we observed earlier that many scholars believe such variables to be less important in explaining public policy than the socioeconomic environment in which governments operate. We want to use our three cases to explore this second perspective as well. Obviously, using comparative analysis to link policy outputs to socioeconomic variables entails making two observations: (1) observations of the environment, or *context,* from which the policies were generated; and (2) observations of the policy *outputs* themselves. Observing the policy context usually involves collecting information on social conditions and economic structure. To describe policy outputs, we need to answer questions about whether and how government provides a particular good or service to the citizenry, how much money it invests, and how it goes about implementing the policy. We then compare national cases, trying to isolate the similarities and differences in order to gain a better understanding, for each individual case, of the relationships that link the environmental context with the policy outputs. Relationships that may escape the analyst's notice in an individual case study may emerge as critical once the initial case is compared with a second and, in this instance, a third case.

In constructing comparative studies of the relationships between policy environments and policy outputs, there are four logical possibilities, as shown in figure 1–1. Of the four comparative studies types, the first appears to be the least interesting. Studies that compare similar policy outputs springing from similar environments offer few analytical opportunities; the absence of significant distinctions among the cases means that we are unable to isolate any particular features of the environment or the outputs themselves for special attention. There are also analytical difficulties associated with Type 4, in which different policies spring from differ-

		In the cases for comparison, the Policy Outputs are:	
		Similar	*Different*
In the cases for comparison, the Policy Contexts are:	*Similar*	Type 1	Type 2
	Different	Type 3	Type 4

FIGURE 1-1 Possible Structures of Comparative Policy Studies, Relating Policy Outputs to Policy Context

ent contexts. Here, there may well be interesting contrasts to observe. But one is likely to end up with what amount to separate case studies, because there are no features of either the environments or the policies to link the cases together. The other two study types are more likely to produce valuable insights. In Type 2 we observe different policies produced from basically similar environments. In comparisons of this kind, where many important elements of the environments being studied are alike, we stand a relatively good chance of identifying the particular ways in which the contexts diverged sufficiently to produce different policy outputs. Type 3 presents the intriguing instance of similar policies being generated out of different environments. In this instance, the overall dissimilarity between the two contexts allows us to limit our consideration to the small number of similarities in environments, among which we can presumably find the factors that account for the similarity in policy outputs.

In this book we are concerned with explaining the presence or absence in our three nations of a particular set of social programs to facilitate working women's dual roles as earners and homemakers. In terms of the policy environments we are dealing with two Western postindustrial democracies that share many important social and economic characteristics. The economic linkages between Europe and America and the homogenization of Western culture have drawn the two continents even closer together than many Europeans would like. On the other hand, it is difficult to imagine a policy environment more divergent from these two than Communist China, on any of the common comparative dimensions: level of industrialization, standard of living, social organization, culture, and religion.

When we turn to examining policy outputs, our cases group themselves differently. In chapter 2 we examine a range of programs including family planning, maternity benefits, child care, and homemaker services. Needless to say, we find that each nation provides a unique package of benefits and services to women. Yet if we concentrate on overall patterns, we must acknowledge that the governments of Sweden and China bear a stronger resemblance to each other than either one bears to the United States. Both foreign governments are unquestionably committed to government-initiated programs aimed at redistributing across the larger society the costs borne by working families, especially by working women. Both governments stress women's universal right of access to family-planning services. The health-service networks of both countries stress universal, low-cost (in Sweden, virtually free) maternity care, and both governments guarantee a woman's right to paid maternity leave. In both societies, national policy makers have emphasized the need to make day care accessible to more working women, and each government has in its own way promoted the construction and expansion of day-care facilities. Finally, each nation has taken steps to "socialize" housework by shifting part of the household burden out of the nuclear family and into the collective realm.

Granted, the programs we have listed have taken rather different forms in the two nations. Sweden provides its elaborate array of benefits and services through a centralized welfare bureaucracy. Eligibility criteria and benefit levels in Sweden's social insurance programs are uniform across the nation, and those administering social services are either professionals or professionally trained staff workers. China, by contrast, has depended on local self-reliance and community self-help projects to meet the need for day care and homemaking services. Typically, factory and residence committees recruit people to contribute time, equipment, and possibly space in a joint effort. The amount of local government or factory support varies from project to project, as does the salary of the staff. The women who work in the day care organizations (there are few male day care workers) are not professionally educated, but are usually chosen on the basis of temperament and inclination, and are trained as apprentices on the job. Despite the contrasting methods of implementation, however, chapter 2 shows that women's programs in the two countries clearly have more in common with each other than either has with the United States.

If we think of this three-nation study as three sets of comparisons—Sweden compared with the United States, Sweden compared with China, and China compared with the United States—we can see that our three comparative pairs fall into three different types, as depicted in figure 1–1. The Swedish-American comparison falls into Type 2 because it involves policy environments that share many important characteristics and yet have generated quite different policies vis-à-vis working women. We would classify the Swedish-Chinese comparisons as Type 3 because two widely divergent contexts have produced women's policies that are strikingly similar. Finally, the U.S.-China comparison would fall into Type 4, in which different contexts have produced contrasting policies. As we observed, the U.S.–China comparison would be unlikely to yield any interesting analysis if presented by itself. But in the interest of rounding out our three-part structure, we do at some points in the text include U.S.–China comparisons.

Let us hasten to assure the reader that we do not intend to hold up either the Swedish or the Chinese model as an ideal type worthy of replication in the United States. For one thing, both foreign models harbor inconsistencies and problems. Most notably, both economies are still sex segregated, despite women's formal right to hold almost any kind of job. Even more alarming is the prospect that expanding social services to working women will *reinforce* sex segregation in the work force because the social service jobs created go disproportionately to women. Perhaps the strongest criticism of either model is that it simply leaves women doing the same jobs they have always done (cooking, cleaning, child care), only now they work for public authorities instead of their own families. Second, we want to avoid implying that any foreign model, however attractive, could simply be grafted on to the American political system. Precisely because policy outputs are so closely linked to their environments, it is impractical to consider wholesale transplanting of foreign models to the United States. Occasionally, programmatic borrowing may be possible on a small scale. But the value of comparative policy analysis lies not so much in its ability to uncover workable alternatives from other societies as in its contribution to our understanding of our own system.

One of the most positive functions of comparative research is to highlight the prevailing assumptions that structure public debate over certain issues in our own system. Once we move outside our culture we often discover that notions we have taken for granted are not necessarily accepted in other systems. We offer some examples below. We would argue that contemporary American feminists have tended to write and debate within the limits of the following assumptions; both are called into question by our investigation of the Swedish and Chinese cases.

1. Public policy can respond to social change but cannot initiate real social change.
2. Women's gains and losses in economic status are tied to their levels of political awareness, organization, and activity. Women make economic gains only when they organize and fight for them.

Our Swedish and Chinese cases also shed light on two more assumptions traditionally accepted by American feminists but now being debated in some feminist circles:

3. Special programs to aid women are invariably regressive in their consequences. That is, public policies that single out women as a special class end up reinforcing women's second-class status.
4. Attitude change must precede any significant changes in women's material circumstances. In other words, liberating women's (and men's) consciousness is the necessary precursor to women's social and economic emancipation.

Obviously, that any of these assumptions may be questioned in other systems does not necessarily invalidate them for the American case. The comparison merely alerts us to be cautious about accepting such assumptions prima facie without asking questions. We raise such questions in the course of our discussion, hoping that all three individual cases can be illuminated by the comparative framework.

WORKING WOMEN'S DUAL ROLES

Readers familiar with the literature on sex roles will have recognized that our study takes off from a view of working women's lives that has drawn considerable criticism from some feminists since the mid-1960s. By opting to look at policies that make it easier for working women to fulfill two roles (wage earner and homemaker), we are in effect opting for a modified form of the dual-role thesis first advanced by Alva Myrdal and Viola Klein in their 1956 book, *Women's Two Roles*.[33] Myrdal and Klein described a pattern that was increasingly common in Sweden in the 1950s: a segmentation of married women's lives into school, followed by a period of employment, then an interruption of employment during child-rearing years, and finally a return to the work force at middle age.

> The most common pattern proposed is for the wife to work while young, leave her job and devote herself to children and home during the years of active motherhood and then pick up the threads of her occupation when the children have grown up.[34]

The 1960s and 1970s brought into prominence a new pattern in which women returned to their jobs much sooner after the birth of their children than they had previously done. Many reentered the work force in only a few months instead of a few years. The expression "dual roles" took on a new meaning—that is, two roles performed simultaneously rather than in sequence.

Originally formulated simply as a way of describing the life situation of most married women workers, the dual-role thesis came under attack in the early 1960s for what were seen to be its prescriptive overtones. In Sweden and the United States, some feminists began to argue that to acknowledge a dual role for working women was to admit that women must shoulder twice the burden of their male co-workers. If this view were accepted as the norm, critics charged, then women would always enter the labor market with a handicap. The Swedish author and feminist Eva Moberg published the single best expression of this criticism in 1961. She rejected both versions of the dual-role thesis, arguing that

> . . . the concept of "double roles" in the long run may have an unfortunate effect. It preserves the concept that woman has an inherent *main function* by which is meant child care and rearing, creating the home and keeping it together. . . . We ought to stop harping on the concept of "women's two roles."[35]

What do critics of the dual-role thesis offer in its place? They advocate an "androgynous" model of sex roles in which the two functions of wage earning and homemaking would be assigned, not on the basis of gender, but on factors such as the preferences, training, and talents of the spouses. It goes without saying that in the ideal androgynous society the socialization process would be altered so that it would no longer assign occupational skills and preferences on the basis of gender. The androgynous model "implies the affirmation and cultivation of formerly sex-linked psychological and social characteristics in both men and women."[36] Theoretically, then, this model would allow for households in which women are full-time earners and men are full-time homemakers. Far more frequently, however, its proponents call for households in which women and men share both functions; in effect, both spouses play a dual role.

The word "androgyny" carries with it some semantic difficulties. Technically it is defined as the possession, by an individual or population, of the characteristics of both sexes. Thus its use necessarily embroils us in the ongoing debate over the existence and importance in the two sexes of genetic temperamental differences that might make true androgyny unrealizable.[37] Hence we prefer to use the expression "symmetry" to identify the family model favored by most critics of the dual-role thesis. Husbands and wives play symmetrical roles when both are employed and are carrying household responsibilities of about equal weight. "Symmetry" carries the connotation that the spouses perform basically similar functions, while not necessarily implying that they share any particular set of personality traits.[38]

It would be difficult for any feminist (among whose ranks the authors count themselves) to disagree with the symmetrical family as a desirable family model. Its appeal lies in the equality built into a relationship in which high-status and low-status, well-paid and low-paid, jobs are evenly divided. Obviously, truly symmetrical families are extremely rare, even in households where both spouses are employed. Working families normally do not attach equal importance to the outside jobs held by wives and husbands, nor do they distribute the weight of household chores equally. But observers who can agree on both the aforementioned propositions (i.e., that symmetrical families are highly desirable and that they are also very rare) nevertheless disagree on the public policy implications of these propositions. Even if we agree that promoting more symmetry in marriage is a legitimate policy goal, we must still ask whether the same policies are required to bring this situation into being as are appropriate to deal with it once it exists. The issue is what model of working women's circumstances should guide policy making on women's issues. Can policy makers more effectively pursue symmetry by (1) basing current legislation on the symmetrical model, expecting that by doing so, they are helping to bring it into being; or (2) recognizing that women workers now face problems different from those of their male co-workers, and drafting programs that respond to women's dual burden?

We often see this issue formulated as a choice between equal treatment for all workers versus special treatment for women workers as a class. Throughout the history of American feminism, political conflicts have arisen because some believed that government policies which officially recognized differences in the family roles of women and men would end up perpetuating and reinforcing those differences. By declaring women workers to be a special class with special needs, government policies would provide employers with a rationale for treating women employees differently from men. We argue in chapter 3 that the women's movement in the United States has placed a much stronger emphasis on equal treatment than it has on special treatment for working women. In fact, public advocates of special treatment for women workers have been labeled "regressive" by many feminists.

Debates over the Equal Rights Amendment illustrate this conflict. The feminists' focus on equal rights, especially the fifty-year campaign waged for the Equal Rights Amendment, was at odds with the unions' desire to preserve "protective" legislation that established special hours and working conditions for women workers. Each time the ERA was introduced in Congress (which happened every single year after 1923), equal rights advocates confronted opposition from women unionists, who accused the amendment's backers of being too middle class to sympathize with the working woman's plight. The ERA's proponents argued that most protective labor laws passed by American states had ultimately worked to women's economic disadvantage because they gave employers an excuse for not putting women into the better-paying jobs and limited women's opportunities for lucrative overtime assignments. This latter argument, it must be noted, did not address the fundamental question whether women workers *should* receive special treatment because of their special burdens. It simply pointed out that once lawmakers had singled out women workers for unequal treatment, that special status had usually worked against them instead of for them. This highly pragmatic argument was ultimately convincing to women unionists, most of whom changed their position in the 1970s and began to support the ERA.

While the earlier disagreements over the merits of protective labor laws seem to have been laid to rest, it is still debatable whether public policies that guarantee women equal treatment in the labor market are really the answer to women's economic problems. In this volume we focus on an alternative approach to improving women's participation and status in the labor force: government benefits and services to ease women workers' dual burden (most notably, maternity and family-planning programs, child care, and housekeeping services). We argue that without such benefits and services, women will not be in a position to compete on an equal basis for jobs, promotions, and wage increases. In a future society in which family roles were symmetrical, these programs would not be viewed as "women's" programs but as "family" programs, since they provide support for functions performed within the family. But under current conditions there is little doubt that the main beneficiaries of such programs are those who carry the greatest responsibility for child rearing and homemaking: women. To acknowledge this reality is not to condone it. We would argue, in fact, that without an accurate assessment of present conditions, we stand little chance of changing them.

ORGANIZATION OF THE VOLUME

Our first task is to examine in detail the policies we have chosen to consider. In chapter 2 we provide a description of all three governments' programs in family planning, maternity benefits, child care, home helps, and welfare assistance to single-parent families. Although we give some consideration to the interaction between national and local governments as it affects implementation, we are primarily concerned in all three cases with assessing the commitment of *national* policy makers to such programs. Our focus at the national level is dictated by our desire to understand the relationships between these social policies and national labor-market policies. Throughout the volume we stress the linkages between policy areas; rather than seeing women's programs as a separate policy sphere, we emphasize their relationships to other economic and social goals of the regimes.

Once we have outlined the policies themselves, we turn to a discussion of the factors that may account for those policies. Our main interest lies in explaining the extent to which the United States lags behind the other two nations in providing public support for women's dual roles. In doing so, we want to avoid the overly simplistic explanations frequently offered for the lack of adequate day care, maternity benefits, home-help services, and so on. Such simplistic explanations usually boil down to some version of the conspiracy argument: "Men control government, and men are opposed to liberating women." Instead, we focus on several systemic factors we believe have strongly influenced American policy on women's issues.

We begin by exploring women's own efforts to improve their political and economic status. Chapter 3 analyzes the women's movements in the three nations, their organizational strategies, and their relative degrees of influence on national policy. In chapter 4 we trace the relationships between women's programs and national policies regarding employment, economic growth, and population growth. In that context we are especially interested in evaluating the extent to which the presence of "socialist" parties in Sweden and China accounts for their commitment to women's policy. Our goal in chapter 5 is to examine the prevailing beliefs in the three political cultures regarding the family's relationship to government. Any public policies designed to shift the balance between women's homemaker and worker roles require some government intervention, either direct or indirect, into the sphere of the family. Hence it is important to know whether the political culture legitimizes such interventions. Finally, the concluding chapter offers some general observations on the relationship of governments to social change and hazards some predictions about future policy directions in the United States.

2

SOCIAL POLICIES FOR WORKING FAMILIES: A COMPARATIVE INVENTORY

The only way to achieve true equality of opportunity for women in the marketplace is to lower the costs of participation imposed on women by finding ways to reduce the burden of the working woman's dual role. One possible solution, favored by many feminists, is to restructure family roles so that the costs of family planning, child rearing, and household maintenance are shared as widely as possible by family members, especially by husbands. Proponents of this position are in effect advocating that males and females assume dual roles. This is an attractive vision of the future precisely because it implies a breaking down of the sex-role stereotypes that have traditionally assigned household duties to one sex. Nevertheless, because the redistribution of household labor depends directly on a reversal of attitudes held by countless generations of women and men, it is not likely to come about quickly. Indeed, it may not come about at all if household members do not perceive women's and men's employment as having equal importance for the household's survival and welfare.

What we are arguing is not that the redistribution of housework and child rearing depends on women working outside the home, for survey after survey shows that women working outside the home continue to carry the primary responsibility for housework. This arrangement persists because families and policy makers see working wives as secondary contributors holding lower-paid, less prestigious jobs than their husbands. American working wives, for example, commonly contribute 25 percent to 40 percent of family income,[1] and only about half of them hold full-time, year-round jobs; the others work part-time or only during certain seasons of the year.[2] Because such working wives cannot lay equal claim to the family breadwinner role, their principal role within the family remains one of homemaker. A rearrangement of household roles will depend on the perception that women's employment is as important to the household economy as men's. Until both husband and wife are perceived as family breadwinners, wives will continue to be identified, and to identify themselves, primarily as homemakers.

The pattern we are describing is a vicious circle. Until women have more than marginal jobs outside the home, they will continue to identify themselves as homemakers. But most women cannot realistically expect to find and hold more than marginal jobs unless they can get some help with their household responsibilities. According to the Labor Department, the major reason why American women work part-time or only part of the year is home responsibilities.[3] We conclude from this that women's equal participation in the labor force cannot await a massive change in attitudes that will permit a redistribution of household responsibilities. We will not see such a change in attitudes *until* women begin to participate equally in the work force. Moreover, the sharing of household labor by two parents is not a viable solution to the problems of one-parent families, whose numbers increase every year. Single heads of household, the vast majority of whom are women, need services that reduce the cost of their dual role.

A wide variety of policies is called for, the most obvious being public support for day-care facilities. In addition, there is a need for public policies supporting maternity leaves with pay and without penalty to the employee; improved access to family-planning services including information, contraceptives, and abortion services; home-help services to care for family members and perform housekeeping chores when an employed parent is unable to do such chores; access to food services to prepare and serve meals for children and adults; and even changes in the design and construction of communities in order to make community planning more responsive to women's needs. The last item, not often listed among the demands expressed by feminists, is nevertheless an important policy consideration. Community design could minimize women's opportunity costs not only by emphasizing construction of housing units for easy maintenance but also by taking account of two major problems facing working mothers: "the meshing of their work schedules with those of day-care centers and other public service facilities" and "access to transportation facilities which enable them to take advantage of employment or recreational opportunities."[4]

This chapter examines the provision of such services in Sweden and China and compares efforts in those countries with the U.S. government. Of our three examples, Sweden has incorporated into its social welfare policies by far the most comprehensive set of programs for women.

Sweden's social welfare system is frequently described as a "safety net" whose fabric of government benefits and services is woven tightly enough to prevent anyone from falling through. An important component of that system is a set of programs aimed at enhancing the welfare of women and children; these programs began taking shape in the 1930s and have continuously changed and expanded. Swedes refer to the programs as their "family welfare policy." The programs have been aimed more and more toward the family with two working parents, which Swedish policy makers have begun to see as the norm.

The interdependence in Sweden between women's programs and other components of the social welfare system is reflected in its maternity and family-planning programs, described in the first two sections of this chapter. Sweden provides the most elaborate maternity and birth-control services (including access to free abortions) of our three cases. At first glance, it might seem paradoxical that the Swedish government provides comprehensive services both to promote and prevent motherhood. This seeming paradox is explained by the observation that both services depend heavily on the existence of a mass health-delivery system offering affordable, easily accessible health care to all. Maternity and birth-control services are administered through Sweden's elaborate public health network; hence, both services partake of the coverage and quality of that network.

Our policy survey of China since 1949 reveals an impressive commitment to women's programs in spite of periodic lapses in the zeal with which the programs have been implemented. Our somewhat mixed review of China's achievements in the fields of day care, home-helper services, and communal mess halls must be weighed against the massive economic problems confronting the Chinese Communists in their drive for rapid industrialization. In China, as in most parts of the world, women have traditionally provided an indispensable array of household services including child care, care of the aged, and care of the sick, not to mention household repairs, sewing, cooking, and so forth. Socializing these services in China would inevitably entail large capital expenditures on buildings and equipment, and salaries paid to women for performing these services tend to inflate the economy, as happened in 1955–1956 and 1958–1960.

The problem of providing support services to working women has been largely dealt with through mutual assistance among women, often undertaken on a voluntary basis or with little pay. Day-care services, in particular, have come into existence largely through the efforts of women's street organizations, coupled with the help of the Women's Department of the All-China Federation of Trade Unions in the cities and by women cadres concerned with welfare services in the countryside. Women have been recruited to solve their own problems.

Undeniably there are problems associated with the Swedish and Chinese approaches to social services for women. In Sweden, the creation of a large public-service sector has bred a class of social service workers, largely women, who are employed by the local government to perform services they formerly would have performed either in their own homes or in other households as domestic workers. Among the social service workers employed by local governments in the early 1970s, fully 95 percent of the social welfare staffs and 86 percent of the hygiene and nursing staffs were women.[5] Moreover, these women service workers are clustered at the low end of municipal pay scales. The lowest two pay grades in municipal employment are overwhelmingly occupied by women; in 1970, women constituted 82 percent of the lowest-paid group and 62 percent of the second lowest. In contrast, women were only 4 percent of the two highest municipal pay grades.[6] One can reasonably ask whether a social service system that gives its low-paying, low-prestige service jobs to women is breaking down or reinforcing sex-role stereotypes.

China's problem is that so many of the services created to support women workers have been makeshift, temporary, and staffed by untrained volunteers. The most common complaint about Sweden's social services is that they are overbureaucratized; the opposite complaint could be leveled at China's. The Chinese government's determination to rely on local initiative means that little guidance, and even less money, comes from the central government. Local service delivery has been susceptible to frequent disruption because it has relied so heavily on voluntary contributions of time, space, and equipment. In China, too, the collective services supplied to working women have been performed most often by other women. Midwife, child-care worker, and cook in the communal dining hall all tend to be women's job categories, even when they are undertaken collectively instead of by the individual housewife.

In establishing day-care centers, communal kitchens, and home-help services, China's government has been almost exclusively concerned with bringing women into the labor market rather than with reshaping sex roles. This reflects an attitude met constantly in the writings of Chinese leaders: household chores and child rearing are the responsibility of the mother. Even when suggesting that husbands treat their wives with respect, as equal partners in the revolutionary cause, party propaganda has not stressed the duty of the man to share equally the burdens connected with everyday life.[7]

Swedish and Chinese policy makers, although they have not yet devised the optimal delivery system for their services to working women, are at least committed in principle to providing those services. Our survey of American programs reveals that national policy makers in this country are reluctant to make such a commitment. They prefer to rely on the private market to furnish working women with medical services, child care, and housekeeping help. This strategy means that women with the greatest need to work—working-class wives and mothers—are least able to afford support services. The other difficulty with this strategy is that the private market provides uneven service delivery. Entrepreneurs choose their locations to maximize their profits and their life-style preferences; this supply problem, well known in the field of health care, also plagues child care and home-help services.

In addition to the private market, national policy makers have relied on state governments to administer whatever public programs are available in maternity and child care, family planning, and home help. State programs have been aimed almost exclusively at the poor in the United States. Like the federal government, states have taken the position that public authorities should have responsibility for providing such services only to people who are too poor to purchase them from private suppliers.

The final section of this chapter examines one additional policy area not mentioned so far. We briefly compare the family assistance, or "welfare," programs of the three countries because these programs service so many female-headed households. The single woman heading a household is probably the clearest example we can find of the woman with a dual burden; she is by definition both breadwinner and homemaker. That so many of these women find themselves depending on public assistance suggests how difficult it is to juggle the two roles successfully.

BEARING CHILDREN: MATERNITY BENEFITS AND SERVICES

The fundamental social policies enabling women to work are those that address women's reproductive function. That many women workers bear children is the most clear-cut indication of women's dual role. First in 1919 and again in 1952, the International Labour Office in Geneva drafted conventions fixing minimum-level maternity benefits for women workers, including six weeks' mandatory leave after the birth of a child, six additional weeks' optional leave, a guarantee that a woman can reclaim her job at the end of the leave, and a cash allowance to assure healthy maintenance of the newborn infant. The ILO convention specifically recommended that the responsibility for paying the cash benefit should *not* fall primarily on employers. Rather, the allowance should be paid out of public funds or through an insurance scheme. In making this recommendation, the ILO was trying to minimize the likelihood of employer resistance to maternity protection policies, recognizing that employers have been almost universally antagonistic to government-sponsored schemes that call for employer contributions. As Evelyne Sullerot has remarked:

> Employers object to women's desire to have their cake and eat it, to reproduce and to go on earning. . . . This desire is considered unrealistic, but in fact, the only way to be realistic in the world of work is to be a man.[8]

The specific provisions of the ILO convention have been endorsed by only eight European nations, but most governments of Europe guarantee women workers some minimum leave of absence with job security and some cash benefit, although the amount of the benefit varies from a lump-sum allowance to 90 percent of the wages a woman would have earned had she stayed on the job. Sweden's system of maternity protection ranks at the top among European nations, rivaling even the elaborate benefits granted by several Eastern European governments.

Sweden

Swedes take pride in the fact that international surveys have consistently rated Sweden among the highest in the world for infant health and among the lowest for infant mortality. By 1973, Sweden had reduced her infant mortality rate (i.e., deaths of infants under one year of age per 1000 live births) to 10, compared with 18 for the United States. Health specialists warn against making the simplistic assumption that health indices of this kind can be directly attributed to variations in health services. Nonetheless, Sweden's health-care system concentrates more of its resources on maternity care and baby care than does the American health-care system (which concentrates resources more on old people).[9] Sweden's maternity services and benefits are a great deal more extensive than those of either the United States or China. Moreover, as figure 2–1 indicates, a dramatic reduction in infant mortality has accompanied the expansion of Sweden's maternity services.

Under Sweden's compulsory national health insurance system, health care is organized and paid for by the government. Under the Medical Care Act, county governments are charged with the responsibility of providing full institutional and outpatient medical services, including obstetrical services, to their residents. Expectant mothers are periodically examined at 621 county maternity clinics by midwives, who also conduct prenatal exercise classes as physical and psychological preparation for childbirth. The clinics offer free laboratory tests and outpatient care for any pregnancy-related illnesses. Unless unforeseen complications arise, midwives also deliver the babies; doctors are brought into the delivery only in problem cases. Under the national health system, all obstetrical care—including the delivery, a one-week stay in the hospital after the birth, and three months' postnatal care—is provided free by county hospitals, and all medications prescribed by obstetricians are dispensed without charge. National government subsidies cover about one quarter of the cost of maternity and infant-care programs; the county governments supply the remainder of the funding.

The most innovative, and to American readers the most intriguing, of Sweden's maternity benefits is the maternity allowance, renamed in January 1974 the Parental Leave. The practice of awarding a lump-sum maternity allowance to every new mother was first introduced in 1931 by the Riksdag in the recognition that "it was reasonable that public assistance should be given to the person who, at great personal risk and economic sacrifice, assured the continuation of society."[10] Designed to cover basic expenses on items required by a newborn child, the allowance was conceived as a universal benefit to which all mothers were entitled, regardless

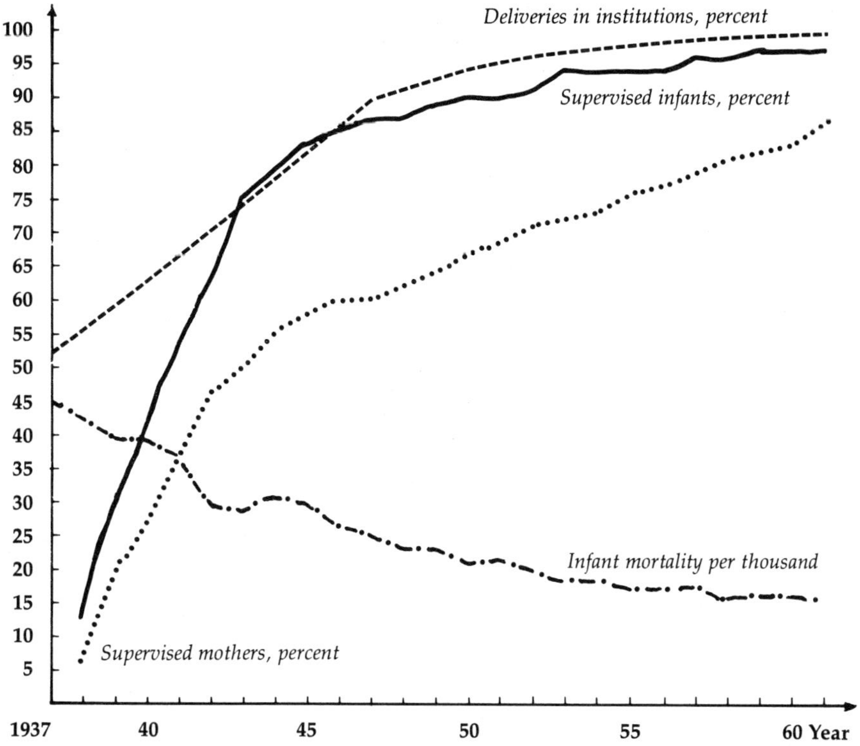

Source: Ragnar Berfenstam and Inger William-Olsson, *Early Child Care in Sweden* (London: Gordon and Breach, 1973), p. 71.

FIGURE 2-1. Percentage of Swedish Babies Delivered in Maternity Institutions, Percentage of New Mothers and Infants Supervised by Social Service Agencies, and Infant Mortality, 1937–61

of their income level and employment status. For four decades, the program operated so that the mother had only to register her baby at birth, and the national government paid the allowance automatically.

In January 1974 the government introduced a new system of Parental Leave. Under this system, every mother caring for a newborn is entitled to a nine-month allowance to meet the extra expenses incurred by the addition of the newborn to the household. The allowance, deliberately titled a "parental," rather than a "motherhood," benefit, goes to whichever parent has custody of the child after its birth. If the child's parents are separated but share custody of the child, then they share the benefits. Normally, the minimum allowance of about $160 a month is given to whichever parent was not employed before the birth of the child. If both parents were working before the birth, the maximum allowance is increased to compensate one of the parents for staying at home with the newborn. In such cases, the parents are entitled between them to a total of nine months' leave of absence from employment at 90 percent pay in order to care for the newborn. Mother and father may split the nine months between them in any proportion they desire; they may even opt to have the father use all nine months, while the mother remains on the job.

Another part of the program gives one parent (again, either mother or father) the right to a certain number of sick days with pay each year, to be taken in order to care for sick children at home. Effective January 1, 1977, a maximum 12 to 18 sick days a year are granted to each household, depending on the number of children in the family. These sick days may also be used by fathers who remain at home caring for older children after the birth of the youngest child.

China

Lacking anything approaching Sweden's national health system, China could not reasonably be expected to deliver comparable maternity services and benefits. Yet the progress made under the Communist party is impressive, especially considering their starting point in 1949. There is almost no way for an American citizen to understand the level of malnutrition and disease existing in China at that time. For women, this meant frequent pregnancies and high mortality rates for both mother and child. Neither the rural nor the urban population was well cared for. The following description was based on an investigation into Wing Chia Village in Honan Province in 1951:

> 132 women, none of whom was in perfect health, had lost 461 of their 646 children before they had reached the age of 16. 447, or 96.5 percent, died before reaching the age of three. . . .
>
> The busy farming season meant death for many children. The chief reason for this was that the women had no way of looking after their children when they went to work in the fields. . . . Sometimes babies were tied down to the bed, and the doors locked. . . . In the village of Pohu in Changko county, four children, left alone to play, fell into a well and were drowned. Accidents of this type, however, were not the only cause of infant and child mortality. Disease was the greatest killer. If children were taken seriously ill, they generally died because their parents had very little money, and there was no doctor or medical facilities in the countryside.[12]

No wonder the saying was prevalent in many areas of China, "Women conceive every year, but no child survives to toddle along the road."[13]

Although hampered by a low level of economic development, the Chinese Communist party set out to alleviate the suffering. One of the first groups to receive attention was the female proletariat or the woman worker. The Labor Insurance Regulations were inaugurated in 1951 and expanded in 1953.[14] These regulations gave the women covered 56 days' maternity leave with full pay, and in cases of difficult labor, 70 days. In her seventh month, the expectant mother was allowed to switch to lighter work. As part of the free medical care extended to workers and cadres, prenatal checkups and delivery were free. Care for dependents of workers was one half the regular fee.

Although these reforms were a boon to working women, their limitations should not be overlooked. Initial regulations did not include bank employees, cadres, and soldiers paid by the "fixed supply" system, and the majority of state employees (e.g., teachers).[15] Coverage was later expanded, but "at the end of 1958, out of a total non-agricultural labor force of 56.9 million, 13.8 million persons had labor insurance and 6.9 million had health insurance; about 12 percent of China's non-agricultural work force was fully covered under industrial health programs. . . . While we do not know exactly how many urban dwellers were covered under various health plans, it is hard to see how the number could have exceeded 25 percent of the total urban population."[16]

In rural areas the principal activity of the party in the early 1950s was to retrain midwives in order to ensure safe childbirth. Practically speaking, attention to this problem was one of the best ways to convince rural women of the party's concern for their welfare. For instance, one woman found it impossible to run literacy classes until the school took up the question of childbirth. As "the wife of the blacksmith Su told her one day, 'I have lost ten of my thirteen children, and my health is bad. I cannot put any heart into this study.' "[17] The midwives' techniques were themselves part of the health problem: "They had infected countless women by probing with unwashed hands and long fingernails." The retraining program was aimed at basic improvements:

> Basic precautions against septicaemia, such as scrubbed hands, and instruments sterilized in locally distilled spirits, drove maternal and infant mortality down. Later, "maternity stations" were built in some villages, so many women, especially those for whom complications were feared, could have their babies in better conditions than their homes could furnish.[18]

The development of medical facilities in the countryside was slow in comparison with the crash program to retrain midwives. Medical care in remote parts of the countryside was inadequate even in the late 1950s, ten years after the Communists took power.[19]

Since 1949, women working in agriculture have been entitled to switch to light work during late pregnancy and to work near home during lactation. Although some communes now give maternity leaves of 30 to 60 days, the leave is unpaid. Because women regularly take time off from work for household chores in the rural areas, it is difficult to view unpaid maternity leave as a bonus. Making shoes and clothes at the season's change, cooking and cleaning for the new year, and coming to work late and leaving early because of daily chores all seem to be reasons for regularly excusing women from work. Women workers on the communes are often awarded only 7.5 work points a day, instead of the 10 points usually given to men, because they have work to do at home and thus spend fewer hours in the fields.

Problems have arisen from the stipulation that women, even pregnant women, should work. During the campaign to develop mutual-aid teams, and especially later during collectivization and communization of agriculture, overzealous cadres caused injury and miscarriages:

> Some people completely ignore women's physical characteristics and household pre-occupations, and often assign to women farm work beyond their capacity. One cooperative in Wu Kiang county, Kiangsu Province, made the erroneous arrangement of offering double pay to pregnant women for farm work done during the childbirth period. This practice actually fostered accidents.[21]

These abuses gave rise to many articles in which work-team leaders were urged to pay more attention to women's state of health in assigning work. "To facilitate such accommodation, mixed work teams were asked to appoint women deputy leaders if their leaders were men, because women found it difficult to discuss intimate matters with men."[22]

Such problems have not been confined to agriculture. In 1957 the complaint was heard that factories were still failing to follow the order to give 56 days' maternity leave to pregnant workers. "In many jointly-operated and some state-operated factories . . . some women workers who had been pregnant for seven or eight months [were] still doing the same amount of work, thus affecting their health."[23] How widespread these abuses were is difficult to assess. Suffice it to say that concern about women's health was sufficiently great to warrant comments by leading women communists at the Eighth Party Congress in 1956.

The Cultural Revolution of 1966–68 brought changes to rural and urban areas in the form of expanded health care. By 1965, every one of China's more than two thousand counties had a "fairly well-equipped and competently-staffed general hospital."[24] Although this represented an eightfold increase in medical facilities over the 1949 level,[25] Mao Tse-tung wanted to decentralize health care even further, to bring medical personnel closer to the people. Located in urban areas, county hospitals were serving approximately 450,000 people, many of whom lived great distances away. According to Mao, "the Health Ministry renders service to only 15 percent of the nation's population [and] . . . should be renamed the Urban Health Ministry."[26]

One method used to accomplish this decentralization was the training of paramedical personnel. Large numbers of women and men were chosen by their fellow workers to train for a short period of time (two to six months) to take care of routine medical problems and complaints. In rural areas these people were called either "barefoot doctors" or "midwives." After training, they returned to their production units, receiving in wages no more than fellow commune members could make. In general, midwives deliver a baby in the peasant's own home and have the job of encouraging birth control. Barefoot doctors also educate women in birth-control techniques and furnish contraceptives.

In the cities, Chinese women now receive prenatal care either through their place of work (many major enterprises maintain clinics) or the neighborhood hospital. Visitors to the mainland report that almost all babies born in the cities are born in hospitals; abortions and contraceptives are free, but prenatal checkups and delivery are not. The greatest compliment to the system came from a pediatrician who visited China in 1973:

> Everyone interviewed, at whatever level in the system, seemed to have been trained adequately for functioning at his or her particular level; they could define the problems they were expected to handle, knew what to do about them, and where to refer problems beyond their own abilities.[27]

United States

The protection of women workers after childbirth has been labeled "among the most widespread and least controversial measures of social welfare legislation."[28] The United States has the distinction of being the *only* major industrialized country in the world that lacks a national insurance plan covering medical expenses for childbirth and is one of few governments in industrialized nations that does not provide any cash benefits to working women to compensate for lost earnings. Only in October 1978, after a two-year legislative battle, did the federal government enact legislation to guarantee that a working woman who bears a child is entitled to sick-leave benefits ordinarily provided by her employer. The Pregnancy Disability Law was introduced in Congress to counteract a major setback on the issue suffered by working women in 1976.

Prior to 1976, progress on pregnancy benefits had been slow but steady. Before the 1964 Civil Rights Act, which outlawed discrimination on the basis of sex, the federal government had left the question of maternity policy in the hands of state governments. States were free to pass or reject legislation requiring employers to pay disability benefits to women for maternity leaves. Only three states passed such laws. Many private insurance companies, which underwrite disability insurance for employers, traditionally excluded payment for any disability arising from pregnancy. Similarly, health and hospital insurance plans often exempted entirely, or limited the coverage for, pregnancy and maternity-related illnesses (despite the fact that such plans routinely cover such male problems as prostate disorders).

In the late 1960s, the Equal Employment Opportunity Commission (EEOC), which had been set up to enforce the 1964 Civil Rights Act, began to focus on denial of maternity leaves as an issue of sex discrimination. In 1972 the EEOC issued guidelines stating that an employer who failed to extend benefits from a company insurance plan to cover pregnancy, miscarriage, abortion, childbirth, or recovery from childbirth was violating the Civil Rights Act. The EEOC's position was not that women should be guaranteed a maternity leave, but simply that whatever benefits a company provided for other physical disabilities must also be provided for pregnancy. Backed by its power to seek federal court orders against violaters, the EEOC began working out agreements with companies around the country.

The EEOC's position was radically undermined by a series of U.S. Supreme Court decisions on pregnancy disability. In 1974 the Court upheld a state decision in favor of a California insurance program that excluded women with normal pregnancies from disability benefits but awarded payments to pregnant women who missed work because of medical complications arising from their pregnancies.[29] In a 1976 ruling the Court decided that employers who provide disability insurance could legally deny women compensation for absence caused by pregnancy, whether it involved complications or not. This ruling, which reversed six lower courts, involved General Electric.[30] GE's sick-pay insurance plan paid benefits for nearly every medical condition except pregnancy. Lower courts had ruled that such an arrangement discriminated against women; the Supreme Court disagreed. The Court's reasoning in the 1974 and 1976 cases was similar. Insurance programs that excluded pregnancy-related disabilities discriminated against a particular medical condition and not against a particular sex; GE did not provide maternity benefits for either sex. Because many women workers, as well as men, were ineligible for such benefits, the program did not single out women, but rather *pregnant* women, as a class.

The only consolation for working women was that the 1976 Supreme Court decision represented only an interpretation of the Civil Rights Act, not a constitutional ruling. It did not make it impossible for either the states or the federal government to pass future laws requiring employers to provide paid maternity leaves. The EEOC began lobbying on behalf of such federal legislation almost as soon as the Carter administration took office in January 1977. By April, representatives from the Justice and Labor departments appeared at hearings of the Senate Human Resources Committee to voice the administration's support for a bill to require employers to treat women affected by pregnancy and pregnancy-related conditions exactly as they treat employees with other physical disabilities. The strategy entailed amending Title VII of the 1964 Civil Rights Act to state that discrimination based on pregnancy, childbirth, or related medical conditions was illegal. Thus the new legislation, finally enacted in late 1978, outlawed a host of discriminatory practices: stipulating larger deductibles for pregnancy than for other disabilities; subtracting maternity leave from an employee's accumulated seniority, although this is not done for other disabilities; paying pregnancy benefits to employees' wives, but not to female employees.

While acknowledging that the bill represents an important victory for women workers, we must also point out that it falls far short of creating a uniform, nationally sponsored maternity protection system. It merely requires that employers extend to pregnant women whatever disability benefits they choose to offer other employees. Moreover, the final version of the bill contained compromise language that allows employers to exclude abortions from their disability plans, even though they must provide coverage for complications arising from abortions. Pregnant employees are now entitled to the same benefits enjoyed by all other disabled employees, with the exception of medical coverage and sick leave for abortion.

Traditionally, employers' arguments against paid maternity leaves have been based largely on the view that pregnancy, unlike other disabilities, is a voluntary condition. This argument, if extended, posits that women can choose not to become pregnant if they want, or need, to continue to earn an income. It is a classic illustration of the more general argument that women who want careers should arrange their lives so as to minimize family responsibilities, and conversely, that women with heavy family responsibilities should be willing to forego certain job rewards. It is an argument against women's dual roles and in favor of mutually exclusive role choices for women.

If we shift our attention to the national government's role in providing maternity services (as opposed to cash benefits), the picture is considerably brighter, or at least it used to be. Maternal and child welfare programs have received enthusiastic federal support since the 1920s. Unfortunately, for the past ten years Congress has been trying to reduce its responsibility by shifting the administration of maternity and infant care programs to state governments. Federal involvement in maternity programs had an auspicious beginning; the Maternity and Infant Protection Act of 1921 (known as the Sheppard-Towner Act) represented the first venture of the national government into social welfare legislation of any kind. Up to that point, maternity services had developed at the local level, and state governments had taken only a passing interest in them. The 1921 bill provided national funds to local health units to provide counseling and care for pregnant women, and it channeled federal funds to state governments for medical aid, hospital care, counseling centers, and visiting nurses. This act has the distinction of being one of the first pieces of federal legislation to arouse the determined opposition of the American Medical Association, on the grounds that it would lead to socialized medicine.[31]

The program stimulated a rapid expansion of state and local maternity services throughout the 1920s until it was allowed to expire in 1929 by Congress and the Hoover administration. But national neglect was short-lived; federal involvement resumed under Title V of the 1935 Social Security Act, which gave the Children's Bureau in the Labor Department large appropriations to administer formula-based grants to help states expand maternity clinics, counseling for pregnant women, and well-baby clinics. In its early years, the Children's Bureau could point to a steadily declining infant mortality rate as evidence that it was fulfilling its mission. But it never reached the "takeoff" point at which it sparked enough interest to command significant increases in its funding. Gradually, through the 1950s, the program received progressively less attention from Washington. Social policy analyst Gilbert Steiner attributes the program's stagnation to its inability "to attract a fair share of attention in an environment dominated by complex issues of social security, unemployment insurance, and public assistance."[32] At President Kennedy's urging, the program was modernized in the early 1960s by adding special grants targeted on low-income urban neighborhoods.

But, abruptly in 1967, Congress mandated that by July 1972 the national government should turn over administrative responsibility for maternal and infant care to the states. The national government would continue to provide funds, but states would henceforth receive the money in a bloc grant and would decide how best to use it. This shift to curtail the national government's responsibility for social service programs was a reflection of mounting congressional enthusiasm for giving states and localities greater discretion in spending federal funds. The trend culminated in Title XX of the Social Security Act, signed into law in 1975. Title XX shifted to the states the chief responsibility for a wide variety of social services to families.

Gilbert Steiner's detailed analysis of maternal and child health programs, *The Children's Cause*, portrays the erratic fortunes of these programs over their 50-year history. Without an organized constituency, they have excited only intermittent interest on the part of national policy makers, usually when they were tied to other, more salient, issues. The temporary boost they received during the Kennedy administration, for example, came about through their identification with the issue of mental retardation.[33] Having traced this uneven history, Steiner concludes that the United States lacks a comprehensive policy on maternal and child health; even more disheartening is his observation that

> there is now no mechanism for formulating such a policy. . . . Programs result more from the momentary strength of a particular group than from systematic consideration of the trade-offs that may be necessary between services and research; federal and state financing; preventive care and treatment.[34]

PREVENTING MOTHERHOOD: FAMILY PLANNING, CONTRACEPTION, AND ABORTION POLICIES

A woman cannot plan and control her work life if she cannot control her fertility. Birth control and family planning are essential services in any society where women pursue employment outside the home. Governments' birth-control policies are obviously linked to their maternity policies, but the former are immeasurably more controversial than the latter. Preventing motherhood is in most societies a highly controversial and intensely political issue. This is not to say that birth control is usually a *partisan* issue. In fact, it is an issue assiduously avoided by party politicians in most competitive party systems; party leaders usually calculate that taking a stand on this volatile question is likely to cost at least as many supporters as it will attract. The stunning defeat of Indira Gandhi's Congress party in India in 1976 is an object lesson to party politicians who would seek to make birth control a partisan campaign issue. Even in a one-party system like China's, a strong birth-control program has been couched in terms of improving the family's quality of life rather than specifically preventing births.

What makes birth-control programs so intensely political? A family's decisions on birth control are among the most private prerogatives the citizenry enjoys in any political system. Government policies on birth control are controversial to the extent that they represent state intervention in this sphere of private decision making. This is true of government policies to promote or suppress information about birth control. There is also the related question whether governments, in making birth control available to all women in a society, are directly supporting its use or merely equalizing access so that all families can make free choices. The ultimate question involved in birth-control policies is how government programs affect the delicate balance between the interests of the state and the prerogatives of individual citizens.

Sweden

In 1910, the same year Sweden passed a law forbidding the distribution of contraceptives and even information about contraception, an organization was formed to fight for free access to family-planning information. The National Association for Sex Education (RFSU) lobbied vigorously for the abolition of the 1910 law, for free contraceptives dispensed to those who could not afford to buy them, and for publicly funded counseling centers. Their first victory came in 1938 with the repeal of the anticontraceptive law. Since then, the RFSU has seen the gradual adoption, one by one, of all its major goals.

Since the 1950s, county maternity clinics have been required to provide information, advice, and contraceptives to all who request them, regardless of their marital status. At these clinics, girls over fifteen years of age can receive birth-control information and contraceptives even without parental approval. Under Sweden's national health insurance system, the cost of providing birth-control counseling at county clinics, the RFSU, or a private physician's office is reimbursed by the national government. Counseling is free to the client. Certain kinds of contraceptives, such as coils and diaphragms, are also provided free at the clinics. Birth-control pills fall under the health system's general rebate on medicines; a woman need pay only the first few dollars of the charge, and the remainder is picked up by health insurance. Contraceptives are also widely sold in drugstores, department stores, and sidewalk vending machines. Moreover, since 1956, the Swedish government has required that sex education be included in the school curriculum as a compulsory subject for youngsters fourteen and older.

The extent of the national government's concern with sex education is reflected in its creation in 1964 of a commission to recommend measures to improve sex education in Sweden. In particular, the commission was charged with rewriting the nationally distributed *Teachers' Handbook* issued in 1956 as a guide to instructors in sex education classes. Among other recommendations, the commission suggested that the *Handbook* should no longer take the position that early sexual experience is either immoral or socially unacceptable. Schools, the commission argued, should not "take sides" on the moral question, but simply portray objectively the risks accompanying early sexual activity, including pregnancy and venereal disease. The commission also recommended that contraceptive information be made available to students at even younger ages because the evidence indicated that a significant minority of Swedish youngsters were sexually active in their early teens.[35]

With its domestic objectives largely accomplished by the 1960s, RFSU shifted a significant portion of its energy to working for family planning overseas, especially in Third World countries. Sweden was the first nation in the world to introduce a government-financed foreign-aid program specifically intended to promote birth control. In addition to financing family-planning programs in Ceylon, Pakistan, and Tunisia, Sweden's government has pressured international organizations, especially UNICEF and WHO, to give family planning a high priority.

Abortion has been no less controversial an issue in Sweden than in the United States. Each successive modification of Sweden's abortion law has been accompanied by widespread and heated public debate. Until 1938, abortions could be legally performed only for medical reasons; through the 1920s numerous attempts to loosen this restriction had failed in the Riksdag. But in the face of an estimated 10,000 illegal abortions being performed each year, the government established a Royal Commission to recommend changes in the law. The resulting reform expanded the legal grounds for abortion beyond the strictly medical to include humanitarian grounds (if, for example, a woman had become pregnant as a minor, a rape victim, as partner to incestuous intercourse, or as a legally insane person) and eugenic reasons (if the offspring were likely to inherit a serious deformity or disease from either parent). Despite this liberalization, estimates taken between 1939 and 1943 showed that although 400–700 legal abortions were performed annually, the number of illegal abortions remained around 10,000.[36] Even with the addition in 1946 of another legally recognized basis for abortion—namely, sociomedical grounds, when childbirth could conceivably injure the mother's physical or mental health—the annual rate of illegal abortion was not reduced. It remained about 10,000 in 1949.[37]

Widespread discontent with the high incidence of illegal abortions forced the national government once again to consider the issue. The report of the 1950 investigative committee included for the first time the startling observation that the total number of abortions performed yearly remained constant. Periodic reforms in the abortion law did not alter the total; they merely removed a certain percentage from the illegal category into the legal. But public opinion in the 1950s was running against any further liberalization, and the 1950 investigation did not produce any changes in the law. In fact, the number of legal abortions granted by the National Board of Health dropped precipitously during the 1950s; in 1960 the board approved 60 percent fewer applications than it had approved in 1951 (see table 2-1.)

As the table shows, the decline in the 1950s was followed by a sharp upswing in the early 1960s, both in the percentage of applications approved and in abortions as a percentage of live births. In large part this can be attributed to a shift in public opinion caused by the dramatic publicity surrounding the deformed "thalidomide babies" of the early 1960s. In response to that tragedy, the government once more expanded the grounds for legal abortion, adding in 1963 the grounds of fetal injury, meaning a high probability that the fetus had been severely damaged or deformed in the womb. The thalidomide experience generated public sympathy for abortion and contributed to an increase in applications to the Health Board.

Even with the addition of fetal injury as the fifth justification for legal abortion, critics of the law were not satisfied. The law was still based on a presumption that, in the absence of some overriding indication to the contrary, a pregnant woman ought to be compelled to carry a child to term. Moreover, the law left the ultimate power to make the decision to abort

TABLE 2-1. Abortions in Sweden, 1951–1972

	Percentage of Applications Approved by National Board of Health	*Legal Abortions as Percentage of Live Births*
1951	84	5.6
1955	71	4.2
1960	62	2.7
1965	86	5.0
1970	97	14.5
1974*	97	27.9

**Last year in which all abortions required official approval.*

Source: Adapted from Rita Liljestrom, *A Study of Abortion in Sweden* (Stockholm: Royal Ministry for Foreign Affairs, 1974), p. 100. Also *Statistisk Arsbok 1978*, p. 298.

with a government agency rather than with the pregnant woman or even the woman's physician. In a widely quoted article on abortion reform in the United States, Garrett Hardin labeled the Swedes' five classifications for justifiable abortion a system for "managing compulsory pregnancy."[38] He urged the U.S. government *not* to adopt it, especially as it did not seem to reduce substantially the number of illegal abortions performed every year in Sweden.

In Sweden, disturbing findings in the mid-1960s concerned children born after applications for abortion had been refused by the Board of Health. One noteworthy study followed 120 such offspring to adulthood and found that, compared with a control group, the unwanted children were more often arrested for drunkenness or criminal or antisocial behavior, received more psychiatric care and were more often exempted from military service because of some defect than wanted children.[39] If Tomasson is correct in his observation that the Swedish government makes greater use of research findings in drafting legislation than does any government in the world,[40] it would be surprising if such studies did not influence legislators toward changing the abortion laws.

A sensational aspect of the Swedish abortion controversy was the widely publicized travel in 1964–1965 by Swedish women to foreign countries, especially Poland, to obtain abortions. The pregnant women, many of whom traveled on charter flights organized by young liberals to protest the existing laws, were risking prosecution; Swedish law forbids citizens to engage overseas in acts classified as crimes on Swedish territory. The publicity surrounding this trend provoked the minister of justice in 1965 to appoint a national Committee on Abortion to reexamine Sweden's abortion laws.

As is typical of Swedish governmental commissions, the Committee on Abortion contained representatives from all the major political parties, as well as professional experts on law and medicines. Even with this varied membership, the committee achieved agreement on some strong recommendations, which were outlined in its 1971 report, "The Right to Abortion." They included recommendations that the woman's wishes should be the primary basis for the decision and that the government should abolish the time limit of 24 weeks, beyond which abortions could be performed only to save the woman's life or health. When finally enacted into law, the reform incorporated the first recommendation but dropped the second. The new law, effective January 1975, put the decision to abort almost entirely in the hands of the woman up through the eighteenth week of the pregnancy. During that period, a doctor can deny an abortion only on grounds that it poses serious risk to the woman's life or health. Moreover, the decision to deny an abortion is referred automatically to the Board of Health for review. One extra condition is imposed after the twelfth week in the form of a special investigation by a social worker to provide the doctor with full information on which to judge the risks. After the eighteenth week, an abortion can be granted only by the Board of Health, again on the basis of a social worker's investigation. The new law has not had a dramatic effect on the total number of abortions performed annually in Sweden. That number increased by only 6 percent in 1975 and then declined slightly in 1976.

China

The official Chinese attitude toward birth control has been less consistent than its attitude toward safe childbirth; birth control for the Chinese has provoked mixed feelings. Because orthodox Marxists view the theory of overpopulation as a capitalist trick, birth control has been a thorny issue. Marxists say that what seems to be too many people trying to survive on too few resources is actually too many people fighting over the crumbs left by the rich capitalists. Few statements emanating from Peking have admitted that a large population might have unfortunate consequences for the development of a socialist country. Rather, when birth control has been emphasized, the dominant theme has been the evil consequences of too many children for the family. As Chang Yun maintained at the Third National Women's Congress in 1957:

> The object of our plea for planned birth-giving is to protect the health of our women and children, to make family life easier and happier and to enable socialist construction to proceed at a quicker pace . . . There is a fundamental difference between the planned birth-giving that we advocate and the (Malthusian) population theory held by the bourgeois rightists.[41]

"This was to become the basic explanation of all future efforts to limit Chinese fertility . . . with Peking stoutly maintaining that 'moderating' the birth rate is entirely different from restricting population growth."[42]

The latest reports from the People's Republic indicate that a significant birth-control campaign has been going on for at least the past ten years. Sporadic attempts at birth control were instituted during the 1950s, but they were halfhearted and penetrated only the upper classes of the cities. By the 1960s the practice of contraception seems to have become widespread among city workers, and during and after the Cultural Revolution, the expansion of medical personnel brought birth control to the peasants.[43] The lowest reported birthrates for China in the early 1970s were in Shanghai; the city as a whole averaged 6 live births per 1000 people,[44] compared with 20 to 30 per 1000 in the rural areas. How astonishing these rates are can be seen from comparison with two other figures: China's annual crude birthrate before liberation was approximately 43 per 1000; New York City's birthrate among whites is 17.1 per 1000, and among nonwhites it is 24.7 per 1000.[45] The apparent target for China is 15 per 1000.

Many obstacles have had to be overcome in expanding birth control. One of the first was the provision of contraceptives to a population as large as China's. "In February 1958, one newspaper admitted in an editorial that the total supply of contraceptives in China was sufficient to meet the needs of only 2.2 percent of all persons in the reproductive ages."[46] Moreover, complaints indicate that quality was low, and inventories were badly coordinated. "Though many dispensaries have supplies of rubber prophylactics and pessaries . . . the contraceptive jelly to be used with these . . . is out of stock for a long time."[47] This situation contrasts sharply with the picture given by more recent visitors. Contraceptives are not only in abundant supply but are readily available through barefoot doctors and Red medical workers (the paraprofessional equivalents of barefoot doctors in the cities). Contraceptives are obtained free of charge. Experimentation with pills and shots effective for periods of three months to a year is also ongoing, as well as the redesigning of mechanical devices to make them less troublesome.

Abortions in China are legal and free. They can be obtained on request of the woman alone and do not make a woman a social pariah. Generally they are performed by a simple suction system in hospitals, although more and more barefoot doctors are being trained to perform them.[48] In the cities, when an abortion is performed within 50 days of conception, the woman has 10 days' leave from work; when it is done from 50 to 120 days after conception, she has 30 days' leave.[49] Although visitors report that abortions are readily available, at least one refugee told of a long waiting list, saying that a woman often needed the intervention of a high official to get an abortion before it was too late.[50] In any case, the emphasis in China is on contraception rather than abortion, and multiple abortions are not condoned.

The idea of birth control flies in the face of previous traditions. As in most other areas of Chinese life, "education" has been extensively used to change people's values. In preliberation days children, especially male children, were a form of social security. Breaking down the belief that many children are a blessing has not been easy, especially among the older people. The National Women's Federation and street residents' committees have conducted meetings and heart-to-heart talks to convince women of the value of contraception. Since the Cultural Revolution, many health stations and production teams even keep charts showing the type of birth-control method each woman is using. The chart is updated by monthly visits from the health worker, who asks about the form of contraception and discusses any problems.[51] The emphasis is on protecting the health of mother and child and enabling the mother to participate in society. Having fewer children will free her to contribute more to the revolution.

Late marriage, as a form of birth control, has also been encouraged. Twenty-five is considered an optimal age for a woman to marry, and thirty for a man. Waiting not only reduces births but also allows women and men to contribute their youth to the "building of the state"; and considering the extent of the physical labor still required in the countryside, vigor and good health are important economic assets. Because of the strongly puritanical nature of Chinese society, the Chinese can be sure that late marriage will reduce births. Premarital sex is almost nonexistent. As one expert pointed out in relation to the Red Guard Movement, China is one of the few countries in which millions of teen-aged boys and girls could travel, demonstrate, and sleep under the same roof without affecting the country's birthrate.[52]

In spite of their successes, the Chinese still have many practical obstacles to overcome. The government has not been able to replace the social welfare services performed by the family—medical help for prolonged illness, old age insurance, and so on—and until it is able to do so, having many children will be considered a necessity.

> This was brought home to one student sent down from Canton City to the countryside. In the village to which he was sent, it was the custom in the summer for the men to gather at a certain spot on the edge of the village after supper, to catch the cool evening breeze and converse. On one of these occasions, the student seized the opportunity to talk about the problems of marrying too early and having too many children. The farmers gathered about quickly retorted that he did not understand their problem. If they were to wait until they were thirty years old to marry, then they would be fifty years old before even their first son would be old enough to be an able-bodied laborer. What would happen in the meantime, if the parents should get sick? Particularly, what would happen if the father became ill with TB or some such disease? There would be no adult male to support the family, and they would sink into poverty. They therefore had to marry as near age twenty as possible.[53]

Moreover, because the woman still marries outside her village and goes to live with the husband's family, she is considered less valuable to her natal family than a son. Her family expends resources needed to bring her up and possibly to educate her, only to lose her services just when she becomes productive. Therefore, the family will keep having children until at least two sons are born, increasing the population. In the last few years, attempts have been made to combat the practice of the daughter-in-law's automatically moving to the husband's family, especially when her own parents have produced only female children. Such efforts, if successful, will reduce the number of children women must bear to ensure the safety of their families. They will help combat the situation Mao described to Edgar Snow in 1970:

> In the countryside, a woman still wanted to have boy children. If the first and second were girls, she would make another try. If the third one came and was still a girl, the mother would try again. Pretty soon there would be nine of them, the mother was already 45 or so, and she would finally decide to leave it at that.[54]

Given these obstacles, the progress made in China in the past thirty years appears all the more remarkable. A recent report sponsored by the

Smithsonian Institution described China's program as virtually unique among the developing nations, in combining (1) a massive political commitment of manpower and resources; (2) the ability of political elites to overrule vested interests in the society, especially physicians; and (3) a health system that relies heavily on paramedical personnel deployed at the urban neighborhood or rural village level. Through such techniques, birthrates in China's urban centers already have been lowered enough to compare favorably with national birthrates in the U.S. (14.5 per 1000 in 1975) and Sweden (13.5 per 1000 in 1975), and progress is steady in the rural areas.[55]

United States

The federal government has taken nothing like the strong interest shown by the Swedish and Chinese national governments in family planning. Federal action in family planning dates only from the 1960s and, unlike federal action in the field of maternal welfare, has been limited to the poverty population. Recent federal policy calls into question even the government's responsibility to provide birth control to the poor.

For most of the last hundred years, the federal government's position on mass birth-control programs has been not simply inactivity but outright disapproval. Federal legislation passed in 1873 (known as the Comstock Law) outlawed any importing of contraceptives, transporting of contraceptives across state lines, or mailing of contraceptives and birth-control information. The law was named after Anthony Comstock, a nineteenth-century exponent of legal bans on contraception and an officer of the New York Society for the Suppression of Vice. Once the federal government had passed such legislation, about half the states enacted similar laws, prohibiting public hospitals, private clinics, and even physicians from dispensing birth-control information. Such laws remained on the books until the 1960s. Planned Parenthood reported in 1968 that 60 percent of the states still had some laws limiting the distribution or display of contraceptives.[56] Several famous court cases of the 1960s publicized the archaic state statutes on contraception. A family-planning advocate was arrested in Boston in 1967 for publicly displaying a contraceptive pill; he waited two years to have his conviction overturned by the Massachusetts Supreme Court. An even more celebrated example was the 1965 *Griswold* v. *Connecticut* decision, in which the U.S. Supreme Court finally struck down as unconstitutional a Connecticut state law prohibiting the use of contraceptives. This decision, which involved a married couple, invalidated the law only for married couples' use of contraception, however; it took until 1972 for the legalization to be extended to unmarried persons.[57]

Most state laws reflect a climate of opinion prevalent in the early twentieth century. After public opinion began shifting, the laws proved strongly resistant to change, in spite of the active agitation of some highly determined reformers. The most famous among them was undoubtedly Margaret Sanger. Based on information she had obtained from Dutch physicians on a trip to Europe, Sanger in 1914 launched a campaign to promote free access to birth-control information. When she began publishing a monthly magazine, she was arrested and indicted for sending birth-control propaganda through the mails. (The federal government eventually dropped the case against her.) In 1915 Sanger founded the National Birth Control League, which continued the fight throughout the 1920s and '30s, eventually changing its name to Planned Parenthood in 1942. Interestingly, Sanger's efforts got little official support from women's organizations in the 1920s. The League of Women Voters, for instance, refused to endorse the struggle.

Throughout the 1950s, the national government staunchly resisted any involvement in birth-control programs. When a presidential commission recommended in 1959 that the U.S. government begin an active campaign to promote family planning in foreign countries, President Eisenhower opposed the idea, specifically labeling birth control a private problem, not a public concern. Specialists in family planning have speculated that the federal government could have introduced public family-planning programs with popular support during the 1950s. A 1956 opinion poll showed that at a time of total federal inactivity in this field, 65 percent of Americans (even 59 percent of American Catholics) favored government action.[58] In the absence of federal action, the problem of unwanted pregnancies grew to massive proportions in the early 1960s. One study showed that from 1960 to 1965, fully one fifth of all U.S. births were unwanted by their parents at the time of conception and would probably have been avoided if the parents had had access to safe contraception or abortion.[59]

When the federal government finally entered the family-planning field in the mid-1960s, it was in programs aimed at the poor. President Johnson's 1966 health policy statement to Congress declared it "essential that *all* families have access to information and service that will allow freedom to choose the number and spacing of their children within the dictates of individual conscience." But when programs were introduced, it became clear that the federal government intended to continue to rely on private physicians or state and municipal clinics and hospitals to provide family-planning services for the vast majority of American women. The national government would confine its efforts to helping the poor. The Medicaid program of 1965 provided federal funds (to be matched by state money) to pay for an array of medical services to the poor, including birth control, if the state chose to include it. (A 1972 amendment to Medicaid *required* that states provide Medicaid coverage for family planning, at a federal-state matching ratio of 90:10.) The Office of Economic Opportunity began in 1965 to issue funds to local antipoverty programs for family-planning assistance. By 1967, Congress had designated family planning a special priority of the OEO program and had amended the Social Security Act to require that states offer family-planning services to public assistance recipients.

The one major piece of national legislation that looked as if it would have an impact not only on the poor but on all American women was the 1970 Family Services and Population Research Act, which put the federal government in the business of providing family-planning services. The bill funded HEW to develop and maintain family-planning programs and to contract for training, research, and the writing of educational materials in family planning. It further required HEW to develop a five-year plan for implementing its social service and research programs. This bill represented a departure from previous ones because it enabled HEW to create federally administered programs rather than channel money to states for their programs.

This gradual acceleration of national interest and involvement in family planning was cut short by the wave of "New Federalism" that swept Washington in the early 1970s. Preferring to shift responsibility for family planning back to the states, the President opposed the extension of the Family Planning Act when it came up for renewal in 1973. Congress halfheartedly renewed it for only one more year.[60]

Abortion, like other forms of birth control, is now accessible in the United States to women who can pay for the procedure in the private medical market. Abortion is one of the oldest forms of birth control; in fact, abortion before the fetus was viable was the legal right of all American women in the early years of the republic. Not until the 1820s did states enact laws prohibiting all abortions except those needed to save the mother's life. Interestingly, these early antiabortion laws were not passed to protect the rights of the unborn, but rather to protect pregnant women from the extremely high risks associated with the primitive abortion procedures in use at the time. Abortions (except to save the mother's life) remained illegal in most states until the late 1960s. Nonetheless, an estimated one million illegal abortions a year were being performed in the late 1960s.[61]

Beginning in 1967, several states revised their laws, broadening the legal justifications for abortion, much as Sweden's government had been doing. But it was a 1973 Supreme Court's decision that dramatically altered the national government's position on abortion. In *Roe* v. *Wade* the Court established rules governing abortion that are at least as liberal as those enacted in Sweden's 1974 reform. During the first 12 weeks, the decision is left entirely to the woman and her doctor; from the 13th to 24th week, states can regulate abortion *only* in ways related to maternal health; only during the 25th to 36th week can the state outlaw abortions altogether (except to save the mother's life). Although U.S. national policy appears at least as liberal as Sweden's, abortions are not as widely available in the United States as they are in Sweden. A national study released by Planned Parenthood in late 1975 revealed that in spite of the liberalized policy, 30 to 50 percent of American women wanting abortions in 1974 did not get them.[62] The two main explanations were geographic disparities and inability to pay. Clinics and hospitals willing to perform abortions are heavily concentrated in major metropolitan centers, as are many health services in the

United States. Large regions in the South and Southwest are virtually without such services. Poor women are the most likely to have abortion requests go unmet.

The problems faced by indigent women seeking abortions were increased by the Supreme Court's ruling in June 1977; under that ruling, states need not cover abortions for Medicaid recipients. At a time when Medicaid funds were paying for about one third of all legal abortions performed annually, the Court's decision doubtless reduced the availability of abortions in many states. Moreover, in December 1977 Congress amended a bill to fund HEW in a way that further discouraged even those states that desired to continue covering abortions with Medicaid payments. The bill withdrew the federal share of subsidies for abortions except when (1) the pregnancy results from rape or incest, (2) a doctor has certified that the abortion is needed to save the mother's life, or (3) two doctors have certified in writing that "severe and longlasting physical health damage to the mother would result if the pregnancy were carried to term."

Once again, as in the cases of maternity care and contraceptive services, the national government moved in the 1970s to reduce its responsibility for making abortion services available even to poor women. That responsibility now lies with state governments. Considering the states' historic position on abortion and their widespread financial problems, the prospects for increasing access to abortion are dim. In October 1978, the National Abortion Rights Action League reported:

> The importance of Congress's restrictive funding legislation in the overall move to cut public subsidy for abortion cannot be denied. Presently, 19 states are funding according to HEW regulations, 12 states are funding only in cases involving the life of the woman, and 5 states (Illinois, Massachusetts, New Jersey, Pennsylvania, and California) are funding "medically necessary" abortions under court order. . . . In almost every other state the funding scenario is similar: severe reduction in Medicaid funding and a significant decrease in the number of Medicaid funded abortions.[63]

We have emphasized that, unlike Sweden and China, the U.S. government has confined its family-planning programs to a limited segment of the population because this point highlights several crucial features of American family-planning policy that distinguish it from other nations' policies. First, the American government does not regard access to birth control as a right, in the sense that the Swedish and Chinese governments do. In Sweden and China, contraception is tied into the national health care systems in a way that makes birth-control information and contraceptives available to virtually every citizen, regardless of the ability to pay. But the program through which the U.S. government reaches the widest clientele—Medicaid—serves only the population on public assistance. The majority of American women are not reached by national programs; instead, they buy their family-planning services on the private market.

The second feature of the system that deserves highlighting is that even if there were a federal commitment to providing universal family-planning services, that goal would be unreachable, given the present health care structure in the United States. Family planning illustrates that we are not set up in the United States to deliver mass personal health services of *any* kind. Frederick Jaffe has made this point forcefully:

> The slow response of the U.S. health system to the change in family planning policy is related to the basic issue of whether a nation should choose to emphasize quality care for the few or basic care services for the many. . . . Family planning, whatever its broad social and health consequences, remains a relatively simple mass personal health service. The current health system offers few rewards for either individual practitioners or agencies to undertake seriously the task of delivering mass personal health services.[64]

Finally, that the national and state governments' birth-control programs are targeted on poor people has provoked suspicion and even hostility among the program's clientele. Many poor people believe the government's primary motivation for providing birth-control services is simply to minimize the cost of welfare payments to poor families. Black welfare recipients suspect a more sinister motive: to contain the growth of the nation's black minority.[65] Such suspicions have been sharpened by periodic disclosures of coercive sterilization performed without the patient's consent during a delivery or abortion procedure or imposed by welfare agencies under the threat of withholding a woman's welfare check. Reports of such cases led HEW in November 1978 to tighten standards for federally funded sterilizations. The new regulations lengthened the waiting period between the time a person consents to be sterilized and the operation to 30 days (from the original 3-day period). They also stipulated that each patient must be given both written and oral explanations of the operation, advice about alternative methods of birth control, "and assurances that no federal benefits will be lost if sterilization is refused." The change was prompted by increasing criticism that federal programs were being selectively used to control the welfare population. Obviously, such public antagonism toward government-provided family-planning services does not exist in the universal service systems in Sweden or China, where no particular groups have been singled out to receive the service.

CARING FOR CHILDREN

Of the services and benefits considered in this chapter, child care is probably the most universally accepted necessity for women's participation in the labor force. The availability of high-quality, reasonably priced child care affects not only a woman's ability to stay on the job but also influences her morale and productivity, her record of absenteeism, and her health and welfare. In other words, it affects her chances for job success and advancement.

In Sweden, day care is clearly a national concern. Local governments administering day-care centers receive large subsidies and considerable national guidance in operating their facilities. In China, national policymakers' serious concern about providing child-care services for working mothers has not been matched by proportionate investments from the national treasury. Instead, national leaders have directed local communities to develop their own day-care services without significant national subsidies, and this has often led to makeshift, low-quality services. The United States is another case of decentralized policy making for day care; control rests at the state level. The federal government has imposed quality standards for facilities receiving federal funds, but Congress has in recent years been cutting back on federal funding. Many observers believe that by combining funding cuts with stricter quality controls, the federal government is actually contributing to a reduction in the supply of publicly funded day care. Meanwhile, there has been significant growth in the private sector, with over half of all licensed day-care services in the United States provided by commercial centers operated for profit.

The greater degree of national supervision in Sweden has been accompanied by a smaller emphasis on parent control or parent participation in the operation of day-care centers. The centers in Sweden are operated by local child welfare authorities, and policy decisions are assigned to child-care professionals. The more decentralized patterns of administration in China and the United States incorporate greater community control. In China, day-care centers are most often set up by neighborhoods or factory workers as self-help projects; they are likely to reflect local values and priorities. In America's commercial day-care market, the parents' leverage over the facility rests in the fees they pay for service. Even in many public and private nonprofit facilities, however, parent involvement is cultivated (e.g., in the Head Start program's strong emphasis on parent participation).

All three countries lack adequate day care. None of them can boast that it has as many places in day-care facilities as there are pre-school children with working mothers. In all, shortages are particularly pronounced outside the major cities. Moreover, all three systems display unevenness in the quality of day care provided by different facilities, from day-care homes to fully equipped centers. The American case is strikingly different from the other two in this important respect: In Sweden and China the national governments are committed to the principle that every preschool child of working parents *should* have access to day care, whereas the U.S. government is not. In Sweden and China, then, the shortages result from inadequate resources to invest in day care. In the United States, national policy makers have not resolved the question *whether* they should commit significant national resources to day care.

Sweden

The place of children in Swedish society presents a paradox. To the foreign observer, Swedish society seems in many ways less child-centered than most other Western societies. For example, compared with American families, the Swedish family's activities are governed to a lesser extent by consideration of the children's preferences and needs,[66] and comparatively greater weight is attached to the parents' preferences and convenience. At the same time, the Swedish government displays a greater concern for child welfare than do the governments of most nations, especially the United States.

The Swedish government provides an impressive array of social services for children. From infancy, county hospitals and clinics provide free medical care. In many cases, the baby's records are sent directly from the maternity ward to the child welfare center (*barnavårdscentral*) so that the staff is advised of any problems or concerns. Most Swedish parents avail themselves of these preventive health-care services until children reach the age of two, but then participation drops off sharply. In response to this tendency of parents to drop the periodic visits to the child welfare center, the government introduced in 1968 the "four-year control." This is an extensive checkup available free to all four-year-olds, which includes a general clinical exam, a dental checkup, hearing and sight tests, and a mental health assessment, all with special emphasis on detecting handicaps. The "four-year control" is voluntary, but when a family does not participate, "a representative of the child welfare center visits the home to try to find out the reasons for this."[67]

Once enrolled in public school, the child receives many services through the school including free medical care and free school lunches. The school meals program was originally limited to children of low-income families, as are most school lunch programs in the United States. In 1946, however, the Riksdag passed legislation providing national subsidies for school lunches for all Swedish children, regardless of income. The change was introduced to ensure a balanced diet (not always assured by adequate family income) and reduce the household work load.

The growth of government-operated preschool facilities on a mass scale is a development of the 1960s in Sweden. Such facilities existed earlier, but they were not expanding rapidly enough to meet increasing demand. Hence a Day-Care Commission was appointed by the national government in 1965 to study the problem and make recommendations. In its 1967 report the commission calculated the need for child-care services on the basis of the number of Swedish children in families with only one parent or with two working parents.[68] This method of calculation doubtless sounds to many American readers as if it overestimates the need for child care, and it is not surprising that the commission report portrayed child care in Sweden as shockingly inadequate.

The commission recommended that by 1975, Sweden must provide 70,000 more places. As table 2–2 shows, by 1974 the growth in child-care

TABLE 2-2. Growth in Swedish Child-Care Facilities, 1950–74

Type of Facility	*1950*	*1965*	*1970*	*1974*	*1980 (est.)*
Day-care centers (*daghem*)	9,700	11,900	33,000	62,000	153,700
Day-care homes (*familjedaghem*)	1,500	8,000	32,000	60,000	70,600
After-school centers (*fritidshem*)	2,400	3,000	6,500	17,000	56,000

Sources: Ake Fors, *Social Policy and How It Works* (Stockholm: Swedish Institute, 1972), p. 23; Elisabet Sandberg, *Equality Is the Goal* (Stockholm: Swedish Institute, 1975), p. 67; and National Labor Market Board, "Equality in the Labour Market: Statistics," September 1977.

services had met and exceeded the commission's recommendations. Between 1965 and 1974, the number of day-care places available to preschoolers increased more than 500 percent. The rate of increase was achieved for both municipally run day-care centers and day-care homes, in which housewives are paid by the local government to take care of other parents' children.[69]

In spite of this progress, the government's 1974 calculations showed a total of 225,000 preschool children in need of day care[70] and places for only about 122,000. The remaining half had to be cared for by relatives and neighbors or by specially arranging the parents' work schedules so that one parent was always at home. Demand for day care is naturally highest in major cities. Where shortages exist, admission priority is given first to children of one-parent households, next to children of working parents with low income, and then to all others.

The shortages in major cities have led the national government to sanction some rather unorthodox arrangements, such as the "three-family system" originated in Stockholm and later spread to other cities. In this arrangement the local government (with national subsidies) provides a trained child-care worker to supervise the children of three families together. Each family takes all the children, plus the child-care worker, into their home every third week. Although they must pay the municipality the same fee they would pay for a place in a day-care center, some parents prefer the three-family system because it maintains a small, stable peer group for the children and keeps them in a home environment.[71]

Sweden drastically increased its preschool education effort in 1975 when, for the first time, the national government required local authorities to offer the option of preschool to all six-year-olds. Nursery schools, called "playschools" (*lekskoler*), have long existed in Sweden. In fact, by the early 1970s, they served as many children as the day-care centers and day-care homes combined. Unlike day care, however, nursery schools offered a child only three hours of supervision each day. Their function has been to enhance child development more than to aid working parents. The necessity for such nursery schools can be easily understood when we consider that a child does not enter Sweden's regular elementary school until the age of seven—a rather late age by American standards. The Riksdag in 1973 passed legislation to provide the preschool option to increasing numbers of preschoolers; the expansion started in the fall of 1975, with places guaranteed to all six-year-olds and to those four- and five-year-olds with special needs (e.g., social skills, language training for immigrant children, and special education programs for handicapped youngsters). These preschools are not intended to replace day care, for they take children only three hours each day. Rather, they reflect the public commitment to child welfare and development.

The principle of expanding day care is no longer controversial in Sweden. There is consensus on the need for more day care. Periodic disagreements do arise over the pace of expansion, the quality standards for day care, the ratio of day-care centers to places in day-care homes, and other tactical questions. The Social Democratic party gave unqualified support to expanding day care in the first half of the 1970s. In May 1976, preparing for the fall election, the Social Democrats promised to create 100,000 new day-care places by 1980; that would represent a 66 percent increase over the number of slots then available. The Conservative party, although not opposed in principle to the expansion, questioned its economic feasibility. The Liberals, also supportive of day care, expressed concern that individual children were being left in day-care centers for too many hours during the day. A government study released by the Family Assistance Commission in 1975 reported that at least half the children in day-care centers in Sweden spent nine hours or more each day in the centers, while a fifth spent ten hours or more. The longer times were especially common for children of either single parents or working-class parents.[72] The Liberals' position was that high-quality day care was absolutely necessary for working parents, but that many Swedish children were spending too much time at the centers. The Liberals feel that no child should be in such care more than seven hours a day; to ensure this, the Liberals proposed measures to shorten the workday for parents.

The Social Democrats were defeated in the fall 1976 election, but no one doubts that day care will continue to expand in Sweden. The pace of expansion may be slower under the current government, however. It now appears unlikely that the target of 100,000 new places, set for 1981 by the outgoing socialist government, will be realized.[73]

Another recent controversy concerned the extension of government-subsidized child care into the evening hours. In 1977, the Swedish Confederation of Trade Unions (LO) demanded that day nurseries be kept open at night for the children of night shift workers. The union demand provoked a storm of protest; opponents argued that the government should not provide an opportunity for parents to leave their children in the care of others at night as well as during the day. This particular debate split even the Social Democratic party, long a champion of increased subsidies for day care.

It is obvious from our discussion so far that although day care and preschool are administered by local governments in Sweden, the national government maintains a keen interest in child care. Data collection, planning, and providing subsidies are the national government's roles. Often, the initiative for new or improved social services to children and mothers has come from government-appointed commissions (see several mentions in this chapter). Usually composed of representatives from all political parties, as well as professional experts, they have investigated such subjects as Support to Incomplete Families; Support to Recent and Future Mothers; Preschools, Child Welfare Guardianship, Childhood Accidents; Society's Childminding Activities—Preschools and Family; Day-Care Homes; and Children's Allowances and Family Increments. Ordinarily, the product of these commissions is a set of legislative recommendations, presented to the Riksdag for action.

The National Board of Health and Welfare sets operating guidelines for day-care centers. For example, national standards for staffing include a staff-child ratio of 1:4 for children under 2½ and 1:5 for children older than 2½. National guidelines have also created job quotas for recruitment and training of male workers in day-care centers. The percentage of men on day-care staffs is small, and a greater male presence among preschoolers is thought to be highly desirable. Job counselors working for the national employment service have been instructed to make their male clients aware of job opportunities in child-care services, and county labor boards have been empowered to give priority in training programs to job applicants from the sex underrepresented in the occupation concerned—in this case, men.

Such direct national intervention into a local government function is possible in Sweden only because the national government heavily subsidizes the cost of day care. Subsidies give the national government considerable leverage over local policy. Part of the cost of day care is of course paid by the parents. Parents' fees are calculated on a sliding scale, according to the family's ability to pay; they range from less than $1 to more than $5 per day. Even the maximum parent fee covers less than half the actual cost of operating the day-care program, and the average fee covers only about 15 percent of costs. Thus the local government pays about 50 percent of the program's expenses, and the national government contributes the remaining 35 percent.

The influence of national subsidies on local service delivery is great. For example, local governments are expected over the next few years to add many more places in day-care centers than they will in day-care homes,[74] even though the cost of providing a place in a day-care home is lower (see table 2–3). This emphasis on building centers can be traced to the pattern of national subsidies: for day-care centers, the national government contributes almost the entire capital cost and nearly half the operating expenditures; for day-care homes, the national contribution is 35 percent of total local government expenditures on the service. Another example of the influence of national subsidies is the shortage of places in after-school centers, which take seven- to ten-year-olds for the portion of the parents' workday when the children are not in elementary school. These centers, also operated by local governments, are in shorter supply than day-care centers. In 1974 they satisfied only about 15 percent of the potential demand.[75] According to table 2–3, after-school centers are less expensive to run than are day-care centers or day-care homes. The local authorities' poorer showing for after-school centers undoubtedly reflects the fact that national subsidies have been less generous for part-time child care than for full-time centers.

In their day-to-day operations, Swedish day-care centers are hardly distinguishable from their American counterparts. The trends in preschool curriculum have followed much the same paths in Sweden as in the United States, having been strongly influenced by the work of Maria Montessori and, more recently, Jean Piaget and Erik Erikson. Nevertheless, an American observer can detect some important differences. For one thing, Sweden's centers lack effective parent participation. Parent groups may have some voice in general policy decisions (e.g., whether to expand a center's capacity or whether to increase fees), but there is little parent involvement in center activities. At least one observer attributed the lack of parent involvement to Swedish parents' "trust in the child-care experts."[76] Another possible explanation is that Swedish parents rely on day care more as a convenience for themselves than as an educational experience for their children, and they are therefore unconcerned about the day-to-day operation of the center.

The most dramatic contrast between Swedish and American centers is

TABLE 2-3. Estimated Cost per Hour of Use for Various Child Care Facilities in Sweden, 1971

Type of Facility	*Operating Cost per Child, per Hour*
Home help, baby sitter	$3.53
Day-care center	1.19
Elementary school	1.00
Day-care home	.86
After-school center	.84
Preschool	.82
Playground	.62
Sports center	.55
Library	.21

Source: *Statens Offentliga Utredningar* (SOU) 1974, No. 24, "Boendeservice 7"

that Sweden's public day-care service is universal. It is not confined to those who can afford to pay full fees, or those with low incomes. The sliding fee schedule accommodates children from all income groups; there is thus no stigma attached to public day care in Sweden.

China

The earliest and most consistent concern of the Chinese Communist party in the area of supportive services to working women has been child care. The plight of urban factory women was the first to receive attention. In 1949, at the National Women's Federation meeting in Shanghai, reports showed how much needed to be done:

> Factory nurseries are one of the major tasks this year. It is understandable that women workers who must spend long hours in factories and care for their families unaided at the same time, cannot have the time or energy to compete freely with men. The double difficulties of women call for special measures.[77]

Attempts to introduce nursing rooms for mothers to nurse their babies and nurseries for children under three progressed most rapidly. These attempts were gradually expanded to include mining enterprises, schools, and government organs. The record of the early 1950s shows a slow but steady increase in this service until by 1956, 6000 nurseries and kindergartens and 1900 nursing rooms were being run under the auspices of the All-China Federation of Trade Unions (see table 2–4). Remember, however, that as with most quantitative information from China, the roughness of the data should not be overlooked.

These particular nurseries were usually organized either by the National Women's Federation (especially in the early 1950s) or the women's department of the local trade union, and were subsidized by the enterprise itself. Their development was uneven, especially because factory management was often hostile to the expense.[78] Women workers were called on to provide support and absorb much of the time and expense themselves.[79] Although little information is available on how staff were recruited in the 1950s and 1960s, it is probable that women workers who liked children were chosen and trained on the job. Consequently, conditions in the nurseries varied widely, depending on the wealth of the factory or organ to which they were attached and the commitment of the relevant party and union personnel to providing day care.

In 1956, at the Eighth Party Congress, Teng Ying-ch'ao, vice-chairperson of the ACDWF, estimated the number of women workers and office employees, plus the number of women cadres and intellectuals, to be 2.7 million.[80] With only 6900 day-care facilities, caring for about 192,000 children, these women had a problem of finding places to leave their children. The party was not unaware of their needs, but the establishment of nurseries by the government meant heavy capital expenditures, which the party

TABLE 2-4. Kindergartens, Nurseries, and Nursing Rooms in Factories, Schools, Mining Enterprises, and Government Organs, 1949–56

Date	*Kindergartens and Nurseries*	*Children Served*	*Nursing Rooms Separately Listed*	*Children in Nursing Rooms*
Pre-1949	136[a]			
1949 (September 1)	81[b]	3,646[b]		
1949 (December 31)	124[c]			
1951 (March 8)	975[d]	38,520[d]		
1951 (October)	1,227[e]			
1952 (December 31)	2,738[f]			
1954	4,000[g]	127,000[g]		
1955 (March 8)	4,413[h]	135,000[h]		
1956 (May)	5,000[i]	158,000[j]	1,900[i]	34,000[i]

Note: Until 1956, nursing rooms seem to have been included in the totals given for kindergartens and nurseries.

Sources: [a]*Chinese Studies in History* 5, no. 2–3 (Winter/Spring 1971–72), p. 102. The October 1951 figure is quoted as being nine times larger than the pre-1949 number. The pre-1949 number is therefore very much an estimate and should be regarded only as an indication that in the late 1940s, urban kindergartens in China numbered somewhere between 50 and 150.

[b]*Ibid.,* p. 122. This figure encompasses the *new* nurseries set up in Peking Tientsin, Shanghai, and Nanking. We use this figure to represent the number of urban nurseries set up throughout China because (1) early efforts were directed almost exclusively at large factories with many women workers, located mainly in Shanghai and Tientsin (Shanghai itself had 70 percent of China's working women); and (2) besides those the communists established, there were very few other nurseries in urban areas.

[c]*Women of China* (Peking: Foreign Language Press, 1953), pp. 1–11, quoting Teng Ying-ch'ao's address to the Second National Women's Congress in April 1953. The 1952 figure of 2738 is quoted as being 22 times the 1949 figure.

[d]SCMP 81, March 9–10, 1951, p. 15; March 8, 1951. According to "incomplete statistics" there were 975 for women workers.

[e]*Chinese Studies in History.*

[f]*Women of China.* Also quoted in *People's China,* No. 11 (June 1, 1953): 6. The figure is further verified by a quote from SCMP 609, July 14, 1953, pp. 9–10; July 11, 1953—"From May 1951 to May 1952, the number of creches for factories and mine workers increased by 14)."

[g]C. K. Yang, *Communist Chinese Society,* vol. 1, *The Chinese Family in the Communist Revolution* (Cambridge, Mass.: MIT Press, 1974), p. 151. Yang is quoting JMJP, August 5, 1955. See also SCMP 1085, July 9–11, 1955, p. 19; NCNA July 9, 1955.

[h]CNA 77, April 1, 1955, quoting JMJP March 8, 1955.

[i]URS 3: 314; KJJP May 31, 1956. "Recently compiled statistics are being used."

[j]SCMP 1309, June 14, 1956, pp. 17–18; May 30, 1956.

wished to avoid. In 1952 the party began a program of street nurseries and mutual-aid teams to help solve the dilemma without heavy cost to either the central or provincial governments. This approach has continued through the 1960s and 1970s, supplementing the various nurseries attached to government enterprises.

In 1954 street nurseries were heralded as "the most popular [day care] for non-industrial working mothers."

> These creches are inexpensive, convenient, and rather easy to set up. Data from 22 cities throughout the country indicate that they are usually initiated and organized by those active in community life. Anyone interested is welcome to help. This includes contributing time, rooms, equipment, toys, and other necessities. In addition, these creches also receive direct guidance and aid from the local governments and women's federations, which provide subsidies and medical services, and train child care personnel.[81]

Figures on these nurseries unfortunately do not confirm such unmitigated enthusiasm. Large numbers of these centers seem to have been created only when there was a campaign afoot. Table 2–5 shows the periodic swings.

The tendency of street nurseries and mutual-aid teams, called by a variety of names (e.g., nursing units, nursing teams, street nursing stations) to disappear when the pressure of the campaign had subsided was probably directly related to campaign methods. Because the government did not want to appropriate large amounts for welfare projects, it found a partial answer in mobilizing women to carry out "mutual aid" most often on a voluntary basis—unpaid. One underlying principle of a socialist society, at least according to the Chinese Communists, is the subordination of individual interests to the needs of the collective. Such unselfishness includes volunteering labor to help one's neighbor overcome her "household burdens." The development of the Hsiaochiao Nursery Station in Kunming, Yunnan, is a case in point. In 1954,

> in the neighborhood of Hsiaochiao Road, women workers . . . in some factories, as well as some primary school women teachers, had either to lock up their children when they went to work, or to take the children along to the workshop, because they could not possibly afford to employ babysitters.[82]

The Hsiaochiao Residents' Committee and the Women's Committee decided to start a nursery, funded through voluntary contributions by the people on the block. Some residents were "persuaded" to give up their houses, and the nursery moved in. In general, salaries in street nurseries seem to have ranged from minimal to nonexistent, thus creating a problem of sloppy work, where morale and ideological motivation were low.[83]

C. K. Yang has spoken of the temporary nature of the early day-care centers and the lack of finances, equipment, trained personnel, and operat-

TABLE 2-5. Street Nurseries and Mutual-Aid Teams, 1952–57

Date	*Street Nurseries*	*Children Served*	*Mutual-Aid Teams*
1952 (December 31)	4,300[a]		
	4,346[b]		
1954 (December 31)	306[c]		
	408[d]		
1955 (August 5)	687[e]	38,000[e]	
1957 (June 1)	2,309[f]		4,316[g]

Sources: [a]C. K. Yang, *Chinese Communist Society,* book 1, *The Chinese Family in the Communist Revolution* (Cambridge, Mass.: MIT Press, 1974), p. 150.

[b]*People's China,* no. 11 (June 1953); 6.

[c]SCMP 819, May 29-31, 1954, pp. 31-32; May 17, 1954—"Creches for children of working mothers in urban areas are now roughly 30 times the pre-liberation figure. One out of every 10 is a street nursery." To find the number of pre-liberation nurseries, we looked to CB 476, October 15, 1957, p. 16; September 10-11, 1957—"26,700 creches in the urban areas is 260 times the pre-liberation figure." This gives a preliberation figure of 102. $102 \times 30 = 3{,}060$. One tenth of $3{,}060 = 306$. Needless to say, this should be considered a very rough figure.

[d]The higher figure of 136 was found for kindergartens, nurseries, and nursing rooms in factories, schools, mining enterprises, and government organs in Table 2-4. $30 \times 136 = 4{,}080$. One tenth of $4{,}080 = 408$. Rather than considering these two figures as opposed to one another, we consider them to be mutually reinforcing; they both indicate a significant drop in street creches from 1952 to 1954.

[e]Yang, *op. cit.,* p. 151.

[f]URS 8: 350; CKFN August 1, 1957.

[g]*Ibid.* This figure is based on preliminary data from only 18 cities and one province.

ing expenses.[84] These problems existed for factory nurseries but were exacerbated in street creches because official support was far more tenuous. Put in perspective, it is difficult to see what alternative the government had in caring for a population which has expanded as quickly as China's. It is sobering to think that better than half of China's 900 million people were born after 1949. The campaign method of rapidly creating day care in the 1950s attempted to overcome the problem of China's scarce resources too quickly and brought about subsequent retrenchment. The voluntary nature of the work made many women resent it, while cadres may have been reluctant to induce families to vacate rooms and contribute equipment and toys without pressure from above.

The Great Leap Forward was the classic example of the campaign method at work. From 1958 to 1960, the Great Leap increased the number of women working in regular industry by 5,000,000 and mobilized additional millions to take part in street industry. The role of the unions in providing day care for the new women workers would best be described as modest. By 1959,the number of nurseries and nursing rooms operated by basic-level trade unions increased only 1.4 times over the 1957 figure, whereas the number of children increased 2.49 times over 1957.[85] These increases work out to 16,906 nurseries and nursing rooms caring for 666,880 children; obviously short of the needs of 8.3 million working women.

The slack was taken up by "mutual-aid" care, often little more than older women baby-sitting in their homes. The figures for Peking are instructive (see table 2–6). The jump from 2800 day-care facilities in 1956 to 20,000 in 1958 occurred mostly in the latter year. If nurseries and kindergartens run by mining enterprises, government organs, factories, and schools followed the pattern of the rest of the country in 1956–1959,[86] there would have been approximately 933 such permanent facilities by the end of 1959. What then were the rest of the 20,000 day care facilities? The most likely explanation, especially given that they were established in a period of only several months, is that they were facilities of the most temporary nature. As in previous years, the increase in temporary mutual aid rose with the pressure of a campaign.

During the campaign, women were pressured to create more day care. "(Urban) commune officials were being told to develop [day care] without state aid."[87] How were they to do it? Houses were made available by the owners, equipment was provided by workers' dependents. These methods were officially sanctioned and held up as models for "some basic level cadres [who] gave over-simple emphasis to objective conditons and were scared by difficulties . . . housing and furniture."[88] In addition, women had to be convinced to work in day-care centers:

> When the mess halls and nurseries were first established, many housewives were unwilling to be assigned as cooks or nurses, feeling that these jobs were not as "honorable" as to participate directly in production. Some others were fed up with cooking and baby nursing because they had always been doing these before. . . . the Party branch convened meetings of all kinds, explaining to the inhabitants that cooking and baby-nursing were glorious assignments.[89]

The problem of attitude was serious enough to be mentioned in the communiqué of the Sixth Plenum of the Eighth Central Committee in 1958.[90]

During the Great Leap, working mothers worried about their offspring and requested extended leave from work when their children fell sick.[91] In October 1959 the rate of attendance of women workers in commercial, trade, and finance departments was reported at a low 70 to 80 percent largely because of the "unsolved question of child care."[92] Newspaper

TABLE 2-6. Day-Care Facilities for Peking, 1949-75

Date	*Facilities*	*Children Served*	*Street Nurseries*	*Facilities Run by Factories, Mining Enterprises, Government Organs, Schools*
Pre-1949	11[a]			
	15[b]	2,300[b]		
February 1951	65[a]			
June 1953	190[c]	9,400[c]		
March 1955				291[d]
May 1956	2,800[e]	55,000[e]		
September 1958	20,000[f]	450,000[f]		
March 1960	18,000[g]	610,000[g]	2,500[g]	
March 1961	17,000[h]		1,800[h]	
July 1975	4,500[i]	200,000[i]		

Sources: [a]C. K. Yang, *Chinese Communist Society,* book 1, *The Chinese Family in the Communist Revolution* (Cambridge, Mass.: MIT Press, 1974), pp. 150–51.

[b]William Kessen, ed., *Childhood in China* (New Haven: Yale University Press, 1975), p. 1; see also SCMP 5898, July 21–25, 1975, p. 68; NCNA English Peking, July 10, 1975.

[c]SCMP 582, June 2–4, 1953, pp. 5–6; NCNA English, June 1, 1953.

[d]*China News Analysis* 77, April 1, 1955; KMJP March 8, 1955, and JMJP March 1, 1955.

[e]URS 3: 314; JMJP May 29, 1956.

[f]SCMP 1848, September 8, 1958, p. 29; NCNA English September 3, 1958. See also SCMP 1971, March 7, 1959, p. 12.

[g]*China News Analysis* 317, March 25, 1960, p. 6; March 8, 1960.

[h]SCMP 2454, March 13, 1961, p. 18; NCNA English, March 7, 1961.

articles hardly promoted the mothers' confidence: "The newly established nursery organizations were mostly started in miserable conditions. Hence, it is essential to find out some means to prevent heat and illness, so that the children may pass the summer safely and comfortably."[93] Some older women reported they feared that under existing conditions, with the ever-present danger of contagion and epidemic, the children could not receive enough care and would be better off with their own families.[94]

With the reversal of Great Leap policies, the number of temporary day-care organizations seems to have decreased. In 1975 Peking reported 4500 permanent child-care facilities caring for 200,000 children. Since 1960 the "blitz" strategy of establishing day care has not been repeated, although mutual-aid is still emphasized. Visitors to the mainland in the 1970s have reported city nurseries to be both clean and healthy. Although no national information is available on the percentages of children attending nurseries and kindergartens in urban areas, official estimates supplied for various cities have recently ranged from 30 to 60 percent. Permanent day-care facilities are still divided between street nurseries and nurseries attached to enterprises, although street nurseries seem to have become far more institutionalized and regularized. Nevertheless, as a recent group of visitors to the People's Republic concluded, "it seems safe to assume that the majority of pre-school-age children are still cared for in a family context."[95]

In rural areas, nurseries have largely been confined to seasonal care, although periodic attempts at year-round care have been tried. Typically, nurseries and kindergartens are set up during campaigns and disintegrate afterward. The available data for day care in rural areas are presented in table 2–7. The reader is again cautioned that these are only rough estimates. The claim of 3.34 million day-care facilities in 1958 should be read with special caution. Visitors in China in the 1970s have suggested that there are at present relatively few nurseries in rural China.[96] This does not mean that all the day-care facilities claimed during the Great Leap Forward year of 1958 were nonexistent, although the possibility is great that the numbers were exaggerated to please superiors. Most day-care arrangements were probably of such a temporary nature that disbanding them cost little effort.

The problem of caring for children while their mothers go out to the fields has long existed for the Chinese during peak work seasons, planting and harvesting time in particular. Because insufficient labor at these times meant no food for the next year, children were left behind in the villages while their mothers worked. Babies were tied down, and toddlers fended for themselves. Even children taken along to the fields fared poorly. "Mrs. Leng's 2-year-old child was taken ill the year before as a result of being brought by his mother to the fields where he was constantly exposed to the sun and often went down to the water to play."[97] And with children to watch, the women obviously worked less efficiently.

Because it has been the avowed policy of the party to increase the number of women working in agriculture, the problem of day care has been critical. To minimize costs, labor exchange has been especially encouraged. Mothers rotate in turn or, before the days of collectivization, exchanged work for child care, especially with older women workers.[98] If labor exchange were not used, the costs would be prohibitive. As one collective explained:

> If the collective paid all the expenses, the members with no children would consider it unfair to them. But a fee which would make the nursery self-supporting would be too high for mothers to pay. So now mothers give the nursery an average one-eighth of their wage for a full day's work, no matter how many children they have, and the difference is made up by the cooperative.[99]

TABLE 2-7. Nurseries and Kindergartens in Rural Areas, 1949–60

Year	*Kindergartens and Nurseries*	*Children Served*
1950	93[a]	
1951	10,000[b]	
1952	148,000[c]	800,000[c]
	148,200[d]	
1956	635,000[e]	6,000,000[f]
1958	3,340,000[g]	36,000,000[h]

Sources: [a]*Chinese Studies in History* 5, no. 2-3 (Winter/Spring 1971–72): 103. The 1951 figure is quoted as being 106 times the 1950 figure.

[b]*Ibid.* Also quoted in C. K. Yang, *Chinese Communist Society,* book 1, *The Chinese Family in the Communist Revolution* (Cambridge, Mass.: MIT Press, 1974), p. 152.

[c]*Ibid.*

[d]*Women of China* (Peking: Foreign Language Press, 1953), p. 5. Also quoted in *People's China*, no. 11 (June 1953): 6.

[e]*China News Analysis* 215, February 7, 1958, p. 1; JMJP September 15, 1957, p. 4.

[f]CB 476, October 15, 1957, p. 16; JMJP Peking September 10-11, 1957.

[g]SCMP 2263, May 6, 1960, p. 20. The previous figure used in 1959 of 4.98 million rural creches had by 1960 been scaled down. The figure was obviously inflated. The figure of 4.98 million was used in SCMP 1971, March 12, 1959, p. 1; JMJP editorial, March 8, 1959.

[h]SCMP 2105, September 29, 1959; NCNA September 22, 1959. "The number of children looked after in nurseries was over 6 times more than in 1957."

Not all cooperatives are willing or able to undertake such subsidization. An analysis of one family's income indicates the problem for parents:

> On the Peing Pu People's Commune outside Shanghai, Chen Yung-kwei, 29, and his wife Ho Hong-ching, 28, told us that their combined earnings were $53 per month. Out of this they pay 70 cents per month for actual rent and $1.50 for monthly maintenance of their two-bedroom house. They also pay $1.00 annually for family medical care and $10 per month for little Chen's nursery school. Grade school is about $2.50 per month . . . Food and clothing together amount to roughly $20 per month.[100]

Out of a combined income of $53 per month, $10 is going for nursery school. It is not difficult to see that at such a rate, two or three children would quickly make it uneconomical for the mother to work.

A strong deterrent to the development of rural nurseries has been the increasing longevity of grandparents. Better medical care and economic security have enabled peasants to live longer than ever before, and today grandparents in the countryside almost invariably live with at least one grown son.[101] The time when daughters-in-law undertake most domestic chores for their mothers-in-law is also fast passing. "In many households, the young wife's source of help is an older woman whose age and state of health preclude her participation in productive labor. This transfer has changed the daughter-in-law/mother-in-law relationship considerably."[102] The older women take care of the children while their mothers earn work points. This alternative is far less costly to the family than a nursery would be.

A second deterrent to collective nurseries, although one less frequently mentioned, is the attitude of women toward day care; they neither like the work themselves nor trust those who do it. Referred to during the Great Leap Forward, this attitude views child care as "the low class job of waiting on others"[103] or, as "certain nurses" declared, "looking after other people's children is a job with no future and it is better to grind rice for others than to look after girls for others."[104]

> "The first day was miserable," said Tien Shu-ying, who now has stopped being a nurse, but talked to me as she came to deposit her own two youngsters. "We couldn't do anything right. Women whose children had never been away from home left their field work to listen at our gate in case their babies were crying . . . Women with children at the nursery claimed that the attendants picked up their own children more than those of the others." So one nurse after another resigned, including Tien Shu-ying herself. "We preferred working in the fields where we women can laugh and have a good time together," she said. "At the nursery we had to bear the constant complaints of our neighbors."[105]

Attitudes of this sort undoubtedly were being referred to in 1960 when it was suggested that "the concern, support, and affection shown and given by the guardians, and especially the mothers, to the nursing and educational undertaking, also play an important role in insuring the development and advancement of the undertaking."[106]

In sum, the most consistent pattern for rural nurseries has been a seasonal one: operating during the few weeks of busy farming every year and closing at other times. Care is usually provided by women too old or sick to work in the fields, women with bound feet, or pregnant women. Work points are given to these women by mothers and, less frequently, nurseries are subsidized by the production team or production brigade. Day care cannot be said to have penetrated rural China to any great extent.

United States

The federal government has confined its efforts in child care to the poor; in fact, at all levels of government in the United States public day care is associated with welfare. The impetus for the early day-nursery movement in the latter half of the nineteenth century was the influx of poor immigrants into urban centers. In the eyes of social reformers, their children badly needed socializing. Upper-class women reformers supported the creation of day nurseries as a response to "the plight of small, dirty, ill-behaved lower-class children who were left alone daily."[107] From the beginning, day care in America has been viewed as an unfortunate necessity to be provided by government only under extreme circumstances.

Federal involvement in day care has been extremely limited in scope and of only two basic varieties: (1) day care as a response to a national emergency, and (2) day care as poverty policy. The largest federal day-care programs were products of the Great Depression and World War II. In the 1930s, during Franklin Roosevelt's first term as President, places for about 40,000 children were set up in day nurseries financed by a combination of federal and state funds. Administered by the Works Projects Administration (WPA), the nurseries were designed primarily to supply jobs for teachers, nurses, nutritionists, and clerical and maintenance workers. Like other public employment programs of the depression, WPA nurseries were phased out once the emergency had passed. Federally funded day care on an even larger scale was introduced by the Lanham Act of 1941, which authorized money to operate day-care centers serving the children of workers in defense plants. The need to employ large numbers of women workers in those plants during World War II supplied the rationale for this program, which included both preschools and after-school facilities for older children. At its peak, the Lanham Act program served about 1.5 million children.[108] That is the largest number of day-care places ever available in the United States. Today about one million places are available, in spite of the day-care boom of the last decade. The World War II program was, in Gilbert Steiner's words, a "win-the-war program, not a save-the-children program,"[109] and federal support was withdrawn at the end of the war.

In addition to these responses to national emergencies, the national government in 1962 began supporting day care as a welfare program. The 1962 Public Welfare Amendments did not provide significant amounts of money, but they did signal a national interest in day care. Nonetheless, federal officials clearly viewed institutional child care as an unfortunately necessary service for deviant families. The Children's Bureau in HEW declared in 1963: "The child who needs day care has a family problem which makes it impossible for his parents to fulfill their parental responsibilities without supplementary help."[110]

One of the "family problems" recognized by national policy makers is the inadequate preparation for school that disadvantaged families give their children. The government's response to the problem was perhaps the single most popular part of the 1960s war on poverty: Project Head Start. Head Start's community-based preschool programs started in the summer of 1965 and have grown continuously, despite numerous attempts by the Nixon administration to cut back funds. Addressed to what the national government calls "culturally disadvantaged" children, the program aims at enriching the children's cognitive and social development, their nutrition, and their general health in order to give them a better chance to succeed in public schools.

A second "family problem" warranting federal attention in the 1960s was the inability of welfare mothers to take jobs because they could not afford the cost of child care. In 1967 Congress amended the Social Security Act to provide funds for 75 percent of the cost of subsidizing child care for mothers receiving public assistance, especially those enrolled in the WIN (work incentive) program. This program contained serious flaws, as Gilbert Steiner has pointed out. Its main limitation was that federal money was not provided for building *new* centers, only for subsidizing AFDC children in existing centers. As of 1970 there were an estimated 638,000 places in all American day-care facilities; even if every one of those places had been given to an AFDC child under six years old, there would have remained another million AFDC preschoolers without day care.[111] The national government's response was not to increase federal responsibility but to shift more responsibility to the states. In 1972 Congress placed a limit on the amount of day-care funds that any one state could receive; states that wanted to spend more than this maximum on day care, Congress decreed, could use their revenue-sharing funds to make up the difference. Of course, ever since 1962 the states had had the option of deciding the extent to which they wished to participate in federal day-care programs. But the 75–25 matching formula created in the 1967 legislation had made day care an attractive option to state policy makers. The effect of the 1972 legislation was to reduce that attraction, by throwing day care into direct competition with many other social service programs for revenue-sharing money.

In the American system, the basic power to license and regulate day care rests with the state governments. Yet when the national government began giving money to the states for day-care services, many state governments had no official standards or licensing programs. In fact, a substantial proportion of federal money for day care has been used to develop and maintain state licensing bureaucracies instead of day-care centers. In 1965, for instance, 43 percent of federal day care money was spent on personnel engaged in licensing.[112] Moreover, state licensing activities carried on in the 1960s distorted the figures frequently used to portray the expansion of day care in the 1960s (see table 2–8) The fivefold increase these figures portray is impressive, even though the one million places available in 1974 could accommodate only one sixth of the six million children under age six with working mothers. But Steiner has cautioned that much of the apparent growth is illusory; the increasing numbers simply represent formerly unlicensed facilities that have been licensed.[113]

The government's problem in enforcing standards through licensing is more difficult in the American system than in the Swedish case because the United States is a federalist rather than a unitary political system, and

TABLE 2-8. Growth of Day Care in the United States, 1960–74

Year	*Children Served by Licensed Day Care*
1960	183,332
1965	310,400
1970	638,000
1972	700,000
1974	1,000,000

Source: Information obtained from Women's Bureau, U.S. Labor Department.

therefore national officials must work through state governments in most social service programs. In addition, national policy makers are faced with a vast private day-care sector, operated for profit. A 1970 survey showed that 60 percent of the day-care centers in the United States were privately operated for profit. Many of these centers are run by business chains and franchise operations, whose critics have called them "Kentucky Fried Children." Under the franchise arrangement, a national corporation sells franchises to local operators who purchase equipment and an operating program from the national corporation. The for-profit market in day care, including both national chains and local independents, serves primarily middle-class families that can afford fees of $5 to $10 per day. The care provided by these centers is not impressive. A national study published in 1972 evaluated only 15 percent of the for-profit centers as "good or superior," ratings given to 38 percent of the public and private, nonprofit centers. Fully 50 percent of the profit-oriented centers were rated "poor," a rating given to only 11 percent of the nonprofit centers.[114]

An even greater quality-control problem is presented by the day-care homes licensed by state governments to handle a significant proportion of the day-care population. As in Sweden, these homes are normally run by housewives who supervise a handful of children in their own homes. If the children's parents are on public assistance, a public welfare agency may pay all or part of the cost. For families not on welfare, the contract is strictly between parents and the day-care mother (in contrast to Sweden, where the local government contracts with the day-care home). Under such circumstances, the public authorities' only leverage over conditions in the day-care home is the licensing procedure, in which "there is often little or no follow-up supervision or conditions for re-licensing."[115]

When governments try to regulate the provision of services through strict licensing standards, without contributing significant amounts of money to their operation, problems are inevitable. This situation is well illustrated by the recent controversy over upgrading federal standards for all day-care centers receiving federal aid. The reader will recall that in 1972 the national government began shifting more administrative responsibility for social services to state governments and enforcing a ceiling on the federal contribution to any state's day-care program. Shortly afterward, in 1974, federal officials introduced more rigid quality standards for centers getting federal funds. They placed particular emphasis on improving the staff-child ratios; the new guidelines required one staff member for *each* infant and one for every four children between one and three years old. Although they were scheduled to go into effect in 1975, the guidelines provoked strong opposition from state governments, on the grounds that they would drastically increase the cost of providing day care while contributing no more federal money to day-care operations. Congress first postponed implementation for six months and then passed a bill giving another six months' extension, with a sum of $125 million to go to the states to help them meet the new standards. This bill was vetoed by President Ford, who explained that he opposed further federal intervention into state affairs. His statement that "the states should have the responsibility and the right to establish and enforce their own quality day care standards"[116] ignored the fact that the states would still have to meet federally imposed standards. They would simply have to do it without federal aid.

The conflict between the President and Congress was resolved by a compromise bill passed later in 1976, which reduced the proposed federal aid to the states to only $24 million but postponed until October 1977 the imposition of the new federal standards. Many observers believe that federal actions, however well-intentioned, will actually reduce the day-care services available to American women because the drive to upgrade quality has not been accompanied by significant increases in federal money.

The Republican administration of the early 1970s resisted several well-publicized attempts by day-care advocates to move the national government beyond its traditional position that public day-care programs should serve only the poor. The first one, the Comprehensive Child Development Act of 1971, retained the subsidized child-care program for poor children but broke down the association between day care and welfare. Introduced by Senator Walter Mondale and Representative John Brademas, the bill called on government to assure "every child a fair and full opportunity to reach his full potential." It provided for a sliding scale of fees to be paid by parents, including middle-income parents, according to their ability to pay. The bill passed Congress, only to be vetoed by President Nixon. The President's celebrated veto message explicitly criticized the program on the grounds that it undermined the American family:

> For the Federal Government to plunge headlong financially into supporting child development would commit the vast moral authority of the National Government to the side of communal approaches to child rearing over against the family-centered approach.[117]

In his exhaustive account of the 1971 Comprehensive Child Development Act, Gilbert Steiner concluded that its passage in Congress resulted from an unusual combination of circumstances that was unlikely to be replicated in the near future.[118] Certainly those circumstances have not been replicated since then, even though Mondale and Brademas introduced a new scaled-down version of the bill in 1974 (the Child and Family Services Act) and again in 1975. In both cases, the bills stipulated that day care, plus a variety of other family services, would be provided free to poor families, with progressively higher fees paid by families with higher incomes. Neither bill made any headway.

The one piece of national policy that does promote day care for other-than-poor families is the tax code. Since 1954, working parents have received tax concessions from the national government for child-care expenses. Until 1976, they took the form of tax deductions available to a maximum income level; in 1976 the deduction was a maximum of $4800 for families with incomes up to $35,000, and a lesser deduction for families earning $35,000 to $42,600. The Tax Reform Act of 1976 replaced the tax deduction with a tax credit (credits are subtracted from taxes owed, whereas deductions are subtracted from income before calculating taxes). The amount of the credit is 20 percent of the working parents' total child-care and housekeeping costs, to a maximum of $400 for one child or $800 for two or more children. The new system treats all income levels identically; there is no income ceiling on the household eligible for the credit, and all households get the same 20 percent of their total outlay for child care. By eliminating the income ceiling, Congress created the only universal child-care benefit offered by the federal government. With this one exception, the United States remains without a national day-care policy that covers any but a small portion of the poor.

SOCIALIZING HOUSEWORK

The daily operation of every household requires a wide array of support services: cooking, washing dishes, changing diapers and feeding children who cannot yet manage for themselves, making beds, cleaning floors, vacuuming carpets, washing bathrooms—not to mention running errands outside the home. Providing the basic necessities for each person consumes many hours every day, and this is true whether the person is a man, woman, or child or whether that person works in the home, outside the home in a part-time job, or in a job demanding 60 or more hours a week. Before anyone can make the contributions society values and remembers, he or she must eat, be clothed, and be sheltered.

Yet the job of housekeeper-childbearer goes unappreciated and unrewarded in many societies. (Many housewives indeed find their tasks rewarding in and of themselves, but this could apply as well to any job outside the home.) In contrast to the private rewards for work, the social rewards (e.g., money, power, and prestige) are sorely lacking for most housekeepers. Although household labor, including child care, accomplishes an enormous amount of socially necessary production, it is rarely recognized as production.[119] This misperception results, of course, from the fact that household production operates outside the money economy; in brief, most women do not receive wages for housework. Yet, recently, economists trying to evaluate the productivity of American housewives in money terms have estimated that the labor of the average housewife with two children, even if it were paid at only $2 an hour, would be worth about $5500 a year.[120]

The indispensability of this household labor quickly becomes evident when the woman of the house takes a job. Hence we include here a discussion of some of the efforts made by governments to lighten the household burdens of working women. These efforts include collectively organizing certain housekeeping functions, as China tried to do in the mess-hall experiment, and also providing government-paid service workers to attend to the needs of individual households, as Sweden has done with its home helps. In addition to these service programs, we include another policy that shapes the dual burden carried by the working woman—that is, housing and urban development policy. We chose to call attention to this particular set of policies because we believe, with Constantina Safilios-Rothschild, that "town and city planning could transform urban networks to give more options to working couples who want to have children."[121]

Past housing and planning policies have created residential and mobility patterns based on the assumption that most women would remain at home. Those patterns now impose restraints on working women. Regrettably, the constraints imposed by urban design are quite literally "fixed in concrete." The urban physical plant represents a massive long-term investment, and decisions to construct roads and buildings have consequences that extend several generations beyond the lives of the decision makers. These planning decisions are based on certain assumptions about the community's needs, habits, and life style: in architectural jargon, the "form" follows the "function." But the form in turn influences the function. The concrete presence of a road or a building influences the life of the community around it, sometimes operating to perpetuate the life-style assumptions on which the plan was originally based. Lewis Mumford put it succinctly: "Through the physical structures of the city, past events, decisions made long ago, values formulated and achieved, remain alive and exert an influence."[122]

Some readers will doubtless question the necessity of government policies to ease the burden of household labor for working women. After all, would not a simpler solution be to redistribute the burden within the household? Why don't working husbands simply assume half the burden, leaving only the other half to be carried by their working wives? We can only speculate as to why they do not. The most likely explanations are that (1) husbands sex-role stereotypes inhibit them from assuming "feminine" duties; (2) that their wives' sex-role stereotypes inhibit them from delegating any "feminine" duties to their husbands; (3) men's jobs are structured on the assumption that such support services will be provided by a spouse; (4) men calculate that their higher earnings fulfill their contribution to the household, while their wives "owe" more unpaid labor to compensate for lower earnings; and (5) men feel the work is beneath them. On this final point, men rightly guess that domestics are badly paid and enjoy low prestige and feel that their time is too valuable to waste on such menial tasks as dishwashing and bed making.

We have to speculate on *why* husbands do not share household labor, but it is indisputably true that they do not. The International Labour Office reported in 1975 that an international survey had shown working women to have less than two thirds the free time enjoyed by their husbands because their combined labor inside and out of the household totaled 70 to 80 hours a week.

> All recent studies of the time budgets of men and women workers show that the time spent by women on household tasks far exceeds that spent by men on such tasks. Married women workers with children are the worst victims of this overwork.[123]

Governments seeking to increase women's participation in the labor force have confronted this apparently universal truth that housework is perceived to be woman's work. Both the Swedish and Chinese governments have claimed to want to change that perception, at least over the long term. But in the short run they have employed two principal ways of getting around it: (1) greater rationalization of housework and of the residential environment itself to minimize the time required for women to play both housekeeper and worker roles; and (2) shifting a large part of the household burden out of the individual family. As difficult as these goals may seem, they may be easier than remodeling people's sex stereotyping of housework. As William Goode has observed for China:

> In certain respects, the development of communal dining halls, nurseries, and kindergartens, laundry services, and so on may be more acceptable to the Chinese male than would be any serious attempt to force him to conform to egalitarian values that would direct him to share the household tasks equally or to give up the services which were traditionally his male right. Under the communal system, he may still obtain these services, even though they are not so individualized as they would be in his own household; at least he does not have to take part in such "women's activities" himself.[124]

China

China's great experiment with collectivizing women's household chores came in 1958–1960 with the Great Leap Forward. During this nationwide campaign to accelerate economic growth, the party saw it as essential that women's participation in socially productive (i.e., nonhousehold) labor be increased: "The labor potentialities of society can be further extracted by liberating housewives from the bondage of the household chores of many years, to participate in production." [125] The commune was to be the foundation of an economic order in which women's household burdens could be markedly reduced so that they could increase their contributions to agriculture and industrial production. It was envisioned as an organic, self-reliant community and at the same time as a production unit, a defense unit, and a social unit. Communes differed from collectives, it was said, because while collectives merely socialized productive life, communes socialized domestic life as well. In the early months of the Great Leap Forward, many party members declared the commune to be a stage of institutional development that more closely resembled true communism than any social or economic arrangement yet seen.

Communes were expected to become the dominant social order in the cities as well as the countryside. In both cases, the commune was to integrate the household's productive life and family life into the larger community effort to pursue the goal of rapid economic growth. In rural communes, peasants were organized into teams and moved around the countryside with militarylike discipline. Formerly private activities, such as raising pigs and chickens, were put under the authority of the commune. Private plots were abolished. In urban communes, organized around factories, residential neighborhoods, government offices, and, infrequently, universities or colleges, cadres tried to build grade schools, mess halls, service stations, nurseries and kindergartens, movie theaters, barber shops, and workshops to enable the average commune resident to live his or her life without having to leave the boundaries of the commune. The workshops (also called "street" or "commune" industry) were meant to incorporate the labor of recently "liberated" housewives into the economic needs of the state. These small and technologically backward enterprises produced handicraft goods and small consumer items, and reprocessed scrap and waste from large state plants.

In both urban and rural areas, the heart of the commune was to be the mess hall, a collective dining facility. In order to pry women out of their homes, the communes would collectively organize meal preparation. When combined with communally sponsored child-care centers, the mess halls were expected to relieve women of the greatest part of their household burden.

> As the most important problem in the livelihood of the masses is the eating problem, the proper running of mess halls should be regarded as the center of the [service] work. It is only when mess halls are well run that the huge labor reserve of women can be further released.[126]

Mess halls first appeared in rural areas during the busy farming seasons, when all efforts had to be bent toward planting or harvesting crops. Occasionally they were also used when shock labor teams were organized to cope with the damage of natural disaster. Extensive use of mess halls began during the winter of 1957–1958, when large numbers of peasants (as many as 100 million by January 1958) were mobilized to take part in water conservation projects.[127] The arrangement appealed to the enthusiasts of the Great Leap, and so in 1958 the party decided to institutionalize mess halls as an integral part of the commune system.

Why did mess halls become the central concern of collective life in 1958–60? Party statements portray mess halls as the indispensable heart of the new form of communism that was to emerge in the Great Leap Forward; they were the first step in creating a whole array of social services—maternity homes, homes for the aged, services such as laundries and shoemaking. Perhaps the most important of the related services was child care. A report from the rural communes makes this clear:

> During our investigations, we probed into the close relationship between the public mess hall and the nursery. To a certain degree we found that it was through the establishment of the public mess that the nursery came to be set up. . . . The mess halls of these production brigades provided the children and workers in the nurseries with meals. The public mess halls supported the growth of nurseries, and the nurseries depended on the mess halls for their existence.[128]

Young mothers who were to contribute their best to production needed child care as well as food-preparation service. In most cases, the women chosen by the commune to work in communal social services were women who normally stayed at home; having become full-time workers themselves, they needed backup help to keep on going. When mess halls were not available to these women, many of them were forced back into their homes to cook, and other collective welfare enterprises folded.

As the center of the commune's social welfare network, mess halls were defended by the party on ideological grounds: "A man's approach to the community mess halls has to do with the solemn question of his [political] stand."[129] We would suggest, however, that the party's commitment to mess halls also rested on grounds other than doctrine. Mess halls were an ideological solution to a practical problem. The disastrous harvests of 1959 and 1960 made eating a central problem for Chinese households. One important function of the mess halls was to control food consumption.

> A central question in providing all around arrangement for the livelihood of the masses is the planned consumption of provisions. . . . In order to enable the masses to live well, it is necessary to observe a planned consumption of provisions and to economize on provisions. The central authorities of the Party have pointed out the need for careful collecting, controlling, and consuming [of] food crops. In our country, production is always planned. Consumption likewise should be planned.[130]

In some rural communes, initially at least, grain was to be provided free to the commune members as an affirmation of the communist principle

"From each according to his/her ability; to each according to his/her need." Grain consumption targets were set up, however, and mess halls were expected to adhere to the targets. When "some people with strong capitalist thoughts took the opportunity to eat lavishly," the targets were exceeded, much to the dismay of party officials.[131]

In addition to food preparation in the mess halls, other replacement services for women were supposed to be introduced in the communes. These included laundry units, sewing and mending teams, barbershops, and public bathhouses. In rural communes, there is little indication that these auxiliary services were widely established. In cities, networks of neighborhood service stations were set up to aid women with the thousand and one miscellaneous chores they performed. It is estimated that by April 1960 the cities of China had over 66,000 such stations, most performing between 60 and 120 odd jobs. In Shanghai, for example, the service stations were of four types:[132]

1. Repair and mending units, to fix water, electrical, and sanitary equipment, and household appliances, and to mend clothing and leather shoes
2. Service units, like barbershops, bathhouses, hot water supply stations
3. Household chore units, to take care of work ranging from washing several pieces of clothing, to taking care of all domestic work (e.g., helping old people to wash their hair, caring for women in confinement, making purchases, sending children off to nurseries)
4. Multi-purpose service agencies, to receive bank deposits, mail letters, book theater, train, and ship tickets, order books and magazines and newspapers, and collect trash

It is even reported that some workers turned over their wages to the service stations, entrusting them to plan the family budget.[133]

China's experiment with socializing housework in mess halls and service stations cannot be judged a success. As with many elements of the Great Leap Forward, the mess halls were set up too quickly, without sufficient consideration of the problems that might arise. In rural communes, in particular, it was extremely difficult to build and staff dining halls. Buildings to house the "new-born things" were built too rapidly. In one county in Szechwan, for example, it was reported that 3850 mess halls were built in three days! Obviously many of the facilities were inadequate, especially for use in the winter months. Nor could peasants be found who had sophisticated bookkeeping skills to keep the accounts. But the most critical problem was that there were few cooks with the technical skills required to feed 30 to 100 households at once. People were drafted who had no special skills or background in mass feeding. Early in the movement, some communes even put to work their "political undesirables" (landlords, rich peasants, and counterrevolutionaries) as a penalty.[134] Needless to say, this did not produce good food.

Given the mess halls' inadequacies, it is not surprising that rural communes encountered resistance to collective dining. A breakdown of supporters and opponents was published in June 1959. Bachelors, young married couples, and young women found eating by themselves more expensive and more troublesome than eating in mess halls; these are the groups that actively participated. Families that were well-off compared to their neighbors often found mess-hall food too simple for their tastes. Families with old people, children, or invalids at home found mess halls inconvenient. Finally, large families with few able-bodied workers found it more economical to eat at home.[135] What is especially interesting about this analysis is that the less-well-off commune members, who were supposed to be particularly aided through the introduction of collective welfare services, were those least willing to participate in the communal dining halls. As those who were wealthier did not want to participate either, this left a very small segment of the communes' residents actively supporting mess halls. As one detractor put it, "The collective welfare enterprises were established prematurely, are in a mess, and unpopular."[136]

In both urban and rural communes, the party's efforts to create mess halls and other household replacement services were hampered by the pervasive belief that such service work was menial. Waiting on others was thought to be "dirty, heavy, and unrewarding" work.[137] Despite major efforts by the Women's Federation to "correct" public opinion in this regard, household labor remained an inferior occupation in the eyes of the Chinese, both men and women. Household workers received lower pay than factory or office workers in the cities or field workers in the countryside. Consequently, the social service workers recruited in the Great Leap Forward were mostly either activist women, ideologically inspired to help their sisters, or women too young, too old, or too burdened by their own children to have other opportunities.

The low status accorded to household labor resulted, in the eyes of the party, from invalid distinctions between mental and manual labor. In direct contrast to the traditional contempt for housework in China, the Central Committee of the party urged that it be considered a glorious task, especially since such labors now served public, rather than private, interests: "Efforts must be made to give positive guidance to public opinion so that the whole of society and the whole communes regard the successful running of community dining rooms, nurseries and kindergartens, and other collective welfare undertakings as noble work of service to the people."[138] The depth and persistence of the disdain for household labor are reflected in the stream of party propaganda exhorting the population to overcome their mistaken notions and giving reports of successful rectification efforts:

> The comrades of the Chengch'ang Laundry and Dyeing Shop explained to the [new personnel] the two different fates of those people who engaged in service labor in the old society and the new society, showing that service labor of today was a part of the glorious socialist construction.[139]

"Mutual aid," a term that appeared more prominently in discussion about service stations than about either mess halls or nurseries, usually meant that some volunteered, or were coerced into volunteering, their services with no thought of financial compensation. Mutual aid was considered a good method of organizing to replace household services; groups of families elected "livelihood service personnel" whose job it was to perform household chores for the families including cleaning floors, making purchases, collecting water and electricity charges, and picking children up from the nursery. Party propaganda lauded such service workers for "not [being] concerned with hours and rewards."[140] What the women actually thought about doing work that was widely regarded as menial, for no pay, is not recorded.

A further hindrance to popular acceptance of mess halls and service stations was the movement's reliance on "self-help" as the solution to supply problems. For example, when mess halls lacked stoves and utensils, they frequently requisitioned such equipment from private homes, even though equipment taken from individual households was seldom suitable for mass feeding operations. The problems faced by service stations in obtaining adequate supplies of soap, thread, sewing machines, brooms, and so forth, were often similarly solved by simply expropriating them from commune residents. Obviously, such strong-arm tactics were not popular.

The combination of problems just outlined led party officials in a few short months to reconsider their campaign to socialize household work. Although in 1958 the era of utopian housekeeping had been proclaimed, by 1959 a more realistic estimate was being advanced: "The socialization of housework does not mean there will be no housework at all. At present, women still have to do some housework; they will continue to be required to do so in the future."[141] Communal organization could be expected only to reduce the woman's burden to the point where it could be handled in her "spare time after social labor."[142] Not only did the party reduce the claims made for the new collective life but it also began to describe participation in mess halls and other collective services as voluntary:

> . . . the majority of toiling masses, especially the family members of workers, earnestly want the organization of collective life. . . . As regards persons who at the moment do not feel the need of collective life and are skeptical of its desirability, we shall not have them participate. What we should do is to create better conditions, so that when they do feel the need of collective life, we may consider taking them in.[143]

By 1961, the use of communal mess halls had declined significantly. In rural communes, social organization for the most part reverted back to the precommune era. Individual families reassumed the responsibility for food preparation and most other household chores. In cities, the urban commune movement was equally unspectacular. We know, for example, that by 1961, in one of the most successful of the urban people's communes in Chengchow, only one fifth of the working women ate in mess halls at lunch, and none ate dinner there.[144] The ideal of integrating community life, household activities, and work life within the urban commune disappeared, and urban organizations reverted to the previous system of residents' committees. Social organization in Chinese cities now centers largely on the neighborhood and is under the direction of the street or residents' committees. These bodies are expected to provide help to families faced with emergencies or temporary problems (e.g., a death or illness in the family). But, in general, working parents work out their own long-term arrangements regarding household responsibilities, care of the elderly, cleaning, cooking, and the like.[145]

We should recognize that making day-to-day arrangements is a good deal easier for working women in China than in the United States. This is true because Chinese community planning since 1949 has emphasized the kind of community ideal that was the keynote of the Great Leap Forward. Zones are spatially organized around a single large work place or a cluster of smaller work places. Housing has been built in close proximity to the factory, office, or other work unit so that workers live within easy walking or biking distance from their jobs. In addition, most of these functional zones contain the important services that families require on a daily or weekly basis: child-care centers, primary schools, health clinics, restaurants, and shops for food and other household items. Shanghai, for example, is reported to have rehoused 2 million people since 1949 in 75 of these new comprehensive developments.[146] For women workers, the advantages of this community planning are obvious. When she need not travel more than walking distance to her job, can leave her child in day care, and can accomplish daily household errands in nearby shops, a working woman carries her dual burden more successfully than when home, work, shops, and services are separated by long distances. The conscious effort on the part of Chinese urban planners to build and renew their cities in ways that minimize congestion, pollution, and energy consumption seem to work in women's favor.[147]

Sweden

Sweden has had no national experience as dramatic as China's experiment with mess halls and other household replacement services during the Great Leap Forward. Nevertheless, Sweden's government has since the 1930s enacted a series of social, housing, and planning policies that have significantly eased women's household burdens and made it easier for them to take employment outside the home. As in the Chinese case, Swedish social planners have not always had working women as their primary concern, but two of their main objectives in the last 40 years—to control urban growth and to promote family life—have worked to the advantage of employed women.

A unique feature of Swedish social policy is the government's willingness to provide public assistance simply to promote the smooth operation of Swedish households. For example, starting in 1938 the government granted marriage loans to newlyweds to help them in setting up a household. These loans, advanced through the Bank of Sweden, became available on the same terms in 1953 to unmarried parents. In 1939, because the vast majority of Swedish households had no running water, the national government introduced subsidies for establishing mechanized laundries all over the country, where families could deliver laundry or do it themselves. Sweden's national network of Home Help Services best illustrates the government's commitment to easing household burdens. Although many Western European governments provide similar services, Sweden's is probably the most elaborate system in the world. It is designed to send a helper (usually a woman) to a family needing assistance in housekeeping, the care of children (or old people or other family members) who are sick, or both.

The idea was brought to Sweden in the 1920s by a private charity—the Red Cross—and some private home-help services still operate in the larger cities. The national government began taking a major responsibility for the program with the passage in 1943 of the Social Home Help Act, which provided subsidies to either local governments or voluntary organizations that recruited home helps, provided certain conditions were met (especially regarding training). Originally, government-supported home-help services were limited to families temporarily in critical circumstances. For example, domestic helpers could be sent into a household when the mother was ill or indisposed so that she was not able to keep house, prepare meals, or look after children. In one-parent households or homes with two working parents, a child-care worker might be brought in to care for a child too sick to attend a regular day-care center. With the rapid growth of the elderly population in Sweden since the 1940s, the service has been expanded to provide long-term care for old and handicapped people living by themselves or with working relatives. By the 1970s, three times more services were being consumed by the elderly and handicapped than by the program's original clients, families with young children. Nevertheless, an estimated 10 percent of young families use the service in Sweden, about half for temporary child care and half for housekeeping.[148]

The government-sponsored home-help services are administered by local governments, although they are financed by an approximately equal combination of national and local subsidies, along with fees from the consumers. Like municipal day care, the program is universal, in the sense that it may be used by households of all income levels. But also like day care, the service is provided free only to low-income families; others pay according to a sliding fee scale based on ability to pay.

The mushrooming of home-help services can be seen in the fact that they now employ about 1 percent of Sweden's total labor force.[149] One reason for the large numbers of people employed is the preponderance of part-time workers among home helpers. The vast majority of them are middle-aged women. Although they receive varying levels of job training, depending on the municipality, they are unorganized, low-status workers. Without a union, their only fringe benefits are supplied by the government's social security system. They are among the unfortunate exceptions in Sweden's otherwise well-organized labor force.

In addition to the social services just described, other government policies have contributed to easing the dual burden for Swedish working women. In particular, we would argue that the approach to community planning has increased women's opportunities. What advantages have Sweden's urban planners conferred on working women?

It may be best to begin by noting one advantage that Swedish working women do *not* enjoy: male partners who share fully in the responsibilities of housekeeping and child rearing. A national government commission investigating the division of responsibilities in Swedish households in 1965 found that the majority of Swedish men did no housework. Furthermore, it was unusual for men to take much responsibility for child care. The men's habits differed only slightly when their wives worked and when their wives were full-time homemakers.[150] Despite periodic media campaigns since the mid-1960s to promote a more equitable distribution of duties between working women and men, the problem has not been solved in most households. Data from Sweden's 1974 Standard-of-Living Investigation were analyzed by Elina Haavio-Mannila, to show the following female-to-male ratios in time spent doing unpaid housework:[151]

	Female:Male
Participated in housework for at least one hour per day	3.14:1
Proportion of meals prepared, of all meals prepared in the household	3.04:1
Proportion of dishes washed up after the meals	2.33:1
Proportion of hours used in washing laundry	5.16:1
Proportion of hours used in taking care of clothes	12.58:1
Proportion of hours used in housecleaning	2.67:1
Proportion of hours used in shopping	1.56:1
No free day from housework	2.66:1

Although women's groups, trade unions, and government agencies continue to promote the sharing of this burden, most working women in Sweden still cope with the inequity. It should also be observed that Sweden has a significant number of single-parent families; they constitute one tenth of all households with children. Over 90 percent of single-parent households are headed by women, who obviously carry total responsibility for both home and work. The practice of hiring domestic help to handle housework has declined in Sweden as elsewhere in the Western world. In sum, Swedish working women continue to play the dual role described by Alva Myrdal in 1956—as workers and as primary managers of home and children. How do they manage it?

First, Sweden's national housing policy has for decades given priority to building apartments rather than single-family detached houses. Swedish builders in the early 1950s were building less than a quarter of their new units as single-family houses.[152] And while the proportion of these houses among construction starts has increased rapidly in recent years (to 45 percent in 1973, 55 percent in 1974, and 63 percent in 1975), the existing housing stock is still dominated by apartments. This is particularly true for Stockholm, whose residential expansion since 1945 has been channeled into a series of satellite communities dominated by large-scale apartment projects.

Apartment living has certain obvious advantages for Sweden's working women, who continue to bear the greater responsibility for household maintenance. The burdens of maintaining the building's interior, exterior, utilities, and greenery all fall to the management rather than to the individual household. But apart from these advantages, enjoyed by apartment dwellers everywhere, Swedes simply have less household space to maintain than American families. Table 2–9 contrasts the size of apartments in Stockholm with apartments in American cities. It shows that in Stockholm, apartments with two or three rooms are the most common; in American cities, the majority of apartments contain four rooms or more.

The reader might assume that the Swedish figures, because they include both old and new Stockholm apartments, reflect the poorer space standards of a less affluent era; under such an assumption, the size of

TABLE 2-9. Apartment Size in Greater Stockholm Compared with Apartment Size in U.S. Metropolitan Areas, 1970

	Stockholm		*United States*	
Apartment Size[a]	*Percent in Central City*	*Percent Outside City Limits*	*Percent in Central City*	*Percent Outside City Limits*
2 rooms	52	21	10	6
3 rooms	25	31	28	23
4 rooms	12	28	31	33
5 rooms or more	11	20	31	38

**Figures for both Sweden and the United States exclude single rooms for rent.*

Sources: Stockholm Real Estate Board, "Housing Renovation in Stockholm," Stockholm, 1973; and U.S. Department of Commerce, Bureau of the Census, *1970 Census of Housing*, vol. 1, *Housing Characteristics for States, Cities, and Counties: U.S. Summary.*

apartments built in future years would be expected to increase. That is not likely to happen. The National Housing Board's building standards for new apartment construction released in 1973 recommended the following standards for projects receiving national subsidies (i.e., about 90 percent of all apartment construction):[153]

1 person:	1 room plus kitchen
2 or 3 people:	2 rooms plus kitchen
4 or 5 people:	3 rooms plus kitchen
6+ people:	4 rooms plus kitchen

As these are presented as "ideal" conditions, it is apparent that Swedish housing authorities do not perceive a need for significant increases in apartment size.

The experiments of Swedish housing developers have gone beyond the conventional multifamily dwelling. In the early 1930s sociologist Alva Myrdal and builder Sven Markelius launched the idea of the Collective House, a new style of living designed specificially for families with two working parents. The Collective House had two main social goals: (1) to free the working woman from as many housekeeping chores as possible, and (2) to promote a sense of community among the residents. It provided collective services for tenants in laundries, communal kitchens, and child-care centers. Although they were encouraged to do so, tenants did not have to eat all meals in the common dining room; they could arrange to have their prepared meals delivered by a food lift from the central kitchen. The buildings contained a common reception area with a permanent "concierge" to take deliveries for all tenants; they also made available to tenants social rooms and exercise rooms.

In 1935 Markelius completed his first Collective House in central Stockholm for a tenants' association. This project, followed a few years later by Markelius's Professional Women's House in Stockholm, was hailed as an important departure in Swedish building styles. It is difficult to know whether the concept would have found an immediate market because building activity in Stockholm came almost to a halt during World War II. But only a handful of Collective Houses, in their original form as tenant communities, were built after the war.

The postwar successor to the Collective House has been the Service House, intended to serve not only the immediate tenant population but also the neighborhood at large. Service Houses are apartment buildings that also contain a wide variety of shops and services. While they retain many of the conveniences of the Collective House, they have shed most of its communal living features. There is, for example, the Fältöversten service center, a high-rise apartment complex in Stockholm's Ostermalm district, which houses on the ground floor a coffee shop, a grocery, a pharmacy, a state liquor store, specialty shops, a small lending library, a laundry, a post office branch, a Social Welfare Department branch office, and a child-care center. Above the ground level, 1600 tenants live in 536 apartments. This imposing triangular block, known affectionately in the neighborhood as "The Red Ugly," services not only its own tenants but the surrounding community as well and has generated about 600 jobs in the heart of this residential neighborhood.

The convenience to working parents of life in a Service House can be easily illustrated by a sample day in the life of one resident family:

7:00 A.M.	Family awakens, and parents prepare breakfast for themselves and two children
8:15 A.M.	Parents drop off the younger child at day-care center in the building
8:30 A.M.	Parents drop off the older child at school
9:00 A.M.	Both parents arrive at their respective jobs
12:00 noon	No need to worry about the children, since even the older child receives a free lunch at school
1:00 P.M.	While they are at work, the building caretaker sends out a laundry order for them, takes telephone messages, and receives delivery of a standing grocery order. In addition, their apartment is cleaned by a building cleaning service
4:00 P.M.	Father arrives home earlier, picking up the younger child in the day-care center. He finds that the child is ill and calls in the building nurse for an examination and to provide a prescription for medicine, which can be obtained from the building pharmacy
4:30 P.M.	When mother arrives home with the older child, all four family members go to eat in the apartment restaurant, where they have purchased a block of tickets for the month. If they prefer, they can take out a prepared dinner to their own apartment.

Without significant government subsidies, this style of housing is clearly a great deal more expensive than the standard apartment, and is therefore accessible only to the well-to-do Swedish family. Since the late 1960s, the Swedish Trade Union Confederation (LO), and the Communist party have shown increasing interest in Service Houses for the working class. In particular, representatives of the women's section of the LO have complained that the growing popularity of single-family suburban houses will undermine women's employment because the life style requires one person to stay at home to manage the house. The issue of reviving Service Houses on a large scale was one of the first pressed by the opposition on the coalition government elected in September 1976. In a December legislative debate on housing policy, the communists even put forth a proposal for special government loans to encourage the construction of more Service Houses, and an appropriation of $22.5 million for experiments with collective building forms. In spite of this support from the left, collective housing is unlikely to gain much ground in a housing market increasingly dominated by single-family construction.

If they have not subscribed wholeheartedly to the collective housing style, Swedish planners have nevertheless carried out a similar idea of the neighborhood service center in much of their suburban development. The best examples of suburban planning are found around Sweden's largest metropolitan area, Greater Stockholm. Unlike the sprawling housing developments that ring America's largest cities, Stockholm's expansion has taken the form of high-density communities radiating out from central Stockholm along the main subway lines. At the center of each satellite is its "miniature downtown," containing the community's shops, services, and community facilities. The difference between this arrangement and the American suburb is evident. Instead of being strung along a main boulevard several miles long, the basic services that residents are likely to need—library, medical and child-care services, subway station, and retail establishments are clustered within a two- or three-block radius. This central district is usually a pedestrian area only; cars must be parked at its edge. Nevertheless, the satellites are planned so that any resident can walk from his or her home to the center in ten minutes.

As consumers, Swedes rely heavily on neighborhood shops and services. For example, one national study published in the late 1960s showed that in large cities, fully 78 percent of the households surveyed shopped for groceries at a store located within a distance of one-quarter mile from their home. They tended to organize their grocery shopping around daily purchases, with 90 percent of the households shopping a minimum of five days a week.[154] Obviously, the mixed-use ground plan found in most of Stockholm's neighborhoods offers maximum convenience for working mothers, who have a minimum of time to devote to shopping, running errands, and picking up children.

The Stockholm planners' determination to control urban sprawl and at the same time plan efficient mass transit systems has also contributed to easing the transportation problems of women workers. For women, who carry the primary household responsibility in addition to their employment, quick and reliable transportation to the work place is essential. In Sweden and the United States, women workers rely less on private automobiles and more on public transportation than do male workers. In both countries, female workers are about twice as likely to travel to work on public transportation as their male counterparts. Of course, the use of public transit for the journey to work is more common in Swedish cities than in American cities for both men and women, but it is clearly the Swedish women who rely on it most heavily.

United States

Americans have constructed a life style that requires a huge labor investment in household tasks, yet Americans continue to hold housework in low esteem. One indication of that low esteem is the low market value of household labor. In her congressional battle to get domestic workers covered by the federal minimum wage law, Representative Shirley Chisholm highlighted the economic status of domestic workers: they are 97 percent female, and earned in 1970 a *full-time* median annual income of less than $2000.[155] Chisholm was finally successfull in 1974 in extending the minimum wage to these workers. Representative Martha Griffiths, working to change tax laws, has confronted the same issue of the low esteem for housework:

> For five years I spent my time in the Committee on Ways and Means every time we had a tax bill, trying to get it set up so that one could deduct the wages paid to domestics. To fail to deduct those wages is in itself sexist discimination. What the gentleman is really saying is that what that woman does in a home is of no worth. I should like to differ with him. What she does in that home is a thing that makes life livable.[156]

We have little evidence that federal policy makers recognize housework as work, let alone indispensable labor. Housewives are not covered by the national pension system in the United States, as they are in Sweden. Nor has Congress given significant attention to creating home-help services on a national scale, to give temporary assistance to households that need to be maintained through emergencies. Home-help services exist in the United States, but they exist in small numbers and only in some communities, particularly the large cities of the Northeast. They are so scattered and understaffed as to have escaped the attention of most Americans. A simple numerical comparison will verify this point: Sweden has the equivalent of one full-time home helper for every 101 citizens; the United States in 1973 had one home helper for every 4709 citizens.[157]

Alternatively labeled "home health aides," "home aides," and "homemakers," these workers are employed by local governments, private businesses, and some combination public-private agencies. Although they started by serving families with young children, these services are consumed more and more by the elderly and handicapped. Not only are home-help services in extremely short supply in the United States; they are also stigmatized:

> Despite the relative frequency of family emergencies and the needs of families who are often far from relatives and friends who might help out, the burden remains on the individual family. People find their own resources and pay for the service out of their own pockets. The [public] homemaker working in families with children becomes a symbol of dependency, neglect, poverty, disorganization—and her assistance is not seen as a necessity similar to medical and nursing care.[158]

Some readers may perceive the Chinese and even the Swedish experiments with socializing housework as so dissonant with American life styles that comparison would serve no useful purpose. Those readers may be surprised to learn that the United States has also had its advocates of socializing housework, although few of them have actually influenced public policy.

In her 1898 treatise, *Women and Economics*, Charlotte Perkins Gilman described the need for living quarters much like the Swedish Service Houses. Basic housekeeping services would be provided by trained and specialized professionals, thus releasing working women from their domestic burdens. In cities, Gilman advocated the construction of apartment buildings with common dining rooms. But she also foresaw the possibility of adapting suburban living to meet the needs of working women:

> In suburban homes this purpose could be accomplished much better by a grouping of adjacent houses, each distinct and having its own yard, but all kitchenless, and connected by covered ways with the eating-house. . . . The cleaning required in each house would be much reduced by the removal of the two chief elements of household dirt—grease and ashes.[159]

The idea of collectivizing housework was also popularized in the United States by several disciples of the influential English planner Ebenezer Howard, whose "garden city" became the model for twentieth-century New Towns in both Europe and America.[160] Howard himself was a proponent of cooperative housekeeping, although this aspect of his work is rarely mentioned by biographers. In 1914, one of Howard's American followers, Alice Austin, designed houses without kitchens for the Llano del Rio community in California. In Austin's design, prepared food was to be delivered through underground tunnels to individual homes.[161] Another disciple of Howard's, Greta Gray, published a book in 1923 that included her plan for Garden Village, done for a steel factory in Canada; in it, she argued against the house as a self-contained unit and against seeing the family as a private institution.[162]

Nevertheless, as we saw for public child care in America, only under national emergencies have these collectivist proposals gained any influence. Cooperative kitchens became popular on the East Coast during World War I, and the *Ladies Home Journal* reported on experiments like "One Kitchen Fire for 200 People: No Necessity Any More for Each Family to Cook Its Own Meals."[163] In World War II, when women were once again needed in the factories, planners began advocating service-oriented housing styles. The designs were to be simple, functional, and easy to maintain; housing units were to be grouped close to neighborhood service centers, where child care, shops, and services would be easily available. As one proponent explained:

> Victory depends on production; production depends on the manpower behind production machines; and men and women cannot work at the top efficiency our situation demands, if they are not housed under circumstances that will assure their continuing ability to stay on the job.[164]

The motivation for such design innovations was clearly the wartime emergency. They were undertaken, not by social reformers, but by employers and military authorities.

After World War II, a few isolated American planners seized on the New Town as the development model of the future. Inspired by the example of British New Towns, built in southeastern England after the war, some American developers promoted the idea of totally planned communities that would contain residential neighborhoods in close proximity to offices and other employment centers, as well as to a full array of basic community services. The New Town was to offer most of the advantages of suburban living without the inconvenience of a long commute to the work place.

The close proximity of home and work place in the New Towns, combined with the convenience of clustered shops and services, would seem to make New Towns an ideal living situation for one-parent families or families headed by two working parents. Research on British New Towns shows that they have employed a significantly larger proportion of their adult female population than they have male residents, within the town boundaries.[165] But the debate over New Towns in the United States has revolved around the difficulties of private financing, the marketability of cluster housing, and New Towns' tendency to exclude low-income and minority residents. Whether New Towns offer a better living environment for working women with families has simply not figured in the planning debate. Rather, New Town planners have simply assumed that "women's roles were defined almost totally by their relationship to a nuclear family."[166] In any case, debates are by now academic: the financial track record of private New Town ventures like Columbia, Maryland, and Reston, Virginia; the economic downturn of the housing market in the 1970s; and the virtual evaporation of federal subsidies for New Towns have discouraged American developers from pursuing the New Town idea.

The suburbanization of American cities is the physical expression of conventional assumptions regarding family roles. It is no accident that the celebrated return to the hearth of middle-class American women portrayed in Friedan's *Feminine Mystique*[167] coincided exactly with the postwar suburban housing boom. Suburban growth was predicated on the assumption that women would play the role of homemaker-childminder. Living comfortably on the urban fringe required that one member of the household be what Galbraith has labeled a "consumption administrator."[168] The family breadwinner was free to pursue a full-time job, usually combined with a time-consuming commute, only because a household manager was on the premises to handle shopping, cooking, child care, arrangements for home and car repair and maintenance, and so forth. Now, when women are challenging these conventional role assumptions, they find that the urban environment we have constructed works against them.

In large measure, this urban environment is the product of public policies. At the local level, zoning policies have increased the amount of time that working women must spend running errands and commuting to work. The use of zoning ordinances as the basic planning instruments of local governments effectively inhibits the creation of small-scale neighborhood service centers within walking distance of residents.[169] Zoning, which tends to segregate uses into large zones, cannot easily create small, multiple land-use districts within residential areas. Instead we see mile after mile of residential development separated from a commercial district, in which shopping centers are lined up for miles along a commercial strip. Under such conditions, even the most casual expedition to shop or run errands requires a car and the time to maneuver in and out of several parking lots.

Even more important than the impact of these local policies has been our national policy to encourage the American "spread city." First, there is the massive federal highway program, which has sealed the fate of public transit in cities. The competition from automobiles has left our cities' mass transit systems underutilized. In combination with rising labor costs, this competition has created insurmountable problems for transit companies in financing and maintaining their services. The decline of public transit in American cities is a grim but well-known story. What is seldom acknowledged is that its deterioration brings greater hardships to female workers than to males. Table 2–10 compares the degree to which men and women workers rely on public transit for their journey to work. In all four categories, women show greater reliance than men on public transit.

The problems created for working women by the absence of safe, efficient public transportation are obvious. First, the crime and violence associated with urban public transit systems discourages those potential riders who feel most vulnerable to attack: women and the elderly. At off-peak hours, public transit is simply not a realistic option for many women. Second, declining service levels on public transit limit women's opportunities because women without cars simply have no access to the greater part of the metropolitan labor market. A 1971 study done in San Francisco showed that in the Bay Area, 36 percent of all employed women lacked access to an automobile, while only 12 percent of employed men were carless.[170] Because many working women in American cities lack effective transportation, one would suppose that women are more pressed than men to seek employment close to home. The supposition is borne out by research showing that a higher proportion of female workers live near their jobs than do male workers.[171]

The other important national influence on suburban sprawl has been our housing policy. In order to encourage homeownership the Federal Housing Administration (FHA) has furnished generous mortgage guarantees for private home building in new subdivisions outside the central cities. Residents of suburbia are the prime beneficiaries of the indirect federal housing subsidies that result from tax deductions by homeowners for property taxes and mortgage interest. These tax deductions, by the Treasury's estimate, amounted to a subsidy of about $5.7 billion in 1971—an amount more than double all other housing subsidies combined.[172] Big-city housing programs in the mid-1970s began to emphasize rehabilitation of central-city properties by lower-middle-income families willing to live in them ("homesteading"), but influence has been minor compared

TABLE 2-10. Percentage of Working Women and Men Using Public Transit in Five Metropolitan Areas,* by Place of Residence and Place of Work, 1970

	Workplace	
Residence	*Central City*	*Outside City Limits*
Central City	Women: 62 Men: 45	Women: 30 Men: 13
Outside City Limits	Women: 44 Men: 28	Women: 7 Men: 3

***Boston, Chicago, Detroit, New York, Philadelphia.**

Source: U.S. Department of Commerce, Bureau of the Census, *Census of the Population, 1970*, vol. 1., *Characteristics of the Population, Books of the States,* parts 15, 23, 24, 34, 40; table 190.

with that of the FHA and IRS in promoting the middle-class exodus to the suburbs.

In short, U.S. governments, local and national, have contributed to the urban sprawl, the predominance of high-maintenance housing styles, and the lack of adequate mass transportation—all of which operate to limit women's participation in the work force. But can we blame these problems entirely on government? Or have American policy makers simply responded to popular preferences?

Our Swedish and Chinese comparisons raise a number of interesting questions about the life-style preferences of Americans. The majority of Swedish and Chinese family living quarters would be considered small by middle-class American standards. Families in Swedish and Chinese cities shop for many goods and services in small-scale neighborhood establishments ("corner stores"); in some of the larger new developments in Shanghai and Stockholm, these shops are located right in the apartment buildings. Finally, Swedes and Chinese rely on the automobile much less than Americans do; this is true even for Swedish suburbanites, because suburban expansion has taken place along the route of an efficient rail system.

Given the choice, would American households, even dual-career households, choose to live this way? It is doubtful. Apartment living is widely perceived by Americans as a transitional life style, suitable either for highly mobile families without roots in the community or for those who cannot afford to buy a house. Indeed, a common criticism of public housing projects is that the high-rise apartment building is a residential form at odds with American housing preferences. One sociologist has caustically described American public housing as a physical symbol of social deviance; the American dream home is a suburban house on its own lot, whereas the public housing family rents a small apartment in a high-density project in the middle of the city.[173]

The widespread decline of small neighborhood shops and services in favor of massive shopping malls suggests that urban dwellers are willing to trade the convenience of corner shopping for the greater variety and lower prices offered by the more distant shopping centers. A 1972 study of a sample of New York City college students as "future housing consumers" reported that only respondents who were poor (annual family income under $2000), black, or living in high-rise buildings considered close proximity to shops as "very important" in determining their choice of residence. Respondents with family incomes over $10,000 and those living in single-family houses rated proximity to shops as only "moderately important."[174]

What about Americans' preference for the private automobile over mass transit—is it amenable to change? Much has been written on the subject, and transit company officials all over the country maintain an optimistic outlook on the question, at least publicly. But the short-range prospect is dubious. After all, land-use patterns that created our dependence on the auto cannot easily be modified. Even as enthusiastic a proponent of mass transit as transportation economist Wilfred Owen has acknowledged that

> In the next few years the automobile itself could become increasingly attractive through measures to achieve greater safety, to eliminate air pollution, and to lower costs through new power sources, longer life, and a reduction in the frequency of model changes.[175]

WELFARE AND FAMILY ASSISTANCE

Welfare programs in modern industrial societies are often perceived as "women's programs" because women constitute such a large proportion of recipients. For many recipients, reliance on welfare is necessitated by the traditional economic dependence of the entire family unit on the earnings of a male breadwinner who is no longer able to support the household because he is disabled, unemployed or underemployed, dead, or absent from the scene. When that happens, it is often impossible for the woman of the house to step into the wage-earner role as a replacement. The factors working against her are many: her self-image as a wife and mother rather than a worker, her lack of training, the structure of the labor market, and the difficulty of replacing her labor in the home as housekeeper and child minder. In many preindustrial societies, a household that had fallen into such distress might well be supported by the resources of the extended family. One consequence of industrialization has been the weakening of the welfare functions performed by extended families. That same distressed household must now be supported either by its own enterprises or public assistance programs. Of our three governments, Sweden deals most generously with such distressed households.

Sweden

The clearest indication of the Swedish government's view that well-maintained families are a valuable asset to the nation, is its treatment of one-parent families. Sweden's one-parent families now constitute almost a quarter of all families with children; and as in America, the vast majority are headed by women. The economic situation of the one-parent family is different in the two nations, however. The difference is obvious from a glance at the extent to which one-parent families rely on public assistance in Sweden and the United States. Table 2–11 shows that the percentage of one-parent families falling into the public assistance category is much smaller in Sweden than it is in the United States. Moreover, the public assistance rate among single parents has actually *declined* in Sweden since World War II. In 1945, 279 out of every 1000 single mothers were receiving public assistance; by 1973, the number had dropped to 192.[176] In part we can attribute this decline to the growing percentage of today's single mothers in Sweden who have never married but simply decided to bear children without marrying. Historically, in Sweden, such women show less likelihood of ending up on public assistance than do divorced mothers.[177] We might speculate that unwed mothers have a lower expectation of becoming dependent on their partners and therefore are less likely to become dependent on the government, even if they become the sole supporters of their children.

Undoubtedly, special conditions in the United States, notably racial inequities, exacerbate the plight of one-parent families; nevertheless, the

TABLE 2-11. One-Parent Families and Public Assistance in the United States and Sweden*

	U.S. (1975)	*Sweden (1976)*
One-parent families as percentage of all families with children	16%	23%
One-parent families as percentage of all public assistance recipients	86%	17%
One-parent families on public assistance as a percentage of all one-parent families	57%	13%

****For the United States figures represent AFDC recipients. For Sweden figures represent relief cases.***

Source: Compiled by authors, using *Statistical Abstract of the United States 1978*, pp. 48, 361, and *Statistisk Arsbok för Sverige 1978*, p. 287.

explanation for the Swedish-American contrast lies in large part in the social welfare programs of the two governments. Sweden's income-maintenance programs keep one-parent families above the public assistance level, whereas American social welfare policies are ill equipped to meet the special problems of one-parent households. The difference in income supports provided to one-parent households in Sweden and the United States is illustrated in table 2-12, which compares the economic circumstances in the two countries of one-parent families and conventional two-parent families. The table reveals the effort made by the Swedish government to equalize the incomes of the two households. The table compares the circumstances of these two different household configurations:

1. A single mother (nonwidow) with two children, one an infant and the other in elementary school. The woman has no job, no personal resources, and no support from the absent father.
2. A conventional two-parent household supporting two children (same ages as in the previous household). The woman has no job, and the man earns the median male industrial wage.

Table 2-12 shows that government support programs in Sweden provide the unemployed single mother with a total income that is much closer to the income of the two-parent household than is the income of the unemployed single mother in the United States.

In addition to the public assistance benefits available in both nations, the Swedish government also provides a family allowance and a child-maintenance grant. The Swedish government began paying out the family allowance in 1948 as a replacement for the earlier system of tax deductions, somewhat similar to the tax deductions for dependents now granted in the United States. Swedish households no longer get any exemptions for dependents; instead they receive an annual tax-free grant of about $500 (as of April 1978) for each child under sixteen years old. The important difference between the family allowance and a tax deduction for dependents is that the amount of the allowance is in no way affected by the family's income. Rather, it is a flat sum granted across the board to all families with children. The rationale offered by its proponents in 1948 was that the community has a clear interest in child rearing and that no family ought to be forced to lower its standard of living in order to perform this valuable service for the larger community.

Besides the universal family allowance, the government may pay an extra child-maintenance grant for children of single parents on the grounds that single parents confront unusual financial difficulties in trying to raise children. The government therefore stipulates that in addition to the family allowance, a single parent should receive an extra $770 a year for each child under eighteen. This supplement is made up of a combination of whatever support payments are contributed by the absent parent plus a contribution from the Child Welfare Board sufficient to ensure a minimum of $770. This supplementary grant, like the family allowance, is universal; it does not depend on the parent's income level. Its payment is administratively integrated with Sweden's system for establishing paternity, granting child custody, and fixing the child support payments owed by the absent parent.[178] Finally, many low- and moderate-income families with children, including single-parent families, are entitled to a housing allowance. For families with incomes under $5225, the allowance is about $15 a month for each child; for families with higher incomes, the amount of the allowance drops as income rises. Lastly, we should point out that table 2–12 portrays only the income-maintenance programs in the two countries. When one considers in addition the in-kind services (especially medical care and day care) available in Sweden, it is clear that single mothers in Sweden are even farther ahead of their American sisters.

From the amounts displayed in table 2–12, one sees immediately that Sweden's public assistance program lacks the strong work incentives built into the American system. The unemployed single parent in Sweden receives from public assistance fully two thirds of what is earned by the male wage earner in the other household, whereas the American unemployed welfare mother receives only a little over one third of that amount. The general observation that Swedish public assistance offers fewer work incentives than the American welfare system is true for all recipients, not just single parents. Table 2–13 shows that a Swedish welfare family of four (two adults, two children), if they live in the municipality with the highest benefit level, can actually receive *more* in benefits than they would earn if

TABLE 2-12. Estimated Monthly Income for Two Model Families, Sweden and the United States (in U.S. dollars)

	Sweden (1976)		*U.S. (1976)*	
	Family 1	*Family 2*	*Family 1*	*Family 2*
Assumed earnings	$ 0.00	$1023.90	$ 0.00	$1160.90
Public assistance	225.00	0.00	236.00	0.00
Family allowance	78.00	78.00	0.00	0.00
Child-maintenance grants	164.00	0.00	0.00	0.00
Housing allowance	119.00	100.00	0.00	0.00
Food stamps	0.00	0.00	75.00	0.00
Less social insurance (social security)	−0.00	−290.00	−0.00	−223.00
Net Income	586.00	911.90	311.00	937.90
Net income as percent of Family 2's Income	64%	100%	33%	100%

Source: Compiled by authors, using *Statistical Abstract of the United States 1978; Statistisk Arsbok for Sverige* 1978; Swedish Institute, "The Economic Situation of Swedish Households," December 1977.

TABLE 2-13. Public Assistance Levels Compared to Median Income (after taxes) of a Family of Four in Sweden and the United States

	Sweden (1973)		*United States (1972)*	
	Lowest	*Highest*	*Lowest*	*Highest*
1. Annual public assistance payments to a family of four with no other income	$3,964	$6,491	$ 1,908	$ 4,524
2. Median income for family of four, only husband working	5,800	5,800	8,389	8,389
3. (1) as a percent of (2)	68	112	23	54
4. Median income for family of four, both parents working	7,257	7,257	11,035	11,035
5. (1) as a percent of (4)	55	89	17	41

Source: Ralph Husby and Eva Wetzel, "Public Assistance in Sweden and the U.S.," *Social Policy* 7, no. 5 (March/April 1977); 30.

the husband were employed at the median wage. They could receive close to 90 percent of what they would earn if both adults were employed at the median wage. By contrast, American benefits are not nearly so generous.

United States

The U.S. government provides no family allowances; with the exception of Japan, it is the only national government in a major industrialized nation that does not. The United States does of course provide public assistance to needy families, in the form of Aid to Families with Dependent Children (AFDC), introduced in 1935 as part of the landmark Social Security Act. As a matching federal-state program, AFDC was set up under broad national guidelines with individual states deciding on their own eligibility criteria and benefit levels. Unlike Swedish public assistance, AFDC is dispensed only to families that meet *both* its main qualifications: (1) low income; and (2) the absence, death, or disability of one or both parents. In about half the states, the breadwinner's loss of job also qualifies a family for aid. The enforcement of the eligibility standards, even by such bizarre tactics as the celebrated "midnight raids" to discover whether a client family was illegally harboring a man in the house, has received a great deal of criticism. Volumes have been written about the flaws in AFDC and the need for welfare reform, but we still have no such reform.

Unlike Sweden's public assistance to families, AFDC can be used to discriminate between married and unwed mothers if states so desire. Throughout the 1950s, state governments enacted laws requiring that AFDC recipients inhabit "suitable homes." This meant that the mother was not to engage in "promiscuity," nor was she to bear any illegitimate children after receiving AFDC payments. If she did, her benefits would be withdrawn. HEW declared in 1960 that states could not legally deny AFDC on the grounds of an unsuitable home as long as children were still living in it. In response, several states began to discourage applications from unwed mothers by a new route, telling them they risked being charged with child neglect and consequently having their children removed to foster homes. In spite of these efforts by some states, the proportion of AFDC children born illegitimate continued to climb throughout the 1960s and early 1970s, thereby contributing to the program's political unpopularity.[179]

The most pointed criticism of AFDC has been aimed at the rule that in order for a family to be eligible, one parent must be disabled, absent, dead or (in some states) unemployed. This rule has led many fathers to leave home so that their families could qualify for aid. For example, a federally financed study done in New York City in 1975 showed that 21 percent of the city's AFDC mothers had either broken up their marriages or pretended to do so in order to get public assistance. The study concluded that AFDC rules result in "gross discrimination" against intact families.[180] More than any other provision, this one is responsible for making AFDC a woman's program. Of the 11.2 million people who received AFDC payments in 1977, only 1.3 percent were men. Another 71 percent were children, and the remaining 28 percent were their mothers. On this particular point, Sweden's public assistance program compares favorably; it furnishes aid even to families with both parents present, and without regard to the parents' employment status. Low income is virtually the only eligibility criterion.

For our purposes the most interesting point of comparison is the heavy emphasis in the American welfare program on work incentives. Since the early 1960s, federal and state officials have voiced constant concern about the problem of "freeloaders" relying on AFDC payments to avoid employment. This concern, that AFDC may discourage able-bodied women and men from working, is reflected in several aspects of the program.

First, the system was based from the outset on the principle of "less eligibility."[181] That is, the AFDC recipient's resources should always be less than the lowest income level for the working poor. That principle continues to get support, both from the general public and in Congress. The average monthly payments to families of four in July 1976 ranged from a low of $60 in Mississippi to a high of $433 in Oregon. Even the Oregon payment fell below the federally established poverty level of $455 per month (for a nonfarm family of four). If we adjust the monthly totals to include the average food stamp benefit received by AFDC families, we find that five states (Oregon, Wisconsin, New York, Connecticut, Michigan) provided a monthly total slightly above the poverty level. Another 43 states in the continental United States supported AFDC recipients with payments below the poverty level. (AFDC payments in Alaska and Hawaii are omitted from this comparison because their cost-of-living and benefit levels are drastically different from the rest of the states.)[182]

Many of the nation's working poor families earn less than the poverty level but are ineligible for assistance because both parents are present in the home. Moreover, welfare specialists Piven and Cloward have argued forcefully that local welfare offices have deliberately adjusted the rules to reduce payment levels below locally available wages in order to ensure a low-cost labor pool for local employers. Offering evidence that AFDC grant levels are highly correlated with the average hourly agricultural wage, they have argued that local welfare offices even resort to withdrawing aid during periods of peak labor demand, such as during harvest season.[183]

Low benefit levels are not the only methods used to ensure that welfare does not become more attractive than work. Congress in 1967 built into the welfare program a rule that allowed welfare recipients to keep the first $30 of earned income each month without any change in their monthly benefit. For every dollar of income they earned beyond the first $30, the welfare check was reduced by 66 cents, thereby leaving the recipient 33 cents ahead of where she would have been had she not been working. This provision was introduced explicitly to give welfare recipients some incentive for working. (Note: The difference between this system and the Swedish is that, in Sweden, all monthly income earned beyond the first 100 kronor reduces the welfare payment by an identical amount; this procedure amounts to a 100 percent tax on earnings.[184])

The most obvious reflections of official concern with freeloading are the numerous programs enacted since 1967 to put welfare recipients to work.

> Work experience, work training, work incentives—whatever the titles and whatever the marginal differences in program content—were all designed, in the catch phrase so often used, to move people off the relief rolls and onto the tax rolls.[185]

For example, the Social Security Amendments of 1967 created the WIN program, which envisioned individual counseling, testing, and job training for all adult AFDC recipients and gave the states permission to impose financial penalties on parents who refused to participate. Under the WIN program, state governments were to decide which adults were eligible for work; many states chose to include mothers of small children. The program was vigorously opposed by welfare rights organizations, which charged that states had neither the resources nor the will to provide the quantity and quality of day care to accommodate the children of working AFDC mothers. The growing level of unemployment made it impossible to find jobs for those who did manage to get training.

These obvious problems aside, the WIN concept was picked up and expanded in Nixon's ill-fated welfare reform proposal of 1969, the Family Assistance Plan (FAP). FAP included a plan to provide assistance to *all* needy families with children, not just families with a missing parent. It proposed to guarantee to all American families with children a minimum yearly income. The amount of the minimum varied in different versions of the bill; in one it was to be $1600 and in another, $2400. Families with no income would receive the full amount of the guaranteed minimum from the government. Families with some income would have their welfare payments reduced, although they would be allowed to earn slightly more than was subtracted. Again, the idea was to leave an incentive for work.

The House Ways and Means Committee report on the proposed FAP concluded that the major impediment to carrying out the work-incentive system in the WIN program was the bureaucrats' squeamishness about enforcing it: "The clear Congressional intent of getting able-bodied welfare recipients (including mothers where there was adequate day care available) into work and training was effectively diluted by federal and state officials who did not share this objective with equal enthusiasm."[186] Thus, in the new bill, the national government explicitly required that all employable family members would have to sign up for work and training except mothers of children under three years old. Recipients would be obliged to take any job available that paid the minimum wage; anyone refusing to participate without a good reason would incur a penalty of $800 a year, taken out of the family's grant. Nixon defended the work provisions of FAP:

> Hard work is what made America great. . . . the "good life" is not the lazy life, or the empty life, or the life that consumes without producing. . . . Let us recognize once and for all that any work is preferable to welfare.[187]

Nixon's FAP (never passed by Congress), like virtually all the work-incentive programs of the 1960s and '70s, assumes that mothers who stay at home are not working. In Nixon's words, they are "consuming without producing."

President Carter's welfare reform proposal, unveiled in August 1977, once again revived the goal of putting welfare recipients to work. The heart of the Carter proposal was a jobs program to create 1.4 million public-service jobs to gurantee a job to every able-bodied American, including those on welfare. Welfare benefits would be structured so that no unemployed welfare recipient would be receiving more income than a working recipient. Thus Carter's proposal clearly endorsed the principle of "less eligibility." It also resurrected the principle that single mothers should be obligated to take employment outside the home, although the proposal limited the work requirement to mothers with children over seven years old. According to Carter's plan, all welfare mothers would be required to go out to work when their youngest child reached age fourteen. Mothers of children between the ages of seven and fourteen would also have to work if adequate day care were available; if such services could not be provided, they would have to accept part-time employment while the children were in school.[188]

China's Street Industry as a Welfare Program

Nixon's censure of those who "consume without producing" would have had a familiar ring to any Chinese leaders who heard it. Despite the propaganda, we can question whether the Chinese Communist party has had any greater respect for household labor, when it has repeatedly called for "consumers to change themselves into producers."[189] The slogan is almost always used in connection with housewives and implies that the housewife produces no valuable commodity for the society. Of course she produces meals, clothes, and educated children, to mention only a few of her "outputs"; the question is not whether she produces anything but who is to pay for her productive labor. Traditionally, in China, the husband has done so. He has paid according to the barter system, supplying her with room and board for her services, and if she is lucky, with more than the basic necessities of life.

Thus China's traditional household arrangement inherently contains the same basic problem that befalls families in the West: What happens when a male fails to pay for the services rendered by a housekeeper-childminder because the male is either incapacitated or absent? Obviously the community must pay her, or the woman will starve. As in the West, this payment is termed "welfare" or "relief", and the Chinese government has not been happy about these payments.

The conflict centers around the need for money to invest in capital versus the need to pay wages to otherwise unpaid housewives. From 1949 on, therefore, the CCP has opted to meet the problem primarily through a program of "salvation through production," limiting outright payments to a very small segment of the population—usually the urban families of dead or permanently handicapped "revolutionary martyrs" which have no member able to work. Instead, the "able-bodied" women have been organized into small enterprises using traditional handicraft methods to enable them to support themselves with reduced government aid or no aid at all. In the cities these enterprises have been called "social welfare production units," and in the countryside "auxiliary production."

These projects are started with almost no capital—at most a few yuan collected among the housewives themselves and perhaps augmented by social relief funds. The city of Chungking provides a thorough description of their beginnings:

> In accordance with social requirements, poor people were gradually organized to take up handicraft work or small processing tasks. In the past, only a small number of the city's poor people were engaged in production of this kind. Early in 1954, the Municipal Relief Branch Association, in cooperation with the departments concerned, conducted discriminate investigations into handicraft production in the city. It formulated a "plan for organizing poor people to help themselves through production," whereby arrangements were made for residents' committees in various districts to educate and mobilize the masses to explore ways of undertaking production according to local circumstances and the qualifications of the poor people. . . . Throughout the various districts, handicraft production, such as the making of cotton thread, chalk, and cloth slippers, and processing work such as the processing of asbestos and ramie cord, have now been successfully organized in 22 places for over 1200 persons.[190]

These projects appeared early in the Chinese Communists' administration. One account, for example, describes a "unified welfare institute," established in Changsha in 1951. "There are more than 10,000 persons in this institute's work projects such as cooperative shoe and sheet factories, and 2270 are engaged in relief projects or productive projects . . . (such as) brick-making, weaving, and dyeing, flour-making, etc."[191] Such projects were particularly strongly promoted during the Great Leap Forward. In fact, by September 1958, it was announced that all the people in the cities who had been on government relief had now turned in their cards and were self-sufficient, thanks to the 75,000 social welfare production units that had been established from May to June 1958.[192] (See table 2–14) While the extent of this claim is probably an exaggeration, it does show the direction of policy.

From 1956 on, women—referred to in Communist Chinese literature as "auxiliary labor"—became the major participants in such production. In October 1956, Tien Hsiang-ting, Director of the Department of Urban Relief, made the following announcement:

> Those who are left now to be organized for production are not to be counted as members of the general unemployed because they are capable only of part-time or auxiliary labor. They are generally in straitened circumstances

TABLE 2-14. Social Welfare Production Units in China, 1953–58

Year	*No. of Production Units*	*No. of People Employed*
1953	901[a]	—
1954	3,300[b]	470,000[b]
1955	2,300[b]	—
1956	—	—
1957 (June)	4,400[c]	260,000
1957 (Dec)	8,009[d]	580,000[b]
1958 (April)	13,709[e]	—
1958 (June)	88,709[f]	Almost all people who had been on relief[f]—approximately 13 million[g]

Sources: [a]SCMP 965 p. 15 1-1-55; NCNA Peking 12-30-54.

[b]SCMP 1823 p. 2 7-31-58; *JMJP* Peking 6-30-58.

[c]SCMP 1562 p. 3 7-3-57; NCNA Peking 6-15-57.

[d]SCMP 1790 p. 7 6-12-58; NCNA Peking 6-6-58.

[e]SCMP 1807 p. 7 7-9-58; NCNA Peking 6-29-58.

[f]SCMP 1872 pp. 6-7 10-10-58; NCNA Peking 9-28-58.

[g]SCMP 1823 p. 1 7-31-58; *JMJP* Peking 6-30-58.

> . . . Our present objectives to be organized consist in the most part of auxiliary labor. To facilitate their participation in production, we must pay attention to organizing scattered activities of production to suit the womenfolk who are kept busy in their homes by housework.[193]

However, even in the People's Republic, the same disrespect toward welfare clients that has plagued the U.S. system has also surfaced.

> Some civil affairs cadres have become indifferent when they see the people left to be organized for production are the poor relatives of martyrs and service men and the destitute ones among the citizens, who are only capable of part-time or auxiliary labor. They regard the work as of little importance and insignificant. This attitude is mistaken.[194]

While it is difficult to determine the number of single-parent families involved in "salvation through production" projects, one fact about China should be kept in mind: such families are very scarce in relation to the total population. The changing family structure so typical of advanced industrialized societies has not come to China. Not only is divorce rare, but many families have more than one generation living together. Even when a husband dies, the wife usually continues to live with her in-laws. While this arrangement increases the economic burdens on the wife (two more mouths to feed), it also prevents the isolation so often experienced in the West, and eases the difficulty of going out to work—an adult remains at home in her absence.

In the countryside, welfare payments are allocated by the production team. The money is taken out of the collective harvest before the harvest is distributed to the households. In addition, families can overdraw grain and then remain in debt to the team until the following year. Or the poor may be assigned extra work, such as tending a buffalo, to give them more income. Occasionally, handicraft production of shoes or embroidery may be collectively organized as in the cities. Welfare payments from the government are rare.

In 1964 welfare constituted about 3 percent of the gross agricultural income in China.[195] One expert has estimated that the welfare fund varies from 1 to 3 percent of the team's budget.[196] Jan Myrdal in 1961 tabulated a list of the recipients of welfare in the village of Liu Ling. Most were families with an insufficient number of males to keep them above the poverty line. In Liu Ling Village Labor Group, seven out of eight cases of social assistance reflected the absence of the husband; in the Labor Group for Vegetable Production, four out of eight cases were caused by the male's absence, and one case resulted from the male's disability. At the brigade level, one out of five cases was caused by the male's absence, and one case was brought about by the male's disability.[197]

Evidently, the problem of women supporting households alone is as real in China as in the West.

CONCLUSION

At first glance, China seems to be the only one of the three governments whose welfare strategies are thoroughly consistent with the other social programs (i.e., family planning, child care, housekeeping service). That is, Communist party propaganda during the great mobilization campaigns has strongly urged women to contribute to socially productive labor, meaning labor outside the family. Even women whose job is cooking, cleaning, or caring for children in the communal nursery are seen to be performing socially productive labor as long as they are doing it for the community rather than for their own families. The devaluation of housework performed within the bounds of the private family is a theme that extends throughout Chinese social policy, including welfare programs. The Chinese government has offered public assistance unwillingly, emphasizing that even single parents should be engaged in socially productive labor. Single mothers are no more encouraged to remain at home with their children than are married women, and few Chinese communities provide a level of public assistance that would make it possible. Instead, the Chinese frequently organize work projects specifically to employ welfare recipients. Thus the party has directed local authorities to provide adequate support services so that all women, including mothers on relief, can work outside the home.

In both Sweden and the United States, we detect inconsistencies between public assistance policies and other social programs. In the United States, state and federal governments provide few support services for the average working woman. American public authorities have not sought to encourage married women to work. Nor have they made any serious attempts to ease the dual burden of women who do choose to work. When it comes to welfare mothers, however, the U.S. government has been enthusiastic in encouraging them to work outside the home. Congress has repeatedly inserted into welfare legislation the provision that recipients be encouraged, and in some cases forced, to take employment.

Swedish social policies also display an inconsistency, although it operates in the opposite direction. The Swedish government offers considerable encouragement to the average Swedish woman to work outside the home by providing an elaborate array of support services for her. Yet, Sweden's public assistance program does not encourage single mothers to go out and work; in fact, the generous welfare benefits actually relieve a single mother of the necessity to get a job in order to support her children comfortably.

How are we to explain the apparent inconsistencies evident in American and Swedish policies toward welfare mothers, as opposed to other mothers? The explanation lies in how policy makers evaluate the labor performed by housewives and mothers. In Sweden, many functions that housewives routinely perform—child care, tending to convalescent or elderly family members, cleaning the house, preparing family meals—have been transformed into job categories, a large proportion of which are performed for government social service agencies. The government's willingness to employ workers to perform these tasks suggests that policy makers recognize the indispensability of these forms of labor in maintaining the family's quality of life. A family that cannot provide these services to itself because both parents work outside the home must obtain them from social service agencies. Given this view, it is not surprising that Swedish officials would perceive a single mother who performs these services for her own family as engaged in socially productive labor. She is, after all, providing services that would be furnished by social agencies if she were to take a job outside the home. Rita Liljestrom, a sociologist at Gothenburg University, explains it this way:

> . . . the care and upbringing of children have increasingly come to be regarded as work necessary to society which, in principle, should be paid in a way comparable to remunerative work. The parent who stays at home to take care of the children should have the same economic status as the parent who earns the money. This attitude has characterized the directives for studies now being done in the field of family policy in Sweden.[198]

In sharp contrast, American policy makers "consistently underestimate the value of work done in the home."[199] Having little regard for the labor performed by the average housewife, they suppose that the housewife's function can easily be dispensed with, as in the case of the welfare family. Thus legislators feel quite comfortable launching a WIN program to put women into jobs without providing adequate child-care services, much less any home-help services.

It perhaps seems odd to the reader that we conclude with a plea that American policy makers recognize the value of labor performed by women employed outside the home and women employed inside the home. Most often, the women's movement has generated debates pitting homemakers against career women, with the homemakers' charging that the career-minded do not appreciate the value of household labor. Our argument is that until society recognizes the indispensability of the household services women have traditionally furnished to the family and finds alternative ways of supplying those services, women will not be able to carry the dual burden successfully.

3

WOMEN'S POLITICS AND POLICY CHANGE

In chapter 2 we examined variations in the social policies pursued by three governments, concluding that in important respects the governments of Sweden and China have demonstrated greater commitment to family programs than has the U.S. government. Our aim in this study is to try to account for policy differences by examining important factors that shape the three governments' family policies. It makes sense to start with the most obvious explanation—women's own efforts to promote government benefits and services for working mothers. Hence, in this chapter we turn to a discussion of feminist political activity in the three nations, stressing the origins and nature of women's politics. We are particularly interested in comparing how feminists in the three systems have organized to influence public policy and in assessing the extent of their influence. In journalistic and scholarly literature one finds the common supposition that women's political activism is responsible for governments enacting women's programs. Stated another way, the assumption is that "liberation cannot be offered; it must be won."[1] Rather than accepting this assumption, we prefer to test its accuracy using our three case studies.

A special concern of this chapter is the connection between the way in which feminist issues have been formulated in the three systems and the political strategies used by women's groups in those systems. Specifically, we believe that the demands feminists can effectively press on government are directly related to the organizing strategies they use to build support. This is most obvious in the Chinese case, where feminists' obligation to organize women under the aegis of the party or party-sanctioned institutions severely limits issues feminists can address and the positions they can take.

Swedish feminists have shown a similar, though much less pronounced, preference for integrationist strategies. Obviously, a major contrast between the two societies is that a much broader range of opinions and interests is reflected in Sweden's organizational life than in China's. Nevertheless, the two cases are similar in that the vast majority of feminist groups in Sweden are sections of larger organizations (e.g., parties, unions, interest groups). This means that, as in China, Swedish feminists have tended to articulate their demands in terms consonant with the goals of the particular organization in which they were operating: Groups of feminists operating within larger interest groups have pressed for more government benefits for female workers, or female students, or female pensioners, more often than they have united to campaign for women as a class.

Historically, American feminists have operated differently, preferring to try to mobilize women into independent, mass-based organizations and concentrating on issues that could unite all women on the basis of gender alone. This accounts in large part for the prominence of the equal rights theme in the American women's movement. The only policy on which *all* women are likely to agree is one that confers benefits solely on the basis of gender—a policy that confers benefits on all women, not just women with children, or low-income women, or women working in industry. Virtually the only policy that conforms to this definition is an equal rights policy. (Even so, as public debate on the Equal Rights Amendment has shown, equal rights is an issue with less than universal appeal to women.)

Each of these organizing strategies has its advantages and limitations. In the final section of the chapter we assess the influence exerted by women's political organizations on public policy in the three systems. We have seen that the governments of Sweden and China have shown more commitment to social programs for working women than has the U.S. government. On that basis, we might be tempted to assume that feminist groups in those two systems are more effectively organized to influence public policy. Such an assumption is not entirely justified; the connections between women's politics and women's policies are considerably more complex than they might at first seem.

WOMEN'S POLITICS: ORIGINS AND ISSUES

Considering the vast cultural and economic disparities among our three examples and the geographic distances that separate them, it is striking that in all three, we find the first important group of feminist thinkers and activists emerging early in the nineteenth century, and the formation of the first broadly based women's organizations deferred until the late nineteenth and early twentieth centuries. In the United States early feminist activity in the 1830s and 40s culminated in the first women's rights convention at Seneca Falls in 1848. Sweden witnessed the flowering of a feminist school of writers at mid-century. In China the issue of women's rights surfaced briefly in the ill-fated Taipeng Rebellion of the 1850s, which attacked the traditional Confucian value system, including its subordination of women. These early manifestations of feminism must be seen as relatively isolated and limited anticipations of the more widespread concern over women's condition that developed in the last decades of the nineteenth century.

We can suggest two probable explanations for this historical coincidence in the emergence of feminism in the three societies. One is simply what social scientists call the "demonstration effect." That is, women (and men) in one nation saw, read, and heard about the activities of social reformers in other nations and were influenced to move in similar directions. Twentieth-century readers may find this hard to accept, given the less advanced communication and transportation technology of the last century. Nonetheless, we know that numerous European and American feminists traveled across the Atlantic to gather information about women in other countries. The Swedish feminist Fredrika Bremer, for example, spent over a year in the United States in 1849–50, observing the problems and progress of American feminists. We also know that early support for women's emancipation in China came from many intellectuals influenced by ideas imported from the West. Thus the historical coincidence may be attributed in some measure to communication between societies.

A more important explanation is the spread of industrialization around the globe, which began in the nineteenth century. It is no accident that in all three cases, the emergence of feminism coincided with the advance of industrialization. Growing interest in the woman question was related to changes in the production process brought about by the new industrial order. Having said that, we must immediately caution against the hasty conclusion that the Industrial Revolution, which came to the United States in the 1840s, developed in Sweden in the 1890s and was imported into China by Western colonials in the late 1800s, somehow "caused" women's movements to form.

Virtually all women's historians agree that industrialization and feminism are linked, but they disagree considerably on the nature of that linkage. For one thing, they disagree over whether the advent of industrialism improves or worsens women's status in a society. In advanced agrarian economies, women fulfill crucial economic functions, mostly those that can be carried on close to home; gardening, tending animals, processing grains, weaving and sewing, and food preparation. The Industrial Revolution centralized the production process in large factories and introduced long and rigid work schedules that made it extremely difficult for women to combine household responsibilities with outside employment. Those women who did take jobs (and many were forced to do so out of economic necessity) underwent extreme hardship. Those who remained at home were increasingly isolated from the production process. These observations have led some to conclude that, compared to men, women's lot has almost universally deteriorated as a result of industrialization.[2] Others reject this gloomy conclusion, arguing that it is based on too "rosy" a view of women's lot in preindustrial societies.[3] Depending on which view one holds, one might see feminism either as an outraged response to women's deteriorating status or as a positive reflection of women's newfound gains.

Second, we cannot be sure that industrialization itself is the only, or even the most important, trend to be observed. Other social trends that tended to occur along with early industrialization may as easily be associated with rising feminism. Three likely candidates are urbanization, declining marriage rates, and declining fertility rates.

Third, we cannot easily establish which is cause and which is effect. Most historians of the West, at least since Marx, have assumed that changes in the production process wrought by the Industrial Revolution have "caused" other social trends, such as the rise in feminism. For both the United States and Sweden, the case for this view is rather easily made. But it is one of the great historical ironies that Marx's living heirs, including the Chinese Communists, have abandoned his economic determinism; instead they have sought to speed changes in the production process by manipulating other societal institutions—chiefly, political and family institutions. In China it is not clear whether economic change is the "cause" of growing feminist awareness or, conversely, if the mobilization of women to abandon their traditional role and work for the revolution is a contributing "cause" of economic change.

With these caveats in mind, we can compare the origins and growth of the women's movements in the three countries. In so doing, we will see an important difference between the American case and the other two. For Chinese and Swedish activists, demands for formal equality for women have taken a back seat to demands for better economic conditions for women. The preference for the latter reflects a recognition that formal equality of rights before the law does not necessarily guarantee women a living wage, decent working conditions, long-term economic security, or adequate health and child-care services. The struggle for these concrete gains—to improve the conditions under which most women live and work—has been labeled "social feminism."

Social feminism is distinguished from the position of equal rights advocates by its emphasis on improved living conditions for women (especially in the form of improved economic conditions) *even if* that means that public and private institutions would treat women "unequally" by providing special forms of support and service for women. In its early guise, social feminism took the form of charitable activities to aid unemployed, abandoned, or wayward women. In recent times, social feminism is reflected in demands for more extensive public-service networks to support working women. Obviously the views of social feminists and equal rights advocates are to some extent represented in the women's movements of all three nations. Nevertheless, the equal rights theme dominates the American movement to a far greater degree than the other two. As William Chafe has pointed out:

> Historically . . . the idea of equality in America has meant procedural rights rather than the substantive sharing of resources. Through most of the 19th and 20th centuries, the twin notions of legal rights and "equality of opportunity" continued to define the country's perception of equality.[4]

In contrast, we will see that while the equal rights theme has been represented in Swedish feminism, the mainstream of the women's movement has focused on upgrading the quality of life for women and families even when this has required special treatment for women by employers or government agencies. China represents yet a third pattern, in which the emphasis on the revolutionary goal of upgrading economic conditions for everyone is given such heavy priority that demands for women's rights have on occasion been labeled "bourgeois." China's leaders have interpreted too singleminded and strident a concern with women's rights to be a threat to party solidarity and economic progress.

China

Revolutionary Chinese women have been variously condemned and applauded for seeking sexual equality within the framework of revolutionary goals, but no one familiar with Chinese politics doubts that China's leaders, female and male, see women's progress as dependent on the success of the revolution. This conviction goes beyond the simple notion that China's economy must expand before the society has sufficient resources to substantially improve living conditions for women (or men, for that matter). More than that, revolutionary doctrine holds that a thorough restructuring of Chinese society is required in order to eliminate the customs and institutions that oppress women—religious superstition, landholding systems, educational admission standards, job discrimination, and especially family patterns.

The history of the Chinese women's movement can largely be seen as an attempt to free women from the restrictive bonds of the family system. Of course, this focus was caused by the almost total absence of other social ties for Chinese women. The multiple group affiliations of modern urbanized women did not exist for Chinese women, who were most often rural and peasant. The primary religious orientation was toward ancestor worship, practiced within and by the family. Voluntary organizations were unheard of, and in any case no respectable woman would leave her home alone to attend a meeting. Visits from friends were few, childhood contacts having been severed a long time before marriage to preserve the girl's "good name." As one working woman explained, "We were not allowed, my sister and I, on the street after we were thirteen. . . . When a family wanted to know more about a girl who had been suggested for a daughter-in-law and asked what kind of girl she was, the neighbors would answer, 'We do not know. We have never seen her.' And that was praise."[5] Even visits to the wife's own parents—the wife customarily went to live with the husband's family—were confined to once or twice a year. Thus it can truthfully be said that the Chinese woman had no existence outside the family.

It should not be assumed that these customs oppressed all Chinese women to the same degree, nor that they were general customs during all periods of Chinese history. In fact, the power wielded by Chinese women has at times been considerable. During the T'ang Dynasty (A.D. 618–907), for instance, one woman even had herself named Empress of the T'ang and ruled with a strong hand for twenty-two years. Since the end of the T'ang, however, the position of women is generally regarded as having deteriorated, until by the last 200 years of the Ch'ing Dynasty (1662-1912) even men began to complain.

Virtually all young Chinese intellectuals in the early 1900s were keenly aware of the discriminatory treatment suffered by China's women. Women's lot in traditional China was deplored by the young radicals who would ultimately lead the Communist revolution of 1949. A modest list of the abuses against women would have to include footbinding; infanticide (a practice which also reduced the number of brides available in later years); the sale of girls into prostitution, concubinage, or servitude no better than slavery; and the sale as child brides of girls too young to be married, but who could be used as servants until they came of age. Many child brides were even bought without the future bridegroom having yet been born, which resulted in women nineteen and twenty years old being betrothed to infants. Even properly married women remained confined to the house, illiterate and unskilled in any but domestic chores, subject to the domination of the male.

The relative strength of the West and the weakness of China during the late nineteenth and early twentieth centuries was a source of both humiliation and determination for change among young Chinese. In search of ways to strengthen China, they borrowed many ideas from the West. Among them were individualism and equality. These ideas, impossible to practice within the hierarchical, restrictive family system of China, became a *cause célèbre* among the educated Chinese youth of the twentieth century, and, naturally, the family system fell into disrepute. Women, indispensable parts of the system, as well as its victims, became targets for change. Roxanne Witke, a scholar in the field, identifies no fewer than 100 journals devoted exclusively to women's problems during the early twentieth century. While the "woman problem" pervaded the literature, however, "serious writers did not deal with the problem as such, but with one or more of its substantive issues: the reform of the family system, marriage reform, divorce, communal rearing of children, chastity, suicide, suffrage, etc."[6] Most of the articles were written by men, for men. One reason was that over 90 percent of Chinese women were illiterate, and most were still unconcerned about the problems of their own emancipation.[7] Given these facts, these early writings were probably less concerned with enhancing the status of women than they were with ensuring that women did not become a blockage to change.

Mao Tse-tung, one of the more prolific writers of the time, illustrates this attitude then and throughout his life. The purpose of life is struggle—to change the unbearable. In several of his early pieces on suicides committed by women seeking to escape arranged marriages, domineering parents, and the like, he clearly described society as the enemy and women as good only insofar as they resisted. Suicide meant surrender to society's evils; living and fighting meant those ills could be changed. The difference between women and men was that women of all classes were especially prone to "superstition, fatalism, and slavish devotion to living authority . . . a vast repository of the old habits of thinking."[8]

While the intellectual ferment of 1910–1930 was dominated by men, women were not completely idle. Feminists concerned with issues of voting and constitutional equality arose from the campaigns to establish the Republic of 1912. The impotent and decadent rule of the Ch'ing Dynasty was brought to an end, in small part through the efforts of the Women's National Army, the Women's Dare-to-Die Corps, and the Women's Assassination Corps. Within months after the establishment of the Republic, several of the women's armies transformed themselves into suffrage societies and were joined by women with no previous military experience.[9] They banded together to fight for women's rights and even stormed the National Assembly when it failed to include an equal rights plank in the constitution. But, this spark quickly died out, and women returned to journalism and teaching and to such long-term concerns as footbinding and suicide; that is, they returned until the May Fourth Movement.

The whole movement from roughly 1917 to 1921 bears the name "May Fourth" from the day in 1919 when students from all over Peking gathered to celebrate "National Humiliation Day." They were protesting the turnover of a large portion of Chinese territory from Germany to Japan. Because of President Woodrow Wilson's statements about national self-determination, the Chinese assumed that they would regain German territorial rights to the Shantung Penninsula at Germany's defeat in World War I. The Japanese differed. Unfortunately, secret treaties signed in 1918 by Japan, Britain, and France assured the territory to Japan. Outraged, the students demonstrated and precipitated a sympathetic response from patriotic Chinese everywhere. Further, they started a great intellectual search for a way out of China's predicaments. One of the elements of this new upsurge of activity was a renewal of interest in suffrage in China's provinces and large cities. But, more important for China's future, radical feminists began moving into the new revolutionary parties—the Communist and the Kuomintang—seeking sexual equality through a restructuring of Chinese society.

Radical feminists have, from that time on, sought female equality through general revolutionary struggle. The first female party members, among them Hsiang Ching-yu and Ts'ai Ch'ang, partly ensured this orientation by their attacks on the feminist-oriented women's rights groups of the 1920s and 1930s.[10] The failure of the women's rights advocates to secure constitutional rights, coupled with the failure of most provincial and national governments even to survive in this period, reinforced the radicals' belief that the struggle for women's rights alone was destined to fail. After the Republic began falling apart in 1916, the once unified state of China fell into the hands of fighting warlords, who were not only closed to suggestions of female equality but were in no position to guarantee those rights, even if granted. What good were laws issued by governments that could change hands any day? "Thus more and more women activists moved towards the position [that] . . . feminist rebellion was meaningless without general political revolution."[11]

The position of the party since 1927 at least, has been that feminist goals, while important, are secondary to more general revolutionary goals. At times this has meant secondary to mobilization of peasant men for military service; at times it has meant secondary to modernization or economic recovery. And at times, when feminist goals have coincided with the greater "revolutionary goals," women's status has progressed, as when the extended family system and the authority of the father-husband were under attack, or when intensive manual labor required more hands than men could provide.

> There was an appreciation of the potential of female participation in the revolution, but female leaders were not recruited to pursue purely feminist goals. Women's issues were not set apart from and indeed could at times be subordinated to more general revolutionary issues. Women at leadership training schools appear to have been treated as individuals rather than as members of a specific interest group. This general policy approach remained right up until 1949.[12]

Indeed, one could say that it remained after 1949 as well. Under this system, women who considered feminist goals to be paramount simply did not survive in leadership positions. The fear of arousing party anger may account for the timidity of the National Women's Federation on certain questions; for example, the federation was accused in 1957 of failing to pursue the problem of death and injury among women during the high tide of agricultural cooperation, as well as failing to implement the marriage reform laws thoroughly.[13]

The happy consequence of such subordination is that on issues that conform to the needs of the party, the full authority of the party and the government is thrown behind the campaign to achieve the goal. The unhappy consequence is that when feminist and general goals conflict, feminist goals are shunted aside. While the party has certainly allowed women more freedom to criticize their treatment than any other group,[14] too great a deviation from party policy has not been permitted. Ting Ling, a prominent woman writer who joined the Communist party in the 1930s, is a classic example. Criticized in 1942 for an article, "Thoughts on March 8th (Women's Day)," she had the audacity to question the dual burden placed on women cadres in Yenan. Women were damned if they wanted a career and damned if they wanted to stay home.[15] For this indiscretion, she was forced to repent. A later example was Tung Pien, editor of *Women in China*. In 1966, at the start of the Cultural Revolution, she was ousted for paying too much attention to the special problems of women (e.g., day care, housework, dual burdens) instead of considering women as part of the larger class struggle. The irony is that at other times—during the Great Leap Forward, and since 1971, for example—the party has dealt seriously with these questions. Consequently, the issue has never been clearly one of feminist versus party goals but rather one of some women advocating some ideas at the wrong times.

From the beginning, the Communists have relied on a special women's section of the party to direct the women's mobilization effort. As early as 1922, the first party bureau was set up to direct the women's movement. By 1945, due to the increasing number of women falling under Communist control, a special 13-member committee was established in Yenan to prepare for women's mobilization in the liberated areas. In 1949 the Preparatory Committee became the All-China Democratic Federation of Women, called the National Women's Committees in that it was a "mass organization," designed to reach and mobilize the millions of women who became citizens of the People's Republic after 1949. Until December 1966, when the NWF was disbanded in the Cultural Revolution, the lowest level at which it kept a permanent office was the administrative district in the cities and the county, or *hsien*, level in the countryside. Every commune within the rural county had a woman in charge of women's work, every brigade had a representative association, and every team had a representative group. But the associations and groups were composed of women who met only infrequently to discuss issues. Thus the lowest full-time cadre for women's work in the countryside was at the commune level,[16] and communes often have up to 50,000 inhabitants. It can easily be seen that NWF organizers simply had too many women to deal with, in both the cities and the countryside. Most Chinese women came into contact with the government, not through the NWF, but through women activists under street committees or production teams. (A production team is the smallest unit in the agricultural commune system, approximately the size of a village, whose members are divided up into work groups of 15–20 members.)

It is an oft-spoken truth in China that most policies would never be implemented among women without the aid of the activist. She is a woman who goes to other people's homes to discuss the current political campaigns with them; she organizes mutual help among neighbors; she creates day-care centers; she keeps a watch on "bad" elements and, as some refugees have attested, may also be a gossip and a busybody. She is not paid for any of this work but may be rewarded by the party with membership and an assignment to the street committee, or in the rural areas may become a team leader or low-level cadre. In the cities, this woman is probably a housewife and probably marginally literate. In the countryside, there is an even greater probability of illiteracy, but the woman generally works in the fields outside her home.

The National Women's Federation is not the only organization dedicated to the interests of women. In a country as bureaucratic as China, overlap is endemic. (Mao himself was known to complain about this tendency in very unhappy language.) In addition to the National Women's Federation, the Communist party maintains its own Women's Committee—presumably to act as a policy-setting body. The lowest level of urban political organization, the street or residents' committee, is composed mostly of activist housewives who carry out projects like nurseries, sanitation, or educating pregnant women. The All-China Federation of Trade Unions has developed a women's section to deal with women workers and dependents of male workers. And lastly, the People's Liberation Army has special party branches to deal with army dependents. Often more than one group will be mobilizing the same population to achieve a party goal, in which case complaints are heard about coordination. At other times, the groups appear to be following contradictory policies, as in 1965. Ts'ai Ch'ang, chairperson of the NWF and ranking member of the Women's Committee of the Central Committee, was urging workers' dependents to go out and work; Chang Wei-chen, secretary of the Secretariat of the Federation of Trade Unions, was praising these same women for being good wives and mothers.[17]

Although the NWF is organized with provincial and local branches, the branches are not only subordinate to higher levels but also to the party committee at their own level. This has produced periodic and possibly chronic antagonism between women's bureaus and party committees. The complaint most often heard is that the party committee responsible for allocating scarce resources at its level does not take the needs of women seriously. The years 1956–1957 produced a spate of complaints. One brave individual in Tsingtao expressed the following views:

1. In cultivating and employing women intellectuals and women cadres, the Party has not seriously implemented the principle of sexual equality and equal pay for equal work. This is because certain leadership personnel think that women have to take care of their household affairs and their children . . . and thus cannot shoulder important and complicated work. . . .
2. Party committees at various levels have failed to give adequate assistance and guidance to women intellectuals and comrades. . . .
3. Special problems of giving care and support to women and some problems of labor protection also existed . . . at present some units still failed

to treat these problems seriously. . . . Originally some units could afford to establish some simple baby feeding and nursery rooms, but the leadership, who did not pay attention to the suffering of the masses, neglected this work, thus making it impossible for some workers to solve the problem of taking care of their children. . . .

4. The district people's council, the street office, and the residents' committees also discriminate against the work of women, and projects proposed by the municipal and district women's federations were often vetoed by them.[18]

Undoubtedly, such attitudes have contributed to the low morale among NWF cadres, which is periodically deplored in the press. Comments such as the following consistently pop up:

> It must be realized first of all that every kind of work is part of the revolutionary work, and that the work of women is an indispensable part. . . . Women cadres should consider the work of women as a glorious task. . . . It is certainly not something of no importance or something which is entirely up to oneself, to do or not to do. The view that work of women is tedious and troublesome, does not involve any policy and does not have any political significance, is wrong.[19]

One of the chief problems for women within the organizational structure of the party and government has been that, once recruited, they have been put in charge of women's work. This has left a dearth of effective, educated women to influence other policy areas. One reason suggested is that

> As with peasants and proletarians, women were best suited to organize and lead their own kind. To have placed male "outsiders" in leadership positions for women's movement work, or vice-versa, would have produced explosive social disruptions dysfunctional for the general revolutionary movement. Like the labor and peasant movements, the women's movement expanded at a rate that outstripped the supply of capable leadership personnel. Thus, qualified female leaders were assigned as fast as they were produced to head mushrooming female mobilization activities.[20]

Despite this past history, China in the 1970s has sought to bring women into other policy areas beyond the traditional women's work. In the efforts to reconstruct party committees during the aftermath of the Cultural Revolution, emphasis was unquestionably placed on the inclusion of women. Lest anyone think the issue was unimportant, the party repeatedly stated that the matter was one of implementing, or failing to implement, Chairman Mao's revolutionary line, and thus showing oneself to be either a revolutionary progressive or a capitalist roader. Such questions have shattered many a career in the People's Republic.

As to the questions that arose regarding the qualifications of the women activists who were being recruited, the party Central Committee would brook no opposition:

> Are women less capable than men? Certainly not . . . a person's ability is not inborn but is acquired. . . . After some women join the leading group, because they had not been so familiar with the conditions and are short of experience in leadership, they have inevitably encountered some problems in work. However, have not men comrades also encountered similar problems? . . . It is [women's] right and obligation to engage in politics and class struggle. It is not a question of whether they can do it or whether they should be allowed to do it.[21]

Special classes were set up for the new women cadres, and party committees were expected to use the recruits for regular work assignments, giving aid and advice when necessary.

Whether such pressure from Peking can make a difference throughout China is not yet clear. One visitor reported in 1972 that women on the revolutionary committees he visited spoke little and poured tea. That was not very equal in his mind.[22] Yet in judging the question whether women can overcome their handicaps to function effectively in the positions to which they have been assigned, it is well to remember the story of Lu Yu-lan. In 1955 the party committee in her village proposed the creation of an agricultural cooperative from the individually held properties of the peasants.

> The regulation required that a woman be elected the deputy director of the cooperative. But no suitable candidate could be found. Somebody then proposed to give the position to little Yu-lan. Thereupon many people said, "What does she know?" Indeed, what could a fifteen-year-old girl know? It was then suggested, "Let her keep the seat occupied at meetings."[23]

Today Lu Yu-lan is a member of the Central Committee of the Chinese Communist party.

Sweden

Like China, Sweden industrialized late. Despite an initial industrial spurt in the mid-1850s, it was not until the 1890s that strong, sustained industrialization came to Sweden. Having emerged late, however, the industrial sector of Sweden's economy grew with phenomenal speed in the early decades of the twentieth century. One indicator of this speed is the change in the composition of the labor force. In 1870, 72 percent of Sweden's work force was still engaged in agriculture; by 1920, the percentage of workers in agriculture had dropped to 44 percent.[24] Obviously then, until very late in the nineteenth century, Sweden was a predominantly agrarian society.

Observers disagree on whether Sweden's late industrialization was a boon or a burden for Swedish women. This disagreement to some extent reflects the more general disagreement about the relative status of women in preindustrial societies. Richard Tomasson, for example, argues that women in Sweden's agrarian society enjoyed relatively high status. Like many agrarian social systems, Sweden's was characterized by a relatively high level of female autonomy and a relatively low degree of sex-role differentiation in the production process. In spite of the clearly patriarchal organization of the rural family, peasant women contributed significantly as producers of food, clothing, and other necessities and thereby gained leverage in family affairs. In the agricultural and fishing communities along the southern coast, men were away at sea for long periods, and women developed a certain amount of economic independence.[25] Tomasson speculates that "it seems reasonable that where life is hard and women have an important economic role to play, they will be less oppressed and will have more equality."[26]

In support of this sanguine view of women's status in preindustrial Sweden, we can also cite the expansion during the first half of the nineteenth century of women's legal rights, including the following:

1842: admission of girls to the newly established nationwide elementary school system
1845: women acquire equal inheritance rights
1846: women acquire the right to practice industrial professions and to carry on business in their own name

It would be a mistake to assume that the Swedish government granted these rights in response to feminist pressures. There was no organized women's rights movement behind these reforms. Some historians have explained the reforms as the product of a conservative parliament influenced by liberal doctrines imported from the European continent. A more convincing explanation is Gunnar Qvist's observation that the Riksdag simply recognized the need for legal changes to accommodate the rapidly changing Swedish economy, especially to accommodate the urbanization and the accompanying reduction in the marriage rate.[27]

Granted, certain Swedish intellectuals of the early nineteenth century did popularize the theme of female independence, especially in the marital relationship. An early example is Carl Almqvist, whose 1839 novel *Sara Videbeck* portrays two protagonists rejecting a formal marriage contract and the idea of economic interdependence to pursue a free-love relationship. By far the best known of the nineteenth-century feminist intellectuals was Fredrika Bremer (1801–1866), an author and world traveler. By 1845, she had founded the first emancipationist organization in Europe; in 1849, she visited American suffragists; she published her famous novel, *Hertha*, in 1856. Comparing the status of women in Sweden and the United States at mid-century, Bremer argued that Swedish women were much less emancipated than their American sisters and advocated equal rights for women in both civil and family life. In 1859 two prominent Stockholm ladies founded the *Home Review*, a periodical advocating advances in women's legal and economic status; this was a journal that became influential throughout Scandinavia in the 1860s and 1870s. Moreover, the works of important male playwrights and novelists like August Strindberg examined the condition of women, particularly within marriage.

This literary movement succeeded in dramatizing women's rights issues for a segment of Stockholm's middle and upper classes, but it was far from being a mass political movement. In effect, these early advocates of women's rights constituted an elite, for whom "the women's rights movement represented first and foremost a demand for the right of ownership within the family, a fight in which the ideological motives appeared as important as the economic ones."[28] Their impact on public policy seems to have been limited. For example, historian Gunnar Qvist has convincingly demonstrated that, contrary to much historical speculation, *Hertha* really had little influence on the legislative reforms for women enacted by the Riksdag in the years immediately following the novel's 1856 publication.[29]

From the early ideological brand of feminism promoted by urban intellectuals two main branches of women's political activity emerged in Sweden. Until the 1890s, both branches were clearly dominated by middle- and upper-class activists, even though they were concerned with different class interests. The equal rights activists were primarily concerned with advancing women's legal status, especially in the realm of property rights. In 1871 two Stockholm women founded the Society for Married Women's Rights to seek national legislation guaranteeing a married woman the right to dispose of her own property, whether in the form of inherited wealth or earned income.[30] In 1884, a group of similarly disposed women founded the influential Fredrika Bremer Association "on a program of equal legal, civic, economic, and political status for women."[31] These status concerns were primarily those of propertied women—not those of either the farm population or the urban lower class, which contained a significant number of self-supporting single women.

For those latter segments of Swedish society, economic conditions at mid-century were bad. Because of Sweden's late industrialization, the rural economy was increasingly strained to support large-scale population increases. While many indigent farmers emigrated to the United States, others migrated only as far as Stockholm to look for work. A household's migration to the city was usually accompanied by a drop in the woman's status: "Where women joined with men in agriculture, they usually had more freedom than in the gradually expanding urban economy, where they were relegated to the duties of the home without escape."[32] Indeed, until 1846, women were legally forbidden to take paid employment, and virtually the only jobs open to young women fleeing from rural poverty were in domestic service, for which they could be compensated with room and board. After 1846, women could receive licenses to engage in shop commerce and street industry. So many did this that by the 1860s most of the small merchants of food and household goods in Stockholm were women, with the shop commerce in the hands of middle-class women while lower-class women carried on the street industry. Aside from these two occupations, women's employment opportunities in the cities were severely limited.

The widespread poverty, misery, and prostitution among young women in the cities became the focus of concern for the second main branch of Swedish women activists—the women's aid advocates. Mostly upper middle class, they organized homes, hospitals, and shelters for their less affluent sisters. They set up dozens of charitable projects including societies for poor relief, child assistance, old-age assistance, shelters for released female prisoners, and organizations to promote female industry. One such Stockholm organization distributed spinning, weaving, and knitting among unemployed women; another opened a salesroom called The Bee Hive to sell the handwork of "females in straitened circumstances."[33]

Upper-class women were in the best position to participate in these early women's activities. There were, however, two concurrent social movements in nineteenth-century Sweden that contributed some middle-class converts to feminism. One was the *Lasariet* Bible study movement of the late 1800s. The Swedish feminist Ellen Key highlighted the important function of this middle-class movement in "spiritually liberating" Swedish women:

> Insofar as the readers took seriously the biblical teaching to set aside the authority of the family for the sake of Jesus, homes gradually become accustomed to the idea that a female member would go her own way.[34]

Another recruiting ground for feminism was the temperance societies, whose membership included not only the middle class but workers as well. Women's strong participation in temperance activities, especially in the free public libraries and study circles established by the societies, often led to feminist activities. The temperance movement produced one of the leading feminist organizers of working women, Agda Ostlund. Readers familiar with the history of American feminism will recognize American parallels to the relationship between religious revival, temperance activities, and feminist organizing. These connections are explored in detail in a book by Ross Paulson, who concludes:

> The working alliance of prohibition, social purity, and women's rights forces in the United States, England, and Scandinavian countries helped to facilitate the eventual reunion of the shattered women's suffrage movement and to boost its cause.[35]

Although in the United States the struggle for the vote was clearly the single most important issue around which feminists organized at the turn of the century, the suffrage question was less central to Swedish activists. There seem to be two reasons for this. The first is the early preoccupation of Swedish feminists with improving women's material circumstances—a goal that seemed only indirectly related to the suffrage. Indeed, to nineteenth-century Swedish feminists, winning the vote seemed a great deal less important than winning equal property rights and the right to earn a subsistence wage in factories. As late as 1884, a Swedish author reporting on women's progress in her country observed, "As regards women's admission to the complete elective franchise, which would confer upon them the right of voting for members of the Diet [national legislature], no demands have been made in this direction nor any meetings held for this purpose."[36]

But a more important reason is that, in Sweden, the issue of votes for women was closely tied to the issue of universal suffrage. Hence women's interests were identified with those of larger organizations seeking general universal suffrage. Two such organizations were the Social Democratic party, formed in 1889 to represent the industrial working classes, and the Liberal party, established in 1902 to represent the lower middle classes, urban intellectuals, and religious nonconformists. Once again Sweden's late industrialization helps to explain why even in 1900 the vote was limited by property qualifications to a very few Swedes. The battle for universal suffrage was thus a battle that cut across the sexes and was led by the nation's two largest political parties. While universal manhood suffrage was legislated first in 1909, the Liberal-Socialist coalition government gave women the vote ten years later.

The struggle for votes for women in Sweden was carried on *within* the major parties rather than being fought, as in the United States and England, *outside* the major parties. It is true that in 1890 a small number of women who were concerned with women's suffrage formed the Universal Suffrage Association of Sweden. But when universal suffrage became the leading political cause of the new Liberal and Socialist parties, the suffrage movement as such became indistinguishable from the mainstream of party politics. In this way, feminism, which had been throughout the nineteenth century a relatively limited upper-middle-class movement, entered the arena of mass politics. The early integration of women activists and women's issues into the major parties helped to overcome the upper-class bias in the women's movement.

Earlier in the chapter we distinguished between equal rights advocates and social feminists, the latter group being more concerned with easing the dual burden of working women than with assuring absolutely equal treatment for the sexes. The history of Swedish feminism has contained both schools of thought. Equal rights advocates were more influential in the early period, stressing in particular women's rights to own and manage property. But social feminism, represented in the late nineteenth century by the women's aid advocates, has gradually become the more prominent doctrine in the twentieth century, especially since the Social Democratic party rose to power in the 1930s. The Social Democrats' commitment to ensuring the health and security of Sweden's population, especially by improving family welfare, virtually guaranteed a strong policy emphasis on social services and benefits for working women. Despite the pronounced influence of Social Democratic ideology on Swedish feminism, the nineteenth-century duality within the women's movement between equal rights advocates and women's aid advocates has persisted to some degree to the present time, with the Fredrika Bremer Association and the Liberal party as the two organizations most closely identified with the equal rights position.

A recent example of the Liberals' commitment to equal rights can be found in their campaign for national legislation to prevent sex discrimination in the marketplace. After examining the substance and impact of American national policy against sex discrimination in employment (Equal Pay Act, Civil Rights Act, and Executive Orders), the Liberal party began agitating in 1975 for similar legislation for Sweden. Surprisingly, until the 1970s there have been no national laws in Sweden against sex discrimination in employment; Sweden did not even have an equal-pay-for-equal-work law. Admittedly, the Swedish government has issued internal directives to government agencies, prohibiting them from discriminating in employment. For example, an ordinance issued by the minister of finance in August 1976 directed government agencies to eliminate personnel policies that gave certain categories of jobs only to women or to men, and to provide equal training and promotion opportunities to both sexes. No national laws require private employers to do the same, however.

Rather than being the subject of government regulation, sex discrimination in the private marketplace has been attacked through contract negotiations between unions and employers. For example, the national Confederation of Employers (SAF) agreed with the national Federation of Labor (LO) in a 1960 negotiation that women should receive equal pay for equal work. The Liberals have argued that such contract provisions have neither the legal force nor do they offer the scope of protection that could be offered by a national law guaranteeing women's equal rights. The dominant Social Democratic party strongly opposed the Liberals' proposed legislation. They defended the tradition of solving such problems through direct negotiation between employers and employees, declaring that government intervention to regulate employers in this regard would set an undesirable precedent. But an even more interesting objection they raised stemmed from their conviction that women deserve *unequal* treatment in the labor market. In the words of Anna-Greta Leijon, assistant minister of labor in the Social Democrat government in 1975, "we think it compatible with equality that women should now be overcompensated in various ways so as to counteract the effects of discrimination in the job world."[38]

Leijon was referring to specific Social Democratic programs of the 1970s that involved compensatory treatment for women. One program created 100 new positions in Swedish public employment offices for employment counselors for women. These new counselors were paid exclusively for handling training and job problems of women. A second program, the Kristianstad pilot project, provided government subsidies in three southern towns to train and employ women in traditionally male industries.[39] The Social Democrats feared that these compensatory programs for women would be ruled illegal under any national statute that prohibited discrimination on the basis of sex. After all, by singling out women for these special investments, the government was discriminating in favor of women but against men. To bolster this argument, the Social Democrats cited the rash of reverse discrimination cases brought in American courts in the mid-1970s.[40]

With the defeat of the Social Democrats in the September 1976 election and the installation of a new government coalition, the issue of legislation against sex discrimination came to the fore. Its revival was the result in large part of the naming of Liberal party leader Per Ahlmark as the new minister of labor. Soon after taking office in 1976, the new government charged the reorganized Committee on Equality, attached to Ahlmark's Labor Ministry, with drafting new legislation against sex discrimination. At this writing, that legislation has not yet been passed. Nevertheless, by June 1977 the National Labor Market Board, an administrative arm of the Labor Ministry, had adopted a long-range program to promote sexual equality in employment. The Labor Market Board is the government's main instrument for manpower planning and training, and for allocating funds for public works employment. Its 1977 program outlined a plan of action to accomplish these objectives:[41]

> To consider in job placement the qualifications and preferences of the individual, irrespective of traditional sex demarcations in the labor market
>
> To encourage individuals to select occupations and training without regard to sex
>
> To harness and develop the individual capacities of men and women through labor market training
>
> To encourage employers to recruit without regard to sex

Among other things, the plan stipulated that the agency's district offices must periodically submit work programs demonstrating that their activities are furthering the objectives outlined above.

Also in the spring of 1977, Swedish unions and employers reached a set of wide-ranging agreements covering most employees in the private sector. According to these agreements between the employers' organization (SAF) and both the LO (blue-collar workers) and the PTK (the cartel of white-collar unions in the private sector), firms are to take planned and purposeful action to further equality between male and female employees in recruitment, training, and promotion. There is to be ongoing evaluation of these efforts, and the unions reserve the right to take disputes arising over sex discrimination either into a grievance procedure (in the case of the LO) or directly to arbitration (in the case of PTK).

United States

It is not our intention here to offer a complete historical account of the women's movement in the United States. That task has been undertaken by several extremely able historians.[42] Instead we highlight only a few features of the American case that are particularly striking in comparison with China and Sweden.

Historians of feminism in America divide its long history into three main periods: (1) the early agitation for women's rights in the 1830s and 40s, (2) the suffrage movement of the early twentieth century, and (3) the women's movement of the 1960s and 70s. While each of these feminist eras displays a unique character, they are unified by a common theme: a consistent and overwhelming concern with formal equality of rights between women and men.

If we compare the rights being sought in the three eras, we find a curious cyclical pattern over the years since 1830. The earliest feminists demanded a range of legal rights; then, from the Civil War to 1920, the focus gradually narrowed to a single issue—an equal right to vote; with the rebirth of feminism in the 1960s, the focus widened once more to encompass the entire spectrum of civil, economic, and educational rights. And one might argue that in the past several years, American feminists have once again narrowed their focus to the Equal Rights Amendment.

The first period of feminist agitation coincides with the beginning of industrialization. It was in the 1830s and 40s that the textile mills, canning factories, and other infant industries began to attract large numbers of women workers including the celebrated mill girls who migrated to Lowell, Massachusetts, to work in the textile plants. William Chafe underlines the importance of industrialization as a trigger for change:

> The industrial revolution acted upon the social and economic system of the early 19th century in America to disrupt the traditional productive role of all women in the household economy.[43]

Chafe further suggests that we should expect the most radical responses to this kind of social disruption to occur when the upheaval is in its earliest stage.[44] The impact of the factory system on women's lives was just beginning to be felt in the 1830s and 40s. Americans had only their first glimpse of the new industrial order, in which working women were even more exploited than they had been in the agricultural production process. At the same time, middle-class women were beginning to perceive their isolation from the production process and their confinement to a purely homemaker role. That glimpse was sufficient to provoke a small band of middle-class women to demand that society take steps to improve women's lot. The most famous among them were Elizabeth Cady Stanton, one of the organizers of the 1848 women's rights convention in Seneca Falls, New York, and Susan B. Anthony. The resolutions adopted by the Seneca Falls convention were based on the principle that "woman is man's equal—was intended to be so by the Creator, and the highest good of the race demands that she should be recognized as such." Thus, this convention and the subsequent public debate provoked by Anthony, Stanton, Lucy Stone, and other activists called into question a broad range of social institutions. They demanded equal rights for women in marriage, in industry, in education, and in politics. Radical in sentiment and small in numbers, these early feminists had only a limited influence on public policy.

The second wave of feminism attracted broader support but for a much more narrow goal—the vote. While its aim was undoubtedly equality between women and men in voting rights, the campaign for women's suffrage resorted to strategies that reflected the influence of social feminists, who wanted the vote to promote social reforms and who accepted the doctrine of "natural" differences between women and men. This is perhaps understandable, given the context in which the suffragists were operating. By the late nineteenth century, the industrial order was firmly enough entrenched to be perceived as the "natural order" by most women and men. The economic and family structure that had been consolidating over the decades of industrial growth was not a particularly hospitable environment for the principle of equality between the sexes. According to Aileen Kraditor, the strong public resistance that met the suffragists' early appeals for equality forced them in the 1890s to shift from an "argument from justice" to an "argument from expediency."[45] That is, they began to argue for universal suffrage not on the basis of women's inherent right to vote but rather on the utility to the larger society of bringing into the political process the reform-minded female electorate. It was an appeal that emphasized the "natural" differences between the sexes, asserting that women's special skills and concerns would humanize American politics. Regrettably, some suffragists also capitalized on nativist sentiments by arguing that granting the vote to women would neutralize the harmful influence being exercised in the political process by the growing masses of urban immigrants. Suffragists who assumed that the right to vote held the key to improving women's economic and social status were disappointed by the events that followed their victory in 1920. The Nineteenth Amendment, heralded by its supporters as the catalyst for a virtual revolution in women's status, produced "little tangible progress toward the goal of economic equality."[46]

The feminist revival of the 1960s and 70s displays once again a predominant concern with formal legal equality for women. As Freeman's account points out, the new women's movement is really two different movements, distinguished by their structure and style. The first is a highly decentralized network of small local liberation groups. Typically, these groups lack any formal structure, they lack official membership qualifications beyond attendance at meetings, they tend to dissolve and reform frequently, and they focus their energies on educational and service projects. Their membership is mainly white, middle class, and college educated. The second movement encompasses the national women's organizations including the National Organization for Women (NOW), the National Women's Political Caucus (NWPC), and the Women's Equity Action League (WEAL). In contrast to the informal local groups, these national coalitions display a formal style of organization with elected officers, bylaws, and boards of directors.

The nationally organized branch of the movement contains the political activists among feminists,[47] whereas the network of small local groups has proved to be "politically innocuous."[48] Whatever policy impact the feminists have had has resulted from the activities of the national organizations and their chapters. And there can be no doubt about the priority accorded by these organizations to winning equal rights for women, especially economic rights. NOW was formed in 1966 to push the infant Equal Employment Opportunity Commission (EEOC) to act on sex-discrimination complaints being filed under Title VII of the 1964 Civil Rights Act. WEAL was established in 1970 to fight court cases involving women's rights. The NWPC formed in 1971 to advance the cause of women's participation in political parties and in government. These groups' most conspicuous successes have been in pursuing equal rights for women in the marketplace and in education, both in securing employment and educational opportunities and in gaining access to credit.

Even in these areas we must be cautious in estimating the impact of feminist groups on public policy. To assume that all such policy was the product of feminist agitation is to ignore other political realities. For example, opinions differ on the relative importance of feminist activity in persuading Congress to pass the 1963 Equal Pay Act. Some observers point out that the measure had been consistently promoted by women's organizations for twenty years.[49] Others argue that Congress was motivated by a desire to upgrade women's wages so that low-paid female labor could not be used by employers as a substitute for higher-paid male workers.[50] Similarly, it is doubtful whether we can attribute the inclusion of sex as a category in Title VII of the Civil Rights Acts to feminist pressure. The sex provision was inserted by a southern representative who hoped that such an unreasonable addition would destroy the bill's credibility with his congressional colleagues. When the bill passed as amended, even the staff of the newly created EEOC refused at first to take the sex-discrimination provision seriously. Nor was Executive Order 11375, barring sex discrimination by government agencies and government contractors, the clear result of women's lobbies; Irene Murphy argues that it was a by-product of federal officials' concern for civil rights.[51] The case for a feminist influence on federal legislation can more easily be made for the period after 1970. For example, pressure from women's organizations had an unquestionable role in the passage of Title IX of the 1972 Educational Amendments, the 1974 Equal Credit Opportunity Act, and the Equal Rights Amendment.

Although observers may disagree about how much influence has been exerted by the national feminist organizations on public policy, there is no doubt about their major goal. They have sought "equal opportunity," defined as a chance to compete with men in the economic and political spheres on an equal footing. In her provocative essay exploring ideological themes in the women's movement, Jean Elshtain points out that by adopting "equal opportunity" as their primary goal, American feminists were merely subscribing to "the prevailing version of equality in American society."[52] According to the "equal opportunity" formula, "all individuals have the freedom to compete for jobs, rewards, status, and position—for whatever it is the society has to offer those who succeed." Elshtain also suggests why the women's movement from the 1830s to the present has consistently formulated its demands in terms of equal rights: because it is America's "predominant social myth." "Blacks, women, and others who wish to make advances are constrained to fit their claims within that framework."[53]

By arguing that the historical continuity in American feminism derives from its primary emphasis on equal rights, we do not want to leave the impression that social feminism has been altogether missing from the American scene. We find instances of middle-class women organizing to help their less fortunate sisters as early as 1798, when a Female Humane Association was formed in Baltimore. The numerous maternal societies of the 1830s and 40s focused their energies on promoting maternal and child welfare and battling prostitution.[54] The famed settlement house movement of the early twentieth century was another example of social feminism, taking the form of private voluntary charitable activity to aid indigent families, in particular to encourage immigrant mothers to feed, clothe, and educate their offspring properly. Jane Addams's Hull House in Chicago and Lillian Wald's Henry Street Settlement in New York were the best known of the settlement houses. Social feminists also dominated the Women's Bureau of the national Labor Department from the bureau's establishment in 1920 up to 1968, promoting protective legislation for women.

And, ironically, the most accomplished theoretician the American women's movement has yet produced—Charlotte Perkins Gilman—was a social feminist. Writing at the peak of the suffrage controversy, Gilman staunchly maintained that the right to vote was of relatively little importance in improving women's economic position. A more important goal, Gilman argued, was to develop support services that would allow women to participate fully in the economic mainstream:

> If there should be built and opened in any of our large cities today a commodious and well-served apartment house for professional women with families, it would be filled at once. The apartments would be without kitchens, but there would be a kitchen belonging to the house from which meals could be served to the families in their rooms or in a common dining-room, as preferred. It would be a home where the cleaning was done by efficient workers, not hired separately by the families, but engaged by the manager of the establishment; and a roof-garden, day nursery, and kindergarten, under well-trained professional nurses and teachers, would insure proper care of the children.[55]

These examples of social feminists, impressive as they may be as individuals, represent a secondary influence in the American women's movement. Although Addams, Wald, Gilman, and other leading social feminists were sympathetic to the suffrage battle, they did not take central roles in the campaign, preferring to "spend their energies on the struggle for social justice. Woman suffrage, while desirable, was not to them of overriding importance."[56] Their influence on the campaign was, as we have observed, more a matter of expediency than of the suffragists' wholehearted conversion to their point of view.

Why has the equal rights theme been so central to American feminism? Beyond the general observation already offered—that equal opportunity is America's predominant social myth—we must appreciate the close historical association between feminism and the black struggle in America. The antislavery societies of the 1830s were perhaps the most important sources of potential feminist leadership at the time. An estimated 100 such societies were operating in the 1830s, with a large proportion of their activities carried on by women. For many of the leading feminists of the time, the two causes were inextricably linked. Those who joined both struggles included Elizabeth Cady Stanton, Lucy Stone, Sarah and Angelina Grimké, and Lucretia Mott. A spirit of organizational cooperation prevailed between abolitionists and feminists. Indeed, some of the leading male abolitionists of the time, including William Lloyd Garrison and Frederick Douglass, vigorously supported the emerging women's movement. In the opinion of historian Eleanor Flexner, "It was in the abolition movement that women first learned to organize, to hold public meetings, to conduct petition campaigns."[57]

The early women's movement borrowed not only the organizational precedent provided by the abolitionist societies but also the abolitionists' firm conviction that to deny the human rights of an entire class of people on the basis of inborn characteristics was intolerable. The connection between the two cases was succinctly argued by Margaret Fuller in 1845: "As the friend of the Negro assumes that one man cannot by right hold another in bondage, so should the friend of Woman assume that Man cannot by right lay even well-meant restrictions on Women."[58] The abolitionist struggle made one other important contribution to the cause of feminism. The sexism encountered by some women as they tried to participate actively in abolitionist politics mobilized those women in support of women's rights. The experience of Lucretia Mott and Elizabeth Stanton, who were denied active roles in the 1840 World Anti-Slavery Convention because of their sex, is said to have sparked their awareness of the feminist problem.

A similar relationship, both organizational and ideological, is observable between the civil rights and women's liberation movements of the 1960s. The dramatic publicity generated by the civil rights marches, sit-ins, and demonstrations had sensitized both policy makers and the general public to constitutional rights issues. Commenting on federal policy makers' relatively greater receptivity to women's demands than to the earlier demands pressed by blacks, Jo Freeman commented:

> It is not for naught that almost all the women's rights legislation involves amendments to or parallels of minority civil rights legislation. The civil rights movement broke the ground.[59]

Like the earlier abolitionist movement, the civil rights movement provided an organizational model for feminists. It trained a certain number of female activists, who then put their experience in the service of the women's cause. It extended public debate over equal rights beyond the political realm and into the economic, by suggesting that so long as a segment of our society remained relegated to the margins of the economy, they could not be said to enjoy first-class citizenship. Unfortunately, the experience of the early feminists who had encountered sexism in the abolitionist camp has its modern parallel also. The sexism that existed within the civil rights movement of the 1960s is best exemplified by Stokely Carmichael's famous quip that "the position of women in SNCC should be prone." Experiencing discrimination from their male co-workers in the civil rights and anti-war movements, women joined the emerging women's liberation movement in considerable numbers.

Why is this connection between the American women's movement and the civil rights movement important? For a century and a half, observers have drawn the analogy between race and sex as sources of oppression. Arguments have raged during most of that period over whether the analogy is justified. In an appendix to his 1944 study of American racism, *An American Dilemma*, the Swedish sociologist Gunnar Myrdal observed that America treated its women and its blacks in much the same ways—attributing to each group some innate characteristics that prevented it from taking full part in the nation's economy and politics.[60] In his recent volume, *Women and Equality*, William Chafe scrutinized the analogy at length in order to evaluate its usefulness for understanding the two movements of the 1960s.

We are not interested here in reviewing yet again the debate over whether blacks and women have experienced similar forms of oppression in the United States. Rather, we have stressed the connection with the civil rights movement in order to explain why, historically, American feminists have been strongly influenced in their organizational strategies by the image (an inaccurate one) of women as a minority group in American society.

FEMINIST ACTION STRATEGIES

United States: A Legacy of Separatism

Obviously women do not constitute a numerical minority in American society. But we would argue that, historically, feminist politics has been so closely associated with the struggle of the black minority that women activists have adopted certain minority action strategies. That is, until recently, American feminists have gone about organizing *as if* they were a minority group. In particular, two aspects of feminist organizing reflect this preoccupation. First, feminist leaders have shown a concern for protecting the purity of the movement by avoiding alignments with organizations and institutions outside the movement. Second, they have worked consistently to maintain the maximum possible following among women, believing that the common bond of gender is sufficient to hold together a highly diverse coalition.

This historical preoccupation with maintaining the movement's purity is most evident in relationship to two central institutions in American politics—political parties and labor unions. Throughout the suffrage campaign feminists favored the strategy of organizing outside the major political parties to act as a check on party actions. The major vehicle for lobbying the Nineteenth Amendment was the National American Women's Suffrage Association (NAWSA), a nonpartisan organization formed in 1890 for the specific purpose of winning the vote. The Congressional Committee of NAWSA staunchly refused any permanent party alignment, remaining "obdurately non-partisan."[61] While they supported the incoming Democrat Woodrow Wilson in 1913 because he expressed sympathy for their cause, they showed their disappointment with the Democratic Congress by organizing national campaigns in both 1914 and 1916 to defeat Democratic congressional candidates. The head of NAWSA's Congressional Committee was militant Alice Paul. So little faith did she have in the regular parties that for many years after women got the vote she advocated forming a separate party composed only of women. While she never succeeded in organizing a mass political party for the female electorate, Alice Paul did found the small band of intrepid women lobbyists (the National Women's party) who maintained constant pressure on Congress from the 1920s to the 1970s in favor of the Equal Rights Amendment.

Having won the Nineteenth Amendment, suffragists debated the question whether women should move toward integration into the established parties or maintain their identity as an independent political force. William Chafe has labeled this question "the central issue" confronting the newly formed League of Women Voters, the organizational heir to the NAWSA. Some prominent feminists within the LWV urged women to become active participants in the Republican and Democratic parties. Carrie Chapman Catt, for example, was so thoroughly opposed to sex segregation that she even wanted to delete "Women" from the title of the organization. But other leading feminists, including Jane Addams, advised women against joining the parties, in which women's impact would be diluted and their cause compromised. Separatists argued that party politics was by nature a corrupt and unsavory enterprise that would force women to abandon their reformist ideals and thereby destroy the unique contribution of females to politics. H. L. Mencken said it most pointedly in his 1922 *In Defence of Women*:

> A woman who joins one of these parties simply becomes an imitation man, which is to say, a donkey. Thereafter, she is nothing but an obscure cog in an ancient and creaking machine, the sole intelligible purpose of which is to maintain a horde of scoundrels in public office.[62]

The controversy within the league ultimately produced an official compromise that called upon women to become "non-partisan and all-partisan."[63] Despite the compromise, it seemed in the early 1920s that feminists had by and large rejected the regular parties as vehicles for expressing their demands. Instead, the most active political arm of the feminists was the Women's Joint Congressional Committee, an umbrella organization that coordinated feminist lobbying activities for a variety of women's organizations but remained outside the party system.

The effectiveness of the separatist strategy depended on the feminists' claim that women voters would retaliate at the polls against a party politician who was unresponsive to their demands. The Women's Joint Congressional Committee wielded this threat to some advantage in the early 1920s, obtaining passage of several important pieces of legislation. But the feminists' influence on party politicians dropped precipitously once politicians discovered that the threat of electoral retaliation from women was an idle threat.

American women did not rush to participate in electoral politics after 1920. Only about one third of eligible women voted in the 1924 election, compared with over two thirds of eligible men.[64] However, female turnout increased in every succeeding decade. By the 1950s, women's turnouts in presidential elections were trailing men's by only ten percentage points, and in more recent elections the gap has closed even further (see table 3–1).

But, if they have increased their participation, American women have not established themselves as a voting bloc. In exercising their vote, women's preferences are better predicted by their socioeconomic position and their husband's preferences than by their sex. Different voting studies have offered different interpretations of this undeniable pattern. In 1964 *The American Voter* concluded that the close correspondence between wives' and husbands' voting patterns reflected the husbands' political influence over their wives.[65] Goot and Reid, in their review of the literature on voting behavior of women, acknowledge the overwhelming correspondence between spouses' voting preferences but argue that we lack

TABLE 3-1. Turnouts in Presidential Elections, 1948–72

	1948[a]	*1952*[a]	*1956*[a]	*1960*[a]	*1964*[b]	*1968*[b]	*1972*[b]	*1976*[b]
Women	56%	62%	69%	69%	67%	66%	62%	59%
Men	69%	72%	80%	80%	72%	70%	64%	60%

Sources: [a]Marjorie Lansing, "Women: The New Political Class," in *Women in Politics* ed. Jane Jaquette (New York: Wiley, 1974), pp. 5–24.

[b]Bureau of Census, Current Population Reports, Series P-20, No. 192, 322.

solid empirical evidence to show that this correspondence is the result of the husbands' influence: "It is one thing for husband and wife to vote alike; it is quite another for this to involve simply reflecting or following the other's preference."[66] Whatever the explanation for the pattern, it has remained unchanged as women's turnout rates have increased. Thus, it is difficult to argue that women's entry into the electorate has made any significant difference in national voting patterns.

The speedy realization on the part of men politicians that the "woman vote" was a myth virtually eliminated feminist influence in the major parties. As a result of their separatist strategy, feminists had made few inroads into either party organization; hence they could exercise little internal influence. (This is not to say that there were no women party officials in either party; there were, but they did not for the most part represent a feminist viewpoint). With the fear of the female electorate dispelled, party leaders could safely ignore feminists' demands. In *Harpers* magazine, a Democratic committeewoman wrote in 1925, "I know of no woman who has a following of other women. I know of no politician who is afraid of the woman vote on any question under the sun."[67]

If we turn to an examination of the early feminists' relationship to organized labor, we find many activists expressing the same suspicion that aligning with the male-dominated unions would require compromising feminist goals. The potential conflict between feminism and unionism was evident starting in the 1860s, when American labor began organizing on a national basis. One labor historian has counted over thirty national trade unions formed from 1863 to 1873, of which only two admitted women to membership.[68] Responding to such exclusionary practices by male unions, nineteenth-century working women organized separate women's unions for textile workers, printers, collar workers, and so forth. Most of these women's unions were formed to work for short-range goals; they often disbanded after those goals were achieved. Women also formed city-wide working women's protective associations to aid all women workers, including the nonunionized. No doubt this early sex segregation in unions resulted primarily from exclusionary practices by men. But, once established, the separatist pattern was supported by some feminists who urged working women to maintain their own unions because of the potential conflict between women's rights and unionism. The strongest expression of the feminist viewpoint came from Susan B. Anthony, who in the 1870s vigorously opposed both mixed unions and protective labor legislation. In 1872 she was expelled from the National Labor Union for condoning the use of women as strikebreakers.

The experience of the Women's Trade Union League (WTUL) in the opening decades of the twentieth century is an instructive example of the historic conflict between feminism and unionism. The WTUL was established in 1903 as an organization to promote unionizing among women workers and provide services to women's unions (e.g., training organizers, running publicity campaigns, subsidizing strike funds, and even providing bail money for arrested strikers). Aligned both with the suffrage movement and with the male-dominated American Federation of Labor under Sam Gompers, the WTUL worked vigorously to get more women organized, mostly in new unions of women wage workers but also in already established unions. At the end of World War I, when men's unions led the fight to fire women who had been hired during the war, WTUL's loose affiliation with the male-dominated AFL was strained. Tension came to a head in 1923, when the WTUL refused to go along with its sister associations in other nations in merging with the International Federation of Trade Unions (IFTU). While the majority of women unionists from other countries felt the merger would strengthen the WTUL, the Americans declared the merger would reduce them to mere appendages of the men in the IFTU. "Putting their roles as feminists ahead of their interests as trade unionists,"[69] the WTUL pulled out of the international.

Surveying women's status in the union movement in the 1920s and '30s, Gail Falk concluded that women were broadly discouraged from joining male-dominated unions by blatantly exclusionary policies and that the unions' stance helped to persuade women that they did not belong in men's unions: "The unions' antiwomen attitudes had the effect of a self-fulfilling prophecy. Unions did not on the whole want women, and women did not on the whole join unions."[70]

The arguments and examples presented so far in this section are intended to establish that the history of American feminism contains a pronounced separatist strain. (This constitutes, as we shall see, a significant difference between the American case and the other two.) But what about the revival of feminism that began in the 1960s? How much emphasis has it placed on separatism as an organizing strategy?

Not surprisingly, we find that many early proponents of women's liberation in the 1960s expressed "an overt female separatist viewpoint, which calls for women to isolate themselves from men in order to come to terms with what it means to be female."[71] In her intellectual history of the contemporary women's movement, Gayle Yates draws a parallel between the Black Power movement's use of the phrase "Black is Beautiful" and the women's liberation slogan coined in 1968: "Sisterhood is Powerful." Both conveyed a sense of group identity; in this sense, the emphasis on "sisterhood" was an emphasis on "female solidarity, respect for women as women, support for all women by women."[72]

The separatist impulses of women's liberationists were also reflected in the widespread popularity of consciousness raising as an organizing strategy. Consciousness raising was the single activity most universally associated with women's liberation in the 1960s and early 1970s. In fact, for many local women's groups, the weekly "rap sessions" constituted the *only* permanent group activity. The benefits, according to its proponents, were to heighten women's awareness of their oppression and confer on group members a collective identity—in other words, to break down isolation. The format for such sessions was well established, conforming generally to the "Protective Rules for Consciousness Raising" published in 1968 by a New York City feminist group called Redstockings, and used all over the country. Invariably, men were excluded from participation.

There is a certain irony in classifying consciousness raising as a "separatist" activity, given the origins of the technique in the Chinese Communist Revolution. The Chinese version of consciousness raising is described in detail later in this chapter; at this point, we simply note that Mao's followers used the method as an instrument of integration to overcome social divisions and cement the participants' loyalty to the revolution. The "consciousness" the Chinese have sought to awaken was the recognition of a fundamental national unity rather than of separation between social groups. Early proponents of consciousness raising within the American women's movement were almost certainly aware of the Chinese antecedents. It is reasonable to suppose that at least the young women who became feminists after participating in New Left political activities in the early 1960s would be familiar with the Chinese model, which figured prominently in the student movement.

At least one account of the American women's movement in the 1960s draws a direct connection between the Chinese experience and the adoption of consciousness raising by American feminists. Susan Brownmiller reports that the two women most influential in introducing consciousness raising as a deliberate method to feminist groups in New York and Chicago were in part guided by Mao's slogan "Speak pain to recall pain."[73]

How then did the American version, as used by women's groups, differ from the Chinese? In the American model, each member of the group (usually limited to 15 participants) is asked to testify in turn regarding some central theme or discussion question. No member may interrupt, criticize, or challenge another's testimony. In the end, the group reaches a collective judgment on the question but not on any individual's testimony. These rules are designed specifically to prevent any individual from being singled out for criticism. Note the striking contrast with the Chinese model, in which group members are encouraged to see themselves as falling short of the group's expectations for them. In the American model, members' hostility is consciously directed outward from the group, against a society that oppresses women. This difference is related to an important difference in goals. The goal in the Chinese case is to mobilize women in the service of established political institutions, whereas the American model seeks to mobilize women against the political establishment.

By the late 1960s, American feminists took for granted the value of consciousness raising to the movement. But the rapid, virtually universal acceptance of consciousness raising after 1968 as the single most important activity of local groups was mirrored in the early 1970s by an equally rapid decline in institutionalized consciousness raising. By 1975, Freeman was reporting that "as a major movement function," consciousness raising was becoming "obsolete."[74] Freeman's explanation for this decline was that feminist consciousness had by that time infused the media and public discussion to such an extent that the organizing of rap groups was no longer seen as necessary.

Our own explanation for the decline is somewhat different. We believe that feminist groups gradually discovered that consciousness raising did not play the role of political mobilizer it was thought to be playing. The theory behind the use of consciousness raising was rarely articulated. But it seems to be this: Individual women have not traditionally perceived their problems as shared problems; instead, they have suffered their lot as individuals and have sought to make individual adjustments to the discrimination they encountered. The rap group, in which each member relates her own experience on the particular question at hand, demonstrates to all present that women hold many problems in common. Once they have achieved that realization, they can act collectively to press their grievances on political and economic institutions. Chafe explicitly states this connection between group discussion and group action:

> For women throughout the country who became active in one form or another of the woman's movement, the discussion group served as the basic forum for developing a sense of strength, solidarity, and commitment. It thereby provided the "social space" for women to grow into a new perception of themselves, and move on to activities devoted to eliminating sex discrimination.[75]

Yates supports this interpretation with her assertion that consciousness raising "is not a therapy but a revolutionary method."[76]

This was the theory behind consciousness raising. Like the Chinese model, the American version was intended "to politicize the personal aspects of people's lives."[77] A raised consciousness would create an awareness of the political content contained in the smallest bits of everyday reality—conversations with family members, watching television commercials, and so on. But in the American case the new awareness seems to have led most commonly to individual-level changes. The primary contribution of consciousness raising has been to bring about emotional and behavioral changes in participants. The feminist psychologist Phyllis Chesler reported these changes in women who had participated in consciousness raising:

> Some women quit their jobs . . . others began job training. . . . Some women started living together; some began living alone for the first time. . . . Some women left their husbands; others began to live with a man, feeling somehow less of a psychological disadvantage than before. . . .
>
> Many women started reading "political" and "scientific" books as passionately as they read novels. . . . Within a small group, women stopped giggling and competing with each other for male attention. . . . Many women found they could think. . . . Some women stopped going to beauty parlors. . . . [They] began to value their time; they needed fewer adornments to "make up" for being female.[78]

Often, consciousness raising has led groups to establish small-scale mutual-aid projects (e.g., neighborhood day care) or community service projects (e.g., female health collectives). One explanation for the prevalence of such projects is that they help to maintain group cohesion and solidarity; they provide a focus around which community women can stay in contact with one another. The projects act as a binding agent. We have little evidence, however, that a consciousness raising experience has mobilized women to push for public policy change. On the contrary, consciousness raising seems to play its most prominent role in those women's groups most inclined to emphasize education projects and least inclined to political activism.

The considerable literature accumulating on the topic of sex-role socialization confirms beyond a doubt the importance of a woman's expectations and self-image as determinants of her life chances. To the extent that feminists are interested in sensitizing both women and men to sexism in the environment and persuading women to upgrade their personal expectations, consciousness raising is an invaluable tool. But as an instrument for influencing government policy, consciousness raising is slow and indirect at best. Its drawbacks are twofold.

First, its usefulness as an instrument for promoting policy change depends on the assumption that a woman with a raised consciousness will become a political constituent who will pressure government officials for policy change. Whether a raised consciousness is likely to be translated into political activism is an empirical question; as far as we know, there is little evidence either confirming or refuting the assumption. One interesting piece of comparative research tested French and American women on three sets of attitudes: their degree of egalitarianism regarding sex roles, their tendency to advocate action when experiencing personal discrimination, and their tendency to advocate action against more general societal discrimination. The researchers were testing the hypothesis that those women holding more strongly egalitarian attitudes (presumably the attitudes fostered by consciousness raising) would be more likely to advocate both kinds of action, personal and collective. Surprisingly, "egalitarian attitudes and action orientation, contrary to expectations, were not found to be strongly interrelated."[79] That is, the research showed that women holding sexually egalitarian beliefs were no more likely than the others in the sample even to *advocate* political action, much less carry it through.

A related drawback is that an emphasis on consciousness raising shifts the burden for change away from government and toward the individual woman. Its feminist proponents may well see social and political institutions as the source of women's problems. But, in practice, consciousness raising encourages women to look to themselves, or to that small group of women with whom they share consciousness, as the source of their "liberation." Consciousness raising is an approach that deemphasizes broad-based social action in favor of a highly personal transformation experience.

Having identified distinctly separatist tendencies in the activities of some local liberation groups, we now turn to the strategies pursued by the national organizations. We have noted that the thrust for legislative reform has come almost exclusively from the national organizations rather than from the local groups. In seeking such reforms, movement leaders perceived the exclusion of feminists from influence in a major party as a serious handicap. Women who have sought political office since 1960 have most commonly resorted to running in primaries to secure a party nomination, often against the opposition of party leaders. Others even further removed from the parties have run as independents. And while women candidates have frequently won elections, they have found in many cases that winning office does not necessarily confer power. In scanning the field of female officeholders in 1973, Susan and Martin Tolchin reported that women officeholders at all levels of government found themselves isolated from power because they remained excluded from the party's "inner circles."[80] Although virtually all state and national parties had formed women's sections, they seldom served any significant function beyond fund-raising. (This situation prompted Betty Friedan to advise a meeting of New York City Democratic women that their first order of business should be to disband).[81]

When feminists decided in the 1960s to enter the political arena on behalf of their sex, they chose not to align with one of the major parties (as blacks and labor had done with the Democratic party) but to form a series of nonpartisan interest groups, of which the first and most important was the National Organization for Women. The organizers of NOW in 1966 were committed to seeking public power for women in order to change public policies in directions more favorable to women. Yet they decided not to seek partisan alliances. A resolution adopted more than a decade later, at NOW's 1978 National Conference, shows that the organization's position has remained virtually unchanged on this particular issue:

> *Whereas*, the National Organization for Women (NOW) has always been an independent feminist organization; and *Whereas*, NOW and its subunits wish to remain independent and free from political party pressure, yet able to endorse individual candidates who support NOW's positions: *Therefore, be it resolved*, that no political party be allowed to use NOW or any subunit of NOW as a vehicle to further its political goals.

The decision to avoid partisan alliances was directly related to NOW's statement of organizational purpose: to serve the interests of *all* women, regardless of their class, their race, their regional, ethnic, or religious background, or their party affiliation. NOW's organizing strategy is simply an organizational reflection of the concept of "sisterhood"; it is based on the premise that all women, no matter how diverse they are in other respects, share the common problems of their sex. Working on this assumption, NOW's leadership has avoided permanent alignments with political parties or any other interest groups whose membership and goals are less inclusive than their own.

The determination to aim for the broadest possible spectrum of interest representation is consciously incorporated into the policy of NOW and other major feminist organizations. According to Chafe, "there developed early in the movement a general policy of not excluding groups or points of view for reasons of political unorthodoxy or social unpopularity."[82] For example, radical lesbians, whose participation in NOW has been viewed by many activists as a political liability for the organization, are incorporated under the umbrella on the grounds that women's rights are indivisible. Irene Murphy suggests that the strategy of organizational inclusiveness dates from the suffrage movement. The vote was an issue that labor leaders, professional women, and social reformers could all support; Murphy implies that it is the suffrage coalition which contemporary feminists are seeking to reconstruct.[83] Although the suffrage campaign may well exert some influence as a model, we would argue that the more proximate model for contemporary feminists, and the more influential, is the civil rights movement. Just as civil rights leaders sought to mobilize as many blacks as possible, asserting that their blackness bound them together as a natural interest group, so feminists have argued that women's shared gender creates a natural community of interest.

This same sense of women's inherent community of interest is reflected in another major national organization—the National Women's Political Caucus, founded in 1971. The group's avowed purpose is to promote a higher level of women's participation in public offices, both elective and appointive. It is organized on a multipartisan basis, working with campaigns for Democratic, Republican, and independent candidates, and lobbying for equal rights measures (especially the Equal Rights Amendment). Needless to say, the assumption behind the NWPC's activity is that women have a shared interest in seeing more women in public office, which can best be advanced by working in both major parties rather than aligning with one of them.

A recent, highly visible instance of the feminist strategy of inclusiveness was the approach taken by the National Commission on the Observance of International Women's Year in organizing the 1977 National Women's Conference in Houston. This national meeting and the 56 preparatory meetings held in the states and territories were funded by the federal government for the express purpose of preparing policy recommendations on ending barriers to women's equality. Organizers, working at the state level, declared that they intended the conference recommendations to represent the interests of *all* groups working to advance women's rights, including women of all ages, income levels, races, ethnic and religious affiliations. The tumultuous conflict that characterized several of these state meetings in the summer of 1977, as well as the national meeting in Houston in November, demonstrated the difficulties inherent in this goal. Meaningful policy recommendations simply could not represent all the divergent viewpoints expressed at those meetings. Fundamental splits occurred in the convention on the issues of abortion, lesbian rights, and the Equal Rights Amendment. While a 25-point National Plan of Action was adopted at Houston, a substantial minority faction left the convention protesting that parliamentary procedure had been selectively used to prevent opposition viewpoints from being heard or incorporated into amending resolutions. Formally delivered to the President in March 1978, the sweeping action plan seems so far to have had little impact on either federal or state policy.

If feminists are seeking to keep public debate on women's issues alive, then the umbrella strategy may be a good one. National conventions of NOW and other organizations provide excellent platforms from which to dramatize women's grievances. But if the goal is to effect policy change, then the strategy of maximizing the coalition works best for those issues that universally benefit supporters—in this case, equal rights issues. For programs whose benefits are less inclusive, the umbrella coalition may not be the optimal strategy.

The ability of any coalition to work effectively for policy change depends on the members' willingness to give higher priority to their common grievances than to any other problems they may have which divide them. American women do not come nearly as close as American blacks did in the early 1960s to sharing a common economic status, or common neighborhoods, or the Protestant denominations, or a cultural heritage. Therefore, women's ability to mount a unified pressure campaign is limited.

An organization like NOW, based on the principle of universal "sisterhood" among women, faces serious difficulties in promoting programs that benefit only certain categories of women (e.g., pregnant women, women who need day care services, retired women, blue-collar workers). All-inclusive organizations are forced to promote many issues at once in order to satisfy their diverse memberships. Resources must be divided among many campaigns. When key issues need to be resolved, consensus is extremely difficult to establish. If they can agree at all on a course of action, it is often on a compromise that dilutes the positions of all constituencies involved in the decision. Even more important, a great deal of the organization's energy is spent in "consummatory" (group maintenance) activities rather than "instrumental" (goal-oriented) activities. Struggling to hold the coalition together becomes the leadership's primary task.

At a national conference on "Women and the American Economy" in late 1975, Betty Friedan called into question the feminists' action strategy of "going it alone." She argued that the women's liberation movement she had helped to found was only a "way station . . . the questions we face now cannot be solved by women alone." Women now need to develop economic alliances with "old people, young people, heart-attack-prone executives, trade unionists, Blacks, and other minorities."[84] In urging cooperation Friedan was arguing, not that feminists' traditional separatism has been misguided in the past, but rather that its utility as an action strategy was now exhausted. To deal with the contemporary economy, women need to align themselves with other organizations and institutions.

Such a shift would almost certainly be marked by less reliance on inclusive strategies and more functional divisions and specialization within the women's movement.

Some observers have already noted such trends. In a 1977 study of four specific policy issues (credit, education, abortion, pregnancy disability), Gelb and Palley observed a growing tendency of feminist groups in the 1970s to forge coalitions with nonfeminist organizations in order to lobby the Congress and administrative agencies. They described, for example, the "pro-choice" coalition linking feminist organizations (Women's Lobby, NWPC, NOW) to other interest groups (Planned Parenthood, ACLU) to counteract groups pressuring Congress to limit Medicaid funds for abortions. Another instance is the coalition of feminist groups, labor, and church organizations activated in December 1976 to back the Pregnancy Disability Act. The formation of such external linkages has led, according to Gelb and Palley, to greater functional differentiation in the women's movement: "Internally, women's groups have developed more effective use of limited resources by developing specialized interests and dividing areas of specialization."[85]

This trend in the direction of greater functional specialization within the movement has been moderated by the protracted battle to ratify the ERA, which has absorbed so much of the time, attention, and money of national feminist organizations. Because of the need to get ratification votes in 38 separate state legislatures, the campaign has of necessity been fought simultaneously on multiple fronts, by backers trying to unite as broad a coalition as possible. In doing so, ERA strategists have called on the various branches of the movement to submerge their differences and devote significant resources to this common cause. Not unlike the suffragists seeking votes for women, ERA proponents have made a universal appeal to women for support on this narrow issue, on the simple basis of their shared sex.

Sweden: Integration

Visitors to Sweden are often surprised to observe that in spite of the high visibility of women's issues in the media and in public debate, a women's liberation movement as such is barely visible. The two women's organizations most closely identified with women's liberation are the well-established and highly respectable Fredrika Bremer Association and the much smaller, more militant Group 8, viewed by many Swedes as an extremist organization. As a nonpartisan voluntary organization, the Fredrika Bremer Association has a little over 9000 members in its local chapters. It falls squarely into the equal rights branch of Swedish feminism, having lobbied consistently since 1884 for equal treatment of the sexes in education, employment, and community life. The association's commitment to absolute equality between the sexes even prompted its leaders in the early twentieth century to oppose the idea of protective labor legislation for women because that concept violated the principle of equal treament. In recent years, the Fredrika Bremer Association has gained most of its publicity for its efforts to increase the representation of women in party leadership and public office.

The other organization, Group 8, can best be described to American readers as the closest Swedish equivalent to the radical women's liberation groups of the late 1960s in the United States. With a markedly leftist orientation, even by Swedish standards, Group 8 has since 1968 attracted its small membership of about 1000 mostly in Stockholm, although a few small branches exist in other cities as well. Its manifesto exhorts members to take an active part in the socialist revolution, and calls for these reforms:

1. Women's legal right to the same working conditions as men
2. Unemployment benefits and free training for all women who are involuntarily unemployed
3. Government scholarship aid for adult students, regardless of their spouse's income
4. Legal protection for part-time employees
5. Day care for all children ages 6 months to 7 years
6. Free abortion and contraceptives
7. Channeling of 25% of all new housing into Collective Houses

Much like women's action organizations in the United States, Group 8 sponsors conferences, workshops, and exhibitions; distributes literature; and assists women trying to organize at their work places and in their communities.

A striking contrast between the activities of women's liberation groups in the United States and Sweden is the much more limited use of consciousness raising by Swedish feminists. Granted, Swedish women's organizations have conducted propaganda campaigns to influence public opinion. One celebrated example is the traveling exhibit shown in the late 1960s titled "Stop Helping Mother with the Housework." Sponsored as a combined effort of the government and the women's sections of national unions and employers organizations, the exhibit portrayed the ideal family as one in which household responsibility was shared so that family members no longer saw their task as "helping mother" but as assuming their rightful share of the household burden.

But, while they have tried to influence mass opinion, Swedish women's organizations have seldom used the rap group to change members' attitudes. Its absence from the Swedish scene is not surprising, given the strong emphasis on materialism in Swedish culture. By materialism, we mean the belief that a society's social, political, and cultural development depends on progress in the material realm, especially in conditions on the job and in the home. While this orientation is expressed by Swedish public officials of virtually all parties, it seems to have originated with the Socialists and to have gradually suffused the entire political system during the many decades of Social Democratic dominance. Whatever its origin, the belief that "the individual's status and potential for self-realization are products of prevailing economic relations"[86] has without doubt strongly influenced the debate on the "woman question."

Swedish feminists express little faith in the possibility of changing social conditions by changing individual consciousness. Consciousness raising seems to them to be a completely backward approach: It is not a woman's consciousness that determines her social circumstances; rather, her circumstances determine her consciousness. Moreover, in Sweden's collectivist culture, an effort to solve women's problems at the individual level is seen as merely disguising the need for structural solutions. What good does it do an individual to "raise" her consciousness if she then cannot find a job because of the structure of opportunities in the labor market or the lack of adequate support services? More than American feminists, Swedes tend to seek solutions at the level of the community and not at the level of the individual, the household, or even the neighborhood. The self-help and mutual-aid schemes so prominent in the United States and China are seen by Swedish activists as no more than short-term, stopgap measures. Using such tactics may actually be counterproductive because they relieve the pressure on government to seek collective solutions to women's problems.

One Swedish feminist interviewed offered another objection to relying heavily on consciousness raising. She pointed out that the stress on "correct consciousness" and the attempt by women's organizations to reconstruct their members' belief systems actually breeds divisiveness among women because it generates hostility from those women who are satisfied with their lot and do not wish to be reconstructed. In Sweden, where consciousness raising is emphasized little, feminists do not encounter the same intense resistance from female traditionalists that American feminists have confronted.

If we are unable to identify either local liberation groups (organized around consciousness raising) or broadly based national women's organizations such as NOW, where does the thrust for women's policies originate? Can we trace it to a highly mobilized and vociferous female electorate? That argument would be difficult to sustain because the female electorate in Sweden displays no significant tendencies toward bloc voting on women's issues or for women candidates. Women voters in Sweden are not apathetic; by comparison with other nations, they are unusually active. Amazingly, there is virtually *no* difference in the turnout rates of the two sexes; women and men have registered turnouts exceeding 85 percent in recent national elections. On other measures of political participation, women rank below men (see table 3–2), although they still rank high compared with female citizens of other nations.

Thus, Swedish women vote and participate in political affairs at a relatively high level. Yet, as in the United States, there is no discernible "female vote" in Sweden. Like Swedish men, women normally vote in accordance with a party affiliation. They even defy the traditional political wisdom that women give disproportionate support to conservative parties;

TABLE 3-2. Percent of Female and Male Survey Respondents Who Reported Participating in Political Ways, 1974

	Women	*Men*
Writing to newspapers	7	15
Expressing self at meetings	16	39
Joining a political organization	16	25
Taking part in a demonstration	12	22
Contacting elected representatives	7	13

Source: Adapted from Elisabet Sandberg, *Equality Is the Goal* (Stockholm: Swedish Institute, 1975), p. 80.

women are as likely to vote for the Social Democrats as are men.[87] This unusual characteristic of the Swedish female electorate would surprise even the suffragists who ardently supported votes for women at the turn of the century. The outspoken suffragist Ellen Key, herself a Socialist, wrote in 1911:

> Even if women are at first on the side of reaction—and in Sweden this would certainly be the case—their direct influence would nevertheless be less dangerous than their indirect and irresponsible influence is now.[88]

The absence of a female vote for women candidates is explained by the mechanics of the electoral system. Because the parties run lists of candidates for election, rather than running a single candidate per constituency, individual candidates win or lose their seats on the basis of the size of the party's vote *and* their ranking on the party's list. The voter does not register support for individual candidates, either male or female. Hence it is not the voter who assures that a female candidate will win the seat, but rather the party leadership that controls the list. This electoral system makes it impossible for individual women candidates to mobilize support for their own personal candidacies apart from their party's electoral fortunes.

As Ingunn Means has observed, Sweden's electoral system can work either for or against women candidates, depending on the party size and party leaders' predispositions toward female candidacies. Progressive, pro-woman party leaders, such as those who have traditionally headed the Liberal and Social Democratic parties in the twentieth century, could add women to their party lists even at times and in constituencies that would be unlikely to elect women directly. On the other hand, parties that have only a small representation in the legislature may be ill disposed to turn over any of their hard-won seats to women candidates.[89]

In the absence of either large-scale women's liberation organizations or even a female voting bloc in the electorate, where should we look for the "movement" in Sweden? The answer is "everywhere." A primary explanation for the low visibility of Swedish feminism is that it is embedded in virtually all the country's major social, political, and economic organizations. The Swedish pattern is totally unlike the American pattern. Rather than having a national women's organization comparable to NOW, feminists in Sweden have worked through the women's sections established in virtually every party, union, professional, social, and religious organization in the nation. Women's sections (*kvinnoförbund*) promote women's interests within the organization and stimulate contacts with women in outside organizations.

The party with the first and most active women's section was the Social Democrats (see table 3–3). Lest the reader equate the Swedish case with either the women's section established by China's Communist party or the traditional fund-raising and service auxiliaries attached to American parties, a brief description of the origins of the Social Democratic Women's Association will serve to demonstrate the differences. First, the Social Democratic Women's Association, initially called the Stockholm Public Women's Club, was organized *against* the wishes of the party's male leadership. August Palm, the founding father of socialism in Sweden, staunchly opposed the idea. The minutes of a party meeting in 1892 report that Palm

> declared his inability to believe that much would be gained by the organization of the women. He was not alone in this opinion. Axel Danielsson, evidently influenced by Strindberg's view of women, declared in spirit of the programme that it was the duty of the party to organize and educate the working woman, so that she would be fit to exercise the civil rights which must one day be granted to her. But as women had not yet reached this point of maturity, he questioned the wisdom of her active participation.[90]

Against the opposition of the leadership, the Social Democrat women formed their association in 1892, and at every party congress they called on the leadership to increase its efforts at organizing women. Finally in 1905

TABLE 3-3. Women's Sections in Swedish Political Parties

Party	*Date Party Formed*	*Date Women's Section Formed*	*Membership in Women's Section, 1973*
Social Democrats	1889	1892	48,700
Liberals	1902	1923	16,000
Conservatives	1912	1920	59,700
Center party	1913	1933	68,000

Source: Information supplied by The Fredrika Bremer Association, May 1976.

the women proposed that the party pay a permanent staff member, preferably a woman, "who would be exclusively concerned with agitation among women." The spokesperson for the women was even driven to threaten the party congress: "Perhaps we women will have to strike to get an agitator."[91] Once recognized, the women's determination to force party leaders to take them seriously led their official magazine, *Morgonbris*, to editorialize in 1909: "Our male colleagues should realize that we have the right to express an opinion both on party issues and other problems which directly concern us."[92] In short, the women's sections were originally organized, not by the party leadership, but by determined women who demanded that a strong women's voice be heard in the party.

Over the past 60 years, the women's sections of the major parties have served an important function as staging areas for female party leaders. Of the 79 women now holding seats in the 350-member Riksdag (elected in September 1976), many gained experience and visibility in their party by working in the women's sections. The women's sections have also directly influenced party platforms. It was, for example, the women's section of the Social Democratic party that originated many of the provisions included in the family policy reform proposed by the Social Democrats the summer before the 1976 election.

A similar picture emerges when we trace women's participation in trade unions. While a separate Women's Trade Union existed from 1902 to 1909, it subsequently merged with men's unions. Since 1909, women have not organized separate unions. Rather than seeing unionism as antagonistic to their cause, working women have created women's sections within the major unions. Women now constitute 33 percent of the membership in the Swedish Confederation of Trade Unions (LO), the central organization that represents about 90 percent of the nation's work force. Women represent 49 percent of the unionized white-collar workers (TCO) and 30 percent of the unionized professionals grouped into the combined Confederation of Professional Associations (SACO) and Federation of Government Employees (SR).[93] In addition to the unions, there are important women's sections in the cooperative movements and in religious and temperance organizations. Our point here is not simply that women's sections exist in every sector of Swedish public life but that they have been the primary locus of debate over, and support for, feminist issues. Since the sex-role debate emerged around 1960 as an important public question, the main initiatives for changes in social welfare programs and labor market policy that would bring more women into the workforce have been generated inside the parties and within labor and professional organizations.

This organizational strategy of joining forces with men to promote women's interests within the various organizations has integrated women into Sweden's political and economic life rapidly. The high levels of female participation in unions, parties, and other organizations are particularly impressive if we remember that the vast majority of women were confined to the home until about 50 years ago. This pattern of cooperation, however, does not appear to have guaranteed that women would gain leadership positions. One is struck by the absence in Sweden of women playing powerful leadership roles in public life. By this, we mean not only that Sweden seems to have no Gloria Steinems or Bella Abzugs—that is certainly true, but anyone familiar with Sweden's political culture would not expect to find women leaders with flamboyant, highly personalized styles—nor men, for that matter. Foreign observers have often remarked on the general absence of strong personalities in Swedish politics—either male or female.[94]

To judge the extent of female participation in leadership roles, we must look to the percentage of leading positions held by women in parties and unions. The figures are not impressive. Of the 19 cabinet positions in the Liberal Party Cabinet formed in October 1978, only 6 went to women. Two of the women are ministers (of transportation and personnel services); one is a deputy minister (of housing and physical planning); the remaining three are assistant ministers responsible for special policy areas that might be regarded as traditionally feminine concerns: services to the handicapped, teacher training, and the status of immigrants and women in the labor market. This total of 6, however, represents an increase over the 5 women in the previous coalition Cabinet. Female leaders in the unions are only slightly more numerous, despite the large representation of women among union members. In 1971 the LO had *no* women on its executive board, and women held only 3 percent of the seats in the representative assembly. In the professional union (SACO) only 12 percent of the executive board members were women, and only 10 percent of the delegates to the assembly. The white-collar TCO showed the highest percentage of women on its executive board: 20 percent. In the same year, women held no offices in the Confederation of Employers (SAF).[95]

In pursuing their strategy of working within established organizations, the leadership of the women's sections of the parties and unions has actively sought to identify women's issues with larger social and economic trends in the nation, especially trends in labor market requirements and in family life (e.g., birth and marriage rates, household size). By and large, Swedish feminists do not view women's concerns as a unique set of issues for political analysis and political action. More often than not, public discussion of women's policies is carried on under the heading of family policy (*familjepolitik*) or labor market policy (*arbetsmarknadpolitik*). Feminists have seen their task as demonstrating women's integration into the economic and social system, emphasizing the close interdependence between women's issues and other public policy concerns. Programs for women, they often argue, are necessary to solve overall problems in the labor market and in the family.

China: Total Assimilation

The gains of Chinese women in almost every area of life have been impressive. The fact that discrimination still exists should not obscure the distance women have come. Yet it *is* possible to ask how responsible Chinese women have been for their own emancipation or lack of it.

Organizationally, from the beginning the party has controlled women's affairs. It has held a tight rein over women's organizations through several devices. First, what might be called "interlocking directorates" is a method common to all mass organizations in China. Communist party members are placed in key positions in organizations outside the party to insure that they remain faithful to party policy. For instance, Ts'ai Ch'ang, chairperson of the Women's Committee of the Party's Central Committee, is also chairperson of the NWF. Teng Ying-ch'ao and Chang Yun, members of the Women's Committee, have also served as vice-chairpersons of the NWF. Yang Chih-hua, a Communist party member and director of the Women's Department of the ACFTU, has also been a vice-chairperson of the NWF. Second, the party controls women's organizations through its control of funds. National budgeting for women's work seems to have been limited; most projects have been funded by individuals or units at the local level, under the control of the party committees. Third, personnel are assigned to the women's federations through central employment agencies. Since China is a "planned economy," the placement of employees, particularly those educated enough to be women's cadres, has not been left to chance. Assignments to the women's federations have not always been received overjoyously. "Graduating from a three-month course [at Hunan Construction College], I was assigned to Nanyang Commune, Hsiangyang county, to take charge of a women's group. . . . That I was now required to do women's work was repugnant to me."[96] Nevertheless, the assignments have been accepted. The result of this situation is that control over policy, money, and personnel has been retained by the party, giving women little independent leverage.

While women have certainly served in many branches of the party and government, neither their numbers nor their positions have been impressive. In 1922 Hsiang Ching-yu was elected the first and only woman member of the policy-making Central Committee of the party. Having died in 1928, she was replaced by Ts'ai Ch'ang at the Sixth National Party Congress. At the Seventh Congress in 1945, Ts'ai was raised from alternate to full-member status, and two new alternates were added. That made 3 women out of a total of 77 members. The Eighth Central Committee progressed to 8 women members out of 195, or 4 percent. And on the Ninth (1969), women numerically advanced to 23 out of 279 members, or 8 percent. However, as Klein and Hager have pointed out, "On the previous Central Committee, all eight [women] had impressive revolutionary credentials and in no case could their election be attributed solely to the fame and importance of their husbands."[97] On the Ninth, only the two women retained from the Eighth—Ts'ai Ch'ang and Teng Ying-ch'ao—had those impressive qualifications. In compensation, however, two women were for the first time named to the Politburo of the Central Committee—Chiang Ch'ing (Mao's wife) and Yeh Chun (Lin Piao's wife).

The Tenth Central Committee (1973) saw 41 women out of 319 members elected and the replacement of Yeh Chun by labor heroine Wu Kuei-hsien as an alternate member of the Politburo. Wu Kuei-hsien is the first Chinese woman to come into the Politburo on her own right and "innocent of any nepotism."[98] This progress, while gratifying, is not overwhelming. Even in Wu's opinion: "The election of women to the Central Committee has come slowly."[99]

With the Eleventh Central Committee (1977), the total membership was reduced to 201 seats, of which 38 were held by women. Thus, the women's representation increased slightly as a proportion of the total membership. The Politburo has maintained one woman alternate, Chen Mu-Hua, who is concurrently serving as Vice Premier of the State Council and Minister of Economic Relations with Foreign Countries. Her election reflected the growing emphasis on modernization in the Politburo.

The process of policy formation in China is a clouded one. Just who decides which issues and why is largely hidden from Western eyes. Yet some light has been shed. General policies that require more participation than the seven-member Standing Committee of the Politburo (the seven most important men in China) seem to be discussed through "work conferences":

> [A work conference] is usually a comprehensive meeting which searchingly reviews past policy and decides upon future tasks. Central ministries hold work conferences annually or semi-annually. . . . The Central Committee also holds a periodic work conference to reassess policies. . . . But the fact is that the final speech is frequently drafted before the conference begins . . . so that the effect of the work conference (particularly at the lower levels in the bureaucracy) is limited to specifying concrete tasks to be performed in the immediate future. . . .
>
> The so-called "central work conferences" are the most important gatherings of this type—and probably of any decision-making format in China. At these meetings the top Party officials gather to evaluate their policy choices.[100]

The clear implication of this description is that the highest officials almost exclusively determine policy, while lower bureaucrats implement it. Since women's participation in the Chinese political process is heavily weighted at the lower levels, it is unlikely that they have had great influence on policy choices.

Although women form caucus-style groups within other organizations, under the auspices of the NWF, these groups seem to be ineffective. As one refugee reported to A. Doak Barnett:

> In some respects, actually, [the women's association] was little more than a paper organization in Ministry "M". Like the Labor Union, it was led by Party members employed in the ministry. Its special responsibility was to implement programs specifically related to women, but like all mass organiza-

> tions, it was also expected to give general support to the Party in carrying out all policies. In this particular ministry, however, its activities were not extensive and it was relatively unimportant.[101]

Thus incentives for both women and men in middle- and higher-level positions of authority are to consider women's issues secondary to other goals and to push for them only when they support general policy.

Such subordination should not be construed as passivity. When splits in the party leadership occur over issues, women may take a determined stand. The most obvious case of this occurred in 1957–58 over the issue of the low number of women party members and cadres. Ts'ai Ch'ang and Teng Ying-ch'ao deplored the situation at the Eighth Party Congress in 1956. To have delivered the reports they did, high elements in the party must have agreed with them.

> Certain leading organs and leading personnel tend to underestimate the strength of, and the positive contributions made by women cadres in revolutionary and construction work. . . . We have even found that a few organs and a few leading cadres tolerate ideas and attitudes which lead to actual discrimination against, and contempt for, women cadres. They think that "even three women are not the equal of one man. . . ." It has even been found in a few cases, that although there have been more women than men among the model cadres elected by the masses, extremely few women are among those promoted.[102]

Yet, in 1957, in a campaign to reduce the number of urban bureaucrats, women were encouraged to quit their jobs and return home. In Shansi Province, for example, over 700 women cadres left.[103] By February 1958, morale among women cadres had become so low that An Tzu-wen, then director of the Organization Department of the Central Committee and a top party expert on organizational questions, published an article in *Women of China* explaining the party's policy. The article was addressed to "people who are against the idea of calling back to their homes those women comrades unfit to work as cadres."[104] An Tzu-wen's defense of party policy provoked a speedy retort from the NWF, whose leadership issued its own circular:

> It must not be construed that in the past women were mobilized for participation in production and now they are only required to do housekeeping . . . the principal aspect [of women's work] is organizing the broad masses of women for direct participation in collective production and socialist construction.[105]

The question dissolved in the campaign of the Great Leap Forward when no one would have dared question the recruitment of women for any task. In a sense, then, women, backed by powerful party elements, won this round.

As independent voices within the Chinese policy process, women, like other special-interest groups, are not quick to speak up. They must wait for an opportunity and then be careful of what they say. Does that mean doing nothing? No. But the methods used to seek their own interests have greater similarity to other Chinese groups than to methods familiar in the West. Passive resistance and noncompliance,[106] manipulation of information,[107] and veiled verbal attacks[108] have all been used. Women's feeble representation at the highest levels, where the most open discussions take place, makes strong statements difficult. Moreover, the type of woman cadre cultivated by the party is unlikely to make an overt push for feminist goals in opposition to general policy. A severe problem therefore remains for Chinese women: Unlikely as it may seem after the strong Maoist line of sexual equality, if Chinese leaders in the future were to decide that revolutionary goals would best be served by women going home to be wives and mothers, who will stop them?[109] To quote the Chinese press during the campaign to recruit women cadres in 1971:

> The broad masses of revolutionary women realize profoundly that they suffered in the old society because they had no power and are happy today because they have power. If women did not have concern for state affairs, take an active part in the three revolutionary struggles, and make their contributions to consolidating the dictatorship of the proletariat, they would lose their power and suffer for a second time.[110]

The party's ability to shift its stance on women's issues, in response to shifts in overall economic goals, is vividly illustrated in its approach to women's consciousness raising. At times women have been organized into small groups to discuss and overcome the problems of going out to work, breaking down traditional barriers, and finding a new identity beyond the confines of the family. The 1973–75 campaign against Lin Piao and Confucius is a prime example. Then women not only discussed present handicaps but historical discrimination resulting from the influence of the Confucian philosophy on Chinese life.

At other times, women's consciousness was to be raised in order to make them into socialist housewives and mothers. In 1955, when urban jobs were scarce,

> in an attempt to get housewives to see themselves as contributing to society through their husbands, their status as dependents was stressed; the word itself was used more often and dependents' conferences were held at which women discussed how best they could maintain their husbands' morale and preserve their strength for their jobs, protecting them from any problems at home.[111]

And again, in the early 1960s, women were once more studying model wives, who cleaned bachelor quarters and darned and washed workers' clothes for free. The five demands they were to internalize:

1. They should provide the workers with adequate and good food, so as to keep them in good health
2. They should allow the workers proper rest and must not interfere with their sleeping time
3. They should encourage the workers to achieve full work attendance and not become absentees
4. They must bring up their children and look after their old people properly and avoid family disputes
5. Economical and planned consumption of grain should be practiced, and there should be no extravagance and waste.[112]

How are we to understand these vacillations in the goals of consciousness raising? Consciousness raising in China derives from Mao's belief that any person, armed with the right ideas, can accomplish miracles. It applies to peasants, factory workers, minority groups—in fact, to everyone. It therefore applies to women. "Mao insists that women are really no different from men and can, if properly motivated, perform the same work."[113] To get women working, then, primary stress should be placed on ideological consciousness. The Communist party determines the goals to be achieved; the individual's job is only to overcome contradictory beliefs or behavior. Cynically put, an individual raises his or her consciousness by overcoming personal preferences and bringing attitudes in line with the requirements of party policy.

Although small-group discussions are a regular part of party life and in schools, government offices, and enterprise management,[114] for the masses of women they occur mostly during campaigns. The group, consisting of no more than 15 members, is organized and led by an activist or cadre assigned by the party. The key aspect of the study group is the "criticism and self-criticism" that require every member to express her views, criticize herself, and submit to the criticism of others in the group.[115] The individuals compare their behavior with that expected by the party and criticize their own inadequacies. They have not been socialist wives, for example, or they have believed the Confucian line on the inferiority of women. If the group leader feels that a member is insufficiently contrite or does not fully understand the intent of the party, she can direct the group to criticize that member. In many cases, discussion can be a pro forma exercise, with everyone going through the required paces and no one expressing candid opinions. In other cases, it can be intensely brutal. And many times, the discussion must be very moving.

> One . . . was a poor peasant and had suffered a bitter life in the old society. She said: "My father died from exhaustion in labor. The landlord still forced us to pay our rent. We had no means to do so. My mother taught me how to spin cotton yarn into threads. We were spinning day and night to earn some money which was not even enough to pay our rent. When I came to fifteen years of age, the landlord forced me into his home in payment of our rent. . . ." She began to cry and could not go on with her story. All the listeners were moved.[116]

Needless to say, the purpose of this particular discussion group was to teach women never to forget class struggle.

Discussion groups in China not only aim at changed attitudes but also at changed behavior. A group that truly internalizes a set of policy goals will be motivated to act, and act in the direction that policy demands. However, a remarkably consistent thread runs through all mobilization attempts aimed at women: Once activated, they are expected to rely on their own resources. If Mao Tse-tung issued the call "Get organized," women set up a street factory from eleven yuan they collected among themselves. If people must learn to hate pests, women are organized into fly-swatting squads. They are not expected to storm the local factory and demand job quotas for women nor picket the local party committee because insufficient funds have been allocated for pest control. Two examples illustrate the approach:

> There was Liu-Tung-hua, a woman of 43. In 1967 she was very ill with a swelling [probably a cyst] in her stomach, and she was told she needed an operation. Her husband was in the factory and she had three small children. The neighbors organized a study class on the theme: "Revolutionary people should love and help each other," and thus they came to her help. Four women took turns, two to go to the hospital and look after her needs, and two to see to the children. The husband did not have to ask for leave from the factory to care for the children. The cyst was extracted and Liu Tung-hua fully recovered.
>
> One day Wang Su-wen became very ill; she micturated blood. Her husband was told her life was in danger. Round her the neighbors grumbled, "Why should we help? She always insults us." But we persuaded them. We opened study classes; again we read Chairman Mao together; and thus a team was organized to help her, including washing her blood-stained garments for her. . . . Thus she began to change when she saw what was being done. . . . Now Wang Su-wen is well and an activist; she has changed completely, a new woman.[117]

During the 1973–1975 anti-Lin Piao and Confucius campaigns, women were again moved to destroy old superstitions stemming from Confucian influence in pre-1949 China, and again by self-reliant activity. They built houses to prove no evil would come of it,[118] and learned plowing to disprove the notion "Women cannot plow the land! The plants will wither and the animals die."[119]

According to the party's view of revolutionary consciousness, the constraints on women are not primarily social but are the chains of their own minds. "Without self-awareness, women will be unwilling to fly, though the sky is high."[120] Consciousness raising has therefore tended to overlook the practical problems women have, once they leave home, whether to take part in labor or community service for no money at all. The very act of being in a study group produces problems. Who takes care of the children while the mother is gone? And once the women have been motivated to open a street factory or have been organized into a group to plow the land, the problems of children and household chores are even greater. It is the classic problem of the dual burden. China's answer has been further self-reliance. The street factory organizes its own nursery and mess hall, if possible, from the profits of the business. Rural women find grandmothers who will work for little or nothing, and whose wages will be deducted from the mother's salary. Women mobilized to join organizations during the Great Leap Forward had to establish women's committees to find day-care places in neighborhoods, dun mothers-in-law for help, and rearrange work schedules.[121]

The dilemma for the Chinese woman is that constraints are not always ideological. The debate on "For What Do Women Live?" in the 1963 issues of the magazine *Women of China* gave a rare view of Chinese women from their own perspective. The letters sent in and published by the editor, Tung Pien, are even more tantalizing because she was denounced in 1966 for failing to censor them.[122] The discussions centered around the conflicts of family and work responsibilities among cadres of the NWF. The first letter presented the problem admirably:

> I was formerly an ambitious girl. [Before having children]. . . . Why is it that now I have only the desire but not the will to be so?. . . . Is it not due to my lack of clearly defined struggle goals that my revolutionary energy has petered out? On second thought, I have practical difficulties, such as household work and children. As a housewife and mother, should I not take care of these things? I think that women cadres, preoccupied with household work and child-care, can in no way compete with men cadres. . . .
>
> Whenever I think of these objective difficulties, I naturally come to the conclusion that the leadership and comrades around me have no understanding of my actual conditions and do not care for my actual difficulties. I think they are even less considerate for imposing on me the same exacting demands as they have imposed on men comrades. But sometimes I also think that the reasons why I have not done a good job of my work could be that I have over-emphasized objective difficulties and that I have had ideological problems. You know I am not willing to lag behind, but are the real causes due to subjective factors and ideological problems or actual difficulties? I cannot get these things straight.[123]

Supporting this woman's view are the comments made by Ts'ai Ch'ang at the Eighth Party Congress: "Certain leading organs and leading personnel . . . have [not] made use of every possibility for the practical solution of problems peculiar to women cadres. Instead, they have left these problems to be solved by the women cadres themselves."[124]

CONCLUSION

We began this chapter with a question: How has women's political activity influenced public policy regarding benefits and services to working women? Having surveyed women's politics in the three systems, we are now in a better position to tackle that question. We begin by observing that there are several ways in which feminists might work to translate their concerns into public policy change: (1) by getting women into key political offices, (2) by mobilizing masses of women to support candidates who favor their preferred policies, and (3) by creating a general climate of opinion favorable to policy reform. We now consider each of these in turn.

Have major policy reforms been won in the United States through the election of women to key public offices? The idea that only women understand the problems of other women is widely used as an appeal to female voters in the campaigns of women candidates. It was the rationale behind the formation in 1971 of the National Women's Political Caucus. But can we trace any obvious legislative victories of the women's movement in the 1970s (e.g., the Equal Credit Opportunity Act, Title IX of the 1972 Education Amendments, passage of the ERA, and extension of the ERA's ratification period) to the presence of feminists in the legislature? Clearly, given the very small female representation in the House and Senate, we cannot credit women legislators with the passage of these bills. We can note that such feminists in Congress as Martha Griffiths, Edith Green, Bella Abzug, and Shirley Chisholm have often led in introducing and then building support for women's issues. What has perhaps been more significant is the growing female presence on the staffs of administrative agencies. Freeman noted in 1975 the emergence of "woodwork feminists" in government agencies and described the network of contact between them and feminist lobbyists as a new "policy system" in Washington. Yet she cautioned against attributing too much power to this policy system; its presence, she acknowledged, was "not sufficient to explain the new policies. Women, let alone feminists, are simply just not that powerful in government or in the private sector."[125]

Nor can the presence of women in policy-making positions be said to explain the prominence of women's issues in public debate in China and Sweden or the greater willingness of those two governments to enact programs that benefit women. In Sweden, although women are numerically well represented in both parties and unions, they hold few top policy-making positions. Similarly, in China, women's strong participation at lower levels is not matched by their representation in high-level decision-making bodies. Only in the 1970s have women begun to make significant breakthroughs into positions of economic and political leadership in either China or Sweden. Hence the major policy initiatives on behalf of women undertaken in Sweden since the 1930s and in China since 1949 must be seen as the products of male-dominated policy establishments. Men have been making "women's policy" in both countries for decades.

Even if we acknowledge that male policy makers might act in the interests of women, we are usually led immediately to assume that such enlightened males must be responding to irresistible pressures from a mass-based women's movement. Can we attribute policy change in our three systems to the mobilization of widespread pressure on policy makers? Two common assumptions among American feminists are that (1) we cannot expect to see legislatures pass women's programs until women are well enough organized to force such programs on reluctant politicians; and (2) in order to maintain effective pressure on policy makers, women must remain outside the policy system as "watchdogs." The work of Constantina Safilios-Rothschild articulates this viewpoint so clearly that we quote at some length from her *Women and Social Policy*:[126]

> Whenever ideology has preceded action, thoroughly permeating a society's entire political system, so as to minimize conflict and protest on the part of the interested parties, the success of implementation of social policies has been less than when an active "watchdog" or protesting group follows the progress of the implementation of legislation and social policies. This basic difference may, for example, explain why the American Black Movement has been more successful . . . than the Sex Role Debate in Sweden. There politicians' campaigns sound like speeches of leaders of the American Women's Liberation Movement. But in Sweden there is no powerful Women's Movement. . . .
>
> [In Sweden] a considerable number of people in power positions—politicians, administrators, educators, and intellectuals—have endorsed the equalitarian sex role ideology due to its social (rather than intrinsic) desirability, and there is no significant Women's Movement to stimulate and bring about changes, to closely examine the implementation of policies, and to help raise the consciousness of women and men.

How do we evaluate Safilios-Rothschild's view that the "success of implementation of social policies" hinges on the presence of a powerful "watchdog" women's movement? Safilios-Rothschild is certainly correct in observing that Sweden lacks an effective mass-based women's movement of the style that American feminists have built. In neither Sweden nor China do feminists represent a mass movement, if by that term we mean a network of grass-roots organizations engaged in mass protest in order to force changes in public policies. As we have seen, Swedish feminists are organized into women's sections inside the major parties, labor unions, professional associations, and virtually all other major interest groups. The women's movement is therefore not a unified movement but is functionally divided along the major political and economic cleavage lines that crisscross Swedish society. Feminists have worked as Social Democratic women or trade-union women instead of simply as women.

In China the NWF is intended to serve as an umbrella oranization to unite women of all regions and economic levels. (In practice, as we have seen, other national organizations have also developed women's sections.) But we could hardly label the NWF a grass-roots organization because it has been organized from the top down: party cadres, guided by directives from the federation leadership, have recruited local members, organized campaigns and projects at the local level. The women's movement in China does not openly agitate for policy changes. More often, women's groups have been a vehicle used by China's leaders to mobilize support for dramatic policy departures initiated by the regime. In short, neither the Swedish nor the Chinese case conforms to the movement model of policy reform, in which political elites act in response to broad-based demands for change voiced by their constituents.

Safilios-Rothschild is by no means the only American exponent of the separatist, mass-based women's organization as the only effective strategy for feminists seeking policy reform. Janet Salaff and Judith Merkle make an argument for China that is similar to Safilios-Rothschild's argument for Sweden. In their widely read analysis of the women's movement in the USSR and China, they concluded that Chinese feminists have been unable to make substantial gains for women since 1949 because they have worked within the structure of the Communist party, thereby allowing women's problems to be overshadowed by other priorities of the party. Whatever progress women have made, they argued, has been an almost accidental by-product of policies introduced for other reasons than to advance women's interests. Salaff and Merkle would clearly have preferred to see Chinese women organized as a unified and independent force in Chinese politics. Instead, they lamented:

> . . . women were not organized *as women* during the revolutionary period. A militant minority, primarily from privileged bourgeois or aristocratic backgrounds, pressed the demands of women, but women were not united in pursuit of equality. Because women did not form a definite power bloc, neither the revolutionary feminists nor the ideological commitment to women's emancipation were powerful enough to maintain the impetus for change.[127]

Implicit in the critiques by Safilios-Rothschild and Salaff and Merkle is the notion that Swedish and Chinese feminists could agitate more effectively for policy change if they would adopt the American suffragists' model of mass-based women's movement, organized independently of the country's major political and economic institutions.

One cannot but agree with Safilios-Rothschild and Salaff and Merkle that integrationist strategies have drawbacks for Swedish and Chinese feminists, who are limited to formulating their demands within frameworks established by larger (and usually male-dominated) organizations and institutions. Yet to prescribe separatist strategies for either Swedish or Chinese feminists is to depart from the dominant political paradigms in those two political systems. For the Chinese case, this point has been elaborated in Nancy Milton's critique of the Salaff and Merkle article[128] and needs no further discussion here. Suffice it to say that *no* group influences Chinese policy by working outside the party umbrella. A similar, though less sweeping, point might be made about the Swedish case. Swedish politics in the twentieth century has been based on a series of compromises between dominant interests and opposition groups seeking change; Hancock calls this Sweden's "assimilationist" tradition, which he describes as the historical willingness of bureaucratic elites "to assimilate representatives of the ascending sociopolitical forces within the leadership stratum."[129] Within parties, interest groups, and major social and political institutions, elite behavior is characterized by "a highly pragmatic intellectual style, oriented toward the discovery of workable solutions to specific problems [that] structures a consensual approach to policy making."[130] By choosing to work within established institutions, Swedish feminists are following the traditional path of outgroups seeking change.

Even in the American context, an organizing strategy that relies on mass-based, separatist women's organizations has its limitations. The need to hold together a widely diverse constituency constrains the choice of issues on which an organization can work. NOW's annual legislative goals have for years included official support for more day care, welfare reforms, services to older women, and a host of other programs targeted at special interests within the organization. But much less of NOW's energy and money has been invested in these programs than in equal rights issues (equal employment, credit, educational opportunity, and the ERA). The common explanation for this imbalance is that equal rights issues are the primary concern of NOW's middle-class membership. We would argue that a strong contributing factor is the leadership's need to find issues whose appeal will transcend the divisions among members.

The irony in American feminists' emphasis on equal rights issues is that these issues engender some of the fiercest political battles in the American system. A demand that government equalize opportunities between groups is, as Freeman has pointed out, a demand for redistributive action; government is being asked to redistribute "life chances." Typically, public debate over redistributive policy is formulated in terms of "winners" and "losers," and therefore mobilizes large classes of people for and against the policy.[131] Thus, by concentrating on demands for equal rights, American feminists have probably generated stiffer opposition than they would have encountered by pursuing more narrowly defined program goals.

Women's activists have recognized another important limitation of mass-based women's organizations—America's governmental machinery is not particularly responsive to mass constituencies. A basic characteristic of America's governmental machinery is that it is constructed to be more responsive to small groups of intensely interested and well-organized individuals than to the mass public. The vast political science literature on interest groups and the policy process reports time and time again that the interests of small groups in the American population can be successfully advanced even at the expense of the majority's interests. Public policy is most successfully manipulated by narrowly defined, well-financed interest groups. The advantages enjoyed by such groups have been evident in the phenomenal successes that right-to-life forces and ERA opponents have had in state legislatures around the country. Organized and financed to fight single-issue campaigns, such conservative groups have often lobbied more successfully than multi-issue organizations like NOW, NWPC, and Women's Lobby.

In *The Politics of Women's Liberation*, Jo Freeman acknowledged that the principal contribution of the mass-based women's movement has not been its ability to secure specific pieces of legislation either by promising (and delivering) massive electoral support for sympathetic male officeholders or by getting enough women into policy-making positions to initiate and pass women's programs. Instead, she contended that the women's movement has generated publicity, creating a "climate of expectations," and assuring policy makers already sympathetic to women's issues that there would be a constituency for any women's legislation they might decide to promote.[132] Hence, although Freeman argues that the women's liberation movement has influenced government programs, her analysis departs from the traditional textbook view of government decision making, which sees demands from the grass roots aggregated (by mass movements, parties, or interest groups) and then pressed upon policy makers, who in turn respond with programs according to their own calculations of self-interest (responding favorably when they expect to make political gains or minimize political losses).

Rather than adopting this simple stimulus-response model of policy making, Freeman seems to explain expansions of social policy in terms of elites acting in anticipation of, rather than in response to, women's political mobilization. Political scientists have sometimes argued that disadvantaged groups in a political system need not achieve a high level of organization in order to attract the concern of policy makers. Political elites, according to this theory, may perceive a general need to compete for the support of various subgroups in the population and may therefore introduce benefits and services aimed at those groups. Under such circumstances, even without being specifically pressured to do so, policy makers might introduce programs to benefit women in order to attract or maintain the support of women.

Could we not use this theory to account for women's gains in Sweden and China, where women do not appear to be strongly and independently organized to press demands on policy makers? It is doubtful, for both nations in recent decades have had virtually noncompetitive political systems. Starting in 1932, the Social Democrats exercised control of the national government virtually uninterrupted until 1976. China since 1949 is an even more striking example of a one-party system. According to the theory we have been advancing, elites would feel little compulsion to compete for mass support under conditions of little or no competition. Thus it is difficult to argue that Swedish and Chinese politicians have been responsive to women's interests because they have seen women as a potentially important constituency.

In sum, none of the standard formulas used to interpret the American experience seems to apply to our foreign examples. In neither Sweden nor China have women's programs been introduced as a result of (1) women occupying key policy positions, (2) mass-based women's movements exerting irresistible pressure, or (3) mass movements creating a "climate of expectations" to which policy makers were responding. Rather, the experience with women's programs in China and Sweden leads us to consider another possibility—that policy makers sometimes introduce policy reforms even when they do not see any immediate (or even long-term) political gains or losses resulting from such changes. Policy research increasingly suggests that the behavior of policy makers, both elected and appointed, can often be explained as a response to a set of environmental conditions rather than to specific demands. In his cross-national study of social security policies, Phillips Cutright concludes:

> A government can act without being told what to do. The scholar operating within a democratic context (and especially that of the U.S.) may tend to view government activities as being dependent upon the demands of secondary groups. A major but tentative conclusion that can be drawn from this study of government activity is that it need not await the petition of secondary groups.[133]

Moreover, the policy process is circular. Some particular feature of the political environment calls forth a response from policy makers in the form of a social program. But once implemented, that social program changes the environment into which it has been introduced. Most social policies have both a primary or intended impact and secondary impacts, which are really by-products of the policy. For example, the primary impact of a labor market policy aimed at increasing female employment is presumably that more women get jobs. But a secondary impact may well be that the policy eventually increases women's economic and political status in the society. This observation reflects the prevailing viewpoint of Swedish feminists, who express the opinion that changing a woman's objective circumstances will eventally lead to changing attitudes and outlooks for both women and men. Rather than promote formal legal equality for women and hope that formal equality will ultimately produce increased employment and economic independence for women, Sweden's Social Democratic government in the late 1960s and early 1970s sought directly to promote greater female employment. Increased female employment, they said, would not only give women greater leverage over the resources in their own households but would also contribute to changing attitudes in the family. And studies have shown that children and husbands of employed women display significantly different attitudes about women's status than do families where the woman is not employed.[134]

The Swedes' argument runs directly counter to the view of many American feminists that "in general, drastic changes in the values and attitudes held by a considerable number of women (and men) are necessary to stimulate, implement, and follow up the reactions to liberating legislative or policy changes."[135] We can surmise that Chinese feminists are in agreement with the Swedes on this point. They would probably even express the point more forcefully: Government policy to liberate women from traditional forms of oppression cannot await a massive shift in men's and women's attitudes regarding sex roles. Rather, public intervention creates attitude changes simultaneous with changes in women's objective circumstances. As Mao explained to Andre Malraux, "Of course it is necessary to give them [women] legal equality to begin with. But from there on, everything still remains to be done. . . . The Chinese woman doesn't yet exist . . . but she is beginning to want to exist."[136] Both Swedish and Chinese cases display a complex interaction between policy makers and their constituents in which constituents' demands sometimes influence policy, but policy also influences consituents' attitudes and demands.

If women's movements have not alone been responsible for the initiation and promotion of women's programs, what other important contributors to women's policy can we identify? Chapter 4 discusses the extent to which social policies for women mesh with more general economic and social goals of the governments in question. Chapter 5 suggests that social policy for women is strongly dependent on the view of the family held by policy makers and in the society at large.

4

NATIONAL ECONOMIC POLICY AND WOMEN IN THE LABOR FORCE

We concluded from our examination of women's political movements in chapter 3 that the numerous policies benefiting working women in China and Sweden have not been exclusively, or even primarily, the result of sustained political pressure exerted by women. Neither the efforts of individual women legislators nor the power of women's mass movements can account for the social welfare efforts made by these two governments in the areas of maternity benefits, child care, canteens, and other replacement services.

One alternative explanation would be to see these programs as responses on the part of mostly male policy makers to the needs of women as they began entering the labor force in large numbers. For example, we see in Sweden that the growth of the welfare state, including the social services and benefits for women described in chapter 2, has taken place since the 1930s. That woman's participation in the labor force has also increased dramatically since 1930 might suggest that the social programs came as the government's response to an influx of women into the labor force. We see a similar temporal coincidence in China. That is, increased social services have been emphasized along with rises in women's employment. One dramatic instance is the Great Leap Forward, when party propaganda stressed both women's obligation to engage in productive labor and the need for expanded support services.

Karl Deutsch posited that new or expanded social services and benefits result from the "social mobilization" of new groups in society, which Deutsch defined as "the process in which major clusters of old social, economic, and psychological commitments are eroded or broken, and people become available for new patterns of socialization and behavior."[1] Surely this formulation is an apt description of the entry of women into the industrial labor force in large numbers. According to Deutsch, "social mobilization brings about a change in the quality of politics, by changing the range of human needs that impinge upon the political process. As people are uprooted from their old habits and traditions . . . they need a wide range and large amounts of new government services."[2] Deutsch's formulation suggests the possibility that in Sweden and China, the entry of large numbers of women into the labor force generated a new set of social needs. Once recognized by policy makers, these needs were met with expanded social services.

This interpretation offers us a variation of the strict stimulus-response model we rejected in the last chapter. Rather than viewing these policies as a direct reaction to constituency pressure, it sees them as a response to problems arising in the policy makers' environment. Thus it is an interpretation consistent with Cutright's observation (quoted in chapter 3) that governments can act on their own without awaiting the petitions of pressure groups. Even accepting our conclusion in chapter 3, that policy makers have not been guided by working women's *demands*, we might still hypothesize that policy makers have been responding to the objective *needs* of working women, as they (the policy makers) perceived those needs. But a closer look at our two cases reveals that even this variation on our original interpretation is too simple.

For Sweden, the relationship between the "welfare state" and women's participation in the labor force is complex. Without doubt, the introduction of Sweden's vast social service network has facilitated women's employment. The benefits and services described in chapter 2 make life easier for working women. But it can hardly be argued that the "welfare state" is a response to the needs of working women because most of the Social Democrats' welfare programs were introduced before women entered the labor force in significant numbers. Both the national requirement that employers grant maternity leaves and the national maternity allowance were introduced in the 1930s. The major liberalization of birth control and abortion laws also came in the 1930s. Family allowances and national subsidies for home helps were legislative products of the 1940s. Sweden's expanding day-care program is perhaps the only program surveyed in chapter 2 that was undertaken after Swedish women began joining the labor force in large numbers in the 1960s.

Nor can we agree with Sondra Herman's declaration that "the welfare state, in itself, prevented the 'retreat to the home' which American women experienced in the 1950s."[3] The figures show that the proportion of Swedish women who stayed home as housewives rather than taking outside employment actually *increased* between 1930 and 1950, while the new social programs were being introduced (see table 4–1). The main explanation for this increase seems to be the rising marriage rate in the 1930s and 1940s. Ever since the onset of industrialization, Sweden had experienced extremely low marriage rates, for reasons related to the social dislocations generated by rapid urbanization and industrialization. As Alva Myrdal explains it, "the increase in mobility during the period of industrialization led to an exceedingly unfavorable sex ratio in different locations"[4] and thus produced a drop in the marriage rate. Starting in the 1930s, the marriage rate began to climb, and with it the proportion of homestaying housewives among Swedish females. The high unemployment and somewhat woman-hostile labor market of the great Depression undoubtedly contributed to women's tendency to stay at home. In fact, the major upsurge in married women's employment did not occur until the 1960s, when the government took deliberate steps to pull women out of their homes. We conclude that, in Sweden, the establishment of the welfare state predated the upsurge in women's employment and did not prevent many working women from leaving the labor force in the 1930s and 1940s.

We have even more difficulty interpreting the Chinese government's interest in replacement services as a response to working women's needs. Ideologically, of course, the party has always recognized the link between support services and the requirements of working women. The problem has come in the sphere of practical economic decisions. Because China is such a poor country, social welfare demands far outstrip available resources. In such a situation, questions other than simple need must decide where the money will be spent. In the case of women, party support for increased social services has been less a response to need than to the perceived value of maintaining and increasing the number of working women. When desire for increased female participation in labor has been strong, so has support for increased replacement services. When desire for increased female participation in labor has been weak, the emphasis on replacement services has receded. While less pronounced in urban areas,

TABLE 4-1. Percentage of Swedish Women (age 15 and over) Occupied as Homestaying Housewives 1910–60

1910	17
1920	18
1930	20
1940	25
1950	29
1960	25

Source: Elina Haavio-Mannila, "Convergences Between East and West: Tradition and Modernity in Sex Roles in Sweden, Finland, and the Soviet Union," *Acta Sociologica* 14, no. 1–2 (1971); 118.

this tendency to use replacement services to produce other social changes has clearly shown itself in the countryside.

The following passage illustrates the instrumental attitude the party has often taken toward day care and mess halls, considering them to be "instruments" with which to produce further change:

> Women's participation in the public socialist production is an extremely important means to their complete emancipation. For this reason, the rural women must be taught to enthusiastically join mutual-aid teams, supply and marketing cooperatives and credit cooperatives. Those who still remain unwilling to take part in the agricultural mutual-aid and cooperation movement . . . must be enlightened and assisted to advance. . . . We should properly arrange, in line with the present needs of national construction, the household duty and production work for women and, where possible, gradually build up public welfare work (such as creches) to relieve women of their household duty and to increase the possibility of their participation in social production.[5]

In rural areas, where sex roles have been much more resistant to change than in cities, increases in women's employment have depended primarily on the party's willingness to commit resources—money, personnel, and prestige—to changing the existing values and mobilizing women for work. Replacement services have been part and parcel of the attempt to change social values. The two major drives to establish day-care facilities in the countryside came during collectivization and communization and were accompanied by immense pressure to get women into the fields. The same holds true for mess halls. The failure of mess halls and nurseries to reappear in large numbers in rural areas after the Great Leap Forward can be explained at least in part by their association with forced social change and their consequent unpopularity.[6] Once they were no longer able to promote women's participation in labor, replacement services were given a low priority. In spite of increasing participation by women in agriculture, implying continuing need, creches and mess halls have not been seriously implemented since the Great Leap.

The cities of China present a far more complicated picture for three major reasons. First, many urban women already worked outside the home prior to 1949, particularly in the textile industries. Consequently, the setting up of day-care facilities and other replacement services was to a much greater extent a response to existing need rather than part of a program to pull women out of their homes. Second, unemployment directives throughout most of the 1950s and economic reports throughout most of the 1960s give the impression that fewer jobs existed than women willing to take them. Thus there was no reason to entice more women into employment. Third, as Hilda Scott points out, the cost of operating facilities like day-care centers is much higher in cities than in the countryside, and consequently their use to pry women out of the home would be much less attractive economically.

> It is no accident that the first Soviet creches that caught the imagination of prewar liberationists were in agricultural areas right on the fields, where the mother could take time out several times a day for nursing. Running such a nursery was relatively uncomplicated. Today . . . nurseries must be a part of every community and every new housing project, within easy walking distance. To meet modern child-care standards they need the services of pedagogical, psychological, medical, and dietary experts, cooks and cleaners, as well as a sufficiently large staff of trained nurses who like their work.[7]

Given these qualifications, the following picture emerges in Chinese cities: a minimal level of support for replacement services based on ideological commitment and need at most times, coupled with a much higher level of support during periods in which female employment was being actively promoted as part of a program of forced social change. The first such period was, of course, the Great Leap Forward; the second was the period of the "criticize Lin Piao and Confucius" movement, during which day-care figures were actually discussed again, after a silence of almost 15 years.[8]

By about 1952, the new government's early enthusiasm for redressing the wrongs done to proletarian women was spent. Thereafter, Chinese press reports painted a picture of perpetual skirmishes between two factions: (1) women workers and their representatives; and (2) factory management, including party cadres responsible for production targets. Yang Chih-hua, director of the Women's Department of the All-China Federation of Trade Unions, captured the essence of the struggle in her speech before the Eighth Party Congress in 1956:

> Yang Chih-hua criticized the view that the employment of women workers was not economical and women workers often presented much of a problem for the management. It was true, she said, that pregnant women had to move to light work and special care had to be taken of them, that they enjoyed maternity leave and breaks during work time for nursing, and that nurseries had to be provided. It was intolerable, however, that some people should complain of this. . . .
>
> Childbirth under the socialist system could not be considered solely as a private matter of mothers, she said. . . . In the interest of mothers and children and the whole country, the utmost possible should be spent on the welfare of mother and children of women factory workers.[9]

The view that support services represented an unnecessary financial drain was reported from many parts of the country. The following report from An Tung in Liaoning Province described the shortages of places, the sickness among the children, and the unnecessarily harsh punishments meted out in local nurseries:

> The principal contributing reason to the emergence of these problems is that the leadership and the basic trade unions in certain units do not place suffi-

cient emphasis on this work, on the pretext that they are busily involved in production tasks and do not have time to attend to these matters. Some individuals even mistakenly believe that it is immaterial whether there should be any care for children or not, so they never or very seldom inquire into the conditions of the nurseries.[10]

The struggle here is clearly over resources: how much women employees are worth versus how much it costs to bring them into the labor market. If men and women were thought to be equally responsible for domestic chores and child rearing, the costs of replacement services would have to be considered a necessary expense of hiring employees. As long as women are considered primarily responsible for the care of the young and for meal preparation, however, the cost of replacement services in the eyes of society must be weighed solely against the benefits to be derived from *female* employment. It is not surprising, therefore, to find that the number of day-care facilities in China has fluctuated according to the emphasis social planners have placed on female employment rather than according to families' needs. Table 4–2 shows that the total number of urban day-care facilities increased from 15,700 in 1951, to 26,700 in 1956. During this time, female employment had roughly doubled. During the Great Leap, female employment increased roughly two and one half times, yet day care expanded over four and one half times.[11]

After the Great Leap ended, emphasis once again was placed on cutting the costs of day-care facilities. Although some pleas were heard for greater numbers of replacement services, particularly from women's organizations,[12] in general the literature of the early 1960s placed the responsibility for family-centered chores squarely on the shoulders of the women. The

TABLE 4-2. Urban Child-Care Facilities

Date	*Child-Care Facilities*	*Number of Children*
December 1951	15,700[a]	520,000[a]
December 1956	26,700[b]	1,250,000[b]
March 1960	66,315[c]	—
May 1960	125,000[c]	5,000,000[c]

Sources: [a]C. K. Yang, *Chinese Communist Society*, book 1, *The Chinese Family in the Communist Revolution* (Cambridge, Mass.: MIT Press, 1959), p. 150.

[b]CB 476, October 15, 1957, p. 16; JMJP Peking, October 10–11, 1957.

[c]CNA 332, July 15, 1960, pp. 1–4.

apparent policy of the state was given in an article on Trade Union work in 1961:

> The number of children increases year by year and the number of creches and kindergartens cannot keep pace with the requirements. The creches and kindergartens can only admit those children who have pressing needs for their service.[13]

This policy dominated despite an apparent rise in the percentage of urban women employed in regular jobs (as opposed to street industry) from 18.8 percent in 1959[14] to 25 percent in 1963.[15]

IS WOMEN'S LIBERATION A BY-PRODUCT OF SOCIALISM?

Instead of viewing social service and maternity policies as responses to working women's needs, we would suggest that they can more accurately be seen as reflections of other policy concerns. That is, in introducing them, policy makers have not been singlemindedly concerned with upgrading women's status in society but have been pursuing other policy goals. Women's gains have come about as a secondary impact of other policy concerns to which women's status is closely connected. What policy goals do we have in mind? To answer this question, we must add the ideological dimension to our discussion.

Some of our readers are doubtless already impatient with us for omitting from our discussion so far the important distinctions between socialist and nonsocialist systems. When we compare government policies regarding working women in the United States with those policies in countries like Sweden and China, we expect that many of our readers will respond, "Yes, but those governments are socialist!" American feminists, looking at women's status in both Sweden and China, have sometimes attributed those governments' efforts on behalf of women to the socialist ideologies of their ruling parties.[16] Behind this assumption lies the belief that socialism as an ideology is inherently sympathetic to the plight of women because women constitute an oppressed class.

Several important socialist tracts of the late nineteenth century articulated this connection between socialism and feminism. Both Marx's *Capital* and the *Communist Manifesto* treated the subject of woman's oppression under the capitalist system of production and property ownership. August Bebel's *Woman under Socialism*, published in Germany in 1883, was more widely read than Marx's own writings because it was written in a "simple and earthy" style much more accessible to the mass readership.[17] Bebel portrayed married women workers as the group most victimized by capitalism:

> The married woman is, as working woman, much more "attentive and docile" than her unmarried sister. Thought of her children drives her to the utmost exertion of her powers, in order to earn the needed livelihood; accordingly, she submits to many an imposition that the unmarried woman does not.[18]

He predicted the disappearance of the stultifying private household, to which many middle-class women were confined:

> The trend . . . is not to banish woman back to the house and the hearth, as our "domestic life" fanatics prescribe. . . . On the contrary the whole trend of society is to lead woman out of the narrow sphere of strictly domestic life to a full participation in the public life of the people.[19]

A few years later, Friedrich Engels published his *Origin of the Family, Private Property, and the State,* which provided a detailed historical interpretation of the connections between the production system, property relationships, and woman's subjugation. Engels analyzed family structure as an outgrowth of the production system, evolving in response to changes in the production process from ancient Rome to the nineteenth century. The family therefore contained "in miniature" all the contradictions that characterized the larger society in each historical period. Engels saw the husband's supremacy in marriage as "the simple consequence of his economic supremacy,"[20] and woman's liberation within the family as dependent on her participation in a public production system. The contemporary American socialist Linda Jenness has summarized the convictions of these socialist theorists this way: They believed that "it was impossible for women to be free short of socialism, and that socialism could not succeed without freeing women."[21]

There is little doubt that these early socialist writings influenced the work of many reformers we have labeled "social feminists." Convinced by the socialists' argument that women's disadvantages in the family and in politics stemmed from their inferior position in the economy, social feminists in Europe and America invested their energies in improving women's material lives. They showed particular concern for the suffering of working-class women and set up charities and settlement houses to offer maternal and child care as well as help for single women who were aging, sick, or unemployed. They campaigned for protective labor legislation for women in factories and for progressive social welfare programs.

Our main question, however, is not whether isolated individual reformers were influenced by socialist theories. Clearly, they were. Rather, we are interested in how socialist ideology regarding women's status in the family and economic system has been translated into government policy by ruling socialist parties in Sweden and China. Immediately we are obliged to introduce two cautionary notes. First, experience shows that, regardless of doctrine, socialist leaders are hardly immune from displaying sexist attitudes in their personal and political lives. By Alice Rossi's account, even

Friedrich Engels was guilty of sexism in his dealings with female socialists.[22] Moreover, when circumstances have forced socialist governments to choose between women's liberation and other important program commitments, women's issues have often taken a back seat. We have a literature on the Soviet Union and Eastern Europe which argues that socialist regimes are just as likely to oppress women as are other political systems.[23] The public agenda of a socialist government, like that of any other government, includes a broad range of priorities that, from time to time, come into conflict with one another. As one of those priorities, women's advancement has not always enjoyed a dominant position.

Second, our two examples in themselves suggest the folly of using the category "socialist" to cover all governments dominated by leftist parties. While it may be perfectly possible to distinguish socialist ideology from other ideologies, the categories become considerably more blurred when we move from a discussion of doctrine to a discussion of practice. In practice, although both governing parties invoke the socialist label, there are enormously significant differences in the strategies used by the Swedish Social Democrats and the Chinese Communists. The most dramatic of these differences lie in the relationship between government and the major sectors of the economy. Upon coming to power in 1949, the CCP inherited a substantial public sector from the previous Nationalist government;[24] beginning in 1952, they moved to enlarge the public sector through pressure on private enterprises. By 1956, fully two thirds of all industry in China was government owned and controlled. The remaining industries were mixed public-private ventures so tightly regulated that they were hardly distinguishable from government-owned enterprises.[25] With the collectivization of agriculture and the absorption of these remaining mixed enterprises during the Cultural Revolution, the economy was effectively nationalized. Chinese socialism, then, is based on the virtual elimination of private ownership over the means of production. In Sweden, by contrast, the means of production are overwhelmingly privately owned. True, the Social Democrats did engage in a halfhearted attempt to nationalize natural resources, some industries, credit institutions, and all transportation and communication systems in the years immediately following World War II. There is some evidence that the party was reluctantly persuaded to advocate this nationalization program by the inroads the Communist party was making into their electoral constituency. In any case, the Social Democrats quickly abandoned this drive when it encountered opposition from the bourgeois parties. Currently, the public sector produces only about 15 percent of the total goods and services produced in Sweden.[26] In this fundamental sense, then, Sweden is not really "socialist" at all.

With all these cautionary notes in mind, let us turn to examining the question whether, and in what ways, the "socialist" complexion of the Swedish and Chinese governments has influenced their treatment of working women. As we have suggested, the programs described in chapter 2 should not be seen as the product of any singleminded concern with upgrading women's status in those societies. Rather, they are clearly related to, and shaped by, other policy concerns. Often the pursuit of other policy goals has been responsible for women's gains in the area of supportive services. In the section that follows, we examine five general policy goals often attributed to socialist parties; each of these has been linked (at least by some observers) to women's gains. They are that socialism (1) seeks revolutionary social change, (2) seeks a more egalitarian society, (3) stresses public over private consumption, (4) seeks to promote sexual freedom, and (5) seeks to promote full employment.

Revolutionary Change

According to one theory, the possibilities for women's advancement are greatest during periods of dramatic social change. Major economic and political dislocations such as wars, the ushering in of new production systems, or the installation of a new political regime create new opportunities for disadvantaged groups in the society, including women. Many elements of a revolutionary situation may contribute to women's gains.[27] Revolutionary social change requires that people be resocialized to adopt new expectations for themselves, their communities, and their government. Breaking with the past means breaking with traditional role definitions and social hierarchies. Revolutionary regimes often attach strategic importance to the family because families have the ability to undermine this resocialization by transmitting "old" values to the new generation. Women's pivotal role in the family assures that, as a group, women will be the object of major propaganda campaigns.

In addition to new family roles, political revolutions prescribe new economic roles for both women and men. Changes in the production system, as well as in patterns of property ownership, loosen the grip of those who formerly controlled the economy and therefore open the way for increased influence exercised by those groups formerly at the margins of the economy. No one would argue that social revolution *guarantees* women more economic power, but it may at least increase the probability. In their search for supporters, revolutionary regimes are likely to try to mobilize groups previously outside the political mainstream. To do so, they may have to offer special appeals in the form of benefits and programs. The view that revolutions are likely to benefit women is summed up by Salaff and Merkle:

> The crumbling of the old regime creates a potential for women's liberation which cannot exist in pre-revolutionary society. To the degree that women are oppressed by the same authority that keeps men in their place and maintains traditional government . . ., revolutions that attack this authority will liberate women. Likewise, when the conditions that oppress women can be attributed to exploitative economic structures, then revolutionary efforts to change the economic system will also liberate women.[28]

In the Chinese case, there can be little doubt about the connection between revolution and women's gains. Prior to 1949, women were more or less confined by a rigid Confucian family structure that strictly limited their opportunities. It narrowly defined the woman's status within the family (i.e., to whom she was subordinate and over whom she had power) and limited her appropriate activities. The Communist revolution, which sought to end the patriarchal Confucian family, inevitably faced the question of what women would do once the restraints of the old society had been loosened. The party opted for increased involvement in the community, equality of the sexes, and employment outside the home.

Once having seized power, the Chinese Communists began to pursue change with revolutionary zeal. They altered the system of ownership in China, the system of education, the legal and moral values, the relationship of the individual to the state, and the role of the family. And through these changes the party tried to enhance women's opportunities to reach the goals of equality, community involvement, and gainful employment. In exchange, of course, the party did not hesitate to demand women's loyalty and adherence to party programs. The continued emphasis in Chinese magazine and newspaper articles on the debt that women owe the party for their advancement indicates the policy-makers' underlying perception of women as a "have-not" group that not only deserves upgrading but has been given new opportunities in exchange for political support.

> In the old society, [women] did not have any political status, and their livelihood was not guaranteed. . . . It was the Party which saved them; and it was the Party which helped them stand up. Just as many women said: "The rich people beg the gods for protection. But we rely on the Party and our emancipation." As a result, they have a clear-cut proletarian stand and firm revolutionary will. They love the Party passionately, listen to the words of the Party, and resolutely follow in its footsteps. Where the Party wants them to go, there they go.[29]

Thus, for practical as well as ideological reasons, revolutionary change has greatly benefited Chinese women.

In Sweden the connection between women's advances and revolution is more difficult to establish. Obviously, Sweden has seen no "revolution" comparable to China's political upheaval of 1949. It is nevertheless true that Sweden's economic modernization occurred much more rapidly than that of other Western societies. Between 1880 and 1920, Sweden was transformed from a predominantly agrarian to a predominantly industrial nation. Rapid industrialization was accompanied by urbanization, changes in the population and family structure, and numerous other social changes. Under such circumstances, it is amazing that no major political upheavals did occur: "In virtue of the magnitude of Sweden's 'great leap forward,' [we] might be surprised that the country had escaped simultaneous political disruption."[30] Yet the unmistakable fact is that Sweden's rapid economic growth did not provoke political or social upheaval. Nor can we argue successfully that Sweden's socialist party has actively promoted sudden or dramatic changes in the economy or the society.

Since the rise of the Social Democrats in the 1930s, Swedish politics has presented a model of stability and gradualism. The socialists' economic policies have uncontestably contributed to that stability. At first glance, this statement may sound strange to the reader. After all, the package of economic programs introduced by the Social Democrats in the wake of the 1930s depression is sometimes portrayed as a dramatic policy departure. To accept this view, however, is to confuse the long-range ambitions of some party theorists with the incremental changes undertaken in practice. In the area of social programs, for example, the government's expenditures increased only gradually. The total transfer payments made by the national government to municipalities and counties to administer social services and benefits amounted to only 3 percent of the national income in 1929, 4.9 percent in 1935, and 5.1 percent in 1940.[31] Like many of Roosevelt's New Deal programs, the Social Democrats' economic policy in the 1930s was designed mainly to revive the business climate in order to stimulate production and employment. To an important degree, such a policy promoted stability rather than change, and reinforced the status quo:

> In the thirties, private enterprise found a better climate, and the power groupings were accordingly made more secure . . . the new policies operated in part to reinforce the ascendancy of entrepreneurs and the owners of capital.[32]

One can even make the case that the socialists pursued economic growth so vigorously from the 1930s to the 1970s because they were seeking social stability and harmony rather than upheaval. They worked "to make the national cake grow bigger and bigger, because then everyone can satisfy his demanding stomach with a greater piece of that common cake."[33]

Our comparison suggests that women's advances may be, but are not necessarily, linked to dramatic or "revolutionary" changes in the surrounding economy and society. In China it seems that Mao's determination to break with the past has indeed contributed to women's gains. The progress realized in Sweden since the 1930s has been made under conditions of extreme stability—a stability carefully nurtured by the dominant Social Democratic party.

Egalitarianism

Socialism, in its utopian form, calls for an equality that gives each individual the possibility of developing his or her talents and capabilities to the utmost.[34] Such equality in everyday life rests on the removal of obstacles that unfairly stand in the paths of some, thereby giving others an advantage. Of course, the problem for women, as for all groups in society, lies in the definition of "unfair." Therefore, Socialist egalitarianism does not *necessarily* benefit women. What the Swedish and Chinese evidence indicates is that policies which reduce differences in income, educational opportunity, job descriptions, political influence, and so forth may or may not aid women; they definitely will aid them only if women's specific problems have been taken into account. In other words, in defining "unfair," policy makers must remember the specific circumstances that handicap women.

In China, for example, women in general share the problems of illiteracy and low skills. Although this situation has been recognized as characteristic of women, the problem has been treated in a general way: Skill levels in general are too low and should be upgraded. Ad hoc literacy classes, factory training classes, and experiments to upgrade agricultural methods have all been used to increase workers' abilities. Unfortunately the result has been that women have participated less than men and consequently have increased their abilities less. Why? Because women are already burdened with domestic chores; learning new skills is a luxury for which they have little time.

> The number of married female workers is increasing gradually. The number of their children is rising increasingly. Their household burden is becoming heavier correspondingly. . . . These changes usually affect directly their perseverance in study and their results of study. . . .
>
> [As Chin Mu-erh, a female worker] said: "Study is important. Production work has to be carried out properly. Household affairs must not be neglected. Weighing them together, I have no other choice but to take care of production work and household affairs." In the past ten years, she joined in study in only two academic terms. She is still illiterate.[35]

Women have fewer hours to devote to jobs and less physical strength; both deficiencies are important in an economy that depends heavily on manual labor. If both men and women are judged by how well they meet these standards, women lose. Rather than change the standards to include areas in which women have traditionally excelled, the Chinese have fostered an egalitarianism that inherently discriminates against women:

> The status of women [in China has been] raised by showing that women are equal to men in their ability to perform the same labor. Since physical strength and the amount of manual labor performed [have been] esteemed more than work zeal and performance of tasks that [are] vital but not based on brute strength, women could not compete with men.[36]

The problem of measuring women's performance against standards that favor men has spilled over into advanced training. If those "outstanding" workers who have contributed the most to the production unit are the ones chosen to learn advanced skills, then women will continue to lag behind men. This is the inevitable outcome as long as the performance criteria favor men. The problem is acknowledged in Chinese campaigns to increase the status of working women.

> Last year [1970] . . . the new Commune Party Committee . . . stirred up a new upsurge of the movement "in agriculture, learn from Tachai." At that time, some cadres of the brigades thought that the movement was mainly to mobilize men, while the women did not show any enthusiasm and were of no importance.[37]

> Some people said, "It does not pay to foster female Party members because they cannot play much of a role after they get married."[38]

Obviously, egalitarian programs that seek to generally upgrade the disadvantaged can have differing effects on men and women unless the problems of women are specifically addressed.

Part of the issue of socialist egalitarianism is the extent to which socialist societies have reduced "credentialism," or the reliance on complex occupational classification systems and specialized training and licensing procedures. It is sometimes argued that women are disproportionately without the credentials that would enable them to assume high-income, high-prestige, powerful positions in the economy. Any efforts to break down credentialism by encouraging amateurism, on-the-job training, or by breaking the hold of professionals over access to their professions will help women.

On this point, China and Sweden differ dramatically because China has stressed repeatedly the importance of the "generalist" versus the expert; the party has actively worked to reduce reliance on specialized training and licensing procedures through much of its 30-year history. Despite this conscious policy, roles for unskilled amateurs seem to be confined to those sectors using relatively unsophisticated technologies.[39] The more specialized the job, the more difficult it is to fill with an unskilled worker. Although large-scale recruitment of amateurs, such as occurred during the Great Leap Forward, obviously helps women to obtain a toehold in the economy, progress depends on upgrading skills. For example, although 15,300 women in Sian were mobilized in 1958 to take over commercial positions previously occupied by men, fully 12,000 of them had to be sent to anti-illiteracy and commercial trade schools to gain the necessary skills.[40]

For China's anti-credentialism to be of permanent value to women, the policy would have to be pursued consistently and vigorously over a long period of time. This seems improbable. Although it is always hazardous to venture predictions about China, we must acknowledge that all industrializing nations up to the present have accepted a high level of occupational specialization as the price of economic progress. The emphasis of the post-Mao leadership on higher standards in the classroom, greater respect for expertise, and improvements in individual productivity seems to reflect a conscious rejection of the policy favoring "red" over "expert." But even without such an overt shift in emphasis, China's economy is likely to continue to relegate unskilled "generalists" to the least advanced, least prestigious, least well-paid segments of the economy, where amateurism is easiest to accommodate.

In Sweden the picture is also complex. There, socialist egalitarianism has been chiefly expressed through income leveling. Numerous social programs have a redistributive impact that favors women. Obvious examples are the social services and public assistance benefits, most of which are either universally available or allocated according to a means test. These include family allowances, child-maintenance grants, housing allowances, child-care home helps, and subsidized medical care (including free maternity and child care). To the extent that domestic and child-care responsibilities are shouldered by women, these programs can be viewed as redistributive programs that aid women. As was shown in chapter 2, they constitute a major form of support for female heads of household. Because they are financed from general revenues collected by a steeply progressive income tax,[41] such services and benefits have a clearly redistributive effect.

The "leveling" effect of Swedish social policy is dampened by certain other social benefits, which are tied directly to earning. These are designed to guard an individual against sudden drops in his or her standard of living. Social insurance benefits are paid to compensate the recipient for income lost because of illness, unemployment, and old age; hence the differences in benefits paid to recipients correspond precisely to the differences in the wages they were earning. This program obviously reinforces rather than reduces income gaps. "In real terms, therefore, the vertical equalization wrought by taxes has fallen short of the distributions shown by the official tax tables."[42]

In Sweden, too, egalitarian programs have sometimes unwittingly blocked women's progress rather than advancing it. The 1971 tax reform was passed specifically to remedy one such injustice. Prior to 1971, Sweden's national income tax had treated households as the taxable units. If both wife and husband earned salaries, their earnings were added together, and because of the highly progressive tax schedule, their combined earnings were taxed at a significantly higher rate than their individual incomes would have been taxed. Since 1971, husbands and wives are taxed separately on their earnings (although their nonwage income from capital gains, property, and the like is still added together). In effect, the government was willing to sacrifice the tax system's progressive treatment of households in order to avoid penalizing wives for entering the labor market.

Among the most significant equalization programs is one developed not by the Social Democratic party but by the Landesorganisation (LO), the national federation of trade unions closely aligned with the Social Democrats. As the primary representative of Swedish industrial workers in bargaining over wages, hours, and fringe benefits, the LO has adopted since the 1950s a "wage policy of solidarity."[43] That is, the LO has consciously pursued agreements that would reduce wage gaps between different classes of workers and different individuals practicing similar occupations.

This strategy is distinct from an "equal pay for equal work" formula and has potentially greater short-run benefits for women. Instead of simply seeking uniform wages *within* a job category, it seeks to reduce income gaps *between* job categories. It therefore has the potential to improve the relative wage position of women workers, who are concentrated in low-paid job categories. Needless to say, this "wage policy of solidarity" has been greeted less enthusiastically by those in higher-paid occupations, especially in white-collar jobs. The issue on which the LO is most sharply divided from the white-collar trade-union federation (TCO) is the TCO's continued resistance to this leveling of wages.

On the matter of credentialism, Sweden diverges markedly from the Chinese model. For Sweden is a highly "credentialist" society, in which there is heavy emphasis on specialized education and training, on titles, and on strong professional associations. To a remarkable extent, Swedish employers (including the government) define work roles in specialized terms and recruit employees on the basis of special training. A broad range of social service professions and paraprofessions not only require training but licensing as well. The highest prestige is accorded to occupations that require the most university training; virtually all Swedes, including labor-union activists, see formal education as the main vehicle for upward mobility. So obvious is the value accorded to credentials, especially formal education, that Sweden has been called a "meritocracy of the educated."[44] This degree of specialization is a function of Sweden's advanced industrialization.

Consumerism Under Socialism

American feminists have suggested that part of women's oppression in our society stems from their role as primary household consumers. In a nutshell, this theory asserts that woman's function as consumer makes her the target of media messages, which heavily reinforce her image as a passive sexual object whose primary satisfaction in life derives from consuming products. In the early 1960s Friedan recognized that increasingly sophisticated appliances would make woman's homemaker role obsolete.

As labor-saving devices have gradually reduced the time necessary to complete basic household chores, American women as home managers have increasingly turned to what Galbraith has called the "functions of consumption administration—in arranging maintenance and repair of the house and of the household machinery and of the automobile and other equipment, in procurement and preparation of food, in supervision of the consumption of the young, in organization and management of social enjoyments, in participation in competitive social display." Indeed, as Galbraith points out, it is absolutely necessary, in an expanding economy based on the production of private goods and services, that levels of per capita consumption continually increase. Women, as consumption administrators, play an indispensable role: "Without women to administer it, the possibility of increasing consumption would be sharply circumscribed."[45] This observation that, in our economy, a high level of production requires constantly increasing levels of private consumption has been labeled "the imperative of consumer demand."[46]

The work of Galbraith and other economists who share his criticisms of the market system suggests that socialism offers a remedy for the economic imbalances created by the "imperative of consumer demand." Socialist economic policies tend to counterbalance the production of private consumer goods with the production of public services and goods. In channeling more resources into the public sector, socialism might be seen as an economic strategy that dampens private household consumption, restrains consumerism, and thereby contributes to women's emancipation from the consumer role.

Predictably, the Chinese Communists have campaigned vigorously to restrain household consumption in order to reduce the demand for consumer goods in the economy. This has been done through a number of mechanisms including rationing, enforced savings, high pricing of all nonessentials, and political campaigns. The government response to most shortages of consumer goods is to promote "self-reliance," by which the Chinese mean that the household should do its best to provide for its own needs without further taxing the state economy. For the housewife, such policies result in the substitution of labor for money. Instead of using wages to purchase goods, the housewife furnishes them through work within the family. Campaigns for self-reliance have done little to combat the image of the woman as the housewife and domestic manager. On the contrary, they have been aimed specifically at housewives as the primary buyers of household food and goods:

> The ACDWF must mobilize the laboring housewives of all strata in the cities and countryside to achieve success in economizing grain. . . . They must promote careful planning, improved methods of cooking and regulation of food among housewives, in order that grain is economized while good food is provided.[47]

From 1955 onward, housewives were exhorted to reduce their families' dependence on collectively produced goods and services. As Chang Yun explained at the Third Women's Congress in 1957, "We must take the attitude of mistresses of the country . . . overcome our own difficulties, reduce the burden of the state and lend support to our socialist construction program."[48] In the same year, at the National Conference of Workers' Dependents, Yang Chih-hua, director of the Women's Department of the All-China Federation of Trade Unions, discussed the shortages of housing and nonstaple foods (i.e., nongrains) with the housewives. To provide more housing, she suggested that families collect funds among themselves to buy materials, organize themselves into work crews, and build new housing units themselves. To overcome food shortages, she suggested that the family women grow their own vegetables, keep sheep and hogs, make bean curd, and so on.[49]

In 1962 a shortage of shoes prompted a similar article about women's responsibility to make footwear themselves.

> If more than 500 million peasants in our economy must get their shoes from factories, then how many shoe-making factories would be required? On the other hand, if those who are able to make their shoes do make them, this can reduce the burden of social production, so that the state can concentrate more manpower, funds, and machines to meet the needs of the more essential production departments, in order to speed up socialist construction. It can be seen that to attend to industriousness and economy in the matter of everyday life is certainly not something that has no importance.[50]

Put succinctly, the CCP's efforts to dampen household consumption have been anything but emancipating for Chinese women. The party has called on women to perform even more zealously their traditional role as producers of goods and services for the household.

If China disproves the theory that reducing consumerism necessarily liberates women, then the Swedish case undermines the rest of the hypothesis by showing that governments controlled by socialists do not necessarily discourage private household consumption. Even as they were expanding public services, the Social Democrats have shown a strong commitment to the Keynesian strategy of stimulating consumer demand for private goods in order to avoid recession. In terms of both public and private goods, Sweden in the 1970s is clearly a materialistic, consumption-oriented society. To be sure, the disposable income available to middle-income households is somewhat lower in Sweden than in the United States. Nevertheless, the strong tendency of Swedes to define "life style" and "quality of life" in terms of goods and services consumed is obvious to any foreign observer. The family car, the boat, and the stereo are as avidly sought after and displayed by Swedish families as by American families.

Nevertheless, at present two trends in Sweden operate to divest *women* of the sole responsibility for administering Sweden's expanding consumption. The first is the growing consensus that men and women must share equally in all household tasks including consumer decisions. (The growing emphasis on "symmetrical" roles for women and men is discussed in chapter 5.) The second factor differentiating Sweden from the United States is the Swedes' greater acceptance of collectively provided services. Consider, for example, the extent to which convenient public transportation could relieve middle-class mothers of the chauffering function they have traditionally performed. The Swedish "service flat" is another example of Swedes' greater willingness to consume prepackaged collective services.

Sexual Freedom

The notion that socialism promotes sexual freedom is traceable to Engels' *Origin of the Family, Private Property, and the State*. Believing that the marriage relationship under capitalism reflected the economic dominance of the male, Engels saw marriage as a bad sexual bargain for the female. Whereas husbands enjoyed opportunities for sex outside marriage, their wives' economic dependence and concern for their children's futures forced them to "put up with the habitual infidelity of their husbands."[51] Once the socialist system of production and property ownership had altered the wife's traditional economic dependence on her husband, she would have no reason except "inclination" to stay with him. Rather than predicting the demise of monogamous relationships, Engels foresaw the full realization of the marriage of sentiment, based on mutual love and satisfaction. Such a liaison would no longer be constrained by economic factors or social pressures. In the socialized economy, the sexual relationship would be open and equal, both inside and outside marriage:

> Society looks after all children alike, whether they are legitimate or not. This removes all the anxiety about the "consequences," which today is the most essential social—moral as well as economic—factor that prevents a girl from giving herself completely to the man she loves. Will not that suffice to bring about the gradual growth of unconstrained sexual intercourse and with it a more tolerant public opinion in regard to a maiden's honor and a woman's shame?[52]

This particular theme in Engels' writing was later amplified and made famous (or infamous) by the Bolshevik revolutionary Alexandra Kollantai, who saw the socialist revolution as one that would release women from their traditional status as their husbands' and lovers' property. She advocated spontaneous, egalitarian relationships between the sexes, which should endure only as long as they were mutually satisfying, and she fiercely championed a woman's right to end a liaison at the first sign that it might restrain her personal freedom: "Love must not crush the women's individuality, not bind her wings. If love begins to enslave her, she must make herself free, she must step over all love tragedies, and go her own way."[53] Kollantai's ideas were by no means universally accepted among the Bolsheviks. Lenin had difficulty condoning Kollantai's version of "free love," and by the late 1920s the Soviet Communist party had endorsed a countertrend toward more stable, more conventional marriage forms, which would "prevent the diversion of energy for social reconstruction into sexuality."[54]

In some ways, Sweden seems to have moved far toward Engels' vision of marriage by "inclination." Increased female employment and social welfare benefits have reduced wives' and children's economic dependence on their husbands. Part of the climbing divorce rate undoubtedly reflects the fact that women who once would not have contemplated divorce can now do so with greater security. Swedish society does, as Engels put it, "look after all children alike, whether they are legitimate or not." In the government's allocation of housing and day-care services, female heads of household are even given preference over intact families. "Loyalty marriage," as the Swedes call an agreement to live together without an official marriage, is chosen by an increasing proportion of the adult population (6 percent in 1974, compared with 1 percent in 1968).[55]

Moreover, ample evidence shows that Swedes take a permissive attitude toward premarital sex. Researchers reported in 1969 that 95 percent to 98 percent of married Swedes had premarital sex.[56] Studies done 10 and even 15 years ago showed that about half of Swedish teen-agers experience intercourse by age sixteen, and subsequent research suggests that sexual activity among teen-agers has risen since then. It was the recognition that many Swedish adolescents were sexually active that prompted the national government in 1964 to undertake improvements in public school sex education. In addition to mandatory sex education, the government supplies adolescents with contraceptives, even without their parents' consent. The pragmatism with which many Swedes view this trend is expressed in this observation: "This young generation does openly what our generation did stealthily and with guilt feelings. Surely, their behavior is more healthy."[57]

Even though it might well have been endorsed by Engels, Kollantai, and like-minded socialists, Sweden's sexual permissiveness cannot be attributed to socialist influence. Historians trace its origins back several centuries to Sweden's agrarian culture. Alva Myrdal has described in detail the village ritual of "night courting," a social custom that allowed sexual experimentation among young people within some widely recognized guidelines. Because of Sweden's late industrialization,

> the habit of fairly lax authoritarian inhibitions of the sex life of youth, which stemmed out of the agrarian society, persisted so long that it was paralleled by more modern patterns and thus strengthened before its ultimate decline.[58]

In China, in spite of some experimentation with free love in the Soviet base areas of the early 1930s, socialism has failed to modify significantly the traditional Chinese restraint in sexual matters, which formed an integral part of China's cultural history for many centuries. In fact, it might be said that the traditional Chinese culture has modified China's socialism because the Chinese Communist party has at least twice altered its marriage program to meet criticisms that it was encouraging sexual permissiveness.[60] If sexual restraints remain, however, the reasons for them have changed. In accord with the finest puritanical standards, sexual discipline in post-1949 China has been linked with economic advance and the good of the collective through slogans like "Making love is a mental disease which wastes time and energy."[61] Not surprisingly, "flirtations and affairs are so severely frowned upon by the authorities that infringements of this rule can lead to expulsion [from a university]."[62] To quote one scholar expert in matters of population control,

> In pre-communist China, premarital sexual intercourse was regarded as extremely reprehensible, and chastity held a high place on the list of womanly

> virtues. This is one of the traditions of old China accepted and nurtured by the Communists and the "liberation" of Chinese women does not extend to the endorsement of free love.[63]

For reasons of economic security and family stability, the Chinese revolution has enforced highly disciplined asceticism in the area of sexual relations. Socialism in China has definitely not meant free love.

Full Employment

We come finally to what we see as the single most important policy goal in Sweden and China that contributes to government programs to alleviate women's dual burden. The conscious pursuit of full employment, more than any other single priority of these governments, accounts for the willingness to treat womanpower as a national resource.

Cross-national comparison is often instructive not just for what it tells us about other societies but because it can highlight for us some of the assumptions so fundamental to our own approaches that they escape our notice. In this case, a glance at manpower policy in Sweden and China throws into relief two common assumptions underlying American policy debates on women's programs. One is the assumption that policy makers must choose to recognize either motherhood *or* employment as women's primary role, and draft policy accordingly. Do we want women in the home or on the job? The question reflects the prior assumption that the two roles are mutually exclusive choices, at least for individual women. Outdated as this view is, it still seems to shape our public debate on women's programs. In this respect, the Swedish case is particularly intriguing because it shows the Social Democrats' simultaneous efforts to promote motherhood (and thereby increase the birthrate), and to promote women's employment (and thereby increase productivity). The second assumption is that policy makers should decide whether our government should put people to work *or* continue to provide social services and benefits to unemployed and underemployed families. One often hears this dilemma formulated as a choice between large expenditures on social programs or large expenditures on employment programs. Again, the Swedish and Chinese cases provide interesting contrasts because of both governments' determination to use manpower policy and social policy in mutually reinforcing ways.

China's Full-Employment Policy. Given the magnitude of China's population, hovering around 900 million by 1975, any attempt to realize full employment would require a massive effort, but especially an attempt that includes pulling women out of the home and putting them into the work force. Yet this has been the goal of the CCP ever since it took power in 1949, and particularly since 1957. What the party has recognized is that China, short of investment capital, short of machinery, short of educational institutions and technical skills, and in fact short of almost every ingredient needed for rapid economic growth, has nonetheless one crucial factor of production: its people. Mao's emphasis on "man as the primary factor" has come about not only because of ideological faith but also because of necessity. According to Mao, people armed with the right ideas can accomplish anything. Using their labor, they have generated capital (e.g., using hands, shovels, carrying poles, and baskets to construct dams or irrigation ditches). Because of the stress on primitive accumulation through hard work, women's labor power has been considered valuable. Every new increment of labor brings China closer to full industrialization.

Fluctuations have occurred in the emphasis put on female employment, but the fluctuations have been much more pronounced in the industrial sector than in the agricultural. Moreover, one would be mistaken in assuming that a deemphasis on women's employment also meant a deemphasis on their labor contribution outside the home. The party's almost constant preference for normative rather than remunerative appeals has extended to women. Women are expected and encouraged to provide a great deal of "social labor" for little or no material reward. For instance, the economic crisis of 1961 brought a call to workers' dependents to forget gainful employment as a primary goal and concentrate on helping their neighbors. Models like Liu Hsiu-lan were held up:

> Chao Yu-chen was part of the management personnel of the mess hall, and had more domestic work on hand than she could handle. Liu Hsiu-lan frequently went over to Chao Yu-chen's home to look for work. Sometimes she mended and washed the working suit for Chao Yu-chen's husband, and sometimes she helped to prepare their meals. . . . Knowing that the workers would be too tired to fetch water after work, while she herself had time to spare in the day, she carried water for those households where both husbands and wives were occupied in work. When worker Wang Huan saw Liu Hsiu-lan deliver a load of water to his door, he felt so awkward that he shut the door. Liu Hsiu-lan said: "You are tired after work in the pit and should rest more so that you can produce more coal tomorrow. I just love it if there is anything I can do for people."[64]

Such public spiritedness is promoted through street work, once described as "a day-to-day, minute-to-minute slogging match in which patience, modesty, good temper, ingenuity, and above all infinite ability to persuade with tact, dozens of other women to be educated, to improve, to work together, to organize."[65] Yet street workers get no salary. Moreover, a lack of jobs in the cities has not necessarily meant that women are allowed merely to stay home. There have been recurring campaigns to send unemployed wives to their relatives in rural areas, where, in Mao's view, additional hands can always be used. China can justly be characterized as a society in which laziness is akin to evil.

Although the substitution of labor for the scarcer ingredients of industrialization has not been equally prominent at all times since 1949, it has always been an element in China's industrial program. Granted, there has been an apparent controversy between the more radical Maoists, who emphasized mobilization and amateurism, and the planners, economists, and technocrats, who emphasized technical considerations and requirements, material incentives and professional skills.[66] But the Maoists never completely rejected professionalism, nor did the technocrats ever completely reject mobilization. The problem was rather one of how much weight to give one set of policies versus the other, and that problem depended on the answers given to two different questions: (1) Is it possible to provide the necessary labor through "mobilization," which rests primarily on ideological appeals? and (2) To what extent and how long can increased amounts of labor be substituted for professional expertise and modern machinery?

The first question is important because of the consequences to productivity. A "properly" mobilized worker in Communist China is one who has internalized the objectives, values, and preferences of economic planners and made them his or her own. Such values invariably include working as much as possible for the good of the collective as an end in itself—regardless of the money, power, or prestige gained—or not gained—through the job. As long as such normative appeals to one's conscience succeed, a high level of productivity is ensured. But when they do not succeed, either other incentives, particularly material, must be used, or else "normative" appeals shade off into coercion. Yet, the greater the reliance on coercion, the lower the productivity. The possible consequences of using coercion among women were illustrated during the Great Leap Forward when many women were mobilized, apparently against their will, to run rural creches.

> At present, all of the 1300 and more nurses in [P'an] *hsien* [Kweichow Province] are undergoing training. . . . In view of the fact that certain nurses entertain the erroneous idea that looking after other people's children is a job with no future and that "it is better to grind rice for others than to look after girls for others," the training includes debates among nurses over the question of for whom are the children looked after and what kind of people shall the children be brought up to be. After the debates . . . they have come to take pride in the nursing work. . . .
>
> In accordance with the directive of the CCP P'an *hsien* committee, women's federation cadres at the *hsien* level and in the various people's communes personally take charge of the important points, give examples and help the various kindergartens to consolidate and improve. While on night duty at *T'anchienwan* kindergarten, Chang Lu-hsiu, cadre of the Women's Federation of Red Flag People's Commune, found that children who wet their trousers were not changed and washed on time, and that some individual nurses did not sufficiently feed the children for fear they might have to defecate in the middle of the night.[67]

Too high a level of coercion obviously breeds bad work.

The second question concerns how long, and to what extent, increased amounts of labor can be substituted for professional expertise and modern machinery. Ideological mobilization is by definition a blunt economic instrument; normative appeals at their best make people *want* to do a good job, but they do not provide the expertise to get the job done efficiently. The most zealous peasant cannot build a nuclear bomb, nor can the most zealous 10,000 peasants, without a grounding in atomic theory. And that would take years of education. Moreover, increased mobilization of labor may at some point lead to a much more inefficient use of resources. For example, constant overwork can shorten the life of the laborer by many years or cause accidents to both herself and machinery. In addition, most machines have an optimal productive life under certain ideal conditions. The less ideal the conditions, the lower the amount that the machine produces during its life. Increased use of machinery caused by increased labor input may in the long run reduce the value of that machinery to the economy. This definitely happened during the Great Leap Forward.

> Under heavy pressure to increase output during the Great Leap, all industrial enterprises overused or abused their machinery and equipment. Regular maintenance and checkups were reduced to a minimum in order to gain more time for operation. Some machines were operated at such a high speed as to exceed the technically permissible limit. It was also very common in the transportation system that vehicles were overloaded and kept running with little or no normal maintenance.[68]

The disagreement between the Maoists and the technocrats, then, came not over the question *whether* labor could be substituted for scarcer resources in China. Obviously it could. The question was: Under what circumstances would the substitution be most beneficial? Here the Maoists opted for a broader range of circumstances. The most clearly realizable benefits of increased labor came in economic areas already dependent on labor-intensive methods. Because such production methods necessitated large inputs of labor, further increases were for the most part helpful and not disruptive. These areas included agriculture, handicrafts, and service industries. Massive labor mobilization to increase output in capital-intensive industries, such as steel, was almost exclusively the work of radical Maoists and usually disruptive.

> There is a great deal of evidence to suggest that Mao looked upon economic development as the conquest of a series of obstacles, obstacles that could be stormed and overcome by zeal, dedication, and commitment. It seems that Mao and many of his colleagues in the top leadership did not fully appreciate the fact that the kinds of qualities required to engineer a civil war and a communist revolution may be quite different from those needed to manage a growing economic, social, and political system, particularly one that is trying to launch a country on the path to modernization, to an industrial and technical revolution.[69]

Because increased labor has been seen both as a way of generating capital and a way of substituting for scarcer resources, women in China have been encouraged to join the work force. In spite of severe population pressure, the low technical level among women, and their chief responsibility for household chores, women's labor has still been considered valuable. Nevertheless, since that value lies mostly in labor-intensive industries that advance accumulation through hard work, Chinese women find themselves concentrated in labor-intensive, low-pay jobs or labor-intensive, no-pay jobs. A broader commitment to women, giving them the chance for greater equality in the economy, is hindered primarily because Chinese women have not been viewed as the principal carriers of economic development; men have. Women's labor has been seen as supplementary, less important because women still shoulder the majority of tasks in the home.[70] Consequently, the same vision that has seen a place for women in the work force has also hindered their advancement.

Nonetheless, the CCP's commitment to draw women into work beneficial to the collective has been useful for women. It has provided entry-level jobs for a group that was systematically excluded from labor outside the home and given them new skills on which to build. Moreover, the fact of women working has been instrumental in promoting an increase in social welfare programs and replacement facilities. From 1949 on, the spirit of developing social services to "aid production" epitomized the programs bringing help to Chinese working women. "The basic starting point of the transformation of domestic labor into social labor is that it stems from production and serves production."[71] The important emphasis here on production rather than on women should not be missed. Social services were started to "aid production," not to "aid women." The translation of this spirit into practical programs has meant that replacement services were created not so much because working women needed them but because the state needed working women. The difference between these two attitudes was of great significance to women. The first would have implied maximum support, to ease the dual burden on working women, while the second implied minimal support, only what was absolutely necessary for economic growth. The second attitude encouraged women to rely on themselves, and left no doubt that in the area of economics, as in other areas, women's interests were subordinate to overall goals.

This concern with maximizing economic growth resulted in a shifting of social services out of the area of economic planning and into the area of social organization. If women could organize themselves and provide day care through mutual assistance, the cost of bringing them into the work force would be greatly reduced. While state- and factory-financed day-care centers and mess halls have definitely been developed, they have never come close to meeting the needs of Chinese working women. Moreover, collective mutual aid was far more in line with the communist spirit of self-sacrifice and primitive accumulation through hard work. Women in the home were viewed as "a vast reserve of working power . . . [to be] tapped and used in the struggle to build a mighty socialist country."[72] Ideally, the party has thought that if a few housewives took over child care and meal preparation for others, many women would be freed to work outside the home. Because the jobs these newly freed women would be performing were likely to be low-paid, the support services had to be low-cost. Otherwise, too much money would be siphoned off from paychecks, discouraging the less ideologically oriented housewives from leaving home. Consequently, the work women have done in the area of social services has also tended to be labor-intensive and low-paid.

Although a very poor country, China has attempted an economic transformation by turning possible liabilities into assets. A huge population that could retard industrialization through growing consumption has been one of these potential liabilities, and therefore people have been pleaded with, cajoled, and threatened to produce more than they consume. Women and men have been reached, and have been provided with rewards for their success. Where day-care facilities have proved vital to enlisting women's support outside the home, they have been expanded and improved. And because of this, they have often become a carrot to encourage proper social behavior and reinforce the values of hard work and sacrifice for the collective. Joyce Kallgren, in her study on social welfare and China's industrial workers, came to this conclusion:

> Facilities such as nurseries and creches are designed to facilitate the employment of women and still maintain acceptable standards of labor discipline. In these cases, need is shared by all claimants, so the administrator must make his decision either on a graded scale of need among a group of needy individuals, or on the basis of alternate and important political values. The latter is what generally happens. Thus, the welfare program acquires a conservative quality; it is used to reinforce societal values which the regime considers central.[73]

Under these conditions, there are obvious advantages to becoming an "advanced worker" with proper "redness."

Not unexpectedly, the Chinese Communist values of hard work and commitment to the collective permeate the system of social services as they do the rest of the economy. They are reflected in the way social services are set up and the way they are dispensed. There can be no question that work and replacement services reinforce each other in the People's Republic. Community mess halls and day-care facilities are designed to help women combine hard work and mothering.

Sweden's Full-Employment Policy. As in the United States, Swedish concern with manpower questions was stimulated when the business cycle brought periods of high unemployment. Prior to the Great Depression of the 1930s, manpower policy in Sweden had been limited to work relief programs for the unemployed. Swedish policy makers in the early twentieth century subscribed to the classical economists' view that it was better, morally and economically, to provide jobs for the unemployed than to provide a "handout." Traditionally the work relief programs were operated by local governments, although the national government added its own work relief in 1916.

The rising tide of Social Democratic strength in the 1920s brought with it increased debate over the issue of unemployment policies. Strongly influenced by the ideas of the British economist John Maynard Keynes, the Social Democratic leadership that took over the national government in 1932 was firmly committed to fighting the effects of the depression by expanding government spending rather than by retrenchment. They were convinced that the high unemployment Sweden was suffering resulted from insufficient demand for the goods and services produced by Swedish industry. Their response was to use government expenditures to increase the purchasing power of the citizenry. Sweden's Social Democrats were among the earliest and staunchest converts to the strategy of deficit spending to buy full employment.

The government developed two main strategies in the 1930s to achieve full employment. The first was to increase government benefits, including unemployment insurance, to stabilize or even increase the purchasing power of Swedish households. Thus, beginning in the 1930s, social welfare benefits began to be seen not simply as relief payments to the poor but as instruments of economic policy. Second, the national government undertook a large-scale public works program.[74] National subsidies created jobs in house building, road construction, and related sectors of the economy. Unlike traditional forms of work relief, which had always paid below-market wages, these jobs were paid at market levels.

No special concern with upgrading women's employment status was expressed in the manpower debates of the 1930s. The new jobs created by the public works program were mainly in construction, not a sector likely to hire women. In practice, therefore, women did not benefit directly from much of the government's countercyclical spending.[75] The Social Democratic coalition did at least succeed in defeating a bill introduced into the Riksdag to deny married women the right to paid employment outside the home. Needless to say, the bill had been introduced by traditionalists who viewed married women as a reserve labor pool, to be called out of their homes in an expanding job market but returned to the hearth when jobs became scarce.

The traditionalists' view that government should recognize and encourage women to accept their primary role as wives and mothers was reinforced by the population scare that swept Sweden in the 1930s. Demographers have long recognized that birthrates invariably decline as a society becomes more urban and industrialized. In the years between World War I and World War II, this "natural decline" combined with unstable economic conditions to produce a significant downturn in fertility rates in most of the industrialized West. Among the European governments that enacted policies to encourage higher birthrates, France and Germany exemplified the tendency for pronatal policies to stress women's primary obligation to home, husband, and children. Sweden was the forerunner in developing a pronatalist social policy based on increasing society's, rather than the wife's, commitment to the family.

Swedish interest in the population question can be attributed almost solely to the influence of a single book: Alva and Gunnar Myrdals' *Kris i befölkningsfrågan* (*Crisis in the Population Question*), published in 1934. In this work the Myrdals traced the dramatic decline in Swedish fertility rates from 29 births per 1000 population in 1890 to fewer than 14 births per 1000 in 1934. The fertility rate of the 1930s was significantly below that needed simply to reproduce Sweden's population. Thus the Myrdals forecast a continuous, rapid, and cumulative population decline which, they argued, would create serious economic and social problems. While the authors themselves worried about a wide range of resultant problems, from a decline in the quality of family life to a submersion of Swedish national culture into the cultures of more populous European nations, the arguments with the greatest impact on policy makers were undoubtedly those that forecast the domestic economic effects of population stagnation. First, a declining birthrate changed the age structure of the population, gradually reducing the proportion of economically active persons in relation to the elderly. Second, a shrinking population depressed the economy by reducing investment and consumption.

The Myrdals' views had been publicly expressed before 1934 but given little notice by political and economic elites. In fact, a segment of the Swedish press had laughingly described large families as "Myrdal's families," and even coined the verb "to Myrdal," meaning "to procreate." More seriously, the Social Democratic press had attacked the Myrdals' position as nationalistic and even militaristic, and some Conservatives claimed that the two sociologists' call for government intervention in family life was a backdoor effort to promote socialism. But by 1935 public concern over the population problem had become widespread enough to prompt the government to appoint a Royal Commission on the Population Problem whose first step was to carry out a special mid-decennial census specifically designed to gather data on population and fertility. The 1936 census showed the following reproduction rates for all marriages contracted between 1900 and 1936:

completely childless:	38%
one child:	30%
two children:	17%
three children:	8%
four or more children:	7%

Given an already low marriage rate in Sweden, these reproduction rates meant that only one fifth of all adult women had any child, and only one twelfth had three or more children.[76]

The 1936 census also showed a fascinating new trend in the relationship of family size to income. Western demographers had identified in virtually all industrializing societies a clear negative correlation between family size and family income. That is, larger families tended to have lower incomes than did smaller families. Scholars debated the cause of this connection; some believed that family income determines family size, with more affluent couples more readily choosing to assure themselves a comfortable life style by limiting their families. Others asserted that the fact of having many children depresses a family's earning power by reducing the breadwinner's mobility, his ability to take risks, and his resistance against wage pressure, and by increasing the likelihood that his spouse will stay at home to care for children. Whatever the explanations, it was demonstrably the case in Europe that children became scarce as family prosperity increased. But the detailed income and family information collected by the 1936 census showed that a shift was taking place in Sweden: Family size showed for the first time a positive correlation with family income.[77] That is, it now appeared that low-income families were having fewer children, whereas more prosperous families were producing slightly more children.

The Myrdals and similarly minded reformers used this information as a "crowbar for social reform."[78] Warning that bearing children would increasingly be seen by young couples as an economic liability, they argued that public policy must encourage families to have children without lowering their standard of living. The influence of the Myrdals' arguments on Swedish policy is unmistakable. All the various programs designed to lighten the economic and psychological burdens of childbirth, child care, and homemaking were intended to stimulate the birthrate. This motivation also accounts in large part for the Swedes' tendency to offer flat universal subsidies in maternity and family allowances rather than means-tested benefits; the objective has been not so much to subsidize the needy families as to encourage growth in *all* families.

It is difficult to evaluate the impact of these policies on Sweden's birthrate. Over the long term they have not increased the birthrate, which has hovered around 14 per 1000 population ever since the 1930s. At least one cross-national study has shown that the adoption and expansion of family allowances in various countries has had virtually no impact on fertility.[79] Nevertheless, one could reasonably argue that the pronatalist programs were successful in at least preventing the further erosion of the birthrate, which was predicted by the Myrdals in 1934.

Moreover, Swedish social policy has not succeeded in erasing the economic differences between families with few children and families with many children. Table 4–3 shows that even in the 1970s large families are more likely to need public assistance than are smaller families. One can safely say, however, that without Sweden's social benefits and services, the plight of large families would be considerably worse than it now is.

From a feminist viewpoint, these programs were successful in another important respect. They were implemented without the accompanying *Kinder, Küche, Kirche* ideology that characterized the pronatalist policies of

TABLE 4-3. Number of Relief Cases per 1000 Married Couples, by Size of Family, 1946–1972

	Number of Children in Family	
Year	*1–2*	*3 or more*
1946	27	83
1948	25	67
1951	26	70
1953	27	71
1960	24	77
1969	38	90
1972	60	105

Source: Walter Korpi, "Poverty, Social Assistance, and Social Policy in Sweden, 1945 – 1972," in *Readings in the Swedish Class Structure,* ed. Richard Scase (New York: Pergamon, 1976), p. 138.

other European governments in the 1930s. Sweden's family policy did not seek to confine women to the motherhood role. For one thing, the fertility decline suffered since the 1890s did not appear to hinge on women's employment outside the home; as late as 1930, only 5 percent of married women worked outside the home.[80] Evidently, keeping women at home did not guarantee that they would produce children. Second, as Alva Myrdal argued, it was precisely the families with children that carried extra financial burdens; they should therefore have the maximum opportunity to increase their earning power: "For economic reasons, the married women must have the opportunity to contribute to the support of the family."[81] Thus, despite a strongly pronatalist social policy in the 1930s, the consensus on full employment forged by the Social Democrats entailed a commitment to "employment for everyone seeking a job," including married women.

Building on this policy consensus, policy makers began in the post–World War II era to refine the instruments for fighting unemployment. In 1948 the government created the National Labor Market Board to coordinate its manpower policy. In addition to administering emergency public works projects and national unemployment insurance, the NLMB also developed a set of programs designed to fight "structural unemployment" (i.e., unemployment that results because workers have inadequate or outdated skills or live in the wrong place to fill available jobs). These programs include vocational guidance and counseling; job training or retraining for those whose skills are no longer in demand; job placement centers to direct unemployed workers to other regions where jobs are more plentiful; and moving allowances to encourage unemployed workers to relocate their families. Unlike the more general countercyclical spending programs introduced in the 1930s, here was a set of programs that could be used to assist specific subgroups within the population—like women.

The first big step to highlight the special problems involved in guaranteeing full employment to women was taken in 1951 when the Joint Female Labor Council was established. This was not a government body but an investigative and advisory council formed by the largest trade-union organization in the country, the LO, and the Swedish Employers' Confederation (SAF). Its officially stated purpose was "to watch official measures affecting women in the labor market, in order to influence these measures to be formed in a way that suits the women and the labor market. It should also in every field watch and encourage measures facilitating women's entry into the labor market." With publications, conferences, exhibitions, and lobbying, the Joint Female Labor Council agitated for better conditions for part-time workers, more and better child care, nonsexist vocational counseling in public schools, and many other concerns of working women.

The council's influence is reflected in the labor market training programs introduced by the National Labor Market Board. Job training is available to any Swede who is unemployed or in danger of becoming unemployed and who cannot find a job with his or her current qualifications. The training is entirely publicly funded; even training courses offered by private firms are subsidized by the national government. In addition to the course work, trainees may receive tax-free stipends, rent subsidies, dependents' allowances, and compensation for travel, clothing, and books. From a small percentage of women participating in the late 1950s, the vocational training program has served increasing numbers of women (see table 4-4). Of the women enrolled, many are housewives entering the labor force for the first time (e.g., housewives comprised 12 percent of the female trainees in 1973).[82] However, women continue to be disproportionately represented in the courses training for traditionally female occupations (e.g., health care or clerical work), despite deliberate efforts to lure women into courses outside the traditional range.

TABLE 4-4. Women and Men Participating in Sweden's Labor Market Training, 1960–73

Year	*Number of trainees*	*Percentage of Women*
1960	6,600	14
1965	16,000	36
1970	34,000	46
1973	110,000	50
1976	96,000	53

Sources: National Labor Market Board, *Labor Market Statistics,* No. 5B 1972, "Labour Market Training 1970"; and National Labor Market Board, "Equality in the Labour Market: Statistics," September 1977.

Sweden's low birthrate in the twentieth century has contributed to a more or less constant labor shortage in the post–World War II period, as a diminishing proportion of the population has fallen into the 16–64 age group and school-age children and the elderly have constituted an increasing share of the population. The labor demand was met in the 1950s and early 1960s mostly by importing foreign workers (the largest numbers from Finland). But in the mid-1960s policy makers began to recognize housewives as their largest untapped labor supply, more easily integrated into the labor force than immigrant workers.

In large measure, this realization on the part of policy makers stemmed from the growing labor demand in the service sector, where women had always supplied a large proportion of the manpower. The expansion of health and social welfare services delivered by local governments, as well as the burgeoning retail and service industries in the private sector, led policy makers to conclude that their wisest course of action would be to pull housewives into the work force. Among the government policies designed to do that, the most dramatic was the 1971 reform of the income tax laws (described earlier in this chapter). This tax reform to lower the tax burden on working couples was consciously conceived as an economic incentive to get more married women into the labor market. In 1972 the national government appointed a special advisory panel to the prime minister, known as the Advisory Council on Equality between Men and Women, whose function was to recommend other policies to increase women's participation in the economy. A 1973 report by the Advisory Council recommended several new programs subsequently introduced by the Social Democratic government. They included

1. Hiring a cadre of government employment counselors specifically to assist women in obtaining jobs
2. Stipulating that the government subsidies extended to business firms for locating in regions of high unemployment would go only to firms that agreed to employ roughly equal proportions of women and men
3. Paying subsidies to private employers who introduced women into occupations traditionally dominated by men

The Joint Female Labor Council stopped meeting in 1975 when its union and employer membership saw that women's issues were being successfully promoted by the prime minister's Advisory Council. This latter body is one of the many Social Democratic policy instruments retained by the coalition government that took office in 1976. Reorganized and fortified (at the urging of the Liberal party), the new Parliamentary Committee on Equality continues to work on policies to integrate women into the labor force.

One bit of evidence suggesting that the government is likely to continue the present policy is government planners' projections regarding Sweden's labor force requirements in the coming decades. The Long-Term Planning

Committee reported in 1970 that Sweden would see only a weak growth in manpower resources in the 1970–1990 period, with married women supplying the most significant increases (see table 4–5).

TABLE 4-5. Sweden's Employment Forecast for Persons 15 to 64 Years Old, 1975–90

Year	*Percent of Employment*		
	Men	*Women*	*Married Women*
1975	84	60	60
1980	84	62	64
1985	83	64	67
1990	83	66	70

Source: Statens Offentliga Utredningar 1971, No. 8, "Manpower Resources 1965–1990," Appendix 1.

Other evidence that women, even married women, are in Sweden's work force to stay is their performance in the last two major recessions. During Sweden's 1971 business slump, when unemployment temporarily rose, women's employment continued its steady growth. More recently, in the 1975 recession that hit all the major industrial nations of the West, female employment increased even as male employment was declining. The major explanation for this pattern is in the sex segregation that still characterized Sweden's labor market in the mid-1970s. Women workers are disproportionately concentrated in the service sectors; they participate less in manufacturing and construction, the two sectors hardest hit in the recession. Women were therefore insulated from the high unemployment that accompanied the recession in those fields.[83]

Our brief review of Sweden's full-employment policy has shown that social spending has been closely related to manpower policies. Expansion of social services creates jobs, as well as accommodates the needs of working families. We can say that expanding social services and full-employment policies have been mutually reinforcing in Sweden's postwar economy.

American Contrasts. A parallel examination of American economic policy reveals that the level of social spending is related to labor market policies in the United States as well, although with different outcomes. The years immediately following World War II augured well for proponents of full employment. The American experience with mass unemployment in the Great Depression had been even more devastating than Sweden's. And, like Swedish leaders, American policy makers expressed anxiety over the possibility of a depression following World War II. Not surprisingly in this atmosphere, Congress was moved to consider legislation to avert another such national disaster. The full-employment bill introduced in 1945 proposed that the national government guarantee to every American "the right to useful, renumerative, regular, and full-time employment." The original legislation clearly acknowledged the federal government's responsibility to sustain economic conditions in the country consistent with full employment. But, the bill finally passed by Congress, the Employment Act of 1946, was significantly different from the original draft. Conservative opposition diluted its original force to such an extent that it did no more than state congressional support for employment; it provided no real means for attaining that desirable goal. Some observers even regarded its passage as a *defeat* for full employment:

> The defeat of the Full Employment Bill was a strong and purposeful affirmative action against a national commitment to full employment, and against the idea of government action either by fiscal spending actions or job creation to guarantee jobs for all. It represented a defeat for the whole body of thought and political influence that had pursued the idea of strong government intervention, planning, and economic action to eliminate unemployment.[84]

Even a more measured interpretation of these events would have to conclude that the American version of Keynesian economics has stressed the health and welfare of business first and workers second. The contrasts with Swedish policy are instructive.

First, American administrations, even under the Democrats, have been willing to tolerate unemployment levels close to three times those of Sweden. Annual unemployment rates for the 1960s and '70s are presented in table 4–6. One can easily see the implications for working women of this higher tolerance for unemployment in the United States. In an economy with high unemployment, creating a large labor reserve, many workers are faced with a situation of lower job security, weakened bargaining power (even if they are unionized), and lower incomes than they would enjoy in a tighter labor market. It is hardly surprising that workers in such circumstances express resentment and resistance to women's participation in the labor force. Two sociologists have in fact described the American labor market as one in which jobs are "rationed," according to a set of widely accepted beliefs regarding "who in society has the greatest obligation to work and the greatest right to a job."[85] In this job-rationing system, married women, especially those with young children, rank very low. They are perceived and even perceive themselves as having less claim to jobs than other workers. Hence, when unemployment is high, the job-rationing system operates against working wives and mothers.[86]

Second the United States does not have an active manpower policy comparable to Sweden's. The United States has dealt with unemployment for the most part as a matter of insufficient demand, placing much less emphasis on the problems of structural unemployment that arise because people have no skills, have obsolete skills, or live where they cannot get to available jobs. The 1946 Employment Act was supposed to assure jobs for

TABLE 4-6. Percentage of Labor Force Unemployed, United States and Sweden, 1961–77

	United States			Sweden		
	Total	*Women*	*Men*	*Total*	*Women*	*Men*
1961	6.7	7.2	6.4	1.5	1.8	1.4
1963	5.7	6.5	5.2	1.7	2.3	1.4
1965	4.5	5.5	4.0	1.2	1.8	.8
1967	3.8	5.2	3.1	2.1	2.3	2.0
1969	3.5	4.7	2.8	1.9	2.0	1.8
1971	5.9	6.9	5.3	2.5	2.8	2.4
1973	4.9	6.0	4.1	2.5	2.8	2.2
1975	8.5	9.3	7.8	1.6	2.0	1.3
1977	7.0	8.2	6.2	1.9[a]	2.3[a]	1.6[a]

[a]*First quarter of 1977*

Sources: National Labor Market Board, "Equality in the Labor Market: Statistics," September 1977; and U.S. Department of Labor, Employment and Training Administration, "Employment and Training Report of the President," 1978, p. 210.

all workers. But the history of postwar economic policy shows a gradual shift in policy makers' interpretation of that mandate, away from assuring jobs and toward assuring that aggregate demand would be sufficient to expand markets. The federal government has made liberal use of fiscal and monetary stimulus policies to give incentives for production and consumption, hoping that new jobs would be created in the process. To this extent, American policy parallels Sweden's conversion to Keynesian strategies for managing aggregate demand.

But, unlike Sweden, the United States has not supplemented such macroeconomic policies with a manpower policy to match up unemployed individuals with available jobs. The federal government has subsidized a certain number of training programs, but these have been aimed at small segments of the work force; individual programs have focused on disadvantaged urban youth, the disabled, veterans, Indians, ex-prisoners, and so forth. These programs have almost invariably been connected to income-maintenance programs. That is, they have been forms of workfare designed to reduce welfare costs.[87]

In 1973, the federal government embarked, perhaps unintentionally, on what was to become the largest public employment program since the 1930s depression. The Comprehensive Employment and Training Act (CETA) was initiated in much the same spirit as previous federal manpower programs. It consolidated various training programs into a single system of bloc grants to local governments and provided money for states and localities to hire the unemployed in public-service jobs. Although it began as a small-scale effort targeted on the severely disadvantaged, CETA has expanded to become an indispensable source of revenue for many big cities. And in the process, the program's emphasis has shifted away from structural unemployment among the unskilled and disadvantaged and toward minimizing the impact of the recession on local governments.

Instead of paying for new services for communities, CETA has been used largely to pay salaries of existing employees who were previously paid with local funds. Thus, instead of helping the disadvantaged (women, minorities, and the educationally deprived), CETA pays wages to people who are "mostly white, male, and educated."[88] And instead of preparing participants for the private sector, CETA programs transfer their participants mostly to public-sector jobs. One analysis of the program concluded that "in practice, CETA has become a disguised form of federal subsidy for local government operations."[89] Thus, while the CETA program offers an American parallel to Swedish stimulus policies, it does not effectively address the problem of structural unemployment. The United States has no universal programs comparable to Sweden's national system of jobs counseling, training, retraining, and placement, much less any benefits comparable to the Swedish moving allowance that helps unemployed workers relocate their families.

In a book published in 1963, Swedish economist Gunnar Myrdal alerted Americans to the fact that their national unemployment problem was increasingly becoming a structural problem. It reflected, he wrote, "an unfortunate backwardness in American economic policy"[90] that policy makers seemed to believe a simple stimulation of production would guarantee increased employment and decreased unemployment. Without public investment in training, retraining, and relocation of workers, a scarcity of workers located in the right place and possessing the right skills would dampen any rise in production, no matter how much "pump priming" was done.[91] Myrdal lamented the "tendency to nearsightedness of American economists, politicians, and the whole articulate public,"[92] arguing that the longer this structural unemployment problem were left untreated, the more difficult it would be to cure. Ultimately, however, Myrdal was forced to acknowledge that the kind of unemployment cure he was proposing, which was being pursued successfully in Sweden, was based on a government mechanism for long-range planning to forecast needs and make investment choices. A system of national manpower planning that would begin matching workers' skills and preferences with existing jobs would require a level of central coordination and planning that has so far proved politically unacceptable in the United States.

Finally, in contrast to Sweden, the American government has chosen at critical junctures in the postwar period to stimulate business expansion by tax cuts rather than by increased spending. Andrew Martin has convincingly argued that American business elites supported President Kennedy's landmark decision to undertake deficit spending in the early 1960s precisely because Kennedy's version of Keynesian economics relied on tax cuts instead of increased expenditures; this choice, made several times over since 1960, has had a crucial effect on social welfare spending: "The basic choice between an expenditure increase or tax cut approach is a choice for or against enlarging the public sector share of GNP."[93] Whereas Sweden has chosen to fight unemployment by enlarging social spending, the United States has not. The results are displayed in table 4–7, which portrays the faster rise of social spending in Sweden compared with the United States. When this information is combined with that in table 4–6, we see the contrasting patterns of Swedish and American policy since World War II. The Swedish pattern combines close to full employment, high inflation, and heavy increases in social spending to bolster purchasing power, create service jobs, and serve the needs of working parents for a wide array of social services. The American pattern combines a higher tolerance for unemployment with lower inflation rates and lower social spending.

The American case can also be usefully compared with China's on the question of how government policy affects the balance between labor-intensive and capital-intensive economic activity. Chinese economic policy has clearly stressed the importance of substituting labor for other factors of production, notably capital and fuel energy; this substitution has been a cornerstone of China's full-employment policy. American national policy operates in several important ways to encourage "relatively more capital-intensive techniques and probably less employment of low-wage workers than would exist in their absence."[94] One example is federal tax policy, which gives businesses investment tax credits in order to encourage them to buy new machines or equipment; the tax code also encourages investors to buy state and local bonds by exempting their interest earnings from taxation. Thus, it encourages states and localities to spend money on capital projects, which can be funded through these tax-exempt bonds, whereas social services must be financed from general revenues. These tax laws are just two examples of numerous federal policies that actually dampen employment by promoting capital-intensive economic activities.

TABLE 4-7. Nonmilitary Public-Sector Spending as a Percent of GNP, Sweden and the United States

Year	*Sweden*	*United States*
1950	21.5	17.8
1960	28.4	21.5
1970	38.9	23.7

Source: Andrew Martin, *The Politics of Economic Policy in the U.S.* Paper in Comparative Politics 01-040, (Beverly Hills: Sage Professional, 1973), p. 15.

There are those who argue that the American economy will become more labor-intensive in the next few decades, not because of public policies encouraging such a shift, but because of some inevitable trends in the economy:

1. The rising costs of energy may lead to the increasing substitution of labor for capital.
2. The increasing scarcity of capital in our "debt economy" may lead to more labor-intensive enterprises.
3. The continued shift from an industrial-based economy to a services base will create more jobs.
4. Environmentalist pressures will exacerbate the shift away from capital-intensive "dirty" industries toward "cleaner" labor-intensive health, education, and other services.

Such trends might even generate a labor shortage similar to Sweden's: "It is possible that within the next 30 years, employment rates may be reported negatively, reflecting a situation in which demands for workers exceeds supply."[95] In such a scenario, unemployment caused by insufficient demand would no longer pose a large problem. Structural unemployment might well persist, offering a continuing rationale for government manpower programs. In an economy where labor began to be substituted for machines and fuel, it is conceivable that a large portion of the labor force would face the employment problem now faced by many educated women: overqualification for their jobs.

THE PRICE TAG FOR SOCIAL PROGRAMS

Even if the American Congress were to achieve consensus on a full-employment policy that included jobs for all married women who want to work (an improbable prospect, at least in the foreseeable future), how would Congress and the states finance the increased social services that would be needed by working women? A glance at our other two cases suggests that, in both countries, support services to working women are financed in ways that would probably be unacceptable to many Americans, even women workers themselves.

To support their welfare system, Swedes pay taxes that are high even by Western European standards. The burden carried by Swedish taxpayers is not only considerably higher than that carried by Americans but it has grown at an increasingly rapid rate since the 1950s (see table 4–8). This steep increase is evident when we observe that taxation absorbed over half the new wealth produced in Sweden in the late 1960s, whereas in the United States taxes absorbed less than a third of new wealth in the comparable period.[96]

TABLE 4-8. American and Swedish Tax Revenues as a Percentage of GNP, 1955–71

	United States	Sweden
Mid-1950s	25.4	29.1
Early 1960s	26.7	33.8
Late 1960s	27.4	39.6
Early 1970s	27.8	41.8
Increase, 1955–71	2.4	12.7

Sources: A. J. Heidenheimer, H. Heclo, and C. Adams, *Comparative Public Policy* (New York: St. Martin's, 1975), p. 228; and R. Musgrave, *Fiscal Systems* (New Haven: Yale University Press, 1969), p. 140.

Most forms of "social insurance" in Sweden are financed by payroll taxes that require contributions from both the employer and the employee. These contributions pay for the various benefits distributed according to income level including sick leaves, maternity leaves (now called "parental leaves" and available to both sexes), leaves granted to care for sick children, unemployment, disability. Compared with many other forms of taxation, these payroll taxes excite less resistance from taxpayers, probably for two reasons: (1) the worker sees his or her employer contributing a share, usually equivalent to the worker's (although it is reasonable to assume that the cost of the employer's share is ultimately borne by the worker through lower wages than would otherwise be paid); and (2) the worker perceives the tax as a personal insurance premium that assures his or her eligibility for benefits.[97] Although the Swedish government collects substantial revenues from these payroll taxes, it actually relies no more heavily on them than U.S. governments do (see table 4–9).

TABLE 4-9. Revenue from Various Taxes as Percentage of Total National, State, and Local Tax Revenues, 1971

	United States	Sweden
Personal income tax	35	46
Corporate income tax	13	4
Payroll taxes on employees	9	7
Payroll taxes on employers	10	12
Sales, excise, customs taxes	19	28
Property tax	12	—
Other	2	3

Source: Heidenheimer *et al.*, *Comparative Public Policy*, p. 232.

As the table shows, there are significant differences in the revenue sources tapped by the two governments to finance public programs. Sweden's government relies much more on the personal income tax and less on corporate taxes than do American public authorities. Sweden derives a much larger share of its revenues from sales taxes, with particularly heavy excise taxes on tobacco, alcoholic beverages, automobiles, and gasoline. In shifting more toward the sales tax in the past decade, Sweden is following a trend in Western Europe. Although the sales tax is generally viewed as a regressive tax, taking a larger share of the income of poorer households, its one important advantage is that it is collected in small amounts on individual purchases and therefore meets less taxpayer opposition than other forms of taxation. Table 4–9 also indicates that there are virtually no property taxes levied in Sweden, even at the local level. Since the late 1920s, local governments have relied almost exclusively on local income taxes and national government subsidies as their revenue sources. This particular Swedish-American contrast is of considerable importance for the delivery of social services to working women. In America the provision of many social services by local governments (e.g., maternity and family-planning clinics, child care, and home helps) relies heavily on the property tax as the major source of local revenues. Widely recognized to be a regressive tax levied on a constantly shrinking urban tax base, the property tax has encountered steadily more vociferous opposition from local taxpayers in the 1960s and 1970s. The financial squeeze on American local governments is one reason why the efforts of national policy makers to get local governments to assume more social service responsibilities have been less than successful.

Sweden's heavy tax burden is most dramatically visible in the steep personal income taxes paid by all wage earners. The income tax pays for universal benefits and services not geared to income; these include such cash grants as family allowances, housing allowances, and old-age pensions to housewives, and services like health care and child care. Table 4–10 displays the tax paid by some low- and middle-income families in the two systems. Although the lower-income families pay considerably smaller tax bills in Sweden than in the United States, the rates accelerate rapidly above $6000. At $23,000, a Swedish family is already paying over half its income for national income taxes; local taxes and social insurance contributions push the total even higher.

Throughout the 1960s, it appeared that Swedish taxpayers were willing to pay the price for the expanding services provided by the Social Democratic government. But in the 1970s we see signs that the tax rate may be pushing the outer limits of taxpayer tolerance. The 1973 election, in which the Social Democrats suffered losses, was widely interpreted as an expression of dissatisfaction with rising taxes; having barely maintained control, the Social Democrats introduced moderate tax reductions after the 1973 election. Taxes surfaced again as a major issue in the 1976 election, especially after the celebrated case of a woman author, Astrid Lindgren, was

TABLE 4-10. National Income Tax Burden for One-Earner Families in Sweden and the United States, 1976

	Sweden		United States	
Taxable Income	*Tax Paid*	*Percent*	*Tax Paid*	*Percent*
$ 3,000	—	—	$ 454	15
3,400	$ 236	7	522	15
4,500	565	13	720	16
6,800	1,322	19	1,157	17
11,300	3,714	33	2,101	19
22,600	11,552	51	5,209	23

Sources: U.S. Internal Revenue Service, "1976 Federal Income Tax Forms, Tax Rate Schedules"; and "Taxes in Sweden," Swedish Institute, March 1976.

publicized. Because of a quirk in Swedish tax law regarding self-employed persons, Lindgren's tax bill amounted to 102 percent of her annual income. Acknowledging that Lindgren's case was something of a fluke, the antitax forces nevertheless made political mileage from it. The three main opposition parties campaigned vigorously against higher taxes, and their surprise victory over the Social Democrats in September 1976 can be attributed, at least in part, to this issue.

China's social services have been financed much less systematically than Sweden's, and certainly Americans would find some of the methods used even less acceptable than Sweden's tax burden. Because day care is by far the most universal service, we will focus on it here. As might be guessed from the great stress on "making do" and self-reliance, the physical facilities housing kindergartens and nurseries in China vary greatly. Visitors to China in 1973 described newly constructed buildings, converted residential apartments, stores, and the house of a former well-to-do merchant now serving as day-care centers. Most of these kindergartens, they said, were begun in the late 1950s,[98] and this would coincide with newspaper accounts which suggest that many people at the time vacated housing to provide room for preschoolers. Equipment has been variously described in the press as being donated by the parents, bought with contributions from neighborhood residents, financed by a factory, or provided by the local branch of the National Women's Federation. Clearly given this mosaic, it is difficult to pin down consistent patterns of financing. The few patterns that can be isolated are discussed here.

First, it seems universally true that parents pay for a part of their children's preschool care. Exactly how much this care costs, and what percentage they pay, varies greatly. In 1961 Edgar Snow noted a 40 percent difference in the cost of a neighborhood nursery in Chengchow and the best nurseries in Peking,[99] and Ruth Sidel noted a similar difference in 1972.[100]

Differences are caused not only because of regional variation but because of the type of care provided: Twenty-four-hour care is obviously more expensive than less prolonged care. In addition, differences are caused by the extent to which the nursery or kindergarten is subsidized.

Nurseries and kindergartens attached to factories, government offices, schools, and mining enterprises are generally subsidized by the unit concerned. This kind of day-care has been available to only a minority of children. In 1957, for example, although 1.25 million urban preschool children were being cared for collectively,[101] fully 1 million of these children were in creches established by street committees and workers' family associations, not in day-care facilities attached to production units.[102] Although some of these creches had connections with local factories, not all of them did. Relations seemed to have been closest when all the residents living in the area were employed at the same plant.

Lastly, we come to the pattern of social mobilization, which has been used extensively to organize day care in both rural and urban areas. Because replacement services have been created chiefly to "serve production," a problem has resulted for women: The value of their labor to China's economy has been weighed against the costs of replacement services. If the costs run too high, then obviously it is not economically worthwhile for women to work, and the problem has been exacerbated because women are concentrated in labor-intensive industries with a low rate of productivity per worker. The difficulty of establishing day-care centers and mess halls from the profits of street industries during the Great Leap Forward is only one example of the plight of marginally productive, labor-intensive industries. To solve the problem of reducing the economic costs of women's employment, the party has relied to a large extent on social control. It has been argued that an efficiently organized system of social control can give greater flexibility to economic planning,[103] and this certainly has been the case with women. Women have been encouraged to work but have been told to reduce the costs of their employment through organization. In particular, the Women's Department of the All-China Federation of Trade Unions, the National Women's Federation, and the street committees have been given the responsibility to organize extra creches, promote mutual aid and volunteer work, talk obstinate grandmothers into baby-sitting for their grandchildren, convince husbands to pitch in, and educate women on more efficient methods of housekeeping.

The possibilities for abuse in such a system, which will be obvious to any American, have periodically occurred, particularly during the Great Leap.

> When a commune intended to run a school, a nursery or a home for the aged, the Party committee at the upper level always compulsively took away the houses and furniture of the peasants under the principle that "all obey the collective body." This resulted in the phenomenon that "what is in my possession belongs to the commune and what the commune has still belongs to the commune" . . . [and] made the peasants think that it was all the same whether they worked hard or not and it was better to rest than work.[104]

That abuses have occurred is less astounding than the success the Chinese have had in using such methods, particularly in urban areas. The accounts of all recent visitors to the People's Republic leave no doubt that many urban creches formed in the late 1950s have been built up into a regularized system of day care that provides a clean, healthy, and loving environment for children to grow in. It is highly debatable whether the Chinese could have come even this far without such heavy reliance on social mobilization.

USING SOCIAL POLICY TO PROMOTE ECONOMIC DEVELOPMENT

Admittedly, the necessity for increases in taxation would present a serious obstacle to introducing large-scale support services for working women in the United States. Yet another obstacle lies in the attitudes prevailing among U.S. policy makers regarding the legitimate functions of social policy. A great deal of the difference between American policy and that of both China and Sweden lies in the "instrumental" approach applied by both those governments in using social services and benefits to pursue economic development.

The Chinese case is the more striking example of this willingness to shape social policy so as to mesh with, and even to speed, the government's production goals. The Communist party has focused its attention on support services for women because changing women's role in the family and enlarging women's participation in "productive labor" are consonant with the party's economic goals. The proof of that statement is that during those periods when increased female employment was not perceived as contributing to economic targets, government concern about providing support services dwindled. In Sweden, too, the national government has demonstrated this willingness to use social policy to advance the regime's economic goals. Sweden's government has introduced numerous benefits and services to stimulate the birthrate (largely, we have argued, for economic reasons), and increase women's labor force participation in times of labor demand.

American policy makers have a different approach to providing social services and benefits. As the work of Larry Hirschhorn demonstrates, social services in the United States are reactive; they serve a "mop up" function rather than being used as instruments to shape the economy.[105] American health and welfare programs aim at relieving the worst distress suffered by the marginal members of society—the poor, the unskilled, and the disabled. But they do little to help move their clients from the margins of society back to the mainstream. "Instead, they appear as permanent 'holding grounds' or reservations in which human talent and faculties are permitted to stagnate."[106] Our social welfare bureaucracy is charged by policy makers with the minimum maintenance function of sustaining the economic marginals in a stagnant state. Hirschhorn refers to the welfare bureaucracy as "an army of domestic pacification," whose job is "to insure some minimal degree of social cohesion and social peace."[107] The consequence of relegating social policy to this mop-up function is "that the productive potential and capacities of the economy itself are repressed, with that repression best expressed in the underutilization of human beings."[108]

In contrast, Hirschhorn envisions a "developmental" role for social policy in which social services help individuals to adapt to the demands of a changing economy. Although Hirschhorn's work does not give specific attention to women workers as a clientele group, it is obvious that the provision of social services to support working women would be the kind of "developmental" use of social policy he advocates. Support services can be used not only to upgrade women's skills but also to enable families to adjust to the absence of a full-time homemaker-childminder. Even health care can be viewed as serving a developmental function, to the extent that it upgrades the human factor of production.[109] Our survey of American social welfare programs in chapter 2 suggested that Hirschhorn's developmental view of social services is not widely shared by policy makers. Public services in family planning, child care, home help, and job training have been virtually limited to the poor; they have served a mop-up function, sustaining those women who could not afford to purchase services on the private market.

The view that social policy should bolster economic development at one time exerted considerable influence over American policy makers. The Progressive social reformers at the turn of the century popularized the view that social services ought to function so as to integrate the individual into the nation's economy. Strongly influencing both the settlement house movement and the infant social work profession, these Progressives thought that through work the individual derived both his or her self-esteem and value to the community. Hence the aim of social policy should be to support the family unit in providing a stable environment for the jobholder, and to organize community resources so that productive households would have access to all the necessities of life.[110] In short, social policy should be designed to help integrate individuals into the industrial order.

The Progressives' long-term influence on public policy was no greater than was the long-term influence of social feminists (many of whom were themselves Progressives) on American feminism (see chapter 3). Instead of integrating social policy with the long-term requirements of economic development, the prevailing American approach is to see benefits and services as short-term emergency relief measures. This remains the case despite Hirschhorn's observation that, in the current postindustrial economy, we need more than ever a social service system that will help individuals move and adapt to economic shifts without becoming unproductive.

Hirschhorn offers two main explanations why American governments are not using social policy developmentally. One is the so-called crisis of work, defined as a breakdown in the legitimacy our society accords to work, and a related breakdown in social consensus on work roles.[111] It was clear to Progressive reformers what values and skills an individual had to possess in order to be successfully integrated into the industrial order; it is no longer clear in the postindustrial order. Work is viewed as less necessary, work roles are more fluid, and work has less legitimacy as the key to an individual's place in society. Social programs

> can no longer reproduce a certain repertoire of behaviors, nor socialize men and women for a certain set of roles, because the contextual settings that gave such roles and repertoires a coherence have themselves dissolved.[112]

The other explanation Hirschhorn offers is the obsession of American policy makers with Keynesian solutions to economic problems. Here, Hirschhorn echoes Gunnar Myrdal's criticisms of American economic policy, described earlier in this chapter. Hirschhorn agrees with Myrdal that the devotion to Keynesian strategies leads American economic policy to stress short-run actions to smooth out the uneven flow of private investment and consumption. This emphasis on stimulating demand takes the structure of the economy as a given; it is not a policy which contributes to structural change. "It should be clear, however, that service reorganization requires a much more activist intervention, a much more dynamic politics."[113] We arrive once again at the question raised by Myrdal's prescriptions for the United States: Is such "activist intervention" possible in the American setting, given our long-standing aversion to any measure that smacks of social or economic planning?

To supplement Hirschhorn's view, we would offer a further explanation of the unwillingness of American policy makers to use social policy developmentally, at least as regards support for women's participation in the work force. To the extent that social policy were to help women expand and upgrade their work roles, it would at the same time generate tension and change in women's family roles. Social services that enabled women workers to better control their fertility and to shed even a part of their child-minding and housekeeping duties, would have the potential to change women's function in the family. To understand America's lag in providing those services, we must examine American political culture, asking how the American view of the relationship between government and family differs from the views prevailing in Sweden and China. This we propose to do in chapter 5.

5

THE FAMILY IN POLITICAL CULTURE

THE BALANCE BETWEEN FAMILY PRIVACY AND GOVERNMENT INTERVENTION

United States

An American political scientist, analyzing the relationship between family structure and politics, recently wrote that "the right to privacy is the *sine qua non* of modern family life. . . . We usually assume that . . . unless parents and children can transact their business free from public sanction, the whole foundation of family relations will be undercut."[1] His observation expresses a fundamental value embedded in American political culture, a value that strongly influences public policy affecting women's rights and roles.

Belief in the sanctity of the family and its necessary insulation from government is a relatively modern idea. Historians of the family in Western civilization tell us there was a time when all politics was family politics; the family as an extended kinship system was the single most important political institution in society. In medieval Europe, the state was little more than a collection of families. Within the boundaries of families, property was allocated, punishments were imposed for breaches of the family code, and support services were provided for dependent members of the family. As commerce expanded and geographical mobility increased, extended kinship systems gradually broke down into smaller household units, each headed by a patriarch. Scholarly opinions diverge somewhat on the causes of this breakdown, but most historians agree that one important trigger was the desire on the part of commercially successful family members to free their fortunes from control by the extended family. Beginning in the sixteenth century, the family gradually shed its role as the most important social institution and became increasingly subject to civic and religious tutelage.

The subjugation of the family to civil law and religion was short-lived. Less than a century later, European philosophers began to articulate a new conception of the family that saw marriage as independent of clan and church, and subject only to minimal interference from the state. Prominent European liberals, particularly Locke and later Rousseau, promoted the view that a family was the result of a private contract entered into by a man and a woman. They acknowledged that the state maintained some interest in families but only to the extent that families produced the nation's citizens and soldiers. As long as a family was performing that duty responsibly, the state need have no interest in the internal workings of the family. Locke elaborated the notion (astonishing for the late seventeenth century) that as marriage constituted a private contract, the parties should be able to negotiate some of the terms of their relationship. Rather than accepting traditional role definitions, Locke argued, husband and wife could agree on their rights and mutual obligations by contract. Moreover, Locke asserted that marriages ought to be as easily dissolvable as any private contract. According to Locke's view, the family served three basic functions: procreation, education, and inheritance. Once these functions had been dispensed, the state had no fundamental interest in keeping the family intact if the partners wished to dissolve it.[2] Locke's writings did not stimulate a rash of marriage contracts (such as we see in the 1970s). Nevertheless, his view of marriage as a private contract seriously called into question the government's right to intervene in family matters in order to define the partners' roles and obligations.

It would be difficult to overstate the influence of Locke's ideas on American political culture. Locke's writings so strongly affected the framers of the Declaration of Independence that they occasionally used his phrasing in the document. In the century after Locke's death (in 1704), his philosophy was nowhere more widely popularized than in the United States; its influence was much more rapid and more thoroughgoing in a society unrestrained by the cultural and legal traditions that bound European societies.[3] For example, the liberalization of divorce he advocated proceeded much more rapidly in the New World than in the Old. Under a British law dating from the late 1600s, it was possible to dissolve marriage in England only through a lengthy and expensive proceeding, leading to a parliamentary decree. As a result, divorces were exceedingly rare. This system survived in England until 1858, when the courts were finally permitted to grant divorces on grounds of adultery. In contrast, as early as 1787 a New York law was introduced permitting divorce on grounds of adultery. This measure was seen as a "liberal victory, as it substituted a legal right to divorce for the vagaries of discretionary divorce by the legislature, which seems to have been exercised rarely, if at all."[4]

Locke's defense of the marriage contract against public encroachment was closely related to his defense of private property against public encroachment. In the preindustrial era, the family was the main owner of private property, especially land:

> Most historians of the family agree that in the pre-industrial era the family can be understood best in terms of its control over property as a productive resource. Most major characteristics of the family during this period spring from its role in the system by which productive property was controlled and passed on from generation to generation.[5]

The sole purpose of government, in Locke's view, was to protect its citizens' lives and their liberty (which Locke defined as property rights). The equation of liberty with property rights was not new with Locke; it had been clearly articulated a century earlier by Jean Bodin: "True popular liberty consists of nothing else, but in the enjoyment of our private goods securely. . . . "[6] Bodin had anticipated Locke in seeing the nation as a collection of families whose properties were made secure by the power of the state, which Bodin characterized as "the lawful government of many families."[7] The American Revolution translated these ideas, in their purest form, into law. In American law the family acquired its inviolability because it was the property-holding unit. To encroach on a family's property was to encroach on its liberty.

In the twentieth century we may well question whether the family any longer functions as the property-holding unit. Not all families are property owners, nor is all property family owned. Nevertheless, the corollary of this assumption—that the family must be tirelessly protected against government encroachment—remains among the strongest of American values. Its pervasive influence on policy making has been observed time and time again. The Sheppard-Towner Act of 1921, as the first major piece of national social welfare legislation, drew strong criticism on precisely these grounds. Providing instruction for new mothers on the care and feeding of their infants had strong political appeal. It seemed to be an undeniably humane use of public funds. But its opponents called it "federal midwifery" and "official meddling between mother and baby which would mean the abolition of the family."[8]

This belief in the sanctity of the family has even been shared by many American feminists. In arguing against public provision of child-care facilities in the 1920s, feminist Suzanne LaFollette declared:

> Perhaps the best argument against such a system is that it would not work. If experience teaches anything, it is that what the community undertakes to do is usually done badly. . . . There is no relation more intimately personal than that of parents to the children they have brought into the world; and there is therefore no relationship in which the community should be slower to interfere.[9]

The power of the idea is evident right up to the 1970s. In his 1972 essay on "Family Values and Public Policy," Alvin Schorr cited the individualistic tradition that one's family life is a "private venture for personal satisfaction" and the liberal ideology of limited government as primary explanations for America's lack of any coherent family policy.[10] A recent, widely publicized report of the Carnegie Council on Children described this constellation of values as "the myth of the self-sufficient family," which assumes "that families are free-standing, independent, and autonomous units, relatively free from social pressures."[11] Disputing this myth, the Carnegie Council report argued that families are buffeted by broad social and economic forces beyond their control. Yet the myth has contributed to our government's failure to formulate public policy to help families:

> This myth tells us that those who need help are ultimately inadequate. And it tells us that for a family to need help—or at least to admit it publicly—is to confess failure. Similarly, to give help, however generously, is to acknowledge the inadequacy of the recipients and indirectly to condemn them, to stigmatize them, and even to weaken what impulse they have toward self-sufficiency.[12]

In the United States, even the strongest advocates of public services to families defend the family's privacy as a primary value. Democrat Walter Mondale, who as a senator chaired a subcommittee on children and youth, sponsored numerous family-assistance programs and advocated dramatically expanded federal support for day care, is one of the most active proponents of national funding for family services. Nevertheless, Mondale recently offered this warning to overzealous reformers:

> Above all, we are proceeding with caution. Families involve the most personal and intimate relationships between human beings, and government must be sensitive to that fact. We can't afford any national crusades to "save the family." We don't need or want any new bureaucracies intruding on the privacy of family life.[13]

As important as the views of social scientists and elected politicians are those of the American judiciary, which continues to uphold the family's right to privacy. After examining recent court decisions involving the government's role in protecting children within their families, Mary Jo Bane detects a movement to restrict even further the permissible forms of state intervention; she sees a "faintly discernible tendency in the law to limit the role of the state as protector of children and to re-emphasize the role of parents."[14]

The most important exceptions to this general policy of nonintervention in family life have occurred in government's dealings with the poor. As we saw in chapter 2, the American government's limited efforts to provide family-planning services, day care, and home helps have been targeted almost exclusively at the poverty population. One result of this focus on the poor has been constant criticism of the American welfare system for denying to recipient families the right to privacy enjoyed by other American families.

For instance, the juvenile court system in most American states is empowered to remove children from a family when the court can determine that the children have been abandoned or wilfully neglected by their parents. Most petitions reviewed by the courts in such cases are filed by field workers from welfare agencies, against welfare families.

> Thus, cases of neglect that come to the attention of the courts most often arise in poor, urban, minority families. This has led some to question whether there is, in fact, more child neglect in poor families or whether the system is simply discriminating against the poor.[15]

Critics have scored the welfare system precisely because it denies to poor people the right to defend their homes against invasion by government, a right cherished by the middle class. The most publicized of such invasions have been the surprise visits by welfare case workers to determine whether families receiving AFDC were illegally harboring a man in the house. These so-called midnight raids were only the most dramatic home visits required under the operating rules of most states' public assistance programs. Although the man-in-the-house rule was struck down by the Supreme Court in 1968, the responsibilities of case workers still take them periodically into the homes of their clients. In fact, the home visit constitutes the heart of welfare administration because it is the means by which the case worker provides a wide variety of services to recipient families. Nonetheless, the home visit has been under constant attack from welfare rights advocates, who have won some of their skirmishes. In 1969, a federal court reviewed a case of a welfare recipient who refused to consent to a home visit by a case worker, and the court ruled in the recipient's favor. It declared the home visit to be an unreasonable act of search because it was also used to redetermine eligibility.[16] Thus Bane's observation about the trend in American law toward strengthening family privacy seems to have at least some applicability even to poor families, who have traditionally enjoyed the least privacy.

Sweden

If we turn from the United States to explore the relationship of government to families in Sweden, we observe an intriguing paradox. On the one hand, some Swedish laws, especially those regarding the marriage contract and divorce, seem to be the embodiment of individualist liberalism; these laws leave the decisions to marry and to dissolve a marriage entirely in the hands of the couple, minimizing the government's interference. On the other hand, foreign observers of Sweden have on occasion expressed indignation and surprise at the readiness of government agencies to intervene in other aspects of family life. Roland Huntford, in the *New Totalitarians*, decried the broad authority of local child-welfare boards to intervene when they judge that children are being improperly treated; such authority, in Huntford's estimation, constitutes a "gross violation of the integrity of the citizen."[17] Yet even in denouncing such state paternalism Huntford was forced to admit that "native disapproval of this state of affairs is rare in the extreme."[18] The tension in Sweden's policy arises because liberalism, while undeniably strong in Sweden, is tempered by the prevailing view of the family's main function in society. Forty years of Social Democratic dominance have shaped national policies vis-à-vis the family. Sweden's tax law has discouraged accumulation of family wealth by heavy taxation and strict inheritance laws. The individual is bound more closely to the community as a whole than in America; the family less often mediates between the individual and society. The state, rather than the family, provides a welfare cushion, medical care, old-age insurance, child care, and so forth. Hence the family disposes of relatively fewer resources to meet its own needs. Instead of viewing the family as a property-holding unit, and by extension as the controller of important material resources, Swedish law has given more emphasis to the family's role as caretaker for the next generation.

The historical background of Swedish family law reads surprisingly like the Anglo-American experience. In the early modern period, laws and customs governing family affairs were religiously based. According to the Ecclesiastical Ordinance of 1572, Sweden's clergy was specifically charged with overseeing the marital lives of parishioners. As early as 1686, however, civil authorities began taking some responsibility for adjudicating family conflicts. The Church Law of 1686 provided that persistently "quarrelsome couples" who could not be successfully reconciled by the clergy could be turned over to secular courts for punishment. The same law turned over to secular courts the main responsibility for investigating the eligibility of individuals applying for divorce on grounds of adultery or desertion.[19] At about the same time the Swedish national government began to grant divorce by special governmental dispensation, the equivalent of the English parliamentary decree. As in England, this special dispensation was granted only in rare cases.

As liberal ideas gained acceptance in Sweden in the nineteenth century, laws regarding marriage and divorce changed. Swedish liberalism was strongly influenced by French intellectual and political currents, especially after the importation in 1810 of a constitutional monarch from France to replace the absolutist monarch who had been deposed in a bloodless coup. This new monarch, Jean-Baptiste Bernadotte, was imbued with the reform tradition of the French Revolution. One of his first priorities was to change family law in Sweden through the Royal Edict of 1810, based upon the idea that

> marriage, as a moral union, is founded upon the mutual respect of the spouses, so that, once that mutual respect has vanished, the marriage has ceased to exist in their sentiments and in their conscience, even though there may still exist the appearance of the tie that had once been established.[20]

From that edict grew the notion, shared with the Anglo-American liberal tradition, that the marriage contract is a private agreement whose terms should be of interest to the state only under unusual circumstances. Swedish divorce law illustrates this presumption. Since 1921, divorces have been easily obtained in Sweden; under the 1921 Marriage Law, courts could grant divorces on various grounds other than adultery, including incompatibility, known in Swedish law as "profound and lasting discord." Even if only one partner desired a divorce, it was usually granted after a legal separation of at least one year. The 1973 Family Law Reform rendered divorce even easier, permitting immediate no-fault divorce with no stated grounds required, as long as both busband and wife agree to dissolve the marriage and there are no children under sixteen.

Since the roots of Swedish noninterference are to be found in this view of marriage as a "moral union" rather than a property-holding unit, Swedish family policy has followed a different course from that in America in its treatment of unmarried couples living together and raising families. In this matter Swedish and American public policies have diverged considerably in recent decades. Social historians tell us that, in preindustrial societies, the bans on cohabitation by unmarried couples and on illegitimacy arose mainly out of concern to protect family property against the claims that might be pressed by illegitimate offspring. A body of law was created in Europe to discourage illegitimacy, and much of that law has survived to the twentieth century. One of the problems with such law is that it often ends up penalizing the offspring of unmarried parents as much as it penalizes the parents. Examples of such penalties are found in the welfare regulations enacted by some American states that have periodically tried to deny AFDC payments to indigent children because their mother bore an illegitimate child while receiving public assistance. The welfare reform program inaugurated by the town of Newburgh, New York, in 1961, flatly prohibited assistance to any unwed mother who bore additional children. The widespread public sympathy for this penalty against illegitimacy was reflected in a Gallup poll; it uncovered majority support for the Newburgh reform. The *Saturday Evening Post* editorialized that a community should have "some defense against bankruptcy by bastardy."[21]

Other examples of legal disabilities suffered by "bastards" (the legal term for illegitimate offspring) are the inheritance laws of many states, which bar illegitimate children from inheriting from a father who dies without leaving a will. The last decade has seen numerous challenges to such inheritance laws; many challenges have been argued on the grounds that the laws deny equal protection to illegitimate children. To date, the U.S. Supreme Court's rulings on the issue are fuzzy. In 1971 the Supreme Court upheld a Louisiana inheritance law that limited a bastard's right to inherit from a father (*Labine* v. *Vincent*).[22] Yet, in April 1977 the Court struck down an Illinois statute that similarly denied such inheritance rights (*Trimble* v. *Gordon*).[23] Students of the Court may be forgiven for displaying some confusion in the matter; even the dissenting justices in the 1977 decision charged that the two decisions were in clear conflict with one another.[24]

Although the trend in American law is muddy on this issue, the trend in Sweden is readily apparent. The incidence of voluntary cohabitation by unmarried couples is rising in Sweden, from 1 percent of the adult population in 1968 to about 6 percent in 1974.[25] Responding to this trend, the Swedish government has moved to give unmarried households the same rights and benefits as those in which partners are married when those rights may affect the welfare of minor children. Unmarried couples enjoy equal treatment in regard to low-interest government loans for setting up housekeeping, free prenatal care for expectant mothers, maternity allowances, and annual family allowances for illegitimate children.[26] Furthermore, since 1970, the children of unmarried parents enjoy full paternal inheritance rights.

These government policies square with Swedish public opinion. A 1969 report on an opinion poll commissioned by the national government showed that 99 percent of the population feels that all children, whether born of married or unmarried parents, should enjoy equal rights. And 98 percent of the sample felt that the community ought to treat unwed mothers exactly as it treats married mothers.[27] Partially in response to this current in public opinion, the government appointed in 1969 a committee to consider reforms in Swedish family law. In charging this committee, the minister of justice remarked:

> In my opinion a new law ought to be neutral as far as possible in relation to different forms of cohabitation and different ethical beliefs. Marriage has and should have a central place in family law, but efforts should be made to ensure that legislation in this field does not contain any provisions which create unnecessary difficulties or disadvantages for those who have children and settle down without getting married.[28]

The 1973 Family Law Reform, based largely on this committee's work, did move in the direction urged by the minister of justice, by introducing uniform practices in awarding child custody when parents separate, regardless of whether the parents are married or not. Prior to 1973, children of unwed parents were invariably awarded to the mother unless the mother was explicitly declared unfit. As of 1974, the custody issue—both in connection with divorce and when unmarried parents move apart—is to be determined exclusively with reference to the child's welfare. The 1973 reform caps a trend in Swedish family law that has increasingly equated free cohabitation with marriage. This trend divests the marriage contract of special legal status and relegates it to the status of a voluntary agreement between private parties.

The voluntary agreement is nevertheless always vulnerable to government intervention when the welfare of minor children is at stake. Here, the government firmly takes the position that the community's concern for the children's welfare overrides the family's right to privacy. The parent-child relationship, regarded by many Americans as a relationship to be even more closely guarded against government invasion than that of husband and wife, is considered a legitimate subject of government interest in Sweden. The outlook that sees danger in giving parents sole responsibility for their children's welfare is an old theme in Swedish social policy. The belief that the community shares an interest in the family as the caretaker of the nation's next generation predates the Social Democrats' rise to national power in the 1930s. The institution that most clearly embodies the public interest in the family is the national Child Welfare Board (CWB), created in 1924 as part of the Ministry of Social Welfare. Under the system set up in the 1924 Care of Children Act, the national CWB acts as an overseeing body for a network of local committees appointed by county councils. The composition of local CWBs varies (Stockholm's is larger than others and contains more social work professionals), but all must contain at least the following: one member of the local welfare board, one clergyman, one teacher, and at least two other persons known for their interest in children. Whenever possible, local CWBs should contain legal and medical experts as well.

The local CWB has a general responsibility for all minors up to age eighteen within its jurisdiction. Its specific duties include the care of poor and delinquent children, an activity closely coordinated with the court system. The CWB operates homes for orphans and other public charges, arranges foster homes and operates homes for mothers with newborns if they have nowhere else to stay. Acting on reports from public officials or private citizens (e.g., neighbors), the local CWB can intervene in homes where children are not receiving adequate care. It may confine itself to admonishing family members; it may remove a child from a home if, for example, the danger of infection from communicable disease seems dangerously high. In other words, the CWB is an extremely powerful local institution with a great deal of discretion. (Note that, in contrast to the United States, where the power to remove children from the family is vested in the courts, in Sweden this power is wielded by an administrative agency.)

In addition to this "negative" power of local government agencies to prevent parents from mistreating their offspring, numerous programs reflect the local authorities' positive interest in enhancing the child's environment. For example, every mother of a newborn baby receives at least one visit from a representative of the local CWB, who checks to see that the baby's environment is safe and sanitary, answers questions from the mother and demonstrates good child-care practices. Health checkups are considered a must and are administered free. If a family does not bring its preschooler into the welfare center for a comprehensive health examination at age four, the center sends a field worker out to ascertain why.

This issue of the family's right to privacy versus the community's right to protect its future citizens has surfaced periodically, most recently in the mid-1960s when a controversial newspaper column provoked intense reaction. In 1965 a woman sociologist and poet named Barbro Backberger published a scathing condemnation of the traditional bourgeois family in the Christmas Eve edition of the daily *Dagens Nyheter*. Much of Backberger's criticism of the family focused on the concept of family members as one another's "property." She was especially critical of parents' delusion that they "own" their children: "Parents cling to their children, prevent them from taking steps toward life, toward friends, and their own interests."[29] The same theme was taken up in a widely discussed book published by politician Per Gahrton in 1969. The author once again questioned a parent's right of ownership over his or her offspring, and he outlined an approach to family policy that would allocate responsibility for Sweden's children among three parties: parents, children, and the government.[30] One social worker and political activist in the late 1960s summed up the prevailing view this way:

> Surely it isn't right that only mothers, or even only parents, should be responsible for children? No one should be allowed to "own" another person, least of all one who cannot defend himself and his interests. This is one of the reasons why society, for its children's sake, must share the responsibility for them.[31]

In what many people regard as the most clear-cut case to date of the government's willingness to intervene between parent and child, Swedish policy makers have recently been discussing a national training program for the nation's parents. Since the mid-1950s, municipal and county authorities have been operating various parental training courses, the most common being maternity training at child-care centers. In the 1970s, it seems that publicly provided parent training may be administered nationally. While this move was first sponsored by the Social Democratic majority in the Riksdag, it had clear support from several opposition parties as well. Since 1970, all five major parties have introduced proposals in the Riksdag to implement parent-training programs. The Center and Liberal parties have shown particular interest in encouraging participation by fathers in such training.

In December 1973 a working group known as the Provisions for Children Group was formally directed by the Cabinet to consider the organization and content of a parent-training program to be made available to all Swedish parents with preschool or school-age children. Comments by the group's chairperson, Grethe Lundblad, express the assumption that the community, represented by its government, has a natural interest in family life:

> Parent training is one of the opportunities available to the community to establish contact with the family. . . . We see that things are going badly in the community for many children who have been well provided for materially. No studies are needed; it's obvious that parents training is necessary. Children are the most important asset the community has. It's not only parents who need teaching about children, but everyone in the community.[32]

Lundblad's comments have also showed the group's intention not simply to guarantee adequate physical care but also to tackle the value-laden question of what constitutes a "proper upbringing." It remains to be seen whether the group's report, requested by the Social Democratic government in 1973, will be given serious attention by the current coalition government. One crucial decision to be made before implementing any such program is whether or not the training should be compulsory, an issue that has stirred up considerable public interest.

How can we reconcile the apparent inconsistency between (1) the Swedish government's reluctance to intervene in married life even to the extent of favoring legal marriage over "loyalty marriage," and (2) its willingness to entertain the possibility of mandatory government training for parents? The one consistent thread running through Swedish family policy is the priority placed on child welfare. Governmental concern for child welfare stems to a large degree from the Social Democrats' emphasis on social egalitarianism. This policy guideline was articulated as early as 1941 by Alva Myrdal in *Nation and Family*, which advocated that Sweden's social policy be predicated on

> the desire to safeguard for all children, born and unborn, what are now average environmental conditions for children with regard to housing, food, medical attention, schooling, and so forth. Such a policy has strong moorings in our predilection for greater social justice. If the nation's resources or the social ingenuity for redistribution cannot ensure such average conditions for all children, no additional children should be sought.[33]

Because the Social Democratic party dominated national policy making from the mid-1930s to the mid-1970s, it has influenced Sweden's social policy more strongly than any other party.

The Socialists' commitment to providing every Swede with a minimum standard of living has been applied especially vigorously in the case of young children. All children, legitimate or illegitimate, must be guaranteed protection against marital instability, poverty, and parental neglect. Welfare specialists within the Social Democratic party have long shared the conviction, held by developmental psychologists the world over, that children's life chances are critically affected by the physical and emotional conditions surrounding them during their first three to five years. That observation, combined with the Social Democrats' egalitarianism, produced the party's official position that all Swedish children must be guaranteed by right, if not *equal* home circumstances, at least some *minimum* standard of maintenance to prevent their being permanently disadvantaged. Originally the Socialists' position, this principle is now accepted by all major parties.

China

Of our three cases, China since 1949 has displayed the most thoroughgoing intervention by a government into family life. Because of the central role the family played in pre-Communist China in social and economic welfare, inheritance rights, socialization, and so on, new ways of thought and new ways of living required that family patterns be altered as well. The Marxist blueprint for a communist society called for characteristics within the family, such as equality and the opportunity for all members to work, that could be instituted quickly only through the intervention of an outside force. In attempting to bring about change, the Chinese government has tampered freely and vigorously with family relationships. Loyalty once given to the family must be transferred to New China; work done for the good of the family must now be done for the good of New China. Not only have major national campaigns been directed at the family, but investigation and education teams have been a constant part of the local Chinese scene. Any peasant or worker who has trouble at home can get help from party or government cadres and activists. Often, people who don't want help get it anyway. For, to the Chinese, life within the family is intimately connected with the success of socialism and, ultimately, communism.

Life under the Chinese Communist party has been structured to guarantee that most family business is subject to public pressure. Collectives, factory teams, and street committees all take responsibility for improving the attitudes, relationships, and consumption patterns of family members when those attitudes and practices are considered a threat to socialist progress. Unwanted deviance can include anything from sloppy work habits to improperly dressed children, from child abuse to eating out at restaurants too often. When such deviance is recognized, a family may be sure of receiving a visit—or several visits—from committee representatives to "correct" the trouble. It is assumed that few individuals, when properly informed, would want their actions to impede the building of socialism. When the definition of public business is as wide as the CCP's, almost every action, inside or outside the family, can be thought to influence public welfare.

If the Chinese case contrasts starkly with our two Western examples, we must hasten to point out that the imposition of collective demands on individuals, which is so pervasive in revolutionary China, does not contrast so starkly with China's prerevolutionary society. Family life prior to 1949 had not undergone the drastic privatization so well documented for the Western family by Shorter and other social historians.[34] In China, married couples and their children were not viewed as the center of family life, and few nuclear family units were independent of clan control. Particularly in rural areas, clans performed political and social functions that in Western societies were performed by the state. In China the state neither ruled the clans (or lineage groups) nor was ruled by them. Instead, the family operated as a mediating institution, placed between the government and the citizenry: "From the point of view of the state, a man's obligations to it were in fact both qualified and mediated by his kinship relations."[35] In this sense, the system of obligations and prerogatives embedded within the family system restricted the state's control over its citizens. At the same time, the family acted as an agent of state control: "Lineage organization implied . . . an organization which could be used by the state for political and fiscal control."[36]

Privatization of the family in the West meant that most collective social and political demands had to stop at the nuclear family level. No such barrier existed in prerevolutionary China. The family unit remained tied to a system of collective obligations and rewards that left little protection for the individual against collective demands. The three-generational family owned the land and businesses and arranged marriages. The clans, especially in the countryside, enforced the social and moral order. They ran schools and mediated disputes. Individuals learned from birth that family and clan interests overrode their own. Within the context of traditional Chinese family life, therefore, Locke's notion that the community had no business interfering in a marriage as long as the couple adequately nurtured and educated their children would have seemed absurd.

Despite the historical precedent for strong community pressure on family members, the substance of family life, as it is being promoted by the communist regime, differs drastically from the Confucian family system. The communists have not only reduced the power of lineage groups over three-generational families; they have also sought to reduce the power of the nuclear family over individual members. The new revolutionary family is meant to fit into the new society. Puritanical and hard-working, the ideal young couple fall in love because of admiration for each other's dedication to the state or collective. He stays late repairing machinery; she runs to the city after dark with her production team's broken irrigation pump. Together they go from repair shop to repair shop to locate the right part. Mutual admiration turns to love.

In this context, greater love hath no spouse than to be willing to separate for a period of several years to give both mates a chance to fulfill production targets. Anything less than selfless dedication is considered entanglement in the bourgeois "small family." Parents must not fill their children with notions of personal ambition but should teach them to subordinate their interests to the needs of the larger society. Children with "feudal" or "bourgeois" parents must patiently educate them to accept the new morality.

> What we are required to set up are new-type, revolutionary families. These families should in the first place serve revolutionary needs and be formed on the basis of complete voluntarism and equality. Under the premise of common struggle for the cause of revolution, the husband and wife should aim at a common target, follow the same direction, encourage and help and love each other, and make progress together. . . . It is first necessary for a revolutionary comrade to make herself a good servant of the people, before she can make herself a good wife and a good mother.[37]

Divorce, unavailable to mismatched couples in traditional China, has been introduced by the communists to alleviate the suffering of people locked into unhappy marriages. It has also reduced the control of families over individuals. Nevertheless because the possibility of divorce exists, that does not mean it has become a private matter for the couple involved. It is a matter of community concern. Before a divorce case is even brought to court, several attempts at mediation will have been made by workers' committees, street committees, or women's federations. A case from a 1959 Shanghai court illustrates the process. The wife's fellow worker is giving her opinion of the marriage:

> They haven't got along since 1956; she asked for a divorce then; we tried to mediate; she brought the case to court in 1957; the court mediated but the situation got worse and worse. . . . In my opinion, let the wife have the children during this period; and then when the children are older, the parents can negotiate about them.[38]

At a trial in 1972, Ruth Sidel witnessed the same community concern. Present were the wife and husband, representatives of the revolutionary committee, representatives of both the husband's and wife's work units, the judges, and several comrades and friends. All involved were asked their opinions. In such cases the courts have wide discretionary powers and often direct the couple to go back and try again. That is exactly what happened here. Divorce was not granted.

The Chinese state's strong disposition to intervene in family affairs is caused by the instrumental attitude policy makers take toward the family, whose "purpose is to provide a locus for the raising of useful citizens."[39] In a society bent on revolutionary change, there can be no more critical function than the proper socialization of the next generation.

FAMILY ROLES: INTERDEPENDENCE OR SYMMETRY?

In the previous section we examined the family's external relationship to government in three political cultures. We now turn to a consideration of the legal presumptions present in these societies regarding the roles played by men and women within the family. We find in the histories of all three nations certain similarities in the "guardian" role that has traditionally been assigned to husbands. The role of family guardian entails, first and foremost, the privilege of speaking for the family, especially in the disposition of property.

In the United States, this presumption of husband-as-guardian was inherited from England along with the large body of common law that treated the family as a single person in law. The legal doctrine that the family acts as a unit and is always spoken for by its male head originated in the commercial revolution that began in Renaissance Europe; it was unknown before that time. Historian of the family Carle Zimmerman devotes a good part of his history of the Western family to destroying

> the misinterpretation of the family as having originally been a despotic thing and of the idea that human progress had been directed from despotism toward equality. The conception of arbitrary power being given to the head at the beginning of the rise of the domestic family was legal fiction.[40]

In other words, the legal principle that the head of the family was the sole owner of the family's property was designed for greater convenience in disposing of property. The need for a more fluid system of property transfer led to the legal doctrine of coverture that has influenced so much of American family and property law. The coverture doctrine as presented in Blackstone's *Commentaries* stipulated that the husband and wife became one person in law upon marriage; hence the legal existence of the woman was suspended during marriage, and as a result the woman lost all control and management of her real property to her husband during marriage.[41]

Marriage law in Sweden was first codified as part of the Swedish General Code of 1734, which did no more than set down the customs of the times. Although its tone was somewhat more rustic, the Code of Marriage portrayed the marital union much as it was portrayed at the time in English common law: "Now a man wishes to marry. Let him ask for the bride from her proper guardian and not take her by violence or artifice."[42] Like English common law, the Swedish Code of 1734 held the husband to be his wife's guardian. Unless special agreements had been made, the property of both spouses was brought "into community" by the act of marriage. This common property, including property inherited by the wife, was controlled by the husband alone. Not until 1874 (several decades after such reforms had been introduced in most American states) did Sweden introduce a reform permitting married women to administer certain parts of their property that did not belong to the marital community and permitting women to control their own wage earnings.[43]

In traditional China, too, the patriarch of the family was its "guardian" in matters of property disposition. By the Ch'ing Dynasty (1644–1911), the tradition that a family acts as a unit and that the eldest male speaks for the family was firmly established. Family property was collectively owned by male family members,[44] but management of the property was dominated by the family head. When the male head of the house died, property management fell to the next male heir, or property was divided among the sons. Female descendants had no claim on family property other than a right of unmarried daughters to their dowries. A widow might come into land at the death of her husband, but she could not dispose of it without the consent of her son if she had male children. If she had no descendants, the land could be claimed by her husband's brothers. No divorced woman (and they were rare) was allowed to take any part of her husband's family property into a new marriage or back to her parents'. If a child did not like the patriarch's actions, that was too bad. "It was an offense to accuse one's father or grandfather in court."[45]

In English common law, the corollary of the guardian's right to control the family property was his obligation to support his wife and children. Since he controlled the family's holdings, he assumed absolute financial responsibility for the family's maintenance, even to the extent that he was responsible for debts incurred by his wife. In the preindustrial era, when land was the basic source of wealth, wife and children were to be supported by the family holdings. Later, when wage labor replaced land as the source of income for most families, the husband was obliged to support his wife and children from his earnings. The Industrial Revolution and the growing separation between home and work place firmly consolidated this strict division of labor in the household between breadwinner and homemaker. As Alva Myrdal has pointed out, these role distinctions did not really make sense in the preindustrial agrarian family, for whom family maintenance was a collective undertaking. In the pre-industrial family, "it had not even dawned upon people that anybody should be considered as the supporter. All supported all."[46]

With the advent of market capitalism, the family gradually separated itself from the surrounding community and turned inward, to create a family life based on the values of privacy, domesticity, and isolation from the outside world.[47] In the process, the increasingly specialized roles of husbands and wives were incorporated into law. English law (and, by extension, American law) came to presume that "the husband has a duty to support his wife, that she has a duty to render services in the home, and that these duties are reciprocal. . . ."[48]

As we have seen, Sweden's economic modernization came later than that of either England or the United States. Hence we would expect that the legal recognition of specialized roles for husbands and wives would emerge later in Sweden. Swedish law did not explicitly impose upon the husband "the duty to support his family" until 1853.[49]

As for traditional China, the marital roles were governed by law and by the ethical tenets of Confucianism. Since courts were only infrequently consulted, however, customs played the role of law in much of Chinese life. Confucian ethics, which elaborated the proper rules of behavior for all members of the household, dictated that "the status of a husband carried full authority over the wife, with the wife's correlative duties of obedience and faithfulness."[50] As family head, the husband had a duty to "attend to the needs of the household."[51] That is, he administered the family holdings, from which all members of the household were entitled to be maintained.

The wife's position was not an enviable one. From the moment she married, she was considered subordinate not only to her husband but to her husband's father and mother. As a woman she was responsible for the housework, which she performed under the watchful guidance of her mother-in-law. When her husband left for the office or the fields, his wife remained behind and had to bear the direction, authority, and often intolerant criticisms of the older woman. Of the work the women performed, this has been said:

> In the scale of values, only the labor of acquisition of goods and services or income from primary production was rated high. Household labor, whether in processing food or clothing for consumption, in sanitary activities like washing and cleaning, or in child care, was rated so low that no man would perform it without feeling some sense of inferiority. The difference of value assigned to various types of labor contributed toward the stratification of status and authority of the member of the family.[52]

Communist Intervention in the Chinese Family

The problem with the traditional family role definitions of husband as guardian and wife as homemaker has been a simple one: Separate has not been equal. The female role as child rearer and domestic has been thought of not only as different from the male's but as inferior. Engels described the problem in 1884:

> The very cause that had formerly made the woman supreme in the house, namely her being confined to domestic work, now assured supremacy in the house for the man: the woman's housework lost its significance compared with the man's work in obtaining a livelihood: the latter was everything, the former an insignificant contribution.[53]

In correcting a situation of unequal treatment stemming from role definitions, two approaches are possible: upgrade the status of women's work, to make it equal to man's work in the eyes of society, or integrate the roles so that both sexes perform identical jobs.

The Chinese Communist party has heavily emphasized equal status in the home, but it has been far less insistent on achieving interchangeable roles. To some extent this orientation stems from Marxian notions about collective living; to some extent it has developed because of the scarcity of resources available to train people in a poor country, coupled with inadequate job opportunities. China's intervention in family life has thus been directed primarily at achieving equal rights for both women and men within marriage, rather than redistributing the burden of domestic chores.

The upgrading of women's status began in earnest with the Marriage

Law of 1950, which triggered one of the most intense and sustained efforts at family transformation in human history. The law was based on earlier legal efforts in the Soviet base areas, efforts largely subordinated to the needs of the war.[54] Almost immediately after the communist takeover in 1949, marriage emerged as a central issue, expecially marriage without parental interference. At least one expert has suggested that although the new law actually dealt with "family relations," its emphasis on the marriage aspect was not unintentional. So direct was the new law's attack on deeply embedded values that "to marry according to the Marriage Law required revolutionary courage in the countryside."[55]

What was radical and disruptive about the law? In the context of traditional Chinese family life, almost everything. It made arranged marriages against the will of the bride or groom illegal. It called for equality between men and women, and the abolition of concubinage, child betrothal, infanticide, interference in the remarriage of widows, and the "exaction of money or gifts in connection with marriage" (i.e., the bride price paid to the woman's family for the expenses of raising her). Freedom to divorce, unheard of in traditional marriages, was granted. Women had the right to use their own family names and, more important, the right to equal management of property, a privilege denied in traditional China. In cases of divorce or the remarriage of widows, the woman had the right to take her children, even her sons, with her. Illegitimate children were given the same claim to paternal support as legitimate ones.

While these rights might sound mundane to Americans in the 1970s, to Chinese women they were indeed revolutionary. The previous status of women had been so low that girls were often drowned at birth because they were of so little value to the family.

> Sons shall be born to him,
> They will be put to sleep on couches;
> They will be clothed in robes,
> They will have scepters to play with;
> Their cry will be loved.
> They will be resplendent hereafter with red knee-covers,
> The future kings, the princes of the land.
>
> Daughters shall be born to him,
> They will be put to sleep on the ground;
> They will be clothed in wrappers,
> They will have tiles to play with;
> It will be theirs neither to do wrong nor to do good.
> Only about the spirits and the food will they have to think,
> And to cause no sorrow to their parents.[56]

A girl was devalued by her own family because she would join her husband's family at marriage. After incurring the expense of raising her, parents would lose her services, her loyalty, and her comfort in their old age when she reached maturity. In her husband's family, the daughter-in-law was an intruder, although one who was needed for domestic chores and producing sons. In order to minimize the disruption caused to the family by a new addition, the bride's subordination to her husband's family was made clear from the outset: The marriage ceremony involved paying homage and sacrifice to *his* ancestors. The wedding was celebrated by his family; hers was not even invited. The bride price, paid to her family to help defray the costs of raising her, kept the daughter-in-law in psychological debt to her new family. In rural areas, where 80 percent of the people lived, the woman usually married outside her village to avoid men with the same surname. Moving as a stranger to a new place left her with no contacts, no friends, and no personal ties to bolster her influence. With transportation poor and little time for visiting, returning to her parents for emotional or material aid was difficult.

Divorce was almost unheard of, and in any case, women were strongly encouraged to take only one husband:

> The loyal official does not serve two dynasties
> The virtuous woman does not have two husbands.[57]

During the Ch'ing Dynasty, widows were even praised for committing suicide on the death of their husbands, to avoid losing their chastity to another man. Running away was pointless; until the twentieth century few opportunities were open to women outside the home. Suicide was considered the only proper protest against inhumane treatment. The Chinese saying "When you marry a dog, stick to the dog; when you marry a chicken, stick to the chicken" covered the situation.

Convincing the working and peasant classes of China to abide by the provisions of the new marriage law has not been easy. As thoroughly alien concepts, they have met with great resistance. Substantial education campaigns have been needed to convince the "masses" of the law's value and even to convince the cadres to comply with the law. In rural areas, peasant cadres, while willing to press for land reform and the redistribution of wealth, have balked at the idea of having their patriarchal authority questioned.

> That in the past two odd years the Marriage Law has not been thoroughly implemented in the major part of the country has been chiefly due to the fact that cadres (especially those at the *ch'u* and *hsiang* levels) have failed to attach importance to, failed to carry out, and even resorted to open resistance against, the Marriage Law. Among the cadres there are prevalent those who do not fully understand the Marriage Law, and hold the mistaken view that the law may be dispensed with, that it only benefits women, that it does not suit conditions in the rural areas, and that the interests of the poor and hired peasants must receive special consideration. . . . But apart from these, there are the more serious cases of quite a number of cadres at the *ch'u* and *hsiang* levels who themselves entertain to a great extent feudal concepts and thoughts of resistance against the Marriage Law, and as a result there emerged such illegal and undisciplined practices as open interference with freedom of mar-

> riage, sheltering of criminal elements who violated the Marriage Law, and interference with and hitting men and women who sought to win freedom of marriage. Such cadres interpreted free love as immoral, improper, and acts of loathing, and proceeded to various measures for its restriction.[58]

Until 1953, the campaign to promote the marriage law was vigorous and often violent. Since then, promoting a new kind of marriage has shifted from emphasis on punitive legal enforcement to propaganda and persuasion.

Under the "Rights and Duties of Husband and Wife," the marriage law left open the question of husband as provider and wife as homemaker.

> Article 7: Husband and wife are companions living together and shall enjoy equal status in the home.
>
> Article 8: Husband and wife are in duty bound to love, respect, assist, and look after each other, to live in harmony, to engage in productive work, to care for the children and to strive jointly for the welfare of the family and for the building of the new society.
>
> Article 9: Both husband and wife shall have the right to free choice of occupation and free participation in work or in social activities.[59]

The law fails to specify which spouse, if either, is responsible for support; which spouse is responsible for domestic duties; or if these duties should be split between partners. Apparently permissive in that it grants couples the right to decide these questions, the law in fact fails to provide specific goals on sex roles. In its ambivalence on sex roles, the law reflects the ambivalence that characterizes the CCP.

Overcoming male resistance to performing such duties as washing and changing diapers is not only a problem of changing attitudes (although sex-role stereotypes have been strong in China). Two other obstacles of equal or greater importance remain, even where attitudes have begun to change. First is the question of providing jobs for women liberated from the home. Presumably, if women are to be released from the primary responsibility for the household, they will then use their time to contribute to production. But, as we saw in chapter 4, unemployment has been a chronic problem in China; hence women's opportunities to join the labor force have been circumscribed. Particularly during the 1950s, when China emphasized the growth of capital-intensive heavy industry, women found job hunting a difficult business. For the party a dilemma arose: Marxism postulates a communist utopia in which women "are enabled to take part in production on a large scale" because "domestic duties require their attention only to a minor degree."[60] But if women were encouraged to leave domestic chores behind, to work outside the home, what was to be done with them? If Marxist theory were strictly adhered to, and women's oppression were explained to them as a result of their homemaker role, then the party would create an enormous pool of discontented housewives with nowhere to go. Hence women have often been praised for their role as wife and mother.

The second obstacle to a redefinition of family roles has been China's limited resources for training personnel. Although often overlooked, the efficient performance of domestic chores is a highly skilled job for which women are trained from birth. As economies develop, men are trained for increasingly specialized roles in the economy. At least one authority has suggested that androgyny is a function of industrial development more than a function of political ideology,[61] and this certainly holds true in the problem of retraining. Once a society has expended the resources to train an individual for a job within the economy, is it not in the society's best economic interest to utilize that individual in the job for which he or she was trained? Interweaving the roles of caretaker and breadwinner would necessitate not only spending money to train women for jobs outside the home but also voluntarily cutting back on husbands'work to allow them to learn and to perform household tasks. Developing economies have few resources available for such experiments.

As an employer, the Chinese government has been more committed to training women for employment than to reducing time demands on workers. The result has been that men, who come home tired, tend to rely on traditional norms. They work less around the house and devote more of their energy to employment, even when their wives work. The result for women has been the classic double burden.

> I am 26 years old and have three children. I returned home every night after 10:00, and when I finished washing and took a child from my amah to bed, it was already 11:00. Soon after I was in bed, the child would wet his diaper, and I had to get up again. In the morning, the child woke up at 6:00, and I had to get up. I usually could sleep for no more than six hours. . . . I ought to have time for rest in the afternoon on Sunday, but because I had no time to take a shampoo, to bathe the children, to brief the amah how the children should be taken care of, and even to do my washing on other days of the week, everything had to be done on Sunday. . . . I make my complaint, not because I consider family life and domestic work more important than work and socialist construction. . . . But I feel I should also carry out the duty of a mother to her children and the duty of a wife to her husband in the family. I believe that when the leadership quarters in the organs map out their timetable for work, conference, and other activities, they should have consideration for the practical difficulties of the female comrade.[62]

Although propaganda has periodically encouraged men to take a greater share of chores in the home, until the anti-Lin Piao and Confucius campaign of the mid-1970s there was no sustained effort by the media to convince men that housework was as much their responsibility as women's. During the conservative swings in policy, the caretaker role has specifically been labeled the "natural" burden of women. During the radical phases, such as the Great Leap Forward, household chores have been called "stultifying and oppressive," slogans that would readily convince women to drop these activities but would hardly convince men to devote more time to them. Collective social services have also proved inadequate to meet the needs of the women China has mobilized to work. Moreover, since the individuals recruited to work in social services are almost universally female, the bias toward women as caretakers remains.

Finding themselves in a social system that advocates collective social services it cannot afford, which puts little pressure on husbands to share household chores, and which demands that women join the labor force for their own emancipation, what are wives to do? Stories and articles have painted a picture of ad hoc solutions generated by women themselves. Sometimes the mother-in-law is prevailed upon to help; sometimes the husband helps. At other times, a workers' committee or residential committee steps in to help: a new nursery is established, or a neighbor is persuaded to volunteer her help. The most significant intervention of the party into family life in this area has been to convince mothers-in-law to reduce the burden of domestic chores on their daughters-in-law. Although substantially altering the traditional relationship between the women, the arrangement makes sense for the family unit. The daughter-in-law, who is younger, stronger, and much more likely to be educated, can earn money outside the family. The mother-in-law can do the lighter chores around the home or at least help with them if she is also employed. Predictably, the transition has been difficult for the older women, and evidence indicates that friction between the two generations of women is common.

The failure of the CCP to face the practical problems of budgeting time for work and home has led the Chinese into two contradictory positions. On the one hand, the party can maintain that equality of the status in the family can be gained through attitude changes, without a redistribution of chores:

> By suggesting that a husband should take the revolutionary attitude of equality toward his wife, do we mean that both husband and wife should divide housework equally, or that the husband should devote more of his time and efforts to housekeeping and attend to his wife's other needs? No, this is not so. If housework is divided in this way, it cannot be considered as true equality, for the key to this question does not lie in the form of sharing household chores, but rather in the attitude of the husband toward the wife after he is back home.[63]

On the other hand, they can call women into the work force because labor outside the home upgrades their position within the family. Given inadequate replacement services to ease the burden of employment plus household chores, family women are left with unequal energy and dedication to the world of work and therefore without equal access to responsible and meaningful jobs. Yet without equal access to jobs, women are left unequal inside the home. In this context, Liu Shao-chi's comments about women, though they may be male chauvinist as charged, are at least honest: "There have been only a few women political figures in history. After getting married, women have babies to look after. How can they become political figures?"[64]

Sweden's Campaign for Symmetrical Family Roles

Whereas Chinese policy has left largely unquestioned the woman's primary role as homemaker, the reforms introduced by the Swedish government have not. In this respect we may judge Swedish policy to have pursued even more radical ends than those sought by Chinese policy makers. For much of Swedish policy seeks not merely to lend more dignity to women's traditional role but actually to achieve greater symmetry in the family roles of women and men. That is, instead of maintaining specialized and interdependent roles for the husband and wife, Swedish policy has moved in the direction of making marital roles symmetrical and almost interchangeable. In a purely symmetrical relationship either spouse might work outside the home; either spouse might be the primary homemaker; or both roles might be shared equally. Sweden's minister of justice clearly had this symmetry in mind when he charged the Family Law Reform Committee, which began deliberating in 1969:

> There is no reason to abstain from using marriage and family legislation as one of several instruments in reform toward a society where every adult individual can take responsibility for himself without being economically dependent on relatives and where equality between men and women is real.

Movement in this direction began in Sweden almost 50 years earlier, in the 1921 Marriage Law, which ended the husband's legal tutelage in marriage. The law, progressive for its time, read:

> . . . man and woman owe each other fidelity and support, and shall jointly and in consultation with each other serve the family's best interests. Neither has a greater right to decide than the other, and each shall dispose of his or her own labor.

Under the law, although each spouse remained owner of property held when the marriage was contracted, upon dissolution of the marriage, all property was brought "into community," to be divided in half. This system of individual ownership during the marriage and equal division at its dissolution was automatic; any other arrangement had to be drawn up specifically. Both spouses were assigned the duty to contribute to the family's maintenance to the best of their abilities by working either inside or outside the home. Thus, the law acknowledged homemaking as an economic contribution to family maintenance.

Although it gave formal recognition to the economic equality between husband and wife, the 1921 law nevertheless assumed that the conventional roles of breadwinner and housekeeper would be performed by husband and wife. By implication, the rule that calls upon the spouses to share the same material standard of living imposes a duty of support on whichever party earns the larger income. That support obligation, along with other economic aspects of the marriage relationships including alimony and property rights, was under review by the Social Democratic government's Family Law Reform Committee for the seven years prior to its defeat in 1976. Appointed in 1969 by the minister of justice, the committee's first charge was to review the laws regarding contraction and dissolution of marriage. The output of this first stage of the committee's work was the 1973 Family Law Reform, which changed the divorce procedure and extended some of the laws affecting married couples to cover unmarried couples as well.

In its deliberations concerning the economic roles assigned to married men and women by the law, the committee was unquestionably influenced by the sex-role debate that has been going on in Sweden since the early 1960s. At that time, the role of women held by most "progressives" was the role elaborated by Alva Myrdal and Viola Klein in *Women's Two Roles*, written in 1956.[65] According to this "moderate" view, married women would continue to bear the primary responsibility for rearing children. But since women's life expectancy had increased in the twentieth century, and family-planning techniques had gained in popularity, child rearing occupied a shorter period in the lives of married women. Hence women gained a dual role as mothers and as employed workers outside the home. Myrdal and Klein argued that public policy should be aimed at removing as far as possible the barriers between these two roles and offering women a new life style: first, education and work, then child rearing in the home, followed by a return to the labor market.[66]

This "moderate" view was challenged in 1961 by Eva Moberg, a feminist and Liberal party member. Moberg's essay "The Conditional Emancipation of Women" argued that as long as working women must perform two roles while working men perform only one role, sexual equality can never be achieved. To Moberg, the moderates were willing to give women the opportunity to enter the labor market only on the condition that they maintain their traditional functions inside the family.

Instead, Moberg offered the "radical" proposal that parenthood responsibilities should be shared equally and that men's roles in the family be changed to include work inside the home (housekeeping and child rearing). This "radical" view gained acceptance so quickly in Sweden, at least among political and professional elites, that by 1968 it had become the official position of the Swedish government. The evidence for this is in Sweden's 1968 Report to the United Nations, *The Status of Women in Sweden*. In the report, the government asserted:

> A decisive and ultimately durable improvement in the status of women cannot be attained by special measures aimed at women alone; it is equally

> necessary to abolish the conditions which tend to assign certain privileges, obligations, or rights to men. No decisive change in the distribution of functions and status as between the sexes can be achieved if the duties of the male in society are assumed *a priori* to be unaltered. . . . The division of functions as between the sexes must be changed in such a way that both the man and the woman in a family are afforded the same practical opportunities of participating in both active parenthood and gainful employment.[67]

Sweden's public policy has not changed overnight to implement this egalitarian conception of family roles articulated in 1968. One area in which there has been a concerted effort to initiate change is on the question of awarding child custody when a marriage dissolves. Since the 1949 Parents and Children Code, mother and father have been considered co-guardians of their children; in a divorce, parents have had the option of sharing legal custody of their children. When the parents have not made this special arrangement, the courts have generally awarded the children to the mother. In fact, one source reported in the mid-1960s that although no law so stipulated, divorce decrees usually favored mothers even when the divorce had been granted to the husband on the ground of the wife's adultery.[68] There was, in other words, a strong presumption that mothers were the "natural" caretakers for children, except under extremely unfavorable circumstances.

This presumption was directly addressed in the 1973 Family Law Reform, under which fathers were put on fundamentally the same footing as mothers. That is, when parents separate, the child's welfare determines who gets custody, and there is no a priori advantage to the mother. The same is true with regard to the disposition of the dwelling occupied by a couple upon separation. Rather than favoring either sex, the law now states that the one demonstrating the greatest need for the dwelling should have it.

Laws governing the payment of alimony still reflect to some extent the unequal roles played in marriage. Under the existing system, now being reviewed by the Family Law Reform Commission, courts decide alimony awards on the merits of the individual case. In principle, alimony payments can be awarded to either party; actually, awards made to ex-husbands are rare. Long-term awards to wives have become less frequent in recent years. Usually, if a wife is in good health and capable of earning a living, she receives alimony only for a short readjustment period to enable her to make the transition to the employment market.

Although alimony awards are infrequent, child-support awards are the norm. The parent who does not have custody (usually the father) is required to contribute support payments. However, the single parent's dependence on support payments from a former spouse is not nearly so great in Sweden as in the United States. If payments are not received, the government intervenes to guarantee the child a minimum standard of maintenance by dispensing a "maintenance grant" to the child.

In Sweden's parental-leave program the most dramatic steps have been taken by the government to promote more egalitarian family roles. Sweden had a maternity-leave program that paid benefits to working women who remained at home after childbirth, for up to six months. The amount of compensation varied from 20 to 80 percent of the woman's normal earnings, depending on her wage level. In January 1974 the maternity-leave program was replaced by a new "parental leave" program. Under the new regulations, in force as of January 1978, the parents of a newborn baby have a total of nine months' paid leave,[69] which they can divide between themselves according to their own preferences. Mother and father can allocate the leave time in any way acceptable to themselves and tolerable to their employers; they might take alternate months, alternate days, or even alternate half-days, as long as both of them are not absent from work simultaneously. They may even save up to three months' leave to be used any time up to and including the child's first year in school.

For Swedish parents, as for American parents, there is a financial disincentive for increasing the father's home responsibilities. Since his salary is likely to be higher than his wife's, a husband who takes time off from work sacrifices a larger proportion of family income than his wife does. The parental-leave benefit minimizes this problem by gearing payments to each parent's normal earnings. As table 5–1 shows, even in a family where the husband earns twice as much as the wife, the couple sacrifices only a negligible amount by deciding to split the leave evenly.

The issue of how far the Swedish government should go to *impose* changes in sex roles within the family surfaced during the last months of the Social Democrats' term in office as a controversy dividing the Social Democrats from the bourgeois parties. In the government's May 1976 pro-

TABLE 5-1. Parental Leave for the Svensson Family, 1975

	Normal Annual Income	*Annual Income 1975*	*Parent's Benefit*	*Total Taxable Income*	*Income After Taxes*
Alternative 1: Wife stays home for 7 months					
Mr. Svensson	$13,500	$13,500		$13,500	$ 8,069
Mrs. Svensson	6,750	2,812	3,544	6,356	4,917
	$20,250				$12,986
Alternative 2: Each stays home for 3½ months					
Mr. Svensson	$13,500	$9,562	$3,544	$13,106	$ 7,924
Mrs. Svensson	6,750	4,781	1,772	6,553	5,040
	$20,250				$12,964

Source: Adapted from M. Millgardh and B. Rollen, "Parent's Insurance," *Current Sweden*, no. 76 (April 1975).

posal to extend the paid parental leave after the birth of a baby, the Social Democrats proposed to *require* that the father use at least 2½ months of the total leave allowed. The proposal to add five more paid months to the then established seven-month parental-leave program was formulated in such a way that if a father opted not to use his allotted share of the leave, the time would be forfeited; it could not be used instead by the mother. Opposition parties, notably the Liberals, immediately reacted against this provision, recognizing the Social Democrats' intention to use it as a means of obligating Swedish fathers to assume greater responsibility for child rearing. According to the opposition, the division of child-rearing responsibilities within the family should remain a private decision rather than the object of government policy.[70] The debate was settled by the victory of the bourgeois parties in the fall 1976 national elections. Current regulations under the coalition government do not impose any specific division of the leave between parents.

Family Roles in American Public Policy

In the United States, we can find no real parallel to the comprehensive government reform of marital roles attempted under China's 1950 Marriage Law, nor even to the incremental reform promoted by Sweden's government since 1920. Part of the reason for this difference lies in the structure of American government. Family law in the United States is formulated at the state level. Laws governing partners' roles and rights in marriage are state laws, and reforms must be sought in fifty separate jurisdictions. This fragmentation of governmental authority over family policy slows the pace of reform considerably. But in addition to this structural explanation, we must recognize the ideological bias against any such sweeping public intervention in American family roles. The long-standing defense of the American family as a private sphere, to be protected against governmental encroachment, has virtually prevented either state or federal governments from formulating any activist family policy. Far from using public policy actively to promote changes in family roles, recent administrations have staunchly resisted introducing programs that would have even indirect effects on family relationships. A celebrated instance was the 1972 report of President Nixon's Commission on Population Growth, in which the commission strongly recommended that contraceptives and family-planning services be made more widely available, especially to teen-agers. Nixon rejected his commission's recommendations to expand public family-planning programs on the grounds that "such measures would do nothing to preserve and strengthen close family relations." He preferred to allow families to deal with such matters privately, feeling confident that they would make "sound judgments that are conducive both to the public interest and to personal family goals."[71] It must be noted that this noninterventionist tradition is one to which feminists themselves appeal on occasion. For example, the celebrated 1973 Supreme Court decisions on abortion (*Roe* v.

Wade and *Doe* v. *Bolton*), hailed by American feminists, should be seen not as dramatic departures from, but as reaffirmations of, this public policy tradition. In these cases the Court found that the "right to privacy" guaranteed by the Constitution is broad enough to include a woman's decision to terminate a pregnancy and commented that this same right to privacy also covers related matters such as contraception, marriage, and child rearing. In such matters the right is so fundamental that the state must prove it has a "compelling" interest to justify its intervention.

Our reader will object that it is, practically speaking, impossible for government policy *not* to have had some impact on the American family, despite the self-conscious restraint exercised by policy makers in both the legislative and judicial branches. Government actions affect so many aspects of our lives that it is impossible to imagine that the family could remain untouched. In fact, it does not. The consequence of policy-makers' determination not to tamper with family roles is that a great deal of public policy operates to reinforce the conventional husband-wife roles within the family unit.

American public policy perpetuates the husband's guardian role, both in controlling the family's property and assuming the support obligation. The common-law doctrine of coverture, under which a woman who married lost control over her own property as well as joint property, was at least somewhat eroded by the Married Women's Property Acts passed during the nineteenth century in all American states. These laws varied from state to state, but generally they restored to married women control over their separate assets. That is, wives could now legally control the property they had brought into the marriage and whatever wages they earned by outside employment. These are, no doubt, rights to be prized. Nevertheless, their acquisition did not by any means end the husband's financial dominance in marriage. One commentator has even argued that "these new freedoms were in the main empty rights for most women." [72]

The vast majority of working-class and even middle-class women brought little property into a marriage with them and worked outside the home only sporadically in a secondary wage-earner role, if they worked at all. They therefore accumulated little in the way of "separate assets" to control. Meanwhile, in most states the assets acquired by the couple during their marriage, through the labor of husband outside the home and wife within the home, were controlled by the husband. To this day, in many states, "the common law courts presume that all household goods which do not have documentary title are the husband's." [73] Women who work as homemakers cannot prove "documentary title" because they cannot show that household goods were bought with their earnings. That would be impossible since, as homemakers, they do not have earnings. In other words, in spite of the Married Women's Property Acts, family law in the 42 "common law" states continues to assign to the husband the primary control over family property:

> The current legal doctrine of separation of assets means that a husband may retain for himself all property or income over that needed for family support even though the wife's legal obligation to perform household services may prevent her from acquiring assets of her own.[74]

The traditional view regarding husbands' property rights echoes a theme we developed in chapter 2: American policy makers hold in relatively low esteem the domestic labor done by women in the home. Such labor confers no entitlement to share control of the family's assets. Fortunately, this principle is currently under judicial scrutiny. Thirty-five states have now enacted "equitable property distribution systems" by which divorced spouses are given equal rights to all property acquired during the marriage, regardless of who held the title. Illinois' law, declared unconstitutional by Cook County's Circuit Court, is at this writing under review by the Illinois Supreme Court. A decision on its constitutionality is expected by late 1979. (We should also note that the eight "community property states," which derive their law from French and Spanish rather than English tradition, give each spouse one half ownership interest in the earnings of the other spouse. Since 1922, most of these eight states even give the spouses joint control of community property in addition to joint ownership.)

As for the responsibility to support the family, American states continue to assign this obligation to the husband while assigning the wife no support obligations. So immutable is this principle that courts have not traditionally waived it even in the face of private agreements made by husbands and wives. "Even in cases where the woman had independent wealth and the parties married on the condition that the husband should not be obligated for support, the courts have nevertheless reaffirmed the unalterability of the husband's obligation and held him liable for his wife's support."[75] In contrast, a wife is usually obliged to contribute to child support only if her husband cannot or will not support the child. Her obligations for supporting her husband are even more limited; even the legal obligation to support an *incapacitated* husband is imposed in only a minority of states.[76]

As numerous observers have pointed out, however, the husband's legal obligation to support his family is virtually unenforceable in an ongoing marriage. The American legal system provides no legal action a wife can take against her husband to obtain adequate support while she is still living with him. Only in cases of abandonment, separation, or divorce will the legal system enforce the husband's support obligation. As long as the wife remains in the household, she must accept whatever level of support her husband is willing to offer. The courts' unwillingness to intervene in an ongoing marriage means that a wife must leave her husband in order to invoke the support doctrine.[77] Moreover, even the support payments to which divorced and separated women are legally entitled do not always materialize. A recent study by the child-support project of the Urban Institute in Washington showed that between 1968 and 1973, only 41 percent of female-headed households eligible for child support received support from the fathers of the children. The other 59 percent received *no* assistance whatsoever from the fathers. Other research confirms these findings.[78]

The impetus for federal action on this problem of nonsupport by absent fathers was the discovery by the GAO in late 1974 that a large proportion of children on welfare had fathers who were not providing support even though they could afford to do so. The GAO research, requested by former Representative Martha Griffiths, found that only one quarter of the fathers who had agreed to make support payments actually paid as much as 90 percent of the amount awarded, and that there was no correlation between actual payments and ability to pay.[79] In response to these findings, Congress enacted in August 1975 Title IV-D of the Social Security Act, known as the Parent Locator and Support Program. It imposed on all states, as a condition of participating in the AFDC program, an obligation to try to track down deserting fathers of welfare families. The federal government cooperates fully in this effort by (1) contributing 75 percent of the program's cost; and (2) giving state welfare officials access to social security, income tax, and civil service records, and even authorizing the garnishment of federal employee's salaries (including servicemen). State governments must cooperate with one another in locating fathers who have moved across state borders. In short, the law authorized what would probably be perceived as an intolerable invasion of the absent father's privacy if it were not identified as a welfare program.[80] In fact, the SSA initially resisted the measure, contending that federal privacy laws protected the confidentiality of social security numbers, but this resistance was overruled by HEW Secretary David Mathews.[81] Given the historical strength of legal precedents protecting an individual's privacy against governmental encroachment, it is significant that the federal government would go to such lengths to ensure that the taxpayers are not forced to assume a father's traditional support obligation. What makes the invasion of privacy tolerable to policy makers who might otherwise object is the prospect that it will reduce the government's welfare expenditures. Evaluated on those terms the program has been successful. HEW reported that in fiscal year 1978 the program collected over one billion dollars in support payments from missing fathers, enabling 19,000 families to be removed from the welfare rolls.[82]

Just as American public policy continues to assign the guardian role to the husband, judges and policy makers continue to see the wife as the natural caretaker of home and family. This bias is particularly evident from court actions in divorce cases and in matters of child custody and visitation rights. The courts' preference for the mother of young children in custody cases is not a matter of statute but a matter of judicial presumption. There are many laws built on the same presumption (e.g., laws in some states make a mother's mere absence from her child a crime of abandonment, while fathers are guilty of abandonment only if they wilfully withhold support in addition to leaving the child).

The most notable exception to this bias has emerged, as we would expect, in the government's welfare policy. As we saw in chapter 2, the WIN program created in 1967 was aimed at putting employable welfare recipients to work. In many states, single mothers of small children were obliged to register for job training and placement. The irony is that feminists themselves have expressed indignation at federal welfare programs that presumed to interfere in the parent-child relationship. For example, in congressional testimony against Nixon's 1971 "workfare" proposal, the National Organization of Women (NOW) assaulted the bill's intention to force women into jobs. In so doing, NOW defended the most conventional of wife-mother stereotypes:

> What is it that makes cooking and cleaning the house and washing clothes and getting the kids off to school and taking care of the baby *normal*, in fact *ideal*, when these activities are supported by the income of a husband/father, yet *deviant* when supported by public funds?[84]

But if federal workfare programs like WIN have represented a deviation from policy makers' normal presumptions about family roles, the Carter administration's welfare proposal unveiled in August 1977 displayed an obvious intent to reinforce the traditional family. It was explicitly aimed at removing the father's incentive to abandon his family, which had long been built into the AFDC program. It permitted a single mother with children under seven years of age to remain at home instead of working. It provided only one public job per recipient couple, on the assumption that in the normal family only one parent works outside the home. This assumption was clearly acknowledged in a memorandum from an assistant secretary to the secretary of labor, during the preparation of the proposal:

> One can think of the traditional American family structure with two parents and children in which the family head goes out to work and makes enough of a living to keep the family together. The major thrust of any program ought to be to support this as the predominant situation for Americans.[85]

By giving preference in the awarding of the public job to the parent who worked or earned the most in the preceding year, the proposal would have the effect of favoring men. The Labor Department acknowledged that 50 percent of the public-service jobs would go to men, even though 80 percent of adult welfare recipients are women. Finally, the proposal presumed that parents and children have mutual support obligations; in addition to the assumption that parents must support minor children, the proposal assumed that adult children have financial responsibility for parents living with them. Thus it stipulated that welfare agencies must consider the incomes of all related members of a household when calculating welfare benefits for anyone in the household.

The treatment of marital roles in American family law has received considerable attention from sociologists, feminist and nonfeminist, in recent years.[86] Therefore, we have not attempted a comprehensive discussion of the topic here. We have presented this brief survey of American public policy to highlight the contrast between American and Swedish trends. Swedish policy, as we saw, has increasingly promoted the idea of symmetrical, almost interchangeable, roles for husband and wife in marriage. U.S. policy has been strongly noninterventionist, reserving its interference in the family for poor households or households dissolved through separation or divorce. In these latter cases, public policy has generally reaffirmed the partners' specialized and interdependent roles. Husbands are seen to be the primary guardians, and wives to be the primary homemakers. The only significant exceptions we can identify are the periodic and mostly unsuccessful welfare reforms that have tried to place welfare mothers in employment. In these cases, federal lawmakers' desire to discourage "freeloading" outweighed the conviction that women belong at home.

Earlier, we noted that family law in the United States is the purview of the states. We would not want the reader to infer from that statement that national policy makers are powerless to influence American family law. One bit of evidence to the contrary in recent years was congressional passage of the Equal Rights Amendment, which, if ratified, would remove many of the double standards from state laws on child support, alimony, and child custody. In these matters, the two spouses' rights and obligations would be defined in functional terms, based on their respective earning power, resources, nonmonetary contributions to the marriage, and so forth. Important as these changes are, they would not directly affect the roles and rights of spouses in *ongoing* marriages (as opposed to dissolved marriages).

> The reluctance of courts to interfere directly in an ongoing marriage is a standard tenet of American jurisprudence. As a result, legal elaboration of the duties husbands and wives owe one another has taken place almost entirely in the context of the breakdown of marriage.[87]

The Equal Rights Amendment will not change this.

CHANGING MODELS OF THE FAMILY

Recent research published by federal agencies shows that despite policy makers' commitment to the traditional American family structure, the reality no longer conforms to the stereotype of the traditional family with two parents, at least one child at home, and a husband who works outside the home while the wife stays home. For one thing, over a third of all family households (37.2 percent) have only two persons.[88] In fact, the average number of persons in family households has dropped precipitously from 3.6 persons in 1970 to only 3.4 persons in 1977. Many Americans are now choosing to live alone; between 1970 and 1977, the percentage of persons between the ages of fourteen and thirty-four who lived by themselves actually doubled (from about 2 percent to about 4 percent). Another explanation for the shrinking household size is women's declining fertility rate. The number of children raised by the average American family dropped from nearly four in 1957 to fewer than two in 1977. Even more intriguing than this general decline is the growing incidence of childlessness among women aged twenty to twenty-four; in this age group the percentage of childless women increased from 24 percent in 1960 to over 40 percent in 1977. Finally, of the households containing more than two persons, a growing percentage now deviates from the stereotype because they are headed by single women. The number of female-headed families has increased by one third in the last decade.[89]

Among the factors contributing to the changing family configuration, divorce has been singled out for particular attention by many commentators on the American family. They view the rising divorce rate with alarm as irrefutable evidence that the traditional family is disintegrating. To examine this contention, we must first look at American divorce rates in comparative and historical perspective. The high divorce rate in the United States is not strictly a mid-twentieth-century phenomenon. Divorce figures at the turn of the century were far higher for the United States than for European countries (see table 5–2).

Moreover, as Mary Jo Bane has pointed out, it is more instructive for some purposes to look at the incidence of marital disruption rather than at the divorce rate. If we are concerned about family instability, especially as it affects children, we might well want to examine the proportion of marriages that remain intact over time as an indicator of family stability. Hence we may want to take into account the number of marriages disrupted by a spouse's death, as well as marriages ended by divorce. When Bane compared the proportion of ever-married women living with their first husbands in 1910, 1940, and 1970, she found the percentages surprisingly consistent over time (see table 5–3). The explanation for the consistency is, of course, that as death rates fell, fewer women in each age bracket were

TABLE 5-2. Annual Divorces per 1000 Marriages, United States and Selected European Nations

United States (1902–6)	84
France (1900–1905)	37
England and Scotland (1900–1903)	29
Netherlands (1900–1905)	19
Sweden (1900–1901)	13

Source: Carle C. Zimmerman, *Family and Civilization* (New York: Harper & Row, 1947), p. 594.

TABLE 5-3. Percentage of Ever-Married Women Living with Their First Husbands

Census Year	Age of Women 45–49	50–54	55–64
1910	70.2	64.7	55.0
1940	68.4	64.0	54.9
1970	69.9	65.7	56.6

Source: Mary Jo Bane, *Here to Stay: American Families in the Twentieth Century* (New York: Basic, 1976), p. 30.

widowed. Therefore, fewer families were disrupted by death, even though more were disrupted by divorce.

Although we acknowledge that the divorce rate has climbed significantly since 1910, we must offer the qualifying observation that it has not risen steadily or uniformly. Rather, divorce rose to an all-time high in 1946; fell until 1958; then began rising again, until in 1973 it passed the 1946 level (see figure 5–1). Having sounded these cautionary notes, we still find it impossible to ignore the dramatic nature of recent increases; from the mid-1960s to the mid-1970s, the divorce rate doubled.

Is Women's Employment a Threat to the Family?

What accounts for this rapidly rising divorce rate? There is an abundance of published discussion and disagreement on this question. Explanations cited in the outpouring of recent literature range from large-scale economic and demographic forces to personal psychological changes, especially as regards the spouses' expectations of their partners and their marriage relationship. We do not attempt any definitive answer to this troubling question; that is a job for specialists in the field of family relations. We do find it interesting to consider, in the context of our comparison with Sweden and China, two theories often raised in this debate: (1) women's increasing labor-force participation is responsible for the rising divorce rate; and (2) by providing more social services to the family, government agencies have usurped many traditional family functions and contributed to making the family obsolete.

Long-term trends lend a certain plausibility to the argument that divorces are caused by women's employment outside the home. The dramatic rise in the divorce rate in the early 1940s is often linked to the wartime separation of couples, combined with women's accelerating employment. During the 1950s, when women returned in large numbers to

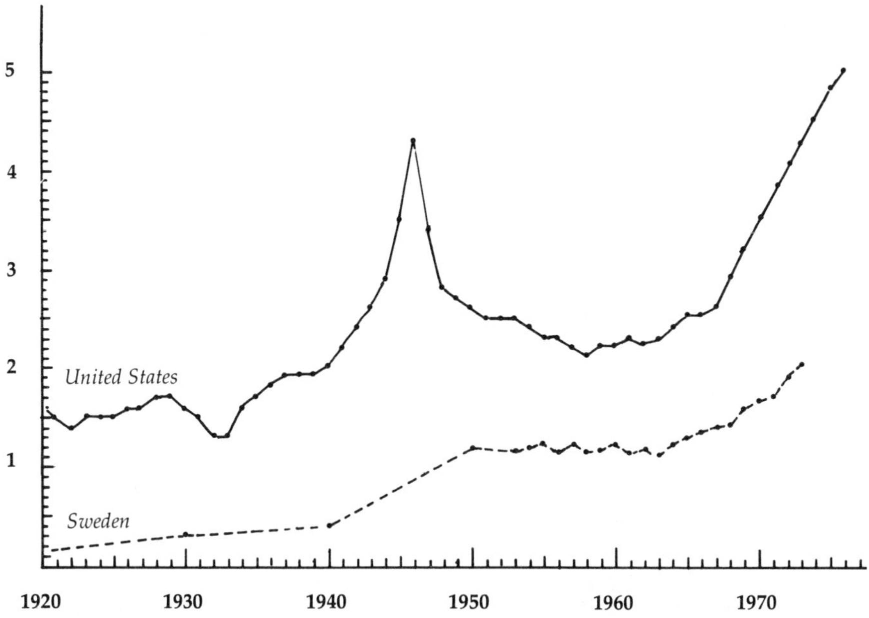

Source: *Statistisk Årsbok för Sverige;* and U.S. Bureau of the Census, *Population Profile of the U.S.*

FIGURE 5-1. Divorces per 1000 Population, 1920–76.

the homemaker role, the divorce rate dropped again. The coincidence in these two trends might well lead one to conclude that they are directly related. Some systematic research has even shown a relationship between the level of wives' earnings from outside employment and the probability of separation.[90] But can we say that women's employment *causes* divorces?

Any social scientists must first respond to that question with the obvious caveats about drawing causal inferences from such data. To say that the female employment rate and the divorce rate are related does not illuminate the causal relationship between them. It is reasonable to assume that in many cases, divorce "causes" women's employment rather than the reverse. That is, a woman who is facing a divorce takes outside employment as an economic or emotional necessity arising out of the divorce. Furthermore, even where we could establish that wives' employment significantly predated their divorces, we could not draw hard-and-fast conclusions about *why* divorce followed employment. The most common conclusion is that wives' employment strains marriages; it may also be true that a wife's job provides the security she needs to end a marriage that has long been strained.

Beyond these preliminary methodological reservations, there are larger questions to be raised about the simple assertion that women's participation in the labor force is responsible for the soaring divorce rate. We must ask why a woman's shift into a productive role should jeopardize the stability of her marriage. History shows that, in the preindustrial era, wives played an integral role in the production process, both in the countryside and in cities:

> Premodern women engaged directly in productive labor. It might not be exactly the same work as that in which men engaged . . . but it did produce goods and/or earn money. In the cities, weavers' wives and daughters prepared thread for weaving, or spun thread themselves, or helped finish the cloth. Wives of urban artisans and merchants often kept accounts. . . . Peasant wives helped with planting and harvesting.[91]

Evidently, at some points in Western history, women's participation in production was perfectly compatible with family stability and even necessary for family survival. Moreover, our Swedish and Chinese cases offer little evidence to support a simple correlation between divorce and women's employment.

True, Sweden's divorce rate, although lower than the American rate, is nevertheless one of the highest in the world. But if we examine closely the long-term trends in the divorce rate in the twentieth century, we find that we can draw no easy conclusions about its relationship to women's employment. As table 5–4 shows, Sweden experienced sharp increases in the divorce rate in the first half of this century. The steady upswing in fact began in the 1870s, as industrialization got under way. In Alva Myrdal's view, this increase was a predictable consequence of the shift away from an agrarian economy, in which the disadvantages connected with any split or mortgaging of landholdings was a strong deterrent to divorce.[92] With the shift to commercial capitalism, divorce became more feasible because a family's assets were more easily divisible. The steepest increases of the century are observable in the 1920s (very probably as a result of the liberalized Marriage Law of 1921), and in the 1940s (particularly in the years immediately following World War II).

When we compare trends in divorce with trends in women's employment, we find no obvious correlation. Women's employment (including married women's employment) remained almost stable between 1910 and 1950. During that period, women's employment hovered around 32 percent, with only about 10 percent of married women employed outside the home. The proportion of women employed began to rise in the 1950s but showed its most dramatic upsurge in the 1960s. During the 1950s, the divorce rate virtually froze, showing no appreciable increase. The rise in

TABLE 5-4. Increases in Divorce and Married Women's Employment in Sweden, 1900–70

	Percentage of Married Women Employed	*Number Divorces per 1000 Population*	*Percentage Increase in Divorces over Previous Decade*
1900	—	.07	40
1910	—	.09	28
1920	—	.16	78
1930	9	.30	87
1940	10	.45	50
1950	11	1.19	164
1960	16	1.20	.8
1970	53	1.40	17

Sources: *Statistisk Arsbok för Sverige*; and Joint Female Labor Council, *Woman in Sweden in the Light of Statistics* (Stockholm: Arbetsmarknadens Kvinnonamnd, 1973), table 3:3, p. 37.

divorces in the 1960s, the decade when married women literally poured into the labor market, is the next smallest increase recorded in the twentieth century. Indeed, if we were to use Swedish data to draw conclusions about the relationship between the two trends, we would have to conclude that divorce is *inversely* related to women's employment. We found at least one observer willing to venture that guess: "The gainful employment of married women has had a stabilizing effect on marriage."[93]

Unfortunately, we do not have comparable data for China, to suggest how the communists' periodic campaigns to increase women's "productive labor" has affected the divorce rate. We know that divorce in traditional China was rare. Wives theoretically enjoyed the right to divorce their husbands, but they faced heavy disincentives for doing so. Upon divorce, a wife left her husband's clan to return to her own family, abandoning any sons and sometimes even her daughters. Children were typically viewed as the husband's property.[94] The family law reforms introduced by the Nationalist government in 1931 contained provisions for divorce by mutual consent. However, the communists' Marriage Law of 1950 and the accompanying propaganda campaign are generally credited with generating the most dramatic upsurge in divorce ever seen in China. In fact, the marriage law brought such a flood of divorces that the population began calling it the divorce law. An overwhelming majority of these divorce actions were brought by wives against their husbands, even in rural areas.[95] The CCP at first viewed this rash of divorces with equanimity and even approval, taking for granted "that the evils of the traditional institution form[ed] the fundamental cause . . . something too obvious to need any statistical proof."[96] After the massive campaign to educate cadres on the marriage law in 1953, however, the party became steadily more sensitive to the criticism that divorce was undermining the social fabric of China. The party started to publish pamphlets to prove otherwise, and letters appeared in the press suggesting that it was becoming increasingly difficult to obtain a divorce. Although it is not complete, table 5–5 gives some indication of divorce trends in the years immediately following the marriage reform.

Recent visitors to China agree that divorce is now far from a common procedure in the People's Republic. Divorces are rarely asked for, and far more rarely given. To some extent, we might attribute this situation to the continuing influence of traditional views regarding marriage. In addition, couples considering divorce are often discouraged by local residents' committees. As one female committee leader explained to Ruth Sidel, "If a couple is quarreling, a member of the residents' committee will go to the home and advise the couple to unite."[97] In the Ching Nian commune in Sian in 1972, out of 9100 resident families, only 17 couples had requested divorces, and only 11 couples had been granted divorces.[98] The Committee of Concerned Asian Scholars has ventured yet another explanation for the rarity of divorce in China. Returning from the People's Republic in 1971, the committee reported that women's ability to work outside the home may actually have a stabilizing effect on marriages:

> Divorce is infrequent because it is discouraged and because couples who do not get along very well can tolerate each other better in China than in the United States . . . incompatibilities can be tolerated in a marriage because the marriage is only one part of life for the woman as well as for the man . . . she has her own work separate from his and she takes part in various afterwork activities alone.[99]

Will Social Services Replace the Family?

If our comparative cases fail to support the view that women's labor-force participation necessarily contrib-

TABLE 5-5. Divorce Cases Heard by Chinese Courts, 1950–56[a]

1950–June 1951	993,000
1952	—
1953	1,170,000
1954	710,000
1955	610,000
1956	510,000

[a] *These figures omit divorces by mutual consent, for which no court hearing is necessary.*

Source: Delia Davin, *Woman-Work and the Party in Revolutionary China* (Oxford, England: Clarendon, 1976), p. 101.

utes to divorce, what about the theory that the expansion of social services to the family undermines the family by usurping its traditional functions? This is an argument commonly used by conservative legislators to oppose government spending for social services. It expresses a viewpoint shared by many social scientists as well. One of its more sophisticated versions is found in a recent essay of political scientist Richard Merelman, who starts from the widely accepted premise that the modern family is less and less a unit of production and is becoming more and more a unit of consumption. In this transformation, he argues, families have become inherently unstable "principally because consumption is almost inherently an *individualistic* pastime requiring little cooperation for its enjoyment.[100] Government has contributed to the tension created within families by family members' consumption activities because government provides a large proportion of the social services consumed by families:

> The state stepped in with a plethora of professionally staffed and impersonally run "helping" organizations in order to provide the educational and social services the family had formerly provided itself.[101]

According to Merelman, social services provided by large bureaucratic organizations not only fail as a substitute for family-provided services, but they actually "subvert" family life because they are administered to consumers on the basis of rational bureaucratic rules and structures totally at odds with the family's emotive style of operation. Bureaucratic service providers seek to satisfy the norms of rationality, efficiency, universality and the like, whereas family members provide services to one another on the basis of sentiment: "The structure of the state's family service production mechanisms is manifestly at odds with its purpose of bolstering the emotive basis of life."[102] Merelman concludes that these services chip away at family solidarity, contributing to its instability.

Inherent in such debates about the influence of social services on traditional family structure are certain assumptions about the nature of families and their proper functions. Within historical memory, families have performed the functions of production, reproduction, education, welfare, and property holding. Presumably, no one any longer believes that production should be transferred back to the family; no one is suggesting that parents undertake to educate their children by themselves or even pay completely to educate their children. Society's stake in a literate citizenry and work force is too great for any politician, conservative or liberal, to suggest that education be left entirely in the family's hands. Our point is simple: The functions of the family change over time, as does family structure. If families are increasingly performing the consumption function, should we view the trend toward new family forms as "instability," or merely as structural adaptation that permits the family to perform its new function?

Moreover, the argument that "consumption is almost inherently an individualistic pastime requiring little cooperation for its enjoyment" is at least debatable. A major part of income in any family is spent for items consumed as a group: living space, furnishings, appliances, utilities, cars, and such food as is shared at meals. A second slice of family income goes for government services like national defense, postal service, and garbage collection, which are also consumed collectively. Furthermore, even the allocation of some part of the family budget for individual consumption requires family agreement on the proper distribution.

Sweden. If Merelman's thesis were true, we would expect the social welfare state constructed in Sweden since the 1930s to have dealt a near-fatal blow to Sweden's families. One might want to argue, for example, that women were encouraged to divorce their husbands in the 1940s by the economic security provided to their children under a 1937 law stipulating that the government would guarantee their child-support payments. If an ex-husband failed to make the payments to which the family was legally entitled, the government would make up the family's loss. This guarantee is a cash benefit rather than a service, but it is precisely the kind of government program opponents of Swedish welfare policy have criticized. It reduces the family's dependence on the father for support, while transferring that dependence to the state.

Sweden's history makes clear that no such simple correlation between social services and the decline of families is possible. Instead of dropping, the proportion of Swedes choosing to live in marriages has actually risen markedly since the 1930s, when the Social Democrats began building the welfare state. In 1930, only 48 percent of the Swedish population was married. In 1974, by contrast, 60 percent of all Swedes were living in marriages. And the latter figure actually underestimates the proportion of Swedes living in marital arrangements because it leaves out those who live in "loyalty marriages," another 6 percent of the Swedish population.[103] While the proportion of Swedes in marriages has risen, the households they have established have changed. Sweden's 1970 census provided a glimpse of what the Swedish household of the future will look like (see table 5–6). The table shows an amazingly high proportion of childless households. Overall, the census showed that more than half (55 percent) of households consisted of only one or two persons. The increase in one- and two-person households in Sweden closely parallels the American trend we noted. Whether the rise in childless couples, loyalty marriages, and single-person households constitutes "family instability" is debatable. Many Swedes regard the changing configuration of their families as no more than a predictable adaptation to changing social and economic trends.

There is also room for disagreement on whether the government's social policies are responsible for Sweden's changing family life. Swedish policy makers we interviewed in 1976 vigorously denied that the national government's social programs had contributed to family instability. With the exception of one Riksdag member representing the Center party, these

TABLE 5-6. Swedish Households, by Number of Children Under 16 Years of Age, 1970

	Percent of Households in Each Category
No children	64
One child	17
Two children	13
Three or more children	6

Source: Joint Female Labor Council, *Woman in Sweden in the Light of Statistics* (Stockholm: Arbetsmarknadens Kvinnonamnd, 1973), table 1:16, p. 16.

legislators perceived Sweden's social policy as a response, rather than as a contributor, to the nation's changing family life. This almost universal perception on the part of national legislators deserves comment. To portray government as a responder rather than initiator of family change is to settle for a short-range interpretation of a complex, long-term interaction between national policy and family units since the 1930s. We pointed out in chapter 4 that the battery of social welfare programs introduced by the Social Democrats, starting in the 1930s, predated the massive entry of women into the labor force. Such programs can be said to have contributed to that influx by providing support services for women working outside the home. Other governmental policies (described in chapter 4) directly aimed at pulling women into the work force. The shift of so many Swedish women into labor market roles brought about changes in the life styles and service needs of many families, which in turn called forth further policy changes from government. In short, today's Swedish legislators may well see recent social policies as responses to family change, but over the longer term family change has been at least in part the result of government actions.

Other trends besides women's employment are contributing to the redefinition of Swedish family structure. One is the trend away from the child-centered family, which is facilitated by certain long-standing cultural norms. Compared with the United States, the mystique of motherhood is comparatively underdeveloped in Sweden. This is particularly noticeable if we contrast the glorification of motherhood that prevailed in the United States in the 1950s[104] with the following observation on Scandinavian women by sociologist Kaare Svalastoga:

> But even if she excels in all these respects [being a good housekeeper and hostess, a loving mother and an attractive spouse], she will reap slight social esteem, because dominant middle class opinion will insist on the superior values of choosing a career outside the home and of cultivating literary and artistic interests.[105]

Studies of Swedish child-rearing practices suggest that Swedish mothers tend to encourage early separation between themselves and their children. They reward displays of self-sufficiency by their children and regard dependency needs as unacceptable.[106] This attitude toward motherhood has doubtless contributed to the widespread demand for public child-care facilities. Such long-standing cultural norms have made the transition from the child-centered family to one centering around dual careers easier.

Sociologist Alva Myrdal, who probably has had more influence over Sweden's family policy during the last two decades than any other individual, recommended as early as 1964 that educators and social welfare officials must recognize the inevitability and even the desirability of eliminating the child-centered family:

> It seems to me about time we accept as a pedagogical objective the conscious preparation of our children to be able to tolerate being set aside to a certain degree. . . . It is extremely desirable that we help our children to develop independence and self-reliance as early as possible and encourage their capabilities to get along on their own inner resources.[107]

More recently, Myrdal has recommended to the Social Democratic government that policy makers accept the dual-career family as the model in formulating family policy from now on; she asserts that family policy that presumes the existence of a full-time homemaker is outmoded.[108]

We find evidence in Sweden's recent social policy that national legislative leaders, not only of the Social Democratic party, but of others as well, have taken seriously Myrdal's advice on recognizing the dual-career family. Nevertheless, social welfare officials have clearly rejected the proposition that government agencies should supply to the dual-career family *all* the services families have traditionally provided to themselves. Even those who may find that desirable have had their enthusiasm for expanded social services dampened by the growing resistance to taxation (credited with contributing to the Social Democrats' defeat in the 1976 elections). Especially with the current governing coalition of bourgeois parties, we should expect to see few new social programs. On the other hand, policies that encourage symmetrical roles for husbands and wives may offer an alternative to large-scale expansion of public services (e.g., the parental leave). Another example is the government's encouragement to many government offices to allow civil servants, male and female, to participate in "flexitime." Under flexitime, an employee may choose to arrive at work any time between 7:00 and 9:00 A.M. and leave at any time between 5:00 and 7:00 P.M., as long as he or she puts in the requisite hours. Moreover, an employee's schedule may vary every day of the week to accommodate his or her family's schedule. If widely used, flexitime could increase families' flexibility and reduce their dependence on outside services. Yet another example is the government's bill (which took effect in January 1979) to guarantee working parents the right to reduce their workday to six hours until their youngest child finishes his or her first year in school. This measure was first suggested by a Social Democratic government commission in 1975[109] and was picked up by the succeeding coalition government as one means of allowing parents to spend more time on home and family. The bill is distinct from the parental leave in that it does not provide the parent with any compensation for lost earnings; it simply entitles parents of young children to request a reduced workday from their employers. Even though it does not involve subsidies, the bill constitutes further proof that the government is seeking to use public policy to bolster and preserve the Swedish family rather than replace it.

China. Since 1949, and to a certain extent even before, Chinese family life has moved in the direction of the "conjugal families" associated with increasing industrialization. The primary characteristic of such family groupings "is that a wide range of in-laws and blood relatives are excluded from the everyday affairs of the nuclear family unit."[110] William Goode has identified this kind of family as the one that dominates most industrialized Western countries and the one that increasingly dominates sub-Saharan Africa, Arabic Islam, India, China, and Japan. All families move in this direction during industrialization, but China's have done so much more quickly.

> The changes toward the conjugal family in most societies occur in a glacial fashion, as education gradually expands, as new extrafamilial employment opportunities develop, as bureaucratic forms of organization and hiring become more dominant, and as ideas of equality and individual fulfillment slowly win favor among the educated urban classes and begin to trickle down to other parts of the population. . . . In China, all of these changes have occurred, but faster, and they have been backed by pressures not generally present in other countries.[111]

The main pressure present in China has been the pressure of a revolutionary government whose desire for change does not admit of "glacial adjustments."

The intervention of the Chinese Communist party into Chinese family life was never intended to break up the family;[112] the task has been modification, changing the family from a "feudal" institution to one more compatible with a socialist society. Attacks have been directed at patriarchy and the privileges of sex and age through marriage law campaigns; at the legal and ethical functions of clans through substitution of central laws and moral standards; at property holding in the family, the accumulation of wealth through inheritance, and families serving as units of production. The family has been left with other important functions and is strongly encouraged to perform them well. This list includes consumption, reproduction, moral education, and welfare. These functions are remarkably similar to the ones fulfilled in Western industrialized countries, but in

China they are to be fulfilled not primarily for the benefit of individual family members but for the benefit of the collective. For in Communist China, the good of the individual and the good of the family are always thought to depend upon the good of the collective.

> In a socialist society, the personal interests of every member of the society are basically identical with those of the collective whole and the state. It is always the policy of the Party and the government to take care of the interests of the state and the collective as well as those of the individual. But at certain times, especially when some members of the society have deserted the interests or when the state and the collective is facing certain difficulties but individual members of the society do not appreciate these difficulties, contradictions will arise between individual interests and those of the state and the collective. At such times we must place the interests of the state or the collective first and make our personal interests subservient to the interests of the state and the collective.[113]

Far from seeking to undermine the family structure, the CCP has relied heavily on the family to continue supplying its members with social services beyond the financial capabilities of the government. In a poor industrializing country that nevertheless wants to maintain a minimum standard of living for its people, only the most essential social services can be offered. Reliance on families to provide primary help and comfort in time of need is imperative. As in the West, most helping services in the Chinese People's Republic (e.g., day care, disability payments, welfare relief) are given only after the family has failed to provide its own. Unlike the West, the People's Republic has gone to great lengths to ensure that the family *will not fail*. Because the notion of the private conjugal family is much less highly developed in China than in the West, the government has been able to apply great pressure to families to encourage them to solve their own problems.

Consequently, parents continue to take care of their children, families care for their sick, and children care for their parents in old age. Families are close because of necessity as well as love. For instance, day-care facilities are not nearly so abundant as has sometimes been suggested. The majority of preschool children are still cared for by the family, and the help of the grandparents solves a critical problem for working mothers. Among rural families, grandparents probably live with their children; among urban families, grandparents may or may not. Three-generational families are still found but are not universal. Interestingly, it seems that at present in the cities, the wife's mother cares for the children, rather than the husband's mother as in the past. And the grandmother may take the children for weeks on end.[114] This report was given by an English schoolteacher who taught in the People's Republic for eight years:

> It is not unknown . . . for urban mothers to be sent for a period of labor in the countryside on a day's notice. In such cases, although very often the father has also been sent away, no official arrangements are made for the mother's

> children. This is considered purely a personal problem, and if the mother seeks exemption from labor on the grounds that she has a sick or a very young child, she may open herself to charges of bourgeois sentimentality. Under these circumstances, she may leave her children to fend for themselves if one is old enough to cook and care for its younger siblings. Or she may place her children in state nurseries, if vacancies can be found, or settle them with relatives. Children hardly able to walk are often entrusted to the care of railway attendants and sent the length of China to join relatives in distant parts.[115]

Other working women choose to leave their children at their mother's for several years. At least one tour guide serving as a translator for foreigners indicated that she preferred to leave her children with her mother, who lived in another city. "The guide was very happy about the arrangement as she found children a bit of a fuss. She preferred her job."[116]

In rural as well as urban China, practical considerations combine to keep the family together. Three-generational families are common and share not only day care but domestic chores. In part, three-generation households persist specifically because of state policies. Because a sharp rise in urbanization could cause a great strain on Chinese agriculture, the government has sharply restricted urban migration. Thus the phenomenon of young people leaving the farm to seek their fortune in the city rarely occurs. While the communists have brought many changes to Chinese life, some things remain unaltered. Most Chinese people, like their ancestors before them, have lived and worked their entire lives in the confines of one or maybe two villages. If the young people stay on the farm, the problem of housing is crucial. In rural areas, it takes around ten years for a couple to save enough money to build a new house, and shortages of building materials increase the amount of time needed to construct one.

> The result of both the expense of building and the occasional shortage of building materials is that most sons must live close to their parents. By the time he is ready to marry in his early twenties, a man will not have been able to save enough money to build a new house. He must therefore either simply stay within his own parents' house, take money from the combined family savings to build a new wing onto the old house, or take even more savings to build a more complete house elsewhere in the village. . . . The most common practice seems to be either to remain with the parents after marriage or to build an additional room or set of rooms very close by.[117]

The Chinese Communist government has stipulated in Article 13 of the Marriage Law that children and parents bear the responsibility for supporting each other in times of hardship and old age. "Neither the parents nor the children shall maltreat or desert one another." Although urban workers have a form of social insurance and medical coverage, any prolonged illness requires the support of family members. Benefits are not sufficient to enable the worker "to go it alone" without additional money from the family and, perhaps, the trade union.[118] In the countryside, the primary social insurance against prolonged illness is the bearing of several sons, as it has been in the past. Although daughters are not considered nearly the liability that they have been in the past, they are still less desired. First, they earn fewer work points. Second, because they join their husband's family, they are a loss to their own. Although the party has recently begun encouraging young men whose parents have many sons to settle with their wives' families, the policy is only in its infancy. Traditional male resistance against being placed in such a subordinate position is bound to make change slow.

Just as it is needed during prolonged illness, the family's support is crucial during old age. "The retiring workers have had a very modest floor for existence. The worker needs additional help from his family, or additional assistance from the trade union, or both, to live out his retirement years." [119] Regarding the countryside, one student from Kwangtung said, "In both Canton and the countryside, one hears it said that if one has several children—male children—one can both retire earlier and live a much more comfortable old age. If one has several children, each need contribute only a few yuan per month, and then one can live quite comfortably." [120] Parents with daughters, on the other hand, are in a very tenuous position. The production team may choose to provide retirement assistance from welfare funds, as if the couple had no children. On the other hand, the team may expect the daughter to contribute to the parents' support. In the latter case, the daughter's husband and his family must cooperate. Having nothing to gain and everything to lose from the bargain, the husband's family is likely to withhold their consent, leaving the girl's parents without any contribution from their offspring. The most favored tactic appears to be to find the daughter a well-to-do husband. Then the couple will be able to support both sets of parents, if the need arises. Given this contrast between the assurance of old-age support from married sons and the possibility that married daughters may provide little or no support, it is easy to understand the widespread preference for sons. [121]

The Chinese Communist government has thus continued to leave many important functions to families. The social services provided by China have not supplanted the family; indeed they do not seek to. Rather, they have contributed help when needed. The primary difference between Sweden and the United States, on the one hand, and China, on the other, has been the extent to which China has been willing to interfere in family life to ensure that family functions are performed properly.

CONCLUSION

A guiding principle in American social policy has been that the private nuclear family is the best, indeed the *only*, acceptable setting for child rearing. But historical surveys of family styles and functions show that the domestic "family of sentiment," centered around child rearing as its pri-

FOLD, TAPE, AND MAIL

NO POSTAGE
NECESSARY
IF MAILED
IN THE
UNITED STATES

BUSINESS REPLY MAIL

FIRST CLASS PERMIT NO. 50745, NEW YORK, N.Y.

FIRST CLASS POSTAGE WILL BE PAID BY

LONGMAN INC.

19 WEST 44th STREET

NEW YORK, N. Y. 10036

COLLEGE DEPARTMENT

PACKING SLIP

LONGMAN INC.
19 WEST 44TH STREET NEW YORK, N.Y. 10036

FREE DESK OR EXAMINATION COPIES FOR

MR. WILLIAM FRAME KENYON COLLEGE	004180 1 240 32800 011880

QTY.	NUMBER, AUTHOR, AND TITLE	SRC
01	280648 MOTHERS AT WORK FREE	

WE HOPE YOU WILL FIND TIME TO USE THE SPACE BELOW TO GIVE US YOUR OPINION OF THESE TITLES, AND TO LET US KNOW ABOUT YOUR PLANS FOR THEIR USE IN YOUR COURSES.

COMMENTS

MAY WE QUOTE YOU? YES ☐ NO ☐

FOLD, TAPE, AND MAIL

mary function, is only one family form, and a relatively recent one at that. Three characteristics of the family we now take for granted—its privacy and isolation from the outside world, the primacy of the child rearing function, and homemaker-childminder as a specialized full-time role—are apparently not immutable at all. The work of both Aries and Shorter suggests that the family's transformation into a private sphere and the family's assumption of child rearing as its central and specialized function date only from the rise of capitalism. Recognizing that fact, we may speculate that the domestic nuclear family is an appropriate form only under the economic and social conditions prevailing in the West during the past 300 years. Indeed, the Chinese case shows few traces of such a private family form, either before or after the Communist Revolution of 1949. In China's preindustrial economy prior to the revolution, the family performed the traditional function as a production unit to which all members contributed their labor. Since 1949, with the push toward industrialization, the production system has undergone significant change. But the party has bent every effort to assure that families do not develop into private spheres of activity removed from the political and economic mainstream.

Sweden has shared in the universal European trend toward the privatized family, although Sweden's late industrialization prolonged the existence of the traditional agrarian family well into the nineteenth century. Our glimpse at contemporary trends in Swedish family life indicates that a new family form has emerged. Rather than performing their domestic functions in isolation from the outside world, Swedish families rely heavily on community services. The high incidence of childlessness and of small family size among Swedish families suggests that child rearing is not the central function of many married women, or even of many family units. Pragmatic Swedish policy makers interpret these trends without the alarm characteristic of American observers. They describe the Swedish family as "adapting" rather than "breaking down." In fact, one Swedish legislator we interviewed speculated that the emerging model of the dual-career family shows much greater survival capacity than the traditional nuclear family. In a society characterized by constant inflation, the mechanization of housework, and increasing life expectancy well beyond the woman's child rearing years, a family in which the woman works outside the home enjoys both financial and psychic advantages over the family in which the woman stays home or is employed only sporadically as a secondary wage earner. The crisis of the "family of sentiment," he argued, is precisely that it breeds emotional and financial dependencies that place too heavy a strain on the marital relationship.[122] The cost to society of maintaining the wife's primary identity as homemaker, with only weak ties to the labor market, is all too obvious in the case of female heads of household. Many such women, without labor skills or significant experience, simply transfer their dependency from their missing husbands to government welfare agencies.

In chapter 4 we described the long-term efforts made by the Swedish and Chinese governments since World War II to pull more women into the labor force. In both cases we observed the governments' willingness to use social services "developmentally" (i.e., to design social programs for women in ways that promoted women's employment). In the United States, it is difficult for feminists to advocate that the government provide special support services to women in order to ease their entry into the labor market. One important reason, which we have explored in this chapter, is the overwhelming cultural value attached to family privacy. What the Carnegie Commission calls the "myth of the self-sufficient family" is shared even by many who sympathize with the need to increase women's work opportunities. Such sympathizers often agree that homemaking and child-care chores should be shared equally by husband and wife, but that such sharing should obviate the need for government-provided services. They believe an internal restructuring of family responsibilities is preferable to government assumption of those responsibilities. Even some feminists suggest that government provision of support services to working women would simply relieve husbands of their proper responsibility for half the household burden. Ideally, these feminists argue, both women and men should work less than a 40-hour week so that both would have time for household chores. Realistically, such a reduction in working hours would put a significant financial strain on many working-class families in which both parents' wages are crucial to the family's standard of living. Moreover, the problem of a reduced workweek would create even more financial strain on single parents.

Another important reason why American feminists find it hard to argue for special social programs to support working women is the historical emphasis in American feminism on equal treatment for the sexes. The argument that women require special services because of their specialized family roles as homemakers-childminders has been labeled a "regressive" position by many American feminists because it assumes that women have the primary responsibility for children and home. Truly liberated women, this argument says, should not need special support services distinct from those required by male parents. The trouble with this argument is that it assumes, as given, symmetrical roles for married men and women that eliminate the need for special women's programs. But, as our Swedish example shows, symmetry in men's and women's family roles is not easily achieved in a society with a tradition of interdependent marital roles. Despite years of encouragement from unions and public agencies, Swedish husbands still do not share equally in household chores. A truly symmetrical sharing of responsibilities is likely to occur only when the household members accord equal importance to wife's and husband's outside employment. Otherwise, as long as the wife's employment is in part-time, low-prestige work, she will continue to assume the homemaker role as her primary identity. In other words, the shift from female dependence toward greater symmetry comes about only *after* women are gainfully employed, not *before*. Without the outside employment, the shift is unlikely to occur. To become so employed, many women need support services because they cannot take for granted their husbands' help.

6

CONCLUSION

MAJOR DETERMINANTS OF GOVERNMENT PROGRAMS FOR EMPLOYED WOMEN

As we observed in the introduction to this volume, American political science has produced a large body of literature stressing the economic determinants of public policy and deemphasizing the political determinants. Economists and political scientists have found the most powerful explanations for government activity in economic development indicators, primarily levels of wealth, industrialization, and urbanization. At the same time, political variables (e.g., party control, interparty competition, popular participation) have been found to be less important in explaining the kinds of programs introduced by governments and the levels of investment in those programs. Indeed, the evidence for the primacy of economics over politics has accumulated so rapidly and so consistently that the tide has been difficult to resist.

In contrast to much of the literature on policy analysis, our study has not emphasized economic development as a critical determinant of government policy. Our three-way comparison of support services for employed women has not produced a clear division between government policies in China's developing economy and policies in the two postindustrial economies. We have found that in many respects Swedish and Chinese policies have more in common than do Swedish and American. The governments of Sweden and China have undertaken in the past 20 years to pull large numbers of women, including married women, into the labor force. To accomplish that goal, both governments have made strong commitments to providing family-planning and maternity services, day care, and home helps. Admittedly, there are important differences in the strategies used by the two governments to deliver services to employed women; here, the vast difference in their levels of economic development is undoubtedly important. Sweden has invested a large proportion of its national budget in a massive public bureaucracy that delivers services to working families. In China's less developed economy, support services have been supplied largely by local self-help projects outside the government bureaucracy and often without government subsidy. In spite of the different delivery systems, we are struck by the fundamental similarity in the policies pursued by these two governments. Nor can we fail to recognize the strong dissimilarities in the approaches taken in Sweden and the United States. The U.S. national government has no active policy to recruit married women, especially mothers, into the labor force, nor does it seek to provide support services for women employed outside the home, except for those women who fall into the low-income category. The prevailing assumption in the United States is that working families will purchase whatever health, day-care, or housekeeping services they need to ease the dual burden carried by employed women. In short, our discovery of significant Swedish-Chinese similarities and significant Swedish-American contrasts suggests that the level of economic development is not a factor with overwhelming importance in explaining governments' policies toward working families. We are thus led to concur with Alexander Groth's observation that "the political orientation of a regime is frequently more important in determining the woman's place in her society than is economic development."[1]

When we move to an examination of the political determinants of policy, we cannot make much use of the political variables most often employed in recent policy studies (i.e. measures of partisan political activity, in elections or within legislatures). We concluded in chapter 3 that it would be inaccurate to see the introduction and expansion of support programs for working women as the result of (1) a high level of interparty competition, (2) a high level of electoral participation by women, or (3) a significant representation of women in policy-making positions. We did not find in either Sweden or China that policy makers have formulated their programs to support working women as responses to overwhelming constituency demand, aggregated either through mass movements or political parties. Conversely, we discovered that the U.S. government, confronted by an independent, mass-based women's movement, has not moved nearly as far as the other governments in providing social support for working women.

In this respect our observations reinforce the findings of much recent policy analysis, which tends to downplay the linkage between policy reform and mass politics (usually defined as electoral politics or party politics). In particular, research on the history of social welfare legislation has called into question the influence mass politics has exerted on social policy. Scholarly interest in this question has focused on the long-standing belief among political observers that massive expansions of social welfare programs inevitably follow from an increase in mass mobilization and political competition in political systems.

Hugh Heclo, in his detailed analysis of income-maintenance policies in Britain and Sweden, described this presumed connection clearly:

> The democratic influence of elections and parties has usually been considered particularly important in the development of modern social policies, because these policies are thought to be of most direct interest to electoral "consumers." The extension of democratic political forms is said to have provided greater popular control of leaders, who responded over the years with the broader welfare policies the electorate wanted. Certainly this interpretation has permeated every debate on wider popular participation, having been shared both by conservatives who feared and by socialists who relished the results of more democratic competition.[2]

Yet Heclo's conclusions minimized the influence of elections[3] or party competition[4] on the introduction and expansion of public pensions and unemployment insurance in Britain and Sweden. In a similar though more general vein, Alexander Groth has pointed out that

> most of the states that in the nineteenth century led the world in terms of the degree of suffrage extended to the population, and in the genuinely open and representative character of their elections, did *not* lead it in terms of welfare programs.[5]

In a contemporary study using 1966 data on 64 nations, Harold Wilensky reported only a weak correlation between social security expenditures and his two measures of political openness: (1) "the degree to which the mass of citizens participate in decision-making," and (2) "the degree to which the state allows or encourages the voluntary action of numerous autonomous groups."[6]

Thus, evidence is accumulating that social policy reforms are not as directly linked to mass politics as we once thought they were. To reject mass politics as the primary determinant of public policy, however, is not to reject politics altogether as an explanation for policy. It is simply to recognize that other features of political systems may have an important impact on policy formation.

In the case of social programs for working women, one critical element is the extent to which those in government see the introduction or expansion of such programs as consonant with other policy goals. We attribute particular importance to the recognition by Swedish and Chinese policy makers that support programs for working women contribute to achieving their goal of full employment. Our reader may object that the commitment to bringing women into the work force as part of the full-employment goal is not really attributable to political factors. Such a commitment, one might argue, is no more than a mechanical response by government to an environmental condition (i.e., a labor shortage in Sweden and a capital shortage in China). Certainly these shortages in Sweden and China over the past 30 years have created a climate receptive to the idea of active manpower policies. The pressure to maintain and increase productivity in both societies may have seemed almost to dictate full-employment policies. But that pressure does not necessarily dictate programs to bring *women* into the work force. To expand the definition of "full employment" to include employable females is a public policy decision that is by no means automatic. Labor shortages have not, always and everywhere, prompted governments to pull women into the work force. Groth spotlights the extreme example of Nazi Germany, which experienced labor shortages during World War II and yet did not respond by mobilizing women workers. The conservative Nazi ideology regarding the woman's place in the family prevented the government from making such a response.[7]

Less extreme examples are several Western European nations that experienced economic booms in the 1950s and 1960s (including, once again, West Germany). Under conditions of acute male labor shortages, a number of these nations imported foreign laborers instead of actively recruiting their female population into the work force. Sweden itself relied on immigrant labor to relieve the post–World War II labor shortage until the mid-1960s. At that point, the Social Democratic government made a conscious decision to shift its manpower effort into recruiting and training its own married women. As Alice Cook has pointed out, this was a decision with long-term policy implications: "Implicit in the Swedish decision is that women should be considered permanent additions to the labor force with appropriate investment in long-range training and placement."[8]

There is no guarantee that women will benefit from the presence of a labor shortage. What we *can* say with certainty is that the political costs incurred by policy makers who decide to promote higher female employment will be far lower under conditions of labor shortage than labor surplus.

But the explanation for the contrasting social policies of the United States and our other two cases hinges not only on the fact that increased female employment has been a goal of Swedish and Chinese governments, whereas it has not been viewed as desirable under American conditions of labor surplus. Perhaps even more important in the long run than this contrast in goals is the difference in the means available to the different governments to promote significant social change. For, as the quote from Alice Cook asserts, that is what is implied by a policy to increase women's long-term participation in the work force.

Our comparison suggests that political ideologies and institutions may either enlarge or restrict the role of government in promoting social change. Two features of politics in Sweden and China that have emerged as particularly important in this respect are (1) prevailing ideologies regarding the proper sphere of governmental activity and influence, and (2) the degree of centralization in the systems that formulate and implement social policy.

Ideologies Regarding the Sphere of Government Activity

Despite the obviously significant differences separating Chinese from Swedish political elites in the twentieth century, we found that they have shared at least two important views intimately related to those governments' willingness to introduce and expand women's support programs.

The first important view is of the family as a legitimate object of governmental concern, interest, and even supervision. Because it performs the indispensable functions of raising and socializing the next generation, the family is seen by Chinese and Swedish leaders as an "agent" of the larger community. This view carries at least two important implications for government policy. First, a social unit with so great a responsibility to the community must be supported; it cannot be allowed to fail in performing its assigned welfare and socialization functions. The commitment displayed by both governments to provide support services for working families can be traced in large part to this conviction that families perform a critical service for the larger community. By promoting family welfare, the state is assuring the collective welfare of its citizenry. A closely related implication is that government agencies have the right, even the obligation, to intervene in families in order to protect the community's interest in the family. In Sweden this intervention is confined to matters involving child welfare; in China community intervention extends even to quarrels between spouses.

On both counts—the state's obligation to support families and its right to intervene in family matters—American policy makers have taken a different view. Most have subscribed to the "myth of the self-sufficient family," convinced that, except for the poor, American families do not need or want the government to provide family services and benefits. In debates about large-scale public services, American officials speak ominously about government "usurpation" rather than government "support" of the family's welfare and childrearing functions. Their chief fear arises from the possibility that government benefits will lead to government interference in family life. Ultimately, the antipathy shown by many American policy makers toward a federal family policy rests on their desire to protect family privacy—an American value discussed at some length in chapter 5.

We have noted throughout our discussion the uncharacteristic willingness of American governments to intervene in the lives of welfare families. This pattern reflects an American tendency to see whatever family policy we do have as a passive, rather than an active, element of federal policy. Richard Rose has offered a distinction between areas of active policy in which "government is positively concerned with approaching specified goals, e.g., economic growth or slum clearance," and areas of passive policy in which "governments are not expected to identify objectives and move toward them, but rather, to respond to requests for services, as and when problems are placed before them."[9] Clearly the plight of welfare families is the "problem" placed before federal policy makers. Their response has not been a comprehensive family policy but emergency public assistance measures.

The second important view in the goverment's willingness to expand women's support programs is an instrumental attitude toward social policy. By this, we mean that Swedish and Chinese leaders regard social policy as a tool to be used by government to bring about desired changes in family life and the economy. We discussed in chapter 4 the use of social services by both governments as a form of leverage, to pry women with children out of their homes and into the labor force. Another example is the willingness of both governments to use social programs to influence fertility patterns in society. In China, public programs have aimed at preventing births by breaking down traditional family obligations, promoting late marriages, and emphasizing strict family planning. In Sweden, the national government has used social benefits and services to encourage births, by making it easier and cheaper to have children.

The American government has not attempted to manipulate social services and benefits to influence fertility patterns, except among welfare recipients.[10] The national significance of fertility patterns is unquestionable. Even a small change in birthrates can have a major impact on public institutions (e.g., schools), government benefits (e.g., social security), and the economy as a whole. The significance attributed to fertility trends is reflected in the close watch maintained by government demographers at the Census Bureau, the national Center for Health Statistics, and a dozen other federal bureaus. Yet American policy makers continue to regard fertility trends as one of the "given" parameters within which they operate. Programs that provide social services and benefits must respond to changes in the birthrate, but they are not seen as an appropriate vehicle for influencing the birthrate. As our previous discussion pointed out, the only exception to this generalization can be found in government treatment of welfare recipients. For this group, the federal government has from time to time invested money to provide family-planning services, and state and local authorities have occasionally even attempted to manipulate welfare benefits to persuade recipients to limit their families. But the motivation to undertake such action has not been the desire to extend government activity in family planning; rather, it has been the desire to control welfare spending.

Are the views toward the family and toward social policy we have just described characteristic of *socialist* politics? Not necessarily. In fact, they are shared by some conservative, and even by some right-wing, regimes. Perhaps this constellation of attitudes is best described simply as an activist conception of government. Political elites in Sweden and China operate on the assumption that public officials, by virtue of their position in government, have an obligation to articulate society's minimum standards for a proper home environment for children and then to see that children are guaranteed at least that minimum. Similarly, it is their obligation to identify the desirable direction of social change and then to use public resources to pursue the goals they have set. Within this activist conception of government, there is room for leaders to take action on the basis of their own perceptions of citizens' needs rather than on the basis of popular perceptions alone. The more such actions involve significant social change, the more elites must work to cultivate popular support for them.

Centralization in Formulating and Implementing Policy

The conception of government we have just described is at odds, not only with the American public philosophy of restricted government but also with the structure of American government. Not that we lack examples in the United States of policies initiated by elected and appointed officials rather than by the constituencies they serve. Clearly, the most important initiators of policy in the American system are actors *within* the government. But what we seldom see in the United States is government initiating policy to promote dramatic social change and then seeking to build broad public support for such change. The American policy process, highly fragmented and studded with veto groups at every level, is more likely to produce incremental adaptations based on widespread bargaining and compromise than it is to produce dramatic departures from the status quo:

> In the normal run of circumstances, American policy adaptations can occur only through the slow, painstaking building of consensus . . . because so much effort is invested in *building* the consensus, the mechanism exhibits very little capacity for *moving* that consensus.[11]

Policies that seek to promote dramatic change in the economy or the society are brought forth only in response to extreme conditions. The easing of working women's dual burden would certainly require dramatic changes in our economy and society, but we see no emergency on the horizon that would provoke government action. In the past, only the labor requirements of a wartime economy have been sufficient to call forth a major government investment in child care. Short of such an emergency, we should expect only incremental changes in federal activity in this area.

Our brief excursion into the labyrinth of American pluralism serves to highlight the importance of consensus building as part of the policy process. Without some agreement on the direction that social reforms should take, policy makers, even those who subscribe to an activist role for government, will be unable to act boldly. Such consensus has been easier to achieve in the Swedish and Chinese systems because of the dominance in each nation of a single party over several decades. We do not mean to imply that either Sweden's Social Democrats or the Chinese Communists constitute a monolithic bloc. Factional splits and leadership changes have occurred in both parties. (In fact, some would argue that internal factionalism increases once a party has ascended to a permanent or quasi-permanent ruling position.) Nevertheless, both can be classified as programmatic parties in which certain commonly accepted principles and purposes underlie the bargaining and reconciliation among factions. Consensus on the directions of desirable social change is easier to achieve under such circumstances than in America's competitive party system, where control alternates between two nonprogrammatic parties.

We should note that, in Sweden and China, the overarching policy consensus that has made possible an activist approach to governing has been eroded in the last few years. In Sweden, that the 40-year-old consensus has been seriously damaged can be seen in the Social Democrats' election loss to the opposition coalition in the fall of 1976. The period following that political shift has been marked by a cautious reevaluation of the Social Democrats' labor market and social welfare programs. While we should not expect to see the welfare state dismantled or even significantly cut back, we may see public services expand less rapidly under the coalition government. In China, Mao's death triggered a period of open conflict between the ideological purists and the pragmatists for control of China's future. With the new leadership, especially Teng Hsiao-p'ing as vice premier, it seems that the pragmatists are in position to articulate the party's vision of social change. In both nations, the recent political changes have commonly been characterized as shifts away from social utopianism toward more emphasis on economic growth and stability. Even if this assessment is correct (and it is really too soon to be sure), it need not mean a curtailment of the women's programs we have been discussing. In fact, if the new elites in both societies place primary emphasis on production goals, the future may bring even more determined efforts to utilize female labor power.

This brings us to another important feature of Swedish and Chinese politics: the degree of central coordination in implementing policies. For, even with an activist conception of government and a high degree of consensus on appropriate goals, political leaders cannot promote social or economic change in their environment unless they control the administrative machinery. How do our three cases compare on the degree of central control over implementation?

The fragmentation of American bureaucracy is thoroughly documented in the literature on public administration and policy. Not only do we have an administrative corps that is vertically divided by the numerous layers of government in our federal system; we also have extreme horizontal fragmentation at any level of government. The prospect of any national coordination of social service programs, has become even dimmer in recent years. As we saw in chapter 2, Congress has since the late 1960s delegated more administrative responsibility for maternal and infant care to the states, has continued to allow family planning programs to be controlled by state governments, and has limited sharply the amount of federal day-care funds any one state can receive. The federal government has increasingly replaced categorical grants for social services with block grants, which increase the discretion of state officials and reduce the possibility of national coordination. Without the administrative capacity to coordinate support services to working families, national leaders would have difficulty easing their burdens even if they could agree on this as a goal. In the United States,

> The economic process has long been integrated nationally. But political authority over policies capable of modifying and offsetting the effects on individuals of participation in, and dependence on, that economic process remains fragmented among a multiplicity of state and local units as well as federal agencies.[12]

The Swedish picture is strikingly different. As in the United States, most social services are administered by provincial and local governments rather than directly by national agencies. The opportunity for national coordination among such programs is much greater in Sweden, however, because of the legal and financial leverage the national government exercises over both province and municipality. Sweden has a unitary form of government in that both lower levels of government are constitutionally subordinate to central authority. The national government appoints key local officials and retains the authority to oversee local government structure and policies. But at least as important as those constitutional provisions is the financial leverage exercised by central authorities. By far the largest share of local budgets is spent on programs prescribed by the national government (most estimates approach 80 percent). National subsidies constitute the largest single source of local revenue, and national agencies constantly monitor the administrative performance of the provinces and municipalities. So many local functions are mandated by national legislation that one observer has labeled Swedish local government "an administrative extension of the central government."[13]

Central control over policy implementation in China is also great, although how great is not uniformly agreed on by China scholars, particularly since the Cultural Revolution.[14] As with many issues in Chinese studies, the evidence is not straightforward. For the purpose of comparative analysis, however, it is appropriate to classify the People's Republic among the most highly centralized governments of the world. In keeping with traditional expectations, as well as its own program of revolutionary change, the CCP has sought to create a political system that encourages maximum responsiveness to central directives. Ideologically, this political system is described as "democratic centralism" or "from the masses, to the masses." On balance, centralism clearly outweighs democracy. Any other mixture for a party dedicated to remaking a society would be improbable, as well as unworkable. Instituting change necessarily involves more attention to setting objectives and demanding compliance than listening to alternative plans and wishes. The greater the pressure for directed change, the lower the tolerance for competitive needs. And in China, there is great pressure for change.

Because China is such a large country, with regional variation in levels of development, population density, resource distribution, customs, and the like, there has obviously been room for diversity in implementing national programs. Nevertheless, the existence of such variation should not obscure the bias toward centralized planning and social control. Both state and party structures are organized in hierarchical, authoritarian patterns, which reflect the doctrine of "democratic centralist discipline." According to the latest constitution, adopted at the Eleventh Party Congress in 1977, this means

> the individual is subordinate to the organization, the minority is subordinate to the majority, the lower level is subordinate to the higher level, and the entire Party is subordinate to the Central Committee.[15]

Once central policy has been formulated, to alter it significantly in deference to local or bureaucratic interests is a serious error, one that has been costly to many cadres. In the end, party loyalty must be the determining factor.

> A communist must never take a liberalist attitude towards the resolutions of Party organizations and the decisions of the leadership, carrying out what is to his liking and refusing to carry out what is not, and must never overtly agree but covertly oppose, feigning compliance while acting differently. . . . All Party members, especially the Party's leading cadres at all levels, must consciously observe Party discipline.[16]

Eliciting compliance with central goals has not been left only to formal organizations, which could allow individual units to develop vested interests in spite of centralized structures and a well-developed system of controls. In addition, people have repeatedly been exposed to informal controls through small-group discussions. Virtually all urban workers and most urban residents have been formed into groups of 8 to 15 members; such groups exist among peasants, too, although it is uncertain how widespread and permanent they are. Through these groups, pressure is applied by "politically correct" activists to elicit enthusiastic support for official policies. These groups discuss the latest policy directives, particularly those which demand their compliance, and the ideological implications of their support.

> In China *hsiao-tsu* [small groups] and the political rituals carried on within them, represent an attempt either to pre-empt or to coopt the autonomous

> primary groups which would ordinarily exist in various organizations and throughout society. Individuals are not left on their own to develop social ties within an organization but are formed into *hsiao-tsu* under the direction of elites. Within these groups individuals who can be expected to support official demands are placed in leadership positions and encouraged to find other group members who will support them. . . . The desired result . . . is a situation in which an individual finds himself surrounded by people who not only comply with higher demands, but also enthusiastically and creatively support those demands.[17]

The extent of such social control may explain why some decentralization of governmental authority has been an acceptable alternative to the CCP on several occasions since 1949.

FUTURE DIRECTION OF AMERICAN PUBLIC POLICY

We close our study with a few modest predictions concerning the likely direction of American policy during the next decade regarding support services for women employed outside the home. Taken as a whole, our observations hold little hope for those who would like to see greater government involvement. We would like to display more optimism, but the evidence is discouraging. A dramatic shift in public policy is improbable for many reasons, but chief among them are these:

1. lack of serious, widespread political support in the United States for a full-employment policy
2. The continuing tendency of American legal and government institutions to assign the breadwinner role to husbands and the homemaker-child-minder role to wives (and, at this writing, the dwindling probability that a national Equal Rights Amendment will be adopted to help break down such a pattern)
3. The traditional reluctance of American policy makers to use social policy "developmentally" (to stimulate social change), rather than "reactively" (to relieve severe social and economic dislocations).
4. The practical difficulties of implementing any nationally conceived social services strategy, given the administrative fragmentation inherent in American government

This picture is disheartening because it suggests a future in which the national government will do little to resolve the problem of overworked wives and mothers.

Some will question whether the government should bother with the difficulties women have in juggling their multiple responsibilities. After all, American women, even women with young children, are employed in larger numbers than ever before. Doesn't their very presence in the labor force in such large numbers mean that they are either purchasing the services they need on the private market or successfully doing without such services? To those who question whether women who work outside the home need help, we answer yes, they do, although the supporting evidence is largely impressionistic at present. The greatest burden appears to be carried by working-class wives and mothers; unable to qualify for publicly provided services, which are designed to aid low-income welfare families, these women can rarely afford to buy services on the private market either. Needing the extra income to maintain the family's standard of living, they must find patchwork solutions, arranging their work around household responsibilities or calling on relatives and friends for help. While many such women manage to cope, the personal costs are almost invariably high. One often overlooked cost is the tendency for these women to remain at the low end of the occupational ladder because they find it impossible to reconcile household demands with the increased demands of a more responsible, better-paying position.

Addressing exactly this problem, the March 1978 issue of *Ms*. magazine featured the query "Can Women Really Have It All? Love, Work, Guilt, and Other Trade-Offs." The magazine's contributors aired a complaint that must concern all people dedicated to upgrading women's position in America's labor force: Is it possible for women to advance to jobs of greater authority if political and social institutions remain unchanged? Are too many feminists guilty of asking women to achieve what is within the reach of only a "superwoman" (i.e., to gain recognition at home and at work simply by trying harder)? How likely are women to achieve such a feat?

> Without equal parenting and more societal responsibility for child care, without equal responsibilities and increased flexibility in the workplace and at home, there is virtually no person who can do it.[18]

Recent opinion surveys offer a clue as to how successfully American women working outside the home are coping with their dual burden. Several have revealed a curious contradiction between women's attitudes and their behavior. Married women, even those with young children, are migrating into the labor force in record numbers. The Census Bureau reported in 1976 that 33 percent of all American mothers with children under three years of age were in the labor force; among mothers with children under six, fully 42 percent were employed.[19] Given this important behavioral trend among American women, it is surprising how many survey respondents continue to express negative views about mothers employed outside the home. A 1977 Yankelovich poll of 1230 American households reported that 69 percent of American parents believe that children of working mothers are worse off than those whose mothers stay home; perhaps even more illuminating, 48 percent of employed mothers *themselves* agreed that the children of working mothers suffer from their mothers' employment.[20] A 1977 poll commissioned by the National Commission on the Observance of International Women's Year showed that over half of American women believe "it is much better for everyone involved if the man is the achiever outside the home, and the woman takes care of the home and family."[21] In a similar vein, a *New York Times*/CBS News poll in November 1977 revealed that 43 percent of Americans believe that marriage is more satisfying if "the husband provides for the family and the wife takes care of the house and children." This last poll sounded an optimistic note, in reporting that *only* 36 percent of American women and *only* 45 percent of American men believe that working women are worse mothers than women who devote all their time to the home. These percentages were somewhat lower than those reported in a 1970 poll by the same organization.[22]

These findings might simply reflect the persistence of traditional stereotypes for husbands and wives. We would suggest an alternative hypothesis. In some measure, these survey findings reflect American women's (and men's) realistic assessment of the problems created for an American family when both parents work. They represent many working parents' perceptions that the wife's dual role is not a comfortable one in an economy that demands a 40-hour week from both employed parents and lacks support services for the family. The experience of many working families is a hardship experience, not likely to encourage positive attitudes toward women's employment.

One possible consequence of these attitudes is explored in an intriguing forecast by a Brookings Institution economist. Michael Wachter hypothesized recently that married women's strong entry into the labor market is not a function of changing attitudes toward employment on the part of women or men; rather, it is a function of the age structure of the American population.[23] As the baby-boom cohort reached adulthood in the 1960s, its entry into the work force intensified America's labor surplus, thereby dampening relative wages and living standards for young people. Young women postponed having children, working instead in order to maintain their expected living standards. Even young mothers migrated into the labor force to supplement family income. While this particular age cohort may always display high participation rates, younger workers will enter an improving labor market and will experience less pressure for two wages. If Wachter is right, and if attitudes do not become more favorable toward employed mothers, then an easing of financial pressure will almost certainly trigger a retreat from the labor force by married women.

Lest the reader conclude that our predictions regarding the future of women's programs are unmitigatedly gloomy, we can point to one probable improvement. We expect to see in the next few years a significant improvement in the status of the American homemaker. If it occurs, such an improvement would ease the double bind described by Lenore Weitzman:

> . . . at the same time that the legal structure of marriages seems to provide incentives and rewards for women who remain in domestic roles, it also penalizes the woman who has done just that if and when her marriage dissolves.[24]

We described in chapter 5 the American legal tradition that has presumed a woman's primary responsibility for her home and her children. Courts have also assigned to the wife a responsibility to render household services; so clear is her family's entitlement to her household services that the family can sue someone who negligently injures her, to recover the value of the service she is unable to perform.

Besides judicial rulings, other forms of public policy encourage women to stay at home, to view themselves as wives and mothers first, and only secondarily as wage earners. The social security system, for example, is built on the one-earner family. Even though it collects payroll taxes from individual workers, it pays benefits by family. A wife who pays social security contributions throughout her working years stands a good chance of forfeiting her entire return, if (as is highly likely) her wages were significantly lower than her husband's. Within the so-called dual-entitlement classification (i.e., recipients who must choose to receive either their own or their spouse's entitlement), 99.9 percent are women.[25] The federal income tax is another example of national policy that gives more favorable treatment to families with one earner than to families with two earning parents. The income-splitting provision available to one-earner families allows the wage earner to split his or her income into halves so that each half is taxed in a lower tax bracket. "The effect of the joint return provisions is to say you get a reward if you marry and take one spouse off the job market."[26] In addition, the tax system encourages women to remain at home by treating "housewife" as a specially favored tax-exempt occupation, while treating other jobs women do as taxable. As a housewife, a woman engages in productive labor whose value is exempt from federal taxation simply because she is not paid with cash. "If a woman wants to leave work as a housewife and go to work at anything else, she has to pay a tax price for it. She is leaving a tax-exempt job and going to a taxable job."[27] Social Security and taxation are just two of the most visible examples of national policies that discourage women's employment outside the home.

Such a discriminatory stance on the part of public authorities would be bad enough in itself. To make matters worse for the American homemaker, a great many public policies deprecate the homemaker role and deny economic security to homemakers. Housework has traditionally been accorded a low value by judicial and legislative policy makers. In many states, it earns a woman no entitlement to family assets. It is a job that is not covered by the social security system. As we argued in chapter 2, housework has not been perceived as useful, productive labor, and therefore legislators have seen little reason to invest public money in replacement services for families without full-time homemakers.

What leads us to expect a change in public policy toward homemakers? We have argued throughout this study that national governments' policies to support working women flow from their overarching economic and social goals. That is, women's programs in China, Sweden, and the United

States are best understood as outgrowths of those governments' more general strategies for the labor market and social services. Compared with Sweden's and China's, the U.S. government's long-term goals are difficult to discern, for we lack programmatic parties to articulate those goals in a clear, systematic fashion. Nevertheless, we would suggest at least three major policy goals relevant to our concerns, which have been endorsed by both Democrats and Republicans over the last decade:

1. To reduce unemployment (Note that this is not necessarily the same as promoting full employment—reducing unemployment may well entail taking some job seekers off the labor market)
2. To curb inflation
3. To hold down social welfare spending

We do not intend here to enter the perennial debate among economists about whether these three goals are mutually consistent. Regardless of whether they represent a consistent national economic program, taken together they suggest a policy climate in which the homemaker's role will be more and more recognized as making a productive contribution to the economy. In our inflationary economy, with wages and prices constantly rising, many families cope with the upward spiral by substituting their own labor and production for the market's. Household members perform services they might otherwise purchase in the market (e.g., canning, laundry, dressmaking, housepainting), and they purchase goods they can assemble and finish themselves. Scott Burns, in his fascinating book on *The Household Economy*, argues that we must shift away from our traditional view of the household as purely a consumption unit and recognize it as a productive economic institution, producing goods and services with tangible economic value. To illustrate its economic significance, he offers an estimate of the total value of goods and services produced by American households in 1965: $300 billion.[28] Furthermore, Burns predicts that "as long as inflation prevails, the household economy will enjoy substantial and growing advantage over the market economy."[29] Policy makers are beginning to recognize this trend. In the last decade, congressional debates on a series of family-assistance and child-care proposals have highlighted the efficiency of the household economy by showing how much money would be needed to provide adequate replacement services, especially child care. This growing realization, combined with the prevailing view in Washington that women entering the labor force are in large part responsible for our current "labor surplus," suggests that national policy makers will move to provide greater security for housewives. What legislation is implied in such a policy shift?

First, we can expect to see (and already are witnessing) changes in pension and property laws to recognize housework as a labor contribution that entitles the homemaker to retirement benefits and to a share in family assets. The state of Massachusetts, for example, introduced in 1978 a reform in its divorce laws that instructed the courts to take into consideration a homemaker's contribution to the family unit when the court decides on alimony and the division of property. Similar reforms are under consideration in other states. Regarding homemakers' pensions, the federal government took the first step in recognizing housework as an occupation in the 1976 Tax Reform Act, by extending the eligibility for the Individual Retirement Account (IRA) to some housewives. Congress had originated the idea to benefit self-employed workers or workers whose employers provided no retirement program. Such a worker can set up an IRA, sheltering up to $1500 annually. As of January 1977, an eligible worker may add a second IRA for an unemployed spouse, setting aside up to $875 per account, or an eligible couple may create a single IRA with two equal subaccounts, sheltering a total of $1750 a year. While the financial significance of this new provision is not great, it is important because it represents an official acknowledgement that homemakers need retirement security of their own. Its passage may foreshadow a shift in congressional sentiment toward social security reforms that would favor homemakers. Under existing law, homemaking is not covered for retirement, disability, or survivor benefits. Dependent entirely on her husband's earnings record for the wife's or widow's benefits, a homemaker may easily forfeit even these benefits, if she is divorced. Several reform proposals have been introduced in Congress in recent sessions; the most comprehensive bill to date has been the Fraser-Keys proposal introduced in 1977 as "Equity in Social Security for Individuals and Families" (H.R. 3247). If passed, the proposal would allow each spouse to build a separate record of contributions. Unemployed homemakers would be credited with 75 percent of their spouses' earnings, and they would maintain their individual record of contributions regardless of whether the marriage remained intact.

Second, we can expect increasing support for "displaced homemakers" programs serving middle-aged women who have worked as homemakers all their lives and who, because of divorce or the death or disability of their husbands, are left without income or employment. Such women do not benefit from the usual unemployment insurance or union benefits other displaced workers may fall back on. Increasingly, policy makers are viewing such persons as members of the work force who have spent their lives in a job not covered by the normal forms of social insurance. In 1975 Representative Yvonne Burke first introduced federal legislation for "Displaced Homemaker Assistance." In its most recent version, the Burke-Hawkins proposal (H.R. 10270) would create multipurpose centers to help women in this situation to become self-sufficient. These centers would offer job training, counseling, placement, health education, financial management, and related programs.

Third, we expect that federal income-maintenance programs will increasingly be geared to supporting mothers of young children who stay at home. American public assistance programs in the future will probably place less emphasis on putting recipients to work and more on paying unemployed parents, especially single mothers, to stay at home, care for their children, and provide household services to their families. National experience with workfare programs in the 1960s and 1970s indicates that rigid work requirements, though politically popular, cannot successfully be applied in an economy with a labor surplus. Moreover, a federal income guarantee that leaves at least one parent in the home is likely to be seen by many legislators as preferable to enlarging the public-service sector. Finally, it appeals to those who believe it would increase the amount of time spent by mothers in child care. There is evidence that a guaranteed income program would reduce the amount of time married women spent working outside the home.[30] Supporters contend that when mothers spend more time in the home, they give their children more attention:

> In particular, mothers of pre-school children in low income families . . . who before the transfer spent a significant amount of time working in the labor market, will spend an increased amount of time in the care of their children. This is, in itself, a desirable goal of public policy (over and above the goal of providing poor familes an adequate income level).[31]

Perhaps the clearest statement of this position is offered by Selma Fraiberg in *Every Child's Birthright: In Defense of Mothering*: "As for poor women, I think federal and state-backed public policy should encourage women to stay at home, when they have young children, rather than go to work."[32] Needless to say, a family policy that encourages married women to stay at home must continue to hold husbands primarily responsible for family support. Not surprisingly, we have recently seen a resurgence of interest in the problem of family support by absentee fathers, with the federal government initiating a large-scale effort to track down absentee fathers whose children are on the welfare rolls (see discussion of this federal program in chapter 5).

The Carter administration's proposal for welfare reform, unveiled in August 1977, carried signs that federal welfare officials are moving in this direction. Despite the strong emphasis placed on jobs in the administration's initial publicity for the proposal, it is significant that the proposal would exempt from the work requirement any mother with children under six years of age and would require only part-time employment from mothers of school-age children who could not find adequate day care. Perhaps even more significant is the proposed job guarantee for only one parent in each recipient family; the underlying assumption is that one parent will remain at home.

At first glance, one might expect that this trend toward greater government recognition and support for homemakers would have drawn opposition from American feminists. Taken together, the measures we have described seem to reinforce women's occupational segregation and perpetuate conventional role stereotypes by paying women to perform their housekeeper-childminder role. Yet these programs have attracted political support from conservatives, liberals, feminists, and staunch traditionalists. Their widespread popular appeal makes it all the more likely that we will see this trend continue and grow in the near future. Their appeal to family traditionalists is obvious: They would help to keep one parent, most likely the mother, at home taking care of house and family. While these reforms *would* entail large cash transfers, both for income maintenance and for social insurance programs, they would not substantially enlarge government social services, a feature that draws support from political conservatives. Many liberals back the guaranteed income because they believe it is a less stigmatized, less coercive form of public assistance than our government currently provides under AFDC.

Finally, this legislative trend is strongly supported by feminists. The National Commission on the Observance of International Women's Year had a Committee on the Homemaker, which investigated the legal status of homemakers in all 50 states and prepared recommendations on inheritance laws, divorce laws, and related areas of discrimination against homemakers.[33] In 1977 the National Organization for Women also established a National Homemakers Rights Committee to promote the interests of homemakers. In recent years, NOW has publicly defended the woman's right to stay at home. For example, in hearings conducted by the New York State Assembly to consider proposed reforms in the diverse laws governing division of property, NOW's representatives emphasized the economic contribution made by homemakers and the right of a woman to remain at home with her children. They argued that marriage should be considered a "legitimate career" for the housewife, whose contribution to the marriage "is equal although not identical to her husband's contribution."[34] In a similar vein, the 1977 National Women's Conference in Houston withheld endorsement for the Carter welfare reform proposal on the grounds that it would require some welfare mothers to work. Even though the Carter proposal exempted mothers of preschool children, the feminist-dominated conference expressed dissatisfaction that any mother be required to take employment, recommending instead that public assistance be considered a wage for homemakers with children.

How do we explain this strong support by American feminists for these various forms of homemaker rights legislation? It appears to be a case of preferring half a loaf to none. Feminists seem to be saying that a society which still confines many of its women to the homemaker role should, at the least, stop penalizing them for playing the role it has assigned.

A Note on the Notes

For the Chinese sections of the book, much of the material used was translated into English by several translation services that publish material originally appearing in the Chinese press. These periodicals are:

CB	Current Background (U.S. Consulate, Hong Kong)
ECMM	Extracts from China Mainland Magazines (U.S. Consulate, Hong Kong)
FBIS	Foreign Broadcast Information Service (U.S. Government)
JPRS	Joint Publications Research Service (U.S. Dept. of Commerce)
SCMM	Survey of China Mainland Magazines (U.S. Consulate, Hong Kong)
SCMP	Survey of the China Mainland Press (U.S. Consulate, Hong Kong)
SUP	Supplement to Survey of the China Mainland Press (U.S. Consulate, Hong Kong)
URS	Union Research Service (Union Research Institute, Hong Kong)

The notes which refer to these periodicals list first the name of the translation series, the number of the periodical, the date and page. The original Chinese source is then listed, the place the material originated (if specified), and the date it was published in Chinese. Thus the note

CB 625, July 6, 1960, p. 14; Peking JMJP April 15, 1960, would be read:

Current Background, serial number 625, published July 6, 1960, page 4; appeared originally in Jen-min Jih-pao (People's Daily) on April 15, 1960, dateline-Peking.

Chinese periodicals cited are as follows:

Antung JP:	Antung Jih-pao (Antung Daily)
Chieh-fang JP:	Chieh-fang Jih-pao (Liberation Daily)
CKCNP:	Chung-kuo Ch'ing-nien Pao (China Youth Newspaper)
CKFN:	Chung-kuo Fu-nu (Women of China)
Hupeh JP:	Hupeh Jih-pao (Hupeh Daily)
HC:	Hung-ch'i (Red Flag)
JMJP:	Jen-min Jih-pao (People's Daily)
Kuang-ming JP:	Kuang-ming Jih-pao (Bright Daily)
Kweichow JP:	Kweichow Jih-pao (Kweichow Daily)
KJJP:	Kung-jen Jih-pao (Workers' Daily)
NCNA:	New China News Agency
Sian JP:	Sian Jih-pao (Sian Daily)
Tsingtao JP:	Tsingtao Jih-pao (Tsingtao Daily)
TKP:	Ta Kung Pao (Impartial Newspaper)

NOTES

Chapter 1

INTRODUCTION

1. Elizabeth Almquist, "Review Essay: Women in the Labor Force," *Signs* 2, no. 4 (Summer 1977): 845.

2. Elise Boulding, *Women in the Twentieth Century World* (New York: John Wiley 1977), chap. 3.

3. Dean D. Knudsen. "The Declining Status of Women: Popular Myths and the Failure of Functionalist Thought," *Social Forces* 48, no. 2 (1969); Alan Sorkin, "On the Occupational Status of Women, 1870–1970," *American Journal of Economics and Sociology* 32 (July 1973): 235–43.

4. Louise Kapp Howe, *Pink Collar Workers* (New York: Putnam, 1977), p. 6. Much has been written about sex segregation in the American labor force. Two of the more important works are Edward Gross, "Plus Ca Change. . . . The Sexual Structure of Occupations Over Time," *Social Problems* 14, Fall 1968; and Valerie Kincaid Oppenheimer, *The Female Labor Force in the United States*. Population Monograph Series No. 5, (Berkeley, Calif.: Institute of International Studies, University of California, 1970).

5. Howe, *op. cit.*, p. 10.

6. Larry Suter and Herman Miller, "Income Differences Between Men and Career Women," *American Journal of Sociology* 78, no. 4 (January 1973): 962–974.

7. Almquist, *op. cit.*, p. 851.

8. Matina Horner, "Women's Need to Fail," *Psychology Today*, (November 1969).

9. Lenore Weitzman, "Sex Role Socialization," in *Women: A Feminist Perspective*, ed. Jo Freeman (Palo Alto: Mayfield, 1975), p. 134.

10. Juanita Kreps, *Sex in the Marketplace: American Women at Work* (Baltimore: Johns Hopkins University Press, 1971), p. 87.

11. Elizabeth Waldman and Beverly McEaddy, "Where Women Work—An Analysis by Industry and Occupation," *Monthly Labor Review* (May 1974), p. 3.

12. Howe, *op. cit.*, p. 253.

13. See especially Margaret Mead, *Sex and Temperament in Three Primitive Societies* (New York: Morrow, 1935); and *Male and Female: A Study of Sexes in a Changing World* (New York: Morrow, 1949).

14. A useful general treatment is Evelyne Sullerot's *Woman, Society, and Change* (New York: World University Library, 1971). Among the most readily available research is that reported in three collections: Michelle Rosaldo and Louise Lamphere, eds., *Woman, Culture, and Society* (Stanford: Stanford University Press, 1974); Lynne Iglitzin and Ruth Ross, eds., *Women in the World: A Comparative Study* (Santa Barbara: ABC Clio Press, 1976); and Ruby Rohrlich-Leavitt, ed., *Women Cross-Culturally: Change and Challenge* (Chicago: Aldine, 1975).

15. Kaare Svalastoga, quoted in Richard Tomasson, *Sweden: Prototype of Modern Society* (New York: Random House, 1970), p. 190.

16. U.S. Department of Labor projection, reported in *New York Times*, May 7, 1978.

17. Elisabet Sandberg, *Equality Is the Goal* (Stockholm: Swedish Institute, 1975), p. 32.

18. *Ibid.*, p. 33.

19. *Daily Report*, March 9, 1978, p. E-11; HC no. 3, 1978.

20. The comments that follow are limited to comparative analysis of policy *formulation* and do not address the growing body of research using comparative methodologies to evaluate policy *impacts* (or "outcomes," as they are often labeled in the policy literature).

21. T. Alexander Smith, *The Comparative Policy Process* (Santa Barbara: ABC Clio Press, 1975), p. 3.

22. Daniel Bell, *The End of Ideology* (Glencoe, Ill.: Free Press, 1960); Robert Dahl and Charles Lindblom, *Politics, Economics, and Welfare* (New York: Harper & Row, 1953); Joseph Lapalombara, "Decline of Ideology: A Dissent and an Interpretation," *American Political Science Review* 60, 5–16.

23. Studies in this vein are too numerous to cite. Three good examples are Richard Dawson and James Robinson, "Inter-Party Competition, Economic Variables, and Welfare Policies in the American States" *Journal of Politics* 25 (May 1963): 265–89; Richard Hofferbert, "Ecological Development and Policy Change in the American States," *Midwest Journal of Political Science* (November 1966): 481–92; and Thomas Dye, *Politics, Economics, and the Public* (Chicago: Rand McNally, 1966).

24. Alexander Groth, *Comparative Politics: A Distributive Approach* (New York: Macmillan, 1971), p. 15.

25. For a theoretical discussion of the operational criteria for democracy, see Robert Dahl, *Preface to Democratic Theory* (Chicago: University of Chicago Press, 1966), p. 84.

26. Jo Freeman, *The Politics of Women's Liberation* (New York: Longman, 1975), pp. 226–27.

27. For a fuller discussion of national–local relationships, see Arnold Heidenheimer, Hugh Heclo, and Carolyn Adams, *Comparative Public Policy: The Politics of Social Choice in Europe and America* (New York: St. Martin's Press, 1975), pp. 97–101.

28. M. Donald Hancock, *Sweden: The Politics of Postindustrial Change* (Hinsdale, Ill.,: Dryden, 1972), p. 111.

29. *Ibid.*, p. 156.

30. Groth, *op. cit.*, p. 15.

31. Michael Oksenberg, "Methods of Communication Within the Chinese Bureaucracy," *China Quarterly*, 57 (January/March 1974): 28.

32. For a general introduction to the Chinese political system, see James Townsend, *Politics in China* (Boston: Little, Brown, 1974).

33. Alva Myrdal and Viola Klein, *Women's Two Roles: Home and Work* (London: Routledge & Kegan Paul, 1956).

34. Edmund Dahlstrom, "Analysis of the Debate on Sex Roles," in Dahlstrom, ed., *The Changing Roles of Men and Women* (Boston: Beacon Press, 1971), p. 176.

35. Eva Moberg, "The Conditional Emancipation of Women," pamphlet printed in Stockholm, 1961.

36. Gayle Graham Yates, *What Women Want: The Ideas of the Movement* (Cambridge, Mass.: Harvard University Press, 1975), p. 117.

37. Judith M. Bardwick, *Psychology of Women: A Study of Bio-Cultural Conflicts* (New York: Harper & Row, 1971).

38. For an application of this concept, see Michael Young and Peter Willmott, *The Symmetrical Family* (New York: Random House, 1973).

Chapter 2

SOCIAL POLICIES FOR WORKING FAMILIES

1. U.S. Department of Labor, Bureau of Labor Statistics, *U.S. Working Women: A Databook*. Bulletin 1977, p. 38.

2. *Ibid.*, p. 13.

3. *Ibid.*, p. 11.

4. Lisa Palm and Allan Pred, "A Time-Geographic Perspective on Problems of Inequality for Women," Working Paper No. 236, Institute of Urban and Regional Development, University of California, Berkeley, September 1974, p. 37.

5. Joint Female Labour Council, *Woman in Sweden in the Light of Statistics* (Stockholm: Arbetsmarknadens Kvinnonämnd, 1973), p. 49.

6. *Ibid.*, p. 56.

7. SCMM 394, December 9, 1963, p. 23; CKFN, November 1, 1963.

8. Evelyne Sullerot, *Woman, Society, and Change* (New York: World University Library, 1971), p. 213.

9. Odin W. Anderson, *Health Care: Can There Be Equity? The U.S., Sweden, and England* (New York: Wiley, 1972), p. 149.

10. Otto Wangson, "Maternal and Child Welfare," in *Social Welfare in Sweden* (Stockholm: Royal Swedish Commission on the New York World's Fair, 1939), p. 49.

11. For further discussion of the Parenthood Benefit, see chapter 5.

12. "Farm Nursery in Honan," *China Monthly Review*, 121, no. 4 (October 1951): 207.

13. Victor and Ruth Sidel, *Serve the People* (Boston: Beacon, 1973), p. 18.

14. Joyce Kallgren, "Social Welfare and China's Industrial Workers," in *Chinese Communist Politics in Action*, ed. A. Doak Barnett (Seattle: University of Washington Press, 1969), pp. 541, 545.

15. *Ibid.*, p. 546.

16. David M. Lampton, "Health Policy During the Great Leap Forward," *China Quarterly*, 60 (October/December 1974): 677.

17. *China Weekly Review*, 117, no. 3 (March 18, 1950): 44.

18. Delia Davin, *Woman-Work: Women and the Party in Revolutionary China* (Oxford, England: Clarendon, 1976), pp. 131–32.

19. *Ibid.*, p. 132.

20. Ruth Sidel, *Women and Child Care in China* (Baltimore: Penguin, 1973), p. 62.

21. SCMP 1299, May 31, 1956, p. 6; JMJP May 16, 1956; editorial.

22. Delia Davin, "Women in the Countryside of China," in *Women in Chinese Society*, ed. Margaret Wolf and Roxanne Witke, (Stanford: Stanford University Press, 1975), p. 259.

23. URS Vol. 8, p. 338; Tsingtao JP June 5, 1957.

24. Sidel and Sidel, *op. cit.*, p. 94.

25. *Ibid.*, p. 26.

26. *Ibid.*, p. 29.

27. William Kessen, ed., *Childhood in China* (New Haven: Yale University Press, 1975), p. 191.

28. Viola Klein, *Women Workers: Working Hours and Services* (Paris: OECD, 1965), p. 57.

29. *Geduldig* v. *Aiello*, 417 U.S. 484 (1974).

30. *General Electric Company* v. *Gilbert*, 45 L.W. 4031 (1976).

31. It must be noted, however, that the bill got enthusiastic backing from organized women doctors, because it duplicated successful Scandinavian programs to cut infant mortality. See J. S. Lemons, *The Woman Citizen: Social Feminism in the 1920s* (Urbana: University of Illinois Press, 1973), pp. 165–66.

32. Gilbert Steiner, *The Children's Cause* (Washington, D.C.: Brookings Institution, 1976), p. 232.

33. *Ibid.*

34. *Ibid.*, pp. 238–39.

35. "State Commission on Aspects of Sex and Personal Relationships in Teaching

and Public Information: Summary of Proposals," *Current Sweden*, no. 43 (October 1974).

36. Rita Liljeström, *A Study of Abortion in Sweden* (Prepared for the Royal Ministry for Foreign Affairs, contributed to United Nations World Population Conference, 1974), pp. 44–45.

37. *Ibid.*, p. 54.

38. Garrett Hardin, "Abortion or Compulsory Pregnancy?" *Journal of Marriage and the Family*, 30, no 2 (May 1968): 246–51.

39. Hans Forssman and Inga Thuwe, "One Hundred Twenty Children Born After Application for Therapeutic Abortion Refused," *Acta Psychiatrica Scandinavica* 42, (1966): 71.

40. Richard Tomasson, *Sweden: Prototype of Modern Society* (New York: Random House, 1970), p. 274.

41. CB 476, October 15, pp. 27–28.

42. Leo A. Orleans, *Every Fifth Child: The Population of China* (London: Eyre Methuen, 1972), p. 39.

43. Han Su-yin, "Family Planning in China," *Japanese Quarterly* 17, no. 4 (October/December 1970): 436.

44. Kessen, *op. cit.*, p. 195.

45. Sidel and Sidel, *op. cit.*, pp. 55, 252–53.

46. Orleans, *op. cit.*, p. 44.

47. Michael Freeberne, "Birth Control in China," *Population Studies*, 18, no. 1 (July 1964): 13.

48. Kessen, *op. cit.*, p. 196.

49. Sidel, *op. cit.*, p. 59.

50. CNA 842, May 21, 1971, p. 7.

51. Sidel, *op. cit.*, p. 53.

52. Orleans, *op. cit.*, p. 46.

53. William L. Parish, Jr., "Socialism and the Chinese Peasant Family," *Journal of Asian Studies* 34, no. 3 (May 1975): 618.

54. Lawrence K. Hong, "The Role of Women in the People's Republic of China," *Social Problems* 23, no. 5 (June 1976): 547.

55. Pi-chao Chen, "The Birth Control Action Program and the Rustication Movement in the People's Republic of China" (Interdisciplinary Communications Program, International Program for Population Analysis, Smithsonian Institution, Washington, D.C., 1976).

56. Planned Parenthood Federation of America, *Laws Relating to Birth Control and Family Planning in the U.S.* (New York: Planned Parenthood, 1968).

57. The most complete history of birth control in the United States is contained in Linda Gordon, *Woman's Body, Woman's Right: A Social History of Birth Control in America* (New York: Grossman, 1976).

58. Leona Baumgartner, "Governmental Responsibility for Family Planning in the U.S.," in *Fertility and Family Planning: A World View,* ed. S. J. Behrman, L. Corsa, and R. Freedman (Ann Arbor: University of Michigan Press, 1969), pp. 435–48.

59. Ruth Dixon, "Hallelujah the Pill?" *Transaction* (November/December 1970): p. 45.

60. David Weinberg, "Family Planning in the American States," in *Population Policy-making in the American States: Issues and Processes*, ed. Elihu Bergman *et al*. (Lexington, Mass.: Lexington Books, 1974), p. 79.

61. Stephen Williams, "Population Policymaking: The Abortion Issue," in Bergman, *ibid*., p. 151.

62. *New York Times*, October 7, 1975, p. 15.

63. Jill Kschinka, "Public Funding in the States: An Overview," *NARAL Newsletter* 10, no. 7 (October 1978): 6.

64. Frederick Jaffe, "Public Policy on Fertility Control," *Scientific American*, 1973.

65. Clinton Jones, "Population Issues and the Black Community," in *Political Issues in U.S. Population Policy,* ed. Virginia Gray and Elihu Bergman (Lexington, Mass.: Lexington Books, 1974), pp. 151–66.

66. Tomasson, *op. cit*., p. 192.

67. Ragnar Berfenstam and Inger William-Olsson, *Early Child Care in Sweden* (London: Gordon and Breach, 1973), p. 75.

68. According to the standard government definition in Sweden, both parents must work 20 hours or more a week in order to be counted as needing day-care services.

69. Although there are rare cases of privately operated day-care centers in Swed-

en, the vast majority are operated by local governments or nonprofit associations receiving local government subsidies.

70. Elisabet Sandberg, *Equality Is the Goal* (Stockholm: Swedish Institute, 1975), p. 67.

71. Berfenstam and William-Olsson, *op. cit.*, p. 103.

72. Statens Offentliga Utredningar 1975, No. 62.

73. Rita Liljestrom, "Integration of Family Policy and Labour Market Policy in Sweden" (paper prepared for Conference on the Implementation of Equal Pay and Equal Opportunity Legislation in the U.S., Canada, and Western Europe, Wellesley College, May 1–4, 1978).

74. Alfred Kahn and Sheila Kamerman, *Not for the Poor Alone: European Social Services* (Philadelphia: Temple University Press, 1975), p. 25.

75. Sandberg, *op. cit.*, p. 67.

76. Kahn and Kamerman, *op. cit.*, p. 33.

77. *Chinese Weekly Review* 116, no. 1 (December 3, 1949): p. 3.

78. SCMP 1381, October 1, 1956, p. 7; NCNA September 26, 1956. See also URS Vol. 3, No. 22, June 15, 1956; Antung JP, May 20, 1956, and SCMP 1258, March 29, 1956, p. 18; JMJP March 8, 1956.

79. *China News Analysis* 77, April 1, 1955, p. 5.

80. *Eighth National Congress of the Communist Party of China: Speeches,* vol. 2 (Peking: Foreign Language Press, 1956), p. 226.

81. SCMP 819, May 29–31, 1954, pp. 31–32; NCNA Peking, May 17, 1954.

82. URS Vol. 3, No. 6, March 28, 1956, p. 325: "Chung-kuo Fang Chin Kung Jen (Chinese Textile Worker)."

83. URS Vol. 3, *op. cit.*, pp. 321, 323; Tsingtao JP January 19, 1956; Yun Nan JP, January 12, 1956.

84. C. K. Yang, *Chinese Communist Society: The Family and the Village*, book 1, *The Chinese Family in the Communist Revolution* (Cambridge, Mass.: MIT Press, 1959), p. 151.

85. SCMP 2089, September 3, 1959, p. 22; NCNA August 26, 1959.

86. An increase of about 50 percent in 1957 and an increase of 1.14 times between 1957 and 1959.

87. CB 625, July 6, 1960, p. 14; Peking JMJP April 15, 1960.

88. SCMP 2263, May 23, 1960, p. 7; Sian JP April 8, 1960.

89. URS, vol. 18, February 18, 1960, p. 329.

90. *Resolutions on Some Questions Concerning the People's Communes* (Peking: Foreign Language Press, 1958), p. 38.

91. Janet Salaff, "The Urban Communes and the Anti-City Experiment in Communist China," *China Quarterly*, no. 29 (January/March 1967): 104.

92. ECMM 186 October 20, 1959, p. 41; CKFN No. 12, June 16, 1959.

93. URS Vol. 20, p. 326; JMJP July 14, 1960.

94. *China News Analysis*, 332, July 15, 1960, p. 332; citing JMJP April 14, 1960, p. 2.

95. Kessen, *op. cit.*, pp. 2–3.

96. *Ibid*. See also Parish, *op. cit.*, p. 620.

97. *Women in China Today*, no. 4 (October 1952): 16–17.

98. SCMP 142, July 25, 1951; NCNA English, July 24, 1951.

99. Sun Tan-wei, "A Village Nursery: How it Grew," *China in Transition* (Peking: Foreign Language Press, 1957), p. 320.

100. Henry and Muffie Brandon, "Communes Keep Food Going to China's Millions," *Smithsonian* (September 1975), p. 104.

101. Parish, *op. cit.*, p. 613.

102. Norma Diamond, "Collectivization, Kinship, and the Status of Women in Rural China," *Bulletin of Concerned Asian Scholars* 7, no. 1 (January/March 1975): 29.

103. SCMP 2024, June 1, 1959, p. 13; Tsingtao JP, March 21, 1959.

104. SCMP 1935, January 16, 1959, pp. 8–9; Kweichow JP December 1, 1958.

105. Sun Tan-wei, *op. cit.*, p. 319.

106. CB 623, June 29, 1960; Peking JMJP April 14, 1960.

107. Margaret Steinfels, *Who's Minding the Children? The History and Politics of Day Care in America* (New York: Simon & Schuster, 1973), p. 41.

108. *Ibid.*, p. 67.

109. Steiner, *Children's Cause*, p. 16.

110. Steinfels, *op. cit.*, p. 72.

111. Gilbert Steiner, *The State of Welfare* (Washington, D.C.: Brookings Institution, 1971), p. 51.

112. *Ibid.*, p. 61.

113. *Ibid.*

114. Mary Keyserling, *Windows on Day Care* (New York: National Council of Jewish Women, 1972).

115. Steinfels, *op. cit.*, p. 154.

116. *New York Times*, April 7, 1976.

117. Quoted in Steiner, *Children's Cause*, p. 113.

118. *Ibid.*, especially chap. 5.

119. For an extended discussion of this point, see Margaret Benston, "The Political Economy of Women's Liberation," *Monthly Review* 21, no. 4 (September 1969): 13–27.

120. Scott Burns, *The Household Economy: Its Shape, Origins, and Future* (Boston: Beacon, 1975), 17–18.

121. Constantina Safilios-Rothschild, *Women and Social Policy* (Englewood Cliffs, N.J.: Prentice-Hall, 1974), p. 24.

122. Lewis Mumford, *The City in History* (New York: Harcourt Brace Jovanovich, 1961), p. 113.

123. International Labour Office, *Equality of Opportunity and Treatment for Women Workers* (Geneva: Report, International Labour Conference, 60th Session, 1975), p. 63.

124. William Goode, *World Revolution and Family Patterns* (New York: Free Press, 1963), p. 302.

125. SCMP 2261, May 19, 1960; Nanking Hsin-hua JP, March 30, 1960.

126. SCMP 2237, April 13, 1960, p. 40; Wuhan Ch'ang-chiang JP, March 13, 1960.

127. Gargi Dutt, *Rural Communes of China—Organizational Problems* (Bombay: Asia Publishing House, 1967), p. 3.

128. SCMP 2235, April 11, 1960, p. 22; Kweichow JP Kweiyang, February 10, 1960.

129. SUP 83, April 6, 1961, p. 8; Hupeh JP December 19, 1960.

130. SCMP 2206, March 1, 1960, p. 4; JMJP editorial, February 21, 1960.

131. CB 538, December 12, 1958, p. 11; Peking JMJP, October 29, 1958.

132. SCMP 2240, April 19, 1960, p. 37; NCNA Shanghai, April 9, 1960.

133. CB 625, April 7, 1960, p. 22; JMJP Peking, April 7, 1960.

134. CB 538, December 12, 1958, p. 25; JMJP Peking November 6, 1958.

135. ECMM 179, August 5, 1959, p. 1; June 25, 1959 Hsin-hua Pan-Yuen-K'an No. 12.

136. SCMP 2157, December 16, 1959, p. 33; Chekiang, November 9, 1959.

137. SCMP 1944, January 29, 1959, p. 10; Peking JMJP January 16, 1959.

138. *Resolutions on Some Questions Concerning the People's Communes*, p. 38.

139. SCMP 2239, April 18, 1960, p. 21; Shanghai Chieh-fang JP, February 26, 1960.

140. SCMP 2242, April 22, 1960, p. 1; Peking JMJP, April 11, 1960.

141. ECMM 173, June 22, 1959, p. 18; CKFN, May 16, 1959.

142. *Ibid.*

143. SCMP 2286, June 28, 1960, pp. 8–9; Tientsin JMJP June 17, 1960.

144. Salaff, *op. cit.*, p. 102.

145. Ruth Sidel, *Families of Fengsheng: Urban Life in China* (Baltimore: Penguin, 1974), p. 75.

146. Graham Towers, "City Planning in China," *Journal of the Royal Town Planning Institute*, March 1973.

147. Rhoads Murphey, "Chinese Urbanization Under Mao," in *Urbanization and Counterurbanization*, ed. Brian Berry (Beverly Hills: Sage, Urban Affairs Annual Reviews, vol. 11, 1976), p. 319.

148. Kahn and Kamerman, *op. cit.*, p. 98.

149. *Ibid.*, p. 94.

150. *The Trade Union and the Family: A Report by the LO Council for Family Questions* (Stockholm: Swedish Trade Union Confederation, 1970), p. 17.

151. Elina Haavio-Mannila, "Differences in the Level of Living of Male and Female Immigrants in Sweden" (paper prepared for Ninth World Congress of Sociology, Uppsala, Sweden, August 1978), p. 14.

152. Economic Commission for Europe, *Le Logement, La Construction, et l'Amenagement en Suede* (Stockholm, 1974), p. 36.

153. A. K. Atmer, *The Swedish Flat* (Stockholm: Almqvist & Wiksell, 1975), p. 49.

154. TCO (Central Organization of Salaried Employees), *Familj och Samhalle: Rapport fran TCOs familjepolitiska grupp* (Stockholm: Prisma, 1970), p. 353.

155. Susan and Martin Tolchin, *Clout: Womanpower and Politics* (New York: Coward, McCann, & Geoghegan, 1973), p. 145.

156. *Ibid.*, p. 144. See also Martha Griffiths, "How Much Is a Woman Worth? The American Public Policy," in *Economic Independence for Women,* ed. Jane Chapman (Beverly Hills: Sage, 1976), pp. 23–38.

157. Information obtained from the National Council of Homemaker–Home Health Aide Services, New York.

158. Kahn and Kamerman, *op. cit.*, p. 106.

159. Charlotte Perkins Gilman, *Women and Economics* (New York: Harper & Row, 1966), pp. 243–44.

160. Ebenezer Howard, *Garden Cities of Tomorrow* (London: Faber & Faber, 1902).

161. Susana Torre *et al.*, *Women in American Architecture: A Historic and Contemporary Perspective* (New York: Whitney Library of Design, 1977).

162. *Ibid.*

163. *Ladies Home Journal*, September 1918. See also Myrtle Fox and Ethel Lendrum, "Starting a Community Kitchen," *Ladies Home Journal*, June 1919.

164. Dorothy Rosenman, "Housing to Speed Production," *Architectural Record*, April 1942.

165. Marion Clawson and Peter Hall, *Planning and Urban Growth* (Baltimore: Johns Hopkins University Press, 1973), p. 208.

166. Michael Johnston, "Public Policies, Private Choices: New Town Planning and Lifestyles in Three Nations," *Urban Affairs Quarterly*, 13, no. 1 (September 1977): 17. For a general discussion of how planners' biases affect women, see "Who Plans for Women?" *Women's Agenda* 2, no. 3 (March 1977): 6–7.

167. Betty Friedan, *The Feminine Mystique* (New York: Dell, 1963).

168. J. K. Galbraith, *Economics and the Public Purpose* (Boston: Houghton Mifflin, 1973), chap. 4.

169. Jane Jacobs, *The Death and Life of Great American Cities* (New York: Random House, 1961).

170. Donald Foley, "Differentials in Personal Access to Household Motor Vehicles" (Working Paper No. 197, Institute of Urban and Regional Development, University of California, Berkeley, 1972), p. 48.

171. John Kain, "The Journey-to-Work as a Determinant of Residential Location," in *Housing Urban America*, ed. Jon Pynoos *et al*. (Chicago: Aldine, 1973), p. 218.

172. Anthony Downs, *Opening Up the Suburbs* (New Haven: Yale University Press, 1973), p. 57.

173. Nathan Glazer, "Housing Problems and Housing Policies," *Public Interest*, Spring 1967, pp. 36–37.

174. M. Hinshaw and K. Allott, "Environmental Preferences of Future Housing Consumers," in Pynoos, *op. cit.*, pp. 195–96.

175. Wilfred Owens, *The Accessible City* (Washington, D.C.: Brookings Institution, 1972), p. 23.

176. Walter Korpi, "Poverty, Social Assistance, and Social Policy in Sweden, 1945–1972," in *Readings in the Swedish Class Structure*, ed. Richard Scase, (New York: Pergamon, 1976), p. 138.

177. *Ibid.*, p. 139.

178. Arnold Heidenheimer, Hugh Heclo, and Carolyn Adams, *Comparative Public Policy: The Politics of Social Choice in Europe and America* (New York: St. Martin's Press, 1975), p. 207.

179. Steiner, *State of Welfare*, p. 42.

180. Blanche Bernstein and William Meezan, *The Impact of Welfare on Family Stability* (New York: New School for Social Research, Center for New York City Affairs, June 1975).

181. F. F. Piven and R. Cloward, *Regulating the Poor* (New York: Pantheon, 1971), p. 36.

182. Barry Friedman and Leonard Hansman, "Work, Welfare, and the Program for Better Jobs and Income." Study prepared for the U.S. Congress, Joint Economic Committee, Washington, D.C., U.S. Government Printing Office, October 14, 1977, pp. 20–21.

183. Piven and Cloward, *op. cit.*, p. 132.

184. Ralph Husby and Eva Wetzel, "Public Assistance in Sweden and the U.S.," *Social Policy* 7, no. 5 (March/April 1977): 30.

185. Steiner, *State of Welfare*, p. 33.

186. Lucy Komisar, *Down and Out in the U.S.A.: A History of Social Welfare* (New York: Franklin Watts, 1974), p. 155.

187. *Ibid.*, p. 160

188. *New York Times*, August 7, 1977.

189. See, for example, Teng Ying-ch'ao, "Report on the Present Course and Tasks of the Chinese Women's Movement." *Chinese Studies in History*, Winter/Spring 1971–72, p. 83.

190. SUP 1008, March 16, 1955, p. 9; Chungking JP, December 17, 1954.

191. *China Monthly Review*, Vol. 122, February 1952, pp. 247–248.

192. SCMP 1872, October 10, 1958, p. 6; NCNA Peking, September 28, 1958.

193. SCMP 1410, November 14, 1956, pp. 8–9; Kuangming JP, October 31, 1956.

194. *Ibid*.

195. Shahid Javid Burki, *A Study of Chinese Communes* (Cambridge, Mass.: Harvard University Press, 1969), p. 19.

196. Parish, *op. cit.*, p. 623.

197. Jan Myrdal, *Report from a Chinese Village* (New York: Pantheon, 1965), pp. 122, 155, 198.

198. Rita Liljeström, "The Swedish Model," in *Sex Roles in Changing Society*, ed. George Seward and Robert Williamson, (New York: Random House, 1970), p. 201.

199. Griffiths, *op. cit.*, p. 33.

Chapter 3

WOMEN'S POLITICS AND POLICY CHANGE

1. Constantina Salfilios-Rothschild, *Women and Social Policy* (Englewood Cliffs, N.J.: Prentice-Hall, 1974), p. 6.

2. Irene Tinker, M. BoBramsen, and M. Buvinic, eds., *Women and World Development* (New York: Praeger, 1976), p. 24.

3. Patricia Uttrachi and Peter Stearns, "Modernization of Women in the 19th Century" (Forums in History Series, FE121, 1973, Forum Press, St. Charles, Missouri), p. 3; and Edward Shorter, "Women's Work: What Difference Did Capitalism Make?" *Theory and Society* 3, no. 4, (Winter 1976): 513.

4. William Chafe, *Women and Equality* (New York: Oxford University Press, 1977), p. 148.

5. Ida Pruitt, *A Daughter of the Han* (Stanford, Calif.: Stanford University Press, 1973), p. 29.

6. Roxanne Witke, "Mao Tse-tung, Women and Suicide," in *Women in China*, ed. Marilyn Young (Ann Arbor: University of Michigan Center for Chinese Studies, 1973), p. 8.

7. *Ibid*.

8. *Ibid*., p. 14 and especially pp. 20–26.

9. Roxanne Witke, "Women as Politicians in China of the 1920s," in Young, *op. cit*., p. 33.

10. *Ibid*., pp. 40–43; see also Susan Leith, "Chinese Women in the Early Communist Movement," in Young, *op. cit*., p. 53.

11. Leith, *op cit*., p. 53.

12. Jane Price, "Women and Leadership in the Chinese Communist Movement, 1921–45," *Bulletin of Concerned Asian Scholars* 7, no. 1 (March 1975): 19.

13. SCMP 1556, June 24, 1957, pp. 2–3; NCNA Peking, June 6, 1967.

14. James Townsend, *Political Participation in Communist China* (Berkeley: University of California Press, 1967), pp. 156–57.

15. Text can be found in *New Left Review*, no. 92 (July/August 1975): 102–5.

16. SCMM 492, October 4, 1965, p. 30; CKFN Number 8, August 1, 1965.

17. SCMP 3433, April 7, 1965, pp. 8–9; KJJP March 19, 1965; and SCMP April 15, 1965, p. 18; KJJP March 31, 1965.

18. URS Vol. 8, p. 337; Tsingtao JP June 5, 1957.

19. SCMM 318 June 18, 1962, p. 25; CKFN No. 2 February 1, 1962.

20. Price, *op. cit*., p. 22.

21. SCMM 713–714, September 27 and October 5, 1971, pp. 77, 75; HC No. 10 September 1, 1971.

22. Jonathan Mirsky, "China After Nixon," *Annals of the American Academy of Political and Social Science* 402 (July 1972): 85.

23. SCMM 532 July 11, 1966, p. 26; CKFN No. 7 April 1, 1966.

24. M. Donald Hancock, *Sweden: The Politics of Postindustrial Change* (Hinsdale, Ill.: Dryden, 1972), p. 23.

25. Richard Tomasson, *Sweden: Prototype of Modern Society* (New York: Random House, 1970), p. 194.

26. *Ibid.*, p. 193.

27. Gunnar Qvist, *Kvinnofrågan i Sverige, 1809–1846* (Gothenburg: Akademiforlaget-Gumperts, 1960).

28. Ronny Ambjornsson, "What Were the Ideas Behind the Early Women's Rights Movement in Sweden?" in *Feminology: Proceedings of the Dutch—Scandinavian Symposium on Women's Position in Society*, ed. R. Silfwerbrand-ten Cate *et al.* (Nijmegan, The Netherlands: University of Nijmegan, 1975), pp. 34–41.

29. Gunnar Qvist, *Fredrika Bremer och kvinnans emancipation: opinionshistoriska Studier* (Gothenburg: Akademiförlaget-Gumperts, 1969), p. 183. For a succinct account of Fredrika Bremer's literary and feminist activities, see Ross Paulson, *Women's Suffrage and Prohibition: A Comparative Study of Equality and Social Control* (Glenview, Ill.: Scott, Foresman, 1973), pp. 98–101.

30. Rosalie Olivecrona, "Sweden," in *The Woman Question in Europe*, ed. Theodore Stanton (New York: Putnam's, 1884), p. 212.

31. Anna-Lisa Kälveston, *The Social Structure of Sweden* (Stockholm: Swedish Institute, 1965), p. 25.

32. B. J. Hovde, quoted in Paulson, *op. cit.*, p. 94.

33. Olivecrona, *op. cit.*, p. 215.

34. Ellen Key, *The Women Movement* (London: Putnam, 1912), p. 84. Original Swedish edition published in 1909.

35. Paulson, *op. cit.*, p. 120.

36. Olivecrona, *op. cit.*, p. 220.

37. Herbert Tingsten, *The Swedish Social Democrats: Their Ideological Development* (Totowa, N.J.: Bedminster Press, 1973). Original Swedish edition published in 1941.

38. Anna-Greta Leijon, "Equality on the Labor Market, in Political and Trade Union Organizations, and in the Home," *Current Sweden*, no. 75 (April 1975): 4.

39. Rita Liljeström, G. Mellstrom, and G. Svensson, *Sex Roles in Transition: A Report on a Pilot Program in Sweden* (Stockholm: Swedish Institute, 1975).

40. For a full government report on this issue, see Ministry of Justice, *PM till frågan om lagstiftning mot Könsdiskriminering* (Stockholm, 1975).

41. *Equality in the Labour Market: Programme adopted by the Labour Market Board* (Stockholm: Arbetsmarknadsstyrelsen, September 1977).

42. Among the histories of the American women's movement, three of the best are Eleanor Flexner, *Century of Struggle* (Cambridge, Mass.: Harvard University Press, 1959); William O'Neill, *Everyone Was Brave* (Chicago: Quadrangle, 1969); and William Chafe, *The American Woman* (New York: Oxford University Press, 1972). For more recent history, Jo Freeman's *The Politics of Women's Liberation* (New York: Longman, 1975) is useful.

43. Chafe, *Women and Equality*, p. 41.

44. *Ibid.*

45. Aileen Kraditor, *The Ideas of the Woman Suffrage Movement 1890–1920* (New York: Columbia University Press, 1965).

46. Chafe, *American Woman*, p. 59.

47. Freeman, *op. cit.*, p. 51.

48. *Ibid.*, p. 145.

49. Irene Murphy, *Public Policy on the Status of Women* (Lexington, Mass: Lexington Books, 1973), p. 17.

50. Freeman, *op. cit.*, p. 176.

51. Murphy, *loc. cit.*

52. Jean Elshtain, "The Feminist Movement and the Question of Equality," *Polity* 7, no. 4 (Summer 1975): 467.

53. *Ibid.*, p. 469.

54. William O'Neill, *The Woman Movement: Feminism in the U.S. and England* (Chicago: Quadrangle, 1971), p. 34.

55. Charlotte Perkins Gilman, *Women and Economics* (New York: Harper & Row, 1966). p. 242.

56. O'Neill, *The Woman Movement*, p. 73.

57. Flexner, *op. cit.*, p. 41.

58. Quoted in Gayle Yates, *What Woman Want: The Ideas of the Movement* (Cambridge, Mass.: Harvard University Press, 1975), p. 16.

59. Freeman, *op. cit.*, p. 229.

60. Gunnar Myrdal, *An American Dilemma* (New York: Harper & Row, 1944), appendix 5.

61. O'Neill, *Woman Movement*, p. 31.

62. H. L. Mencken, *In Defence of Women* (New York: Knopf, 1922), p. 132.

63. Carrie Chapman Catt, quoted in Chafe, *American Woman*, p. 35.

64. "Women in Politics," *Congressional Quarterly Editorial Research Reports* 1, (1956): 121.

65. A. Campbell, P. E. Converse, W. E. Miller, and D. E. Stokes, *The American Voter* (New York: Wiley, 1964).

66. Murray Goot and Elizabeth Reid, *Women and Voting Studies: Mindless Matrons or Sexist Scientism?* (Beverly Hills: Sage Professional Paper in Contemporary Political Sociology 06–008, 1975), p. 13.

67. Emily Blair, "Are Women a Failure in Politics?" *Harpers*, October 1925, pp. 513–22.

68. Alice Henry, *The Trade Union Woman* (New York: Franklin, 1973) p. 15.

69. O'Neill, *Woman Movement*, p. 91.

70. Gail Falk, "Sex Discrimination in the Trade Unions: Legal Resources for Change," in *Women: A Feminist Perspective*, ed. Jo Freeman (Palo Alto: Mayfield, 1975), p. 257.

71. Yates, *op. cit.*, p. 77.

72. *Ibid.*, p. 102.

73. Susan Brownmiller, "Sisterhood Is Powerful," in *Blueprint for the Future*, ed. S. Stambler (New York: Ace Books, 1970), p. 145.

74. Freeman, *op. cit.*, p. 128.

75. Chafe, *Women and Equality*, p. 103.

76. Yates, *op. cit.*, p. 105.

77. Freeman, *op. cit.*, p. 137.

78. Phyllis Chesler, *Women and Madness* (Garden City, N.Y.: Doubleday, 1972), pp. 243–44.

79. Ludwig Geismar *et al.*, "Feminist Egalitarianism, Social Action Orientation, and Occupational Roles: A Cross-National Study." (U.S./France), *Journal of Comparative Family Studies* 7, no. 3 (Autumn 1976): 429.

80. Susan and Martin Tolchin, *Clout: Womanpower and Politics* (New York: Coward, McCann, & Geoghegan, 1973), p. 68.

81. *Ibid.*

82. Chafe, *Women and Equality*, p. 137.

83. Murphy, *op. cit.*, p. 6.

84. *New York Times*, November 3, 1975.

85. Joyce Gelb and Marian Lief Palley, "Women and Interest Group Politics: A Comparative Analysis of Federal Decision-making" (paper delivered at Northeast Political Science Association Annual Meeting, Mt. Pocono, Pa., November 1977), p. 35.

86. Hancock, *op. cit.*, p. 71

87. Tomasson, *op. cit.*, p. 171.

88. Ellen Key, *Love and Marriage* (New York: Source Book Press, 1970), p. 274. Original Swedish edition published in 1911.

89. Ingunn Norderval Means, "Scandinavian Women," in *Women in the World*, ed Lynne Iglitzin and Ruth Ross (Santa Barbara, Calif.: ABC Clio Press, 1976), p. 383.

90. Quoted in Helena Streijffert, "The Women's Movement—A Theoretical Discussion," *Acta Sociologica* 17, no. 14 (1974): 362–63.

91. Hulda Flood, *Den Socialdemokratiska kvinnorörelsen i Sverige* (Stockholm, 1960), pp. 26–27.

92. *Ibid.*, p. 31.

93. Elisabet Sandberg, *Equality Is the Goal* (Stockholm: Swedish Institute, 1975), pp. 77–78.

94. Tomasson, *op. cit.*, p. 275.

95. *Organisationernas kanslier*, 1972.

96. SCMM 437, pp. 33–36, October 5, 1964; CKFN No. 8, August 1, 1964.

97. Donald Klein and Lois Hager, "The Ninth Central Committee," *China Quarterly*, no. 45 (January/March 1971): 46.

98. Roxanne Witke, "Wu Kuei-hsien—Labor Heroine to Vice Premier," *China Quarterly*, no. 64 (December 1975): 739.

99. *Ibid.*, p. 736.

100. Michael Oksenberg, "Methods of Communication within the Chinese Bureaucracy," *China Quarterly*, no. 57 (January/March 1974): 3–5.

101. A. Doak Barnett, *Cadres, Bureaucracy, and Political Power in Communist China* (New York: Columbia University Press, 1967), p. 30.

102. "Speech by Comrade Ts'ai Ch'ang," *Eighth National Congress of the Communist Party of China* (Peking: Foreign Language Press, 1956), 2:283.

103. SCMP 1657, November 22, 1957, p. 19; also November 17, 1957.

104. ECMM 125, April 14, 1958, pp. 14–15; CKFN No. 2, February 1, 1958.

105. SCMP 1726, March 7, 1958, p. 2; NCNA Peking, February 26, 1958.

106. SCMP 2087, September 1, 1959, pp. 19, 21; JMJP, August 20, 1959.

107. Tung Pien, editor of *Women in China*, was accused of refusing to publish the important statements and speeches of party and state leaders, important notices of the National Federation of Women, and articles by its leaders, and refusing to publish any article with a strong political character, class character, or party character. She called them "empty words," "vapid things," "generalizations," and "things the readers do not like." SCMM 543, July 11, 1966, p. 7; CKFN No. 7, July 10, 1966.

108. The support of P'eng Teh-huai's return in August 1962, for example; SCMM No. 330, September 10, 1962, pp. 18–19; CKFN No. 8, August 1, 1962.

109. For further discussion, see Shelah Gilbert Leader, "The Emancipation of Chinese Women," *World Politics* 36 (October 1973): 55–79.

110. URS Vol. 62, No. 25, March 26, 1971, p. 336; Hupeh People's Radio Station, March 10, 1971, 7:00 p.m.

111. Delia Davin, *Woman-Work—Women and the Party in Revolutionary China* (Oxford, England: Clarendon, 1976), p. 170.

112. SCMP 2495, May 12, 1961, pp. 8–9; KJJP, April 6, 1961.

113. Leader, *op. cit.*, p. 79 *n*.

114. Townsend, *op. cit.*, p. 75 *n*.

115. *Ibid*.

116. URS Vol. 38, January 29, 1965, p. 136; Peking JMJP, December 12, 1964.

117. Han Su-yin, "A Housewife," *Eastern Horizons* 9, no. 1 (1970): 8–9.

118. Elizabeth Croll, "The Anti-Lin Piao and Confucian Campaigns: A New Stage in the Ideological Revolution of Women," *Australian and New Zealand Journal of Sociology* 12, no. 1 (February 1976): 39.

119. SCMP 5331–5335, March 12–March 16, 1973, p. 176; NCNA English, March 8, 1973.

120. CKFN November 1, 1960, cited in Croll, *op. cit.*, p. 35 fn.

121. SCMM 304, March 12, 1962, pp. 12–16; CKFN No. 12, November 1, 1961.

122. SCMP 3787, July 11, 1966, p. 8; CKFN No. 7, July 10, 1966.

123. SCMM 374, July 22, 1963, p. 28; CKFN No. 6, June 1, 1963.

124. "Speech by Comrade Ts'ai Ch'ang," *op. cit.*, pp. 281–82 *n*.

125. Freeman, *op. cit.*, p. 229.

126. Safilios-Rothschild, *op. cit.*, pp. 9, 6.

127. Janet Salaff and Judith Merkle, "Women and Revolution: The Lessons of the Soviet Union and China," *Socialist Revolution* 1, no. 4 (July/August 1970): 71.

128. Nancy Milton, "Correspondence: Women and Revolution," *Socialist Revolution* 1, no. 6 (November/December 1970): 135–151.

129. Hancock, *op. cit.*, p. 65.

130. Thomas Anton, "Policy-Making and Political Culture in Sweden," *Scandinavian Political Studies* 4 (New York: Columbia University Press, 1969), p. 99.

131. Freeman, *op. cit.*, p. 172.

132. *Ibid.*, p. 234.

133. Phillips Cutright, "Political Structure, Economic Development, and National Social Security Programs," *American Journal of Sociology* 71 (March 1965).

134. Chafe, *American Woman*, p. 236.

135. Safilios-Rothschild, *op. cit.*, p. 17.

136. André Malraux, *Anti-Memoirs* (New York: Bantam, 1970), p. 465.

Chapter 4

NATIONAL ECONOMIC POLICY AND WOMEN IN THE LABOR FORCE

1. Karl Deutsch, *The Nerves of Government* (New York: Free Press, 1966), p. 385.

2. Karl Deutsch, "Social Mobilization and Political Development," *American Political Science Review* 55, no. 3 (September 1961): 497.

3. Sondra Herman, "Sex Roles and Sexual Attitudes in Sweden: The New Phase," *Massachusetts Review* 13, no. 1–2 (Winter/Spring 1972): 52.

4. Alva Myrdal, *Nation and Family* (rev. ed.; Cambridge, Mass.: MIT Press, 1968), p. 31.

5. SCMP 742, February 6–8, 1954, p. 15; JMJP Peking January 29, 1954.

6. William Parish, Jr., "Socialism and the Chinese Peasant Family," *Journal of Asian Studies* 34, no. 3 (May 1975): 620. Also, ECMM 179, August 5, 1959, pp. 1–5; "Strive to Run the Community Mess Halls Well, Seriously Try to Follow the Principle of Voluntarism"; also SCMM 318, June 18, 1962, pp. 18, 24—"Teaching Material on Duties Relating to Work on Rural Women"; also SCMM—Sup #26, June 27, 1968, p. 2, "A Record of Liu Shao-Ch'i's Crimes."

7. Hilda Scott, *Women and Socialism: Experiences from Eastern Europe* (London: Alison & Busby, 1976), pp. 187–88.

8. See, e.g., SCMP 5898–5902, July 21–25, 1975, p. 68; NCNA English July 10, 1975.

9. SCMP 1381, October 1, 1956, p. 7; NCNA Peking September 16, 1956.

10. URS Vol. 3, No. 22, June 15, 1956, p. 315; Antung JP, May 20, 1956.

11. Based on John Philip Emerson's statistics for female nonagricultural employment, "Employment in Mainland China: Problems and Prospects," in U.S.

Congress, Joint Economic Committee, *An Economic Profile of Mainland China,* vol. 2 (Washington, D.C.: Government Printing Office, 1967), p. 433.

12. Phyllis Andors, "A Look at the Present Socioeconomic and Political Context of the Changing Role of Women and the Family in China," *Australian and New Zealand Journal of Sociology* 12, no. 1 (February 1976): 24.

13. CB 672, November 30, 1961, p. 12; KJJP Peking September 12, 1961.

14. Emerson, *op. cit.*, p. 433.

15. Barry Richman, *Industrial Society in Communist China* (New York: Random House, 1969), p. 304.

16. We are referring, not to Sweden's current governing coalition of nonsocialist parties, but to the Social Democrats who dominated the national government from 1932 to 1976.

17. Lewis Coser, "Introduction to the Paperback Edition" of August Bebel's *Woman Under Socialism* (New York: Schocken, 1971), p. vii.

18. Bebel, *ibid.*, p. 167.

19. *Ibid.*, pp. 186–87.

20. Friedrich Engels, *Origin of the Family, Private Property, and the State* (New York: International, 1942), p. 73.

21. Linda Jenness, "Feminism and Socialism," *International Socialist Review,* March 1976.

22. Alice Rossi, ed., *The Feminist Papers* (New York: Columbia University Press, 1973), p. 475.

23. Marlies Allendorf, *Women in Socialist Society* (New York: International, 1976); Barbara Jancar, "Women Under Communism," in *Women in Politics,* ed. (New York: Wiley, 1974); Juliet Mitchell, *Women's Estate* (Baltimore: Penguin, 1973); and Scott, *op. cit*.

24. Alexander Eckstein, *China's Economic Revolution* (New York: Cambridge University Press, 1977), p. 29.

25. *Ibid.*, p. 84.

26. Norman Furniss and Timothy Tilton, *The Case for the Welfare State* (Bloomington, Ind.: Indiana University Press, 1977), p. 134.

27. A good historical reference on this subject is Sheila Rowbotham's *Women, Resistance and Revolution* (New York: Vintage, 1974).

28. Janet Salaff and Judith Merkle, "Women and Revolution: The Lessons of the Soviet Union and China," *Socialist Revolution* 1, no. 4 (July/August 1970): 70.

29. Supplement to SCMP 87, October 31, 1961, p. 8; Shanghai *Hsin-min Wan-pao,* June 30, 1961.

30. Francis Castles, *Political Stability* (Milton Keynes, England: Open University Press, 1974), p. 20.

31. Kurt Samuelsson, *From Great Power to Welfare State* (London: George Allen & Unwin, 1968), p. 245.

32. *Ibid.*, p. 244.

33. G. Adler-Karlsson, *Functional Socialism: A Swedish Theory for Democratic Socialism* (Stockholm: Prisma Bokforlaget, 1969), p. 18.

34. Donald J. Munro, *The Concept of Man in Contemporary China* (Ann Arbor: University of Michigan Press, 1977), p. 159.

35. SCMP 2570, September 1, 1961, p. 10; Peking KJJP, July 29, 1961.

36. Shelah Leader, "The Emancipation of Chinese Women," *World Politics* 26, no. 1 (October 1973): 66–67.

37. URS Vol. 62, No. 25, p. 341; Chekiang People's Radio Station, March 8, 1971.

38. SCMP 4983–87, September 27–October 1, 1971, p. 8; Peking JMJP September 13, 1971.

39. Alexander Eckstein, *China's Economic Development* (Ann Arbor: University of Michigan Press, 1975), pp. 69–79.

40. SCMP 1899, November 21, 1958, pp. 7–8; NCNA Sian November 18, 1958.

41. National health insurance is financed only partially from general taxation.

42. Samuelsson, *op. cit.*, p. 254.

43. For a general discussion of this wage policy, see Arnold Heidenheimer, "Professional Unions, Public Sector Growth, and the Swedish Equality Policy," *Comparative Politics* 9, no. 1 (October 1976): 49–73.

44. Samuelsson, *op. cit.*, p. 270.

45. John K. Galbraith, *Economics and the Public Purpose* (Boston: Houghton Mifflin, 1973), pp. 36–37.

46. John K. Galbraith, *The Affluent Society* (Boston: Houghton Mifflin, 1958), chap. 10.

47. SCMP 1152, October 19, 1955, pp. 6–7; NCN Peking, October 8, 1956.

48. CB 476, October 15, 1957, p. 25; JMJP Peking, October 10–11, 1957.

49. SCMP 1556, June 24, 1957, pp. 4–5; NCNA Peking, June 4, 1957.

50. SCMP 2765, June 25, 1962, pp. 11–12; CKCNP Peking, May 29, 1962.

51. Engels, *op. cit.*, p. 71.

52. *Ibid.*, p. 64.

53. Alexandra Kollontai, *Free Love,* quoted in Rowbotham, *op. cit.*, p. 156.

54. *Ibid.*, p. 159.

55. Elisabet Sandberg, *Equality Is the Goal: A Report from the Advisory Council to the Prime Minister on Equality between Men and Women* (Stockholm: Swedish Institute, 1975), p. 60.

56. Richard Tomasson, *Sweden: Prototype of Modern Society* (New York: Random House, 1970), p. 182.

57. Birgitta Linner, *Sex and Society in Sweden* (New York: Harper & Row, 1967), p. 26.

58. Myrdal, *op. cit.*, p. 45.

59. See Chi-hsi Hu, "The Sexual Revolution in the Kinagsi Soviet," *China Quarterly,* no. 59, (July/September 1974): 477–90.

60. For information on the Kiangsi Soviet period of the early 1930s, and the stiffening of divorce regulations in the 1950s, see Leader, *op. cit.*, pp. 77–78.

61. Leo A. Orleans, *Every Fifth Child: The Population of China* (Stanford, Calif.: Stanford University Press, 1972), p. 46.

62. K. S. Karol, *China: The Other Communism* (New York: Hill & Wang, 1967), p. 305.

63. Orleans, *op. cit.*, p. 46.

64. SCMM 264, June 5, 1961, pp. 29–30; CKFN No. 5, May 1, 1961.

65. Han Su-yin, "A Housewife," *Eastern Horizon* 60, no. 1 (1970): 8.

66. Eckstein, *China's Economic Revolution,* p. 47.

67. SCMP 1935, January 16, 1959, pp. 8–9; Kweichow JP, December 1, 1958.

68. Kang Chao, "Economic Aftermath of the Great Leap in Communist China," *Asian Survey* 9, no. 5 (May 1964): 855.

69. Eckstein, *China's Economic Revolution*.

70. Irene Eber, "Images of Women in Recent Chinese Fiction: Do Women Really Hold Up Half the Sky?" *Signs* 2, no. 1 (Autumn 1976): esp. 30–32. See also Janet Salaff, "Institutionalized Motivation for Fertility Limitation," in *Women in China*, ed. Marilyn B. Young (Ann Arbor: University of Michigan Center for Chinese Studies, 1973), esp. pp. 109–17.

71. SCMM 145, October 13, 1958, p. 35; HC No. 7, September 1, 1958.

72. *Socialist Upsurge in China's Countryside* (Peking: Foreign Languages Press, 1955), p. 286.

73. Joyce Kallgren, "Social Welfare and China's Industrialized Workers," in *Chinese Communist Politics in Action*, ed. A. Doak Barnett (Seattle: University of Washington Press, 1969), p. 558.

74. Hugh Heclo, *Modern Social Politics in Britain and Sweden: From Relief to Income Maintenance* (New Haven: Yale University Press, 1974), p. 100.

75. Not until the 1970s did the National Labor Market Board take steps to provide emergency public works jobs suited to the skills and experience of unemployed women (especially in social services). Whereas in 1971 only 3 percent of those doing public works jobs were women; by 1974 the percentage had been increased to 17 percent. Sandberg, *op. cit.*, p. 27.

76. Alva Myrdal, "Swedish Women in Industry and at Home," *Annals of the American Academy of Political and Social Science* 197 (May 1938): 219.

77. Alva Myrdal, *Nation and Family*, p. 63.

78. Gunnar Myrdal, "Population Problems and Policies," *Annals of the American Academy of Political and Social Science* (May 1938), p. 201.

79. Leif Haanes-Olsen, "Children's Allowances; Their Size and Structure in Five Countries," *Social Security Bulletin*, 35 (May 1972): 17–28.

80. Alva Myrdal, *Annals*, p. 230.

81. *Ibid*.

82. Sandberg, *op. cit.*, p. 42.

83. Organisation for Economic Cooperation and Development, *The Recession and Employment of Women* (Paris: OECD, 1977).

84. Russell Nixon, "The Historical Development of the Conception and Im-

plementation of Full Employment as Economic Policy," in *Public Service Employment,* ed. Alan Gartner *et al.* (New York: Praeger, 1973), p. 26.

85. Frank Furstenberg and Charles Thrall, "Counting the Jobless: The Impact of Job Rationing on the Measurement of Unemployment," *Annals of the American Academy of Political and Social Science* 418 (March 1975): 49.

86. For a discussion of the recent recession's impact on American women's employment, see U.S. Congress, Joint Economic Committee, *Achieving the Goals of the Employment Act of 1946,* Paper no. 6, "The Impact of Macro-Economic Conditions on Employment Opportunities for Women," January 3, 1977.

87. *Work in America: Report of a Special Task Force to the Secretary of HEW* (Cambridge, Mass.: MIT Press, 1973), p. 168.

88. Congressional Quarterly, *Urban America: Policies and Problems* (Washington, D.C., August 1978), p. 29.

89. *Ibid.*

90. Gunnar Myrdal, *Challenge to Affluence* (New York: Pantheon, 1963), p. 4.

91. *Ibid.*, p. 56.

92. *Ibid.*, p. 25.

93. Andrew Martin, *The Politics of Economic Policy in the U.S.: A Tentative View from a Comparative Perspective* (Beverly Hills: Sage Professional Paper in Comparative Politics, 01–040, 1973).

94. David Warner, "Fiscal Barriers to Full Employment," *Annals of the American Academy of Political and Social Science* 418 (March 1975): 157.

95. James O'Toole, "Planning for Total Employment," *Annals of the American Academy of Political and Social Science,* 418 (March 1975): 80.

96. Arnold Heidenheimer, Hugh Heclo, and Carolyn Adams, *Comparative Public Policy* (New York: St. Martin's Press, 1975), p. 229.

97. *Ibid.*, p. 234.

98. William Kessen, ed., *Childhood in China* (New Haven: Yale University Press, 1975), pp. 74–75.

99. Edgar Snow, *Red China Today* (New York: Vintage, 1971), p. 495.

100. Ruth Sidel, *Women and Child Care in China* (Baltimore: Penguin, 1973), p. 138.

101. CB 476, October 15, 1957, p. 16; Peking JMJP, September 10–11, 1957.

102. SCMP 1556, June 24, 1957, p. 6; NCNA Peking, June 4, 1957.

103. Eckstein, *China's Economic Development,* p. 345.

104. URS Vol. 28, No. 12, p. 198; refugee interview.

105. Our discussion in this section relies heavily on three working papers written by Larry Hirschhorn and published by the Institute of Urban and Regional Development, University of California, Berkeley. They are "Toward a Political Economy of the Service Society," Working Paper No. 229 (February 1974); "The Social Service Crisis and the New Subjectivity," Working Paper No. 244 (December 1974); and "The Social Crisis—The Crisis of Work and Social Services," Working Paper No. 251 (March 1975).

106. Hirschhorn, "Crisis of Work and Social Services," p. 5.

107. Hirschhorn, "Toward a Political Economy," p. 54.

108. *Ibid.*, p. 55.

109. *Ibid.*, p. 73.

110. Hirschhorn, "Social Service Crisis," p. 15.

111. *Ibid.*, pp. 17–30.

112. Hirschhorn, "Crisis of Work and Social Services," p. 14.

113. Hirschhorn, "Toward a Political Economy," p. 79.

Chapter 5

THE FAMILY IN POLITICAL CULTURE

1. Richard Merelman, "Family Structure and Politics: Consensus and Dialectics" (paper delivered at the Annual Meeting of the American Political Science Association, Chicago, September 1976).

2. John Locke, *Two Treatises of Government*, ed. Peter Laslett (rev. ed.; New York: Mentor, 1963), *Treatise* 2, p. 365, discussed in Mary L. Shanley, "Marriage Contract in 17th Century Political Thought" (paper delivered at the Annual

Meeting of the American Political Science Association, Chicago, September 1976), pp. 20–21.

3. The one outstanding example of strict community regulation in the American colonies over family life, that of early Puritan New England, dissolved in the eighteenth century.

4. Lenore Weitzman, "Legal Regulation of Marriage: Tradition and Change," *California Law Review*, 62 (1974): 1201.

5. Merelman, *op. cit.*, p. 47.

6. Jean Bodin, *Six Books of a Commonweale* (Cambridge, Mass.: Harvard University Press, 1959), p. 675.

7. *Ibid.*, p. 9.

8. William H. Chafe, *The American Woman* (New York: Oxford University Press, 1972), p. 27.

9. Suzanne LaFollette, *Concerning Women* (New York: Albert & Charles Boni, 1926), excerpted in Alice Rossi, *The Feminist Papers* (New York: Bantam, 1973), p. 561.

10. Alvin Schorr, "Family Values and Public Policy," *Journal of Social Policy* 1, no. 1 (January 1972): 34–35.

11. Kenneth Keniston and the Carnegie Council on Children, *All Our Children: The American Family Under Pressure* (New York: Harcourt Brace Jovanovich, 1977), p. 9.

12. *Ibid.*, p. 12.

13. Walter Mondale, "The Family in Trouble," *Psychology Today*, May 1977, p. 39.

14. Mary Jo Bane, *Here to Stay: American Families in the 20th Century* (New York: Basic, 1976), p. 108.

15. *Ibid.*, p. 104.

16. *James* v. *Goldberg*, 303, SONY, 1969.

17. Roland Huntford, *The New Totalitarians* (New York: Stein & Day, 1972), p. 84.

18. *Ibid.*

19. Max Rheinstein, "Divorce Law in Sweden," in *Divorce and After*, ed. Paul Bohannan, (Garden City, N.Y.: Doubleday, 1970), pp. 148–49.

20. *Ibid.*, p. 152.

21. Lucy Komisar, *Down and Out in the USA* (New York: Franklin Watts, 1974), p. 85.

22. *Labine* v. *Vincent*, 91 Supreme Court 1017 (1971).

23. *Trimble* v. *Gordon*, 75 Supreme Court 5952 (1971).

24. *New York Times*, April 27, 1977.

25. Elisabet Sandberg, *Equality Is the Goal: A Report from the Advisory Council to the Prime Minister on Equality between Men and Women* (Stockholm: Swedish Institute, 1975), p. 60.

26. For further discussion of social benefits available to unwed single parents, refer to chapter 2.

27. Birgitta Linner, "What Does Equality Between the Sexes Imply?" in *The Women's Movement*, ed. Helen Wortis and Clara Rabinowitz (New York: Halsted, 1972), p. 54.

28. Birgitta Alexandersson, "The 1973 Family Law Reform," *Current Sweden*, no. 8 (September 1973): 2.

29. Backberger, quoted in Frederic Fleisher, *The New Sweden* (New York: McKay, 1967), p. 228.

30. Per Gahrton, *Barn i Sverige* (Stockholm, 1969).

31. Anna-Greta Leijon, *Swedish Women—Swedish Men* (Stockholm: Swedish Institute, 1968), p. 77.

32. Lena Anderfelt, "Public and Compulsory Training for Parents—A Possibility?" *Current Sweden*, no. 62 (January 1975): 2.

33. Alva Myrdal, *Nation and Family* (rev. ed.; Cambridge, Mass.: MIT Press, 1968), p. 108.

34. Edward Shorter, *The Making of the Modern Family* (New York: Basic, 1975).

35. Maurice Freedman, "The Family in China, Past and Present," in *Modern China*, ed. Albert Feuerwerker (Englewood Cliffs, N.J.: Prentice-Hall, 1964), p. 28.

36. *Ibid.*, p. 29.

37. SCMM 390, November 12, 1963, p. 28; CKFN October 1, 1963.

38. Maud Russell, *Chinese Women: Liberated* (New York: Far East Reporter, n.d.), p. 32.

39. Freedman, *op. cit.*, p. 39.

40. Carle Zimmerman, *Family and Civilization* (New York: Harper & Row, 1947), pp. 133–34.

41. Leo Kanowitz, *Women and the Law* (Albuquerque: University of New Mexico Press, 1969), p. 36. See also Weitzman, *op. cit.*

42. Quoted in Folke Schmidt and Stig Stromholm, *Legal Values in Modern Sweden* (Bedminster, N.J.: Bedminster Press, 1964), p. 77.

43. *Ibid.*, p. 40.

44. For a variation on this interpretation, see M. J. Meijer, *Marriage Law and Policy* (Hong Kong: Hong Kong University Press, 1971), p. 10.

45. *Ibid.*, p. 11.

46. Myrdal, *op. cit.*, p. 59.

47. Shorter, *op. cit.*, pp. 205–54.

48. Homer Clark, *The Law of Domestic Relations in the United States* (St. Paul, Minn.: West., 1968), p. 181.

49. Myrdal, *loc. cit.*

50. Meijer, *op. cit.*, p. 6.

51. *Ibid.*, p. 10.

52. C. K. Yang, *Chinese Communist Society: The Family and the Village*, book 1, *The Chinese Family in the Communist Revolution* (Cambridge, Mass.: MIT Press, 1965), p. 140.

53. Karl Marx and Frederick Engels, *Selected Works* (Moscow: Progress, 1968), p. 579.

54. Delia Davin, *Woman-Work—Women and the Party in Revolutionary China* (Oxford, England: Clarendon, 1976), pp. 27–35.

55. Meijer, *op. cit.*, p. 270.

56. Barbara Ward, ed., *Women in the New Asia* (Paris: UNESCO, 1963), p. 384.

57. Paul S. Ropp, "The Seeds of Change: Reflections on the Condition of Women in the Early and Mid Ch'ing," *Signs*, 2, no. 1 (Autumn 1976): 7.

58. CB 236, March 10, 1953, p. 6; NCNA Peking January 31, 1953.

59. Russell, *op. cit.*, pp. 11–12.

60. Marx and Engels, *loc. cit.*

61. Barbara Jancar, "Women Under Communism," in *Women in Politics*, ed. Jane Jaquette, (New York: Wiley, 1974), pp. 217–39.

62. SCMP 1220, February 1, 1956, p. 13; Peking JMJP January 8, 1956.

63. SCMP 3331, November 4, 1964, p. 14; JMJP October 14, 1964.

64. SCMP 4139, March 15, 1968, p. 19; March 13, 1968.

65. Alva Myrdal and Viola Klein, *Women's Two Roles: Home and Work* (London: Routledge & Kegan Paul, 1956).

66. Edmund Dahlstrom, "Analysis of the Debate on Sex Roles," in Dahlstrom, ed., *The Changing Roles of Men and Women* (Boston: Beacon, 1971), p. 176.

67. *The Status of Women in Sweden. Report to the United Nations* (Stockholm, 1968), pp. 5–6.

68. Schmidt and Stromholm, *op. cit.*, p. 46.

69. Compensation during the first eight months is equivalent to 90 percent of the parent's normal income; during the ninth month, compensation amounts to about 32 kronor per day.

70. Interview with Gabriel Romanus, Liberal party spokesman on family policy, Stockholm, May 26, 1976.

71. *New York Times*, May 6, 1972, p. 1.

72. M. Karowe, "Marital Property: A New Look at Old Inequities," *Albany Law Review* 39 (1974): 55.

73. Joan Krauskopf, "Partnership Marriage: Legal Reforms Needed," in *Women into Wives: The Legal and Economic Impact of Marriage,* ed. Jane Chapman and Margaret Gates (Beverly Hills: Sage, 1977), p. 96.

74. *Ibid.*, p. 97.

75. Weitzman, *op. cit.*, p. 1181.

76. Herma Kay, *Sex-Based Discrimination in Family Law* (St. Paul, Minn.: West, 1974) p. 139.

77. Krauskopf, *loc. cit.*; Weitzman, *op. cit.*, p. 1184.

78. Greg Duncan and James Morgan, eds., *Five Thousand American Families—Patterns of Economic Progress*, vol. 5, *Components of Change in Family Well-Being and Other Analyses of First Eight Years of the Panel Study of Income Dynamics* (Ann Arbor: Institute for Social Research, 1977); Marian Winston and Trude Forsher, *Nonsupport of Legitimate Children by Affluent Fathers as a Cause of Poverty and Welfare Dependence*, (Santa Monica, Calif.: Rand., April 1974).

79. U.S. Congress, Joint Economic Committee, Report of the Subcommittee on Fiscal Policy, "Income Security for Americans," December 1974.

80. In actual fact, the locator service is available to nonwelfare mothers who apply, but this fact is not a well-known or well-advertised feature of the program.

81. *New York Times*, April 7, 1976.

82. *New York Times*, February 12, 1979.

83. *Hoyt* v. *Florida*, 368, U.S. 57, 61–62 (1961).

84. Quoted in Komisar, *op. cit.*, p. 165.

85. Memorandum of March 14, 1977, from Assistant Secretary of Labor for Policy Evaluation and Research Arnold Packer, to Labor Secretary Ray Marshall, quoted in David Rosenbaum, "Much More than Dollars Figure in Welfare Costs," *New York Times*, June 26, 1977, p. E3.

86. In addition to Krauskopf, *op. cit.*, and Weitzman, *op. cit.*, see Bane, *op. cit.*, chap. 8.

87. Barbara A. Brown, Thomas Emerson, Gail Falk, and Ann Freedman, "The Equal Rights Amendment: A Constitutional Basis for Equal Rights for Women," *Yale Law Journal* 80, no. 5 (April 1971).

88. The information in the paragraph that follows is taken from the U.S. Bureau of the Census, *Population Characteristics: Household and Family Characteristics, 1977*, (Washington, D.C.: Current Population Reports, Series P–20, No. 326, August 1978).

89. Heather Ross and Isabel Sawhill, *Time of Transition: The Growth of Families Headed by Women* (Washington, D.C.: Urban Institute, 1975), p. 97.

90. *Ibid.*, p. 57.

91. P. Uttrachi and P. Stearns, *Modernization of Women in the 19th Century*, Reprint Series: Forums in History (St. Charles, Mo.: Forum, 1973).

92. Myrdal, *op. cit.*, p. 38.

93. Leijon, *op. cit.*, p. 117.

94. Meijer, *op. cit.*, p. 16.

95. Yang, *op. cit.*, p. 71.

96. *Ibid.*, p. 72.

97. Ruth Sidel, *Families of Fengsheng: Urban Life in China* (Baltimore: Penguin, 1974), p. 73.

98. *Ibid*.

99. Committee of Concerned Asian Scholars, *China: Inside the People's Republic* (New York: Bantam, 1972), p. 281.

100. Merelman, *op. cit.*, p. 56.

101. *Ibid.*, p. 67.

102. *Ibid.*, p. 74.

103. Sandberg, *op. cit.*, p. 60. For a fuller treatment of the issue of "loyalty marriages," see Jan Trost, "Married and Unmarried Cohabitation: The Case of Sweden with some Comparisons," in *Beyond the Nuclear Family Model*, ed. Luis Lenero-Otero (Beverly Hills: Sage, 1977).

104. Betty Friedan, *The Feminine Mystique* (New York: Norton, 1963), especially chap. 8.

105. Quoted in Richard Tomasson, *Sweden: Prototype of Modern Society* (New York: Random House, 1970), p. 190.

106. Herbert Hendin, *Suicide and Scandinavia* (New York: Grune & Stratton, 1974), p. 50.

107. Birgitta Linner, *Sex and Society in Sweden* (New York: Harper & Row, 1967), p. 9.

108. Alva Myrdal, *Towards Equality* (Stockholm: Prisma Bokforlaget, 1971), p. 87.

109. Camilla Odhnoff, "Equality Is for Children Too," *Current Sweden*, no. 98 (December 1975).

110. M. K. Whyte, "The Family," in *China's Developmental Experience*, ed. Michael Oksenberg, (New York: Praeger, 1973), p. 189.

111. *Ibid.*, p. 190.

112. With the possible exception of some policies implemented by the more radical members of the CCP during the Great Leap Forward.

113. SCMP 476, October 15, 1957, p. 20; Peking JMJP September 10–11, 1957.

114. Suzanne Butler, *Impressions of China Today* (Hong Kong: Hamlyn, 1974), p. 85.

115. *Current Scene*, 3, no. 18 (May 1, 1965): 12.

116. Butler, *loc. cit.*

117. William Parish, Jr., "Socialism and the Chinese Peasant Family," *Journal of Asian Studies*, 34, no. 3 (May 1975): 621.

118. Joyce Kallgren, "Social Welfare and China's Industrial Workers," in *Chinese Communist Politics in Action*, ed. A. Doak Barnett (Seattle: University of Washington Press, 1969), p. 555.

119. *Ibid.*, p. 554.

120. Parish, *op. cit.*, p. 624.

121. *Ibid.*

122. Interview with Gabriel Romanus, *op. cit.*

Chapter 6

CONCLUSION

1. Alexander Groth, *Comparative Politics: A Distributive Approach* (New York: Macmillan, 1971), pp. 189–190.

2. Hugh Heclo, *Modern Social Politics in Britain and Sweden* (New Haven: Yale University Press, 1974), pp. 6–7.

3. *Ibid.*, p. 288.

4. *Ibid.*, p. 293.

5. Groth, *op. cit.*, p. 154.

6. Harold Wilensky, *The Welfare State and Equality* (Berkeley: University of California Press, 1975), pp. 21–22.

7. Groth, *op. cit.*, p. 193.

8. Alice Cook, *The Working Mother: A Survey of Problems and Programs in Nine Countries* (2nd ed.; Ithaca, N.Y.: Cornell University, New York State School of Industrial and Labor Relations, 1978), p. 42.

9. Richard Rose, "Comparing Public Policy: An Overview," *European Journal of Political Research* 1 (1973): 88.

10. We should note that some observers have charged the U.S. government with pursuing a covert or unofficial pronatalist policy. See Jessie Bernard, *Women and the Public Interest* (Chicago: Aldine, 1971), pp. 58–59.

11. Arnold Heidenheimer, Hugh Heclo, and Carolyn Adams, *Comparative Public Policy* (New York: St. Martin's Press, 1975), pp. 261–62.

12. Andrew Martin, *The Politics of Economic Policy in the U.S.: A Tentative View from a Comparative Perspective* (Beverly Hills: Sage Professional Papers in Comparative Politics, 01–040, 1973).

13. M. Donald Hancock, *Sweden: The Politics of Postindustrial Change* (Hinsdale, Ill.: Dryden, 1972), p. 93.

14. See for example the Paris Chang–Victor Falkenheim exchange in *Problems of Communism* 21 (July/August 1972). See also the Audrey Donnithorne–Nicholas Lardy exchange in *China Quarterly* 52 (October/December 1972): 61 (March 1975); and 66 (June 1976).

15. *Peking Review*, no. 36 (September 2, 1977): 20.

16. *Ibid.*, p. 32.

17. Martin King Whyte, *Small Groups and Political Rituals in China* (Berkeley: University of California Press, 1974), pp. 10–11.

18. Letty Cottin Pogrebin, "Can Women Really Have it All?" *Ms.* 6, no. 9 (March 1978): 48.

19. Elizabeth Almquist, "Review Essay: Women in the Labor Force," *Signs* 2, no. 4 (Summer 1977): 844.

20. *New York Times*, April 21, 1977.

21. *Philadelphia Bulletin*, May 6, 1977.

22. *New York Times*, November 27, 1977.

23. Michael Wachter, "Intermediate Swings in Labor-Force Participation," Brookings Papers on Economic Activity No. 2 (Washington, D.C.: Brookings Institution, 1977).

24. Lenore Weitzman, "Legal Regulation of Marriage: Tradition and Change," *California Law Review* 62 (1974): 1193.

25. Eleanor Smeal, "Testimony on Equity in Social Security Impact on Women," *Hearings before the U.S. Congress, Committee on Ways and Means, Subcommittee on Social Security*, July 21, 1977.

26. George Cooper, "Working Women and Discrimination in Income Tax Laws,"

in *Women's Role in Contemporary Society*, ed. New York City Commission on Human Rights, (New York: Avon, 1972), p. 381.

27. *Ibid.*

28. Scott Burns, *The Household Economy* (Boston: Beacon, 1975), pp. 5–6.

29. *Ibid.*, p. 141.

30. G. G. Cain and H. W. Watts, eds., *Income Maintenance and Labor Supply* (Chicago: Rand McNally, 1973), pp. 14–20.

31. C. Russell Hill, "Guaranteeing Income and Encouraging Child Care" (University of Michigan Institute of Public Policy Studies, Discussion Paper No. 58, Ann Arbor, 1974), p. 2.

32. Selma Fraiberg, quoted in Robert Coles, "Talk with Selma Fraiberg," *New York Times Book Review*, December 11, 1977, p. 1. The interview concerned Fraiberg's book *Every Child's Birthright: In Defense of Mothering* (New York: Basic, 1977).

33. National Commission on the Observance of International Women's Year, *To Form a More Perfect Union: Justice for American Women* (Washington, D.C.: Government Printing Office, 1977).

34. *New York Times*, September 13, 1974.

INDEX